Forensic Social Work

Psychosocial and Legal Issues in Diverse Practice Settings

About the Editors

Tina Maschi, PhD, LCSW, ACSW, is an assistant professor at Fordham University's Graduate School of Social Service. Her research and practice interests focus on at-risk youth, mental health, juvenile and criminal justice involvement, trauma, mental health, criminality across the lifespan, and community-based research and evaluation. She is also a licensed clinical social worker with extensive practice experience (including the use of creative arts techniques) in correctional, school, and community mental health settings. She currently teaches research and practice courses in the Master's program at Fordham's Lincoln Center campus.

Carolyn Bradley, PhD, LCSW, LCADC, is an Assistant Professor of Social Work at Monmouth University in West Long Branch, NJ. Dr. Bradley's research interests are concentrated in substance use, women, and spirituality. Dr. Bradley has been a clinician maintaining a private practice in clinical social work for over 25 years.

Kelly Ward, PhD, LCSW, LCADC, is an Associate Professor at Monmouth University in West Long Branch, NJ, and is also a private practitioner working with adolescents with substance-abuse issues. She has been involved with forensic social work practice throughout her career.

Forensic Social Work

Psychosocial and Legal Issues in Diverse Practice Settings

Editors

Tina Maschi, PhD, LCSW, ACSW

Carolyn Bradley, PhD, LCSW, LCADC

Kelly Ward, PhD, LCSW, LCADC

SPRINGER PUBLISHING COMPANY

New York

Springer Publishing Company, LLC
11 West 42nd Street
New York, NY 10036
www.springerpub.com

Acquisitions Editor: Jennifer Perillo
Production Editor: Pamela Lankas
Cover design: Steve Pisano
Composition: International Graphic Services

Ebook ISBN: 978-0-8261-1858-5

09 10 11 12 / 5 4 3 2 1

The author and the publisher of this Work have made every effort to use sources believed to be reliable to provide information that is accurate and compatible with the standards generally accepted at the time of publication. The author and publisher shall not be liable for any special, consequential, or exemplary damages resulting, in whole or in part, from the readers' use of, or reliance on, the information contained in this book. The publisher has no responsibility for the persistence or accuracy of URLs for external or third-party Internet Web sites referred to in this publication and does not guarantee that any content on such Web sites is, or will remain, accurate or appropriate.

Library of Congress Cataloging-in-Publication Data

Maschi, Tina.
  Forensic social work : psychosocial and legal issues in diverse practice settings / Tina Maschi, Carolyn Bradley, Kelly Ward.
      p. cm.
  Includes bibliographical references and index.
  ISBN 978-0-8261-1857-8 (alk. paper)
  1. Social workers—Legal status, laws, etc.—United States. 2. Forensic sociology—United States. 3. Evidence, Expert—United States. I. Bradley, Carolyn. II. Ward, Kelly, LCSW. III. Title.
  KF8968.7.M37 2009
  363.25—dc22
                              2009021806

Printed in the United States of America by Hamilton Printing.

Contents

Contents

Contents

Contents

Contents

Contents

Contents

Contents

Contents

Contents

Contents

Contents

Contents

Contents

Contents

Contents

Contents

Contents

Contents

Contents

Contents

Contributors

Leon Banks, PhD, is an instructor with the University of Georgia School of Social Work.

Rosemary A. Barbera, PhD, is an assistant professor in the School of Social Work at Monmouth University.

Carol Cleaveland, PhD, is an assistant professor in the George Mason University Department of Social Work.

Regina Doyle, LCSW, has enjoyed dual careers as an educator and a social worker for the past 35 years.

Johanna Foster, PhD, has held various academic positions over the past 15 years and has coordinated and taught two postsecondary-education programs for women prisoners in the greater New York City metropolitan area.

Sandy Gibson, PhD, MSW, is an adjunct professor at Temple University.

Lauri Goldkind, LMSW, is the Director of Evaluation and Analytics for The Urban Assembly, a nonprofit school support organization in New York City.

Lauren Gunneson, BA, is currently pursuing her master's degree in Professional Counseling at Monmouth University.

Schnavia Smith Hatcher, PhD, is an assistant professor with the University of Georgia School of Social Work.

Christine Heer, Esq, MSW, is an attorney/mediator and collaborative practitioner specializing in family law, estate planning, and professional responsibility for social workers. She also maintains a private therapy practice and is an adjunct professor at Seton Hall University.

Paul Hirschfield, PhD, is an assistant professor in the Department of Sociology and the Program in Criminal Justice at Rutgers University.

Mary Kay Jou, MSW, is pursuing her PhD at Rutgers University, and teaches at both Rutgers and Monmouth Universities.

Laura Kelly, PhD, APRN, BC, has 15 years of clinical experience working in a community-based substance-abuse program; has worked for 5 years with juveniles in a county detention center, and for 3 years has been a nurse interventionist working with families.

Mary Lou Killian, MSW, PhD, is currently Director of Operations for a community-based agency for survivors of domestic violence and sexual assault.

Kenneth J. Lau, LCSW, is presently the president of the New York State chapter of ATSA.

Leah K. Lazzaro, MSW, LSW, is the Coordinator of Field and Professional Education in the School of Social Work at Monmouth University.

Janet Mahoney, PhD, RN, APN-BC, is an associate professor and associate dean at Monmouth University.

Lisa Maietta, BA, is currently pursuing her master's degree in social work at Monmouth University.

Marie Mele, PhD, is an assistant professor with the Department of Criminal Justice at Monmouth University.

Nancy J. Mezey, PhD, is an associate professor of sociology at Monmouth University, where she serves as the Sociology Program Coordinator.

Thomas J. Morgan, PsyD, is an assistant research professor at Rutgers University, Center of Alcohol Studies.

Keith Morgen, PhD, is an assistant professor of psychology at Centenary College.

Patricia O'Brien, MSW, PhD, is an associate professor at the University of Illinois at Chicago, Jane Addams College of Social Work.

Audrey Redding-Raines, MSW, MPA, is a doctoral student in the School of Public Affairs and Administration at Rutgers University (Newark).

Rosemary Richards, MSW, has been a social worker for 28 years. She worked in the child protective agencies and the juvenile justice system prior to her experience as a School Social Worker/Student Assistance Coordinator.

Edward A. Risler, PhD, is an associate professor with the University of Georgia School of Social Work. He was recently appointed for a second term by the Governor of Georgia to be a member of the Georgia Department of Juvenile Justice board of directors.

Jennifer Ristow is currently earning her MSW at Monmouth University, in West Long Branch, New Jersey.

Morris Saldov, PhD, MSW, is an associate professor at Monmouth University in West Long Branch, NJ.

Rebecca Sanford, PhD, is Assistant Professor in the Department of Communication at Monmouth University. She has 10 years experience as an instructor and program administrator for education programs administered to male and female incarcerated students.

Nancy Scotto Rosato, PhD, is a research scientist at the New Jersey Department of Health and Senior Services.

Nora Smith, PhD, LCSW, has taught at Monmouth University for 8 years and is the coordinator for the Post Master's degree in the Play Therapy Program.

Anne Sparks, PhD, is an assistant professor in the Department of Social Work at Ohio University.

Eileen C. Treacy, PhD, is co-founder of Bronx Women Against Rape, and founder of the Kingsbridge Heights Community Center's Child Sexual Assault Counseling and Prevention Program.

Katherine van Wormer, PhD, is a professor of social work at the University of Northern Iowa.

Nancy M. Violette, PhD, LCSW, LCADC, is an assistant professor at Rutgers University, Center of Alcohol Studies.

Preface

Social workers are found in most community and institutional settings, including social services agencies, schools, hospitals, substance-abuse and mental health programs, child welfare agencies, and courts and prisons throughout the world. Regardless of the location of practice, to be effective practitioners social workers must share common professional needs. We need to have the skills to assist and empower clients who may be struggling with an array of problems, including legal issues, unfair policies, and/or lack of legal protections. We also must be able to work collaboratively with other professionals and stakeholders to help clients sort through a mixture of financial, psychological, emotional, social, and legal concerns.

This book targets the important and emerging practice area of forensic social work, an area that is often overlooked or misunderstood. The book builds on prior work in this area by providing a broader view of forensic social work to include the knowledge and skills needed to practice effectively with clients in the sociolegal environment. We define "forensic social work" to include not only a narrow group of victims and offenders involved in the juvenile justice and criminal justice settings, but all the individuals and families involved with family and social services, education, child welfare, mental health, and addictions programs, in which they are affected by federal and state laws and policies. Examples include social workers advocating for legal protections for undocumented workers, those assisting individuals and families in need as they apply for entitlements such as Medicare or Social Security disability benefits, and those providing mental health treatment to inmates with special needs in a correctional setting.

This book fills a critical gap in social work education. Interdisciplinary practice and legal knowledge are essential for social workers to ensure that clients are effectively served. Yet the implications of legal issues are rarely addressed and/or integrated in social work education in a meaningful and practical way. This book addresses this perceived oversight. This volume, made up of 26 chapters written by forensic professionals, enlightens readers with state-of-the-art, practical knowledge in collaborative forensic social work practice. Readers of the book will become more confident and competent in integrating sociolegal knowledge and skills, especially collaboration and advocacy, into their professional practices.

Organization

Forensic Social Work is structured so that the reader can make the most of its contents. It is divided into seven parts that move from the broad discussion of collaborative forensic practice to specific fields of practice. Part I, Overview of Collaborative Forensic

Practice, prepares the reader with a definition of collaborative forensic social work practice. Assuming a social justice systems approach, we define this specialty practice area to include all practice fields that operate in the sociolegal environment. These fields range from social and mental health services to the juvenile and criminal justice systems. Readers are guided on a journey through the history of forensic social work from its roots in the charity and corrections movements to its current manifestation as the work of professional clinicians and policy advocates. The use of a social justice systems approach helps readers visualize their practice within the sociolegal system. A comprehensive description of civil and criminal law helps readers understand the legal issues and court proceedings that affect clients and professional practice. This section concludes with a discussion of multidisciplinary practice, which provides practitioners with knowledge and skills that can be applied to any field of practice.

In Parts II through VI, readers are introduced to specific fields of practice affected by the sociolegal environment. In these sections, readers learn what it means to use legal knowledge and skills in practice areas, such as family and social services, education, child welfare, mental health and addictions, juvenile justice, criminal justice, and immigration systems. Readers also have the opportunity to hear from seasoned practitioners and experts about the types of clients or practice issues they may encounter in a specific practice field.

Part II, Forensic Practice in Family and Social Services, begins with an overview of which is followed by a discussion of forensic practice with female victims of partner violence and older adults victims of abuse. The educational system is another area in which social workers must know federal and state policies and other service systems that influence their students' success. Part III, Forensic Practice in Education, addresses the relationship between school social work and the law. The unique school reentry needs of juveniles being released from secure care in the juvenile justice system are also addressed.

As clients' problems become more serious, such as child maltreatment and neglect, social workers often become involved in the child welfare system. Part IV, Forensic Practice in Child Welfare, tackles specialized practice in the child welfare system. It provides readers with an overview of this system as well as a detailed account of the theory and practice of forensic interviewing with alleged victims of child sexual abuse.

Mental health and addictions are practice areas filled with legal quagmires. Part V, Forensic Practice in Mental Health and Substance Abuse, helps prepare social workers in this arena by making readers aware of the psychological, social, and legal issues affecting their clients and their professional practice. This section addresses the knowledge and skills required for practice with clients presenting with mental health and/or addiction issues in the community and the criminal justice system. Specialized topics addressed include social work practice with drug-court-involved clients, mothers in addictions treatment at risk of criminal justice involvement, and suicidal clients in jail settings.

In Part VI, Forensic Practice in Juvenile and Criminal Justice, readers learn about systems traditionally associated with forensic social work. Social workers in these systems often work with clients who have a multitude of social, psychological, financial, and legal issues involving delinquency or a criminal law violation. Three chapters provide insiders' portraits of the continuum of care for juveniles and adults that range from the courts to prisons to community reentry. Social justice issues, such as the disproportionate waiver of minority youth into the adult system, as well as the use of the restorative justice approach for victims and offenders are highlighted.

The book concludes with Part VII, Diversity, Human Rights, and Immigration. A detailed discussion linking human rights to forensic social work is presented. Special topics, such as social work practice with undocumented workers and refugees and victims of human trafficking, prepare social work practitioners to address the diverse sociolegal needs of these clients.

After reading this book, social workers will be better positioned to intervene with clients within and across various fields of practice. They will also be better prepared to integrate specialized knowledge and skills in interdisciplinary collaboration with other professionals. Additional resources found in the book enable the lifelong learning process of forensic social work practice with a variety of populations across a wide range of practice settings.

Acknowledgments

There are many people who helped shape this book idea into a reality. We are most indebted to the practitioners and clients who shared their experiences. Special thanks are extended to David Estrin and David Follmer for their editorial words of wisdom. We also acknowledge Professor Reba Brown and her undergraduate students at the University of North Carolina-Charlotte for adopting a draft version of this manuscript. The feedback provided by Professor Brown and her students was invaluable. We also thank our friends and family members for making this collaborative effort easier. We hope you know who you are!

Part I
Overview of Collaborative Forensic Practice

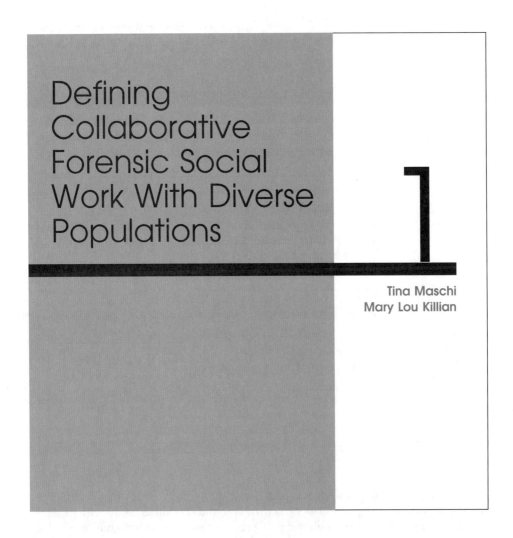

Defining Collaborative Forensic Social Work With Diverse Populations

1

Tina Maschi
Mary Lou Killian

As a professional social worker, inevitably you will encounter diverse individuals, families, or communities affected by social/environmental and legal issues. Poverty, homelessness, parental divorce, exposure to family or community violence, and juvenile or criminal offending are just some of the hardships clients face. Frontline social workers in a variety of settings (e.g., community-based child and family services, health care, education, child welfare, mental health, substance abuse, social services, juvenile justice, and criminal justice systems) interact daily with clients who have multiple problems, including legal ones. For example, a social worker may have a client who is a single father facing allegations of child neglect. He knows little about the child welfare policies and laws affecting his family or how to navigate the court system. Thus, it is imperative that social workers supplement their specialized practice expertise with knowledge of the laws and policies that influence their client populations. The practice of collaborative forensic social work is ideal because social workers are positioned to take action in a sociolegal environment.

We argue that all social workers across all fields of practice, not just those in juvenile and criminal justice settings, often assist clients affected by laws and policies

1.1

A broad definition of social work.

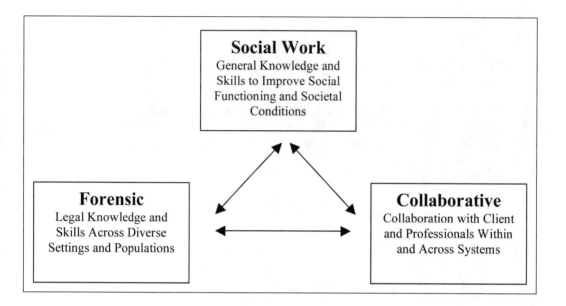

or problems in accessing resources. Therefore, it is imperative that practitioners integrate their understanding of collaboration, the law, and specialized skills with generalist social work practice. This book will help prepare practitioners with the knowledge, values, and skills to navigate the social and legal issues that affect clients.

We also argue that effective, collaborative forensic social work practice requires a two-pronged approach to helping clients. This dual approach involves intervening with clients on both an individual level to address a client's social well-being (e.g., referral to mental health counseling) and/or at the legal or policy levels (e.g., representing a youth in court as a child advocate or participating in lobbying efforts to advocate for legislation that addresses special population needs). We define collaborative forensic social work as an *integrated (i.e., generalist, specialized, and collectivistic) approach to social work practice with diverse populations across diverse practice settings in the sociolegal environment*. Figure 1.1 illustrates this definition. This figure depicts a broad definition of forensic social work that integrates the knowledge and skills of generalist and specialized social work, forensic social work, and collaboration. We refer to this specialty area as "collaborative forensic social work."

The integrated role of collaborative forensic social workers allows us to assume multiple professional roles, functions, and activities. This strategy is designed to improve clients' social functioning and environmental conditions through collaboration with clients, professionals, and other stakeholders within and across different systems of care. The "forensic" or "legal" aspect of the work situates social workers in a position to honor their professional commitment to social justice through the use of legal knowledge and skills, including advocacy and policy practice.

Definitions

Generalist Social Work

Embedded in our definition of collaborative forensic social work are the general principles of social work practice, such as the International Federation of Social Work's (IFSW) definition. According to the IFSW:

> The social work profession promotes social change, problem solving in human relationships, and the empowerment and liberation of people to enhance well-being. Utilizing theories of human behavior and social systems, social work intervenes at the points where people interact with their environments. Principles of human rights and social justice are fundamental to social work. (IFSW, 2000)

Forensic Social Work

There are a number of definitions of forensic social work. They range from general to specific and they may focus on one or more practice settings or populations. For example, Barker and Branson (2000) placed forensic social work in a broad "legal" environment, and they defined it as a "professional specialty that focuses on the interface between society's legal and human service systems" (p. 3). In contrast, Hughes and O'Neal (1983) defined forensic social work as specifically relating to the intersection of mental health and law, in which social workers "function in this space in which mental health concepts and the law form a gestalt" (p. 393). Roberts and Brownell (1999) described forensic social work in terms of the knowledge and skills needed for the specific populations served, particularly victims and offenders. In this case, forensic social work is the "policies, practices, and social work roles with juvenile and adult offenders and victims of crime" (p. 360). In comparison, Green, Thorpe, and Traupmann (2005) defined forensic social work more broadly as "practice, which in any manner may be related to legal issues and litigation, both criminal and civil" (p. 1).

Barker (2003) and the National Organization of Forensic Social Workers (1997) provide even broader definitions of forensic social work. Barker's definition addresses both civil and criminal law issues:

> The practice specialty in social work that focuses on the law, legal issues, and litigation, both criminal and civil, including issues in child welfare, custody of children, divorce, juvenile delinquency, nonsupport, relatives' responsibility, welfare rights, mandated treatment, and legal competency. Forensic social work helps social workers in expert witness preparation. It also seeks to educate law professionals about social welfare issues and social workers about the law. (p. 166)

On their Web site, the National Organization of Forensic Social Work (NOFSW) (1997) offers the broadest definition:

> Forensic social work is the application of social work to questions and issues relating to law and legal systems. This specialty of our profession goes far beyond clinics and

psychiatric hospitals for criminal defendants being evaluated and treated on issues of competency and responsibility. A broader definition includes social work practice which in any way is related to legal issues and litigation, both criminal and civil. Child custody issues, involving separation, divorce, neglect, termination of parental rights, the implications of child and spouse abuse, juvenile and adult justice services, corrections, and mandated treatment all fall under this definition. (para 1)

For more on the ethical issues of social work, see chapter 4, "Understanding Civil and Criminal Law."

Collaboration

As the various definitions suggest, social workers who practice in a sociolegal environment must be well versed in collaboration. This includes working with other professionals (e.g., attorneys, doctors and nurses, and victim advocates), law enforcement personnel, and clients, family members, and other stakeholders.

Historically, social workers have practiced in a variety of "host" agency settings, such as hospitals, schools, industries, psychiatric clinics, police departments, and court and criminal justice settings (Brownell & Roberts, 2002; Jansson & Simmons, 1986). (See chapter 2, "A History of Forensic Social Work in the United States.") With the increasing intricacies of social problems and dwindling resources, social workers' involvement in interdisciplinary collaboration within and across agencies is often unavoidable (Bronstein, 2003; Graham & Barter, 1999; Guin, Noble, & Merrill, 2003; Payne, 2000).

In particular, forensic social workers often work with interdisciplinary teams. When they do, the elements of interdisciplinary team practice often consist of:

- a group of professionals from different disciplines,
- a common purpose,
- the integration of various professional perspectives in decision making,
- interdependence,
- coordination and interaction,
- communication,
- role division based on expertise (Abramson & Rosenthal, 1995).

The ability to work interdependently with others is critical to achieving successful client outcomes. As Bronstein (2003) noted, interdisciplinary collaboration is an "effective interpersonal process that facilitates the achievement of goals that cannot be reached when individual professionals act on their own" (p. 299). Social workers who incorporate interdisciplinary collaboration into forensic practice are able to address sociolegal issues with the help of a variety of professionals in a group problem-solving process, which makes it possible to examine the problem from all angles (Abramson & Rosenthal, 1995).

In addition to multidisciplinary practice skills, multicultural competence is critical for forensic social work practice in which diverse populations are served. The following section underscores the important role of diversity in social work practice.

Underscoring Diversity in Forensic Social Work

"Diversity" or other related terms, such as "multiculturalism," "cultural competence," and "vulnerable populations" are commonly used in social work practice (Barker, 2003; Beckett & Johnson, 1995; Logan, 2003). *The Social Work Dictionary* defines diversity as "variety, or the opposite of homogeneity" (Barker, 2003, p. 126). Diversity within social organizations commonly refers to the "range of personnel who more accurately represent minority populations and people from varied backgrounds, cultures, ethnicities, and viewpoints" (Barker, 2003, p. 126). (See chapters 23 through 26 for a detailed discussion of diversity issues, especially those related to immigrants and refugees.)

The Diversity Dilemma

How can collaborative forensic social work develop a "way to be" that is affirming and inclusive of diversity? Many of the professions that collaborate in correctional settings are struggling with this question. In law, attorneys speak of "antioppressive legal practice" and the activation of "privilege and disadvantage" (Kafele, 2005). (See chapter 4, "Understanding Civil and Criminal Law.") In psychiatry, a leading text reminds the reader that cultural considerations should be paramount, for example, when offering expert assessment in areas such as competency to stand trial, the presence of mental illness, or the use of psychological testing across cultures (Tseng, Matthews, & Elwyn, 2004). In mental health treatment, the U.S. Department of Health and Human Services Substance Abuse and Mental Health Services Administration [SAMHSA] published extensive guidelines in 2001 mandating that correctional settings create comprehensive plans for addressing cultural practice in their settings.[1] In medicine and health care delivery, practitioners discuss the importance of "providing care within a framework of cultural meaning," expecting all colleagues to do so as standard practice (Hufft & Kite, 2003). And in social work, the core of our ethics mandates cultural competence, even when correctional institutions may not seem responsive to such concepts.[2] (See Part V, "Mental Health and Substance Abuse.")

Diversity and the Justice System

A glaring example of the lack of cultural competence, indeed the lack of acknowledgement of the role of privilege and race in the U.S. justice system, can be found in the overrepresentation of persons of color and persons from communities in poverty among the incarcerated population. James (2000) provided a good overview of some of these issues, citing rates of arrest for working-class versus typical "white-collar" crime; the use of those in prison as a source of labor; the overrepresentation of African American men in justice system "supervision" (e.g., probation, incarceration, or parole); uneven statistics for lengths of sentences and state executions; and inconsistencies between the U.S. justice system and some provisions of international human rights. James (2000) also noted that when state justice systems deny political rights (including, at times, the right to vote) to those who are or have been incarcerated, this disproportionately affects people of color and the poor. Addressing these issues is squarely within the realm of "diversity practice," and it is social work's responsibility to respond, as a profession that is based on an ethics of human rights.

Diversity in Practice

Diversity and collaborative forensic social work practice encompass several overlapping mandates. At the micro end of the spectrum, recruitment and retention of personnel throughout service and justice systems should reflect the diversity of the communities in which those systems operate. Those systems must also accommodate all individuals who are participating, whether accused, aggrieved, or employed, and respond to their diverse characteristics and abilities. Forensic social workers are ethically bound to develop practice skills grounded in an understanding of clients in their contextual identities and lives. In the mezzo section of the spectrum, social service programs and services must be vigilant regarding unintended structural biases that favor or accommodate individuals with certain backgrounds or characteristics over others. This extends to governmental agencies as well, whose policies and procedures may rise to the level of regulation or law and thus have even more impact on individuals' and families' lives. Finally, at the macro end of this continuum, the intersection of forensic social work with considerations of diversity points to the need to work for the improvement of human rights conditions throughout all nations. Wherever a forensic social work practitioner finds herself or himself on this continuum, the remaining segments cannot be ignored (see chapters 23 to 26).

Summary and Conclusions

The broad definition of collaborative forensic social work incorporates the knowledge, values, and skills of social work, policy practice, the law, collaboration, and diversity. Consistent with the mission of social work, collaborative forensic social work involves a two-pronged approach to assessment and intervention with diverse clients in a sociolegal environment. With the increased complexity of social problems, adopting this approach will help increase social and justice outcomes for the diverse populations we serve.

Notes

1. These can be accessed at http://mentalhealth.samhsa.gov/publications/allpubs /sma00–3457/ch2.asp
2. See, for example, Van Wormer (2001) on the conflicting paradigms of the two arenas.

References

Abramson, J. S., & Rosenthal, B. S. (1995). Interdisciplinary and interorganizational collaboration. In R. L. Edwards (Ed.), *Encyclopedia of social work* (19th ed., pp. 1479–1489). Washington, DC: NASW Press.

Barker, R. L. (2003). *The social work dictionary* (2nd ed.). Washington, DC: NASW Press.

Barker, R. L., & Branson, D. M. (2000). *Forensic social work: Legal aspects of professional practice* (2nd ed.). Binghamton, NY: Haworth Press.

Beckett, J. O., & Johnson, H. C. (1995). Human development. In R. L. Edwards & J. G. Hopps (Eds.), *Encyclopedia of social work* (pp. 1385–1405). Washington, DC: National Association of Social Workers Press.

Bronstein, L. R. (2003). A model for interdisciplinary collaboration. *Social Work, 48*, 296–306.

Brownell, P., & Roberts, A. L. (2002). A century of social work in criminal justice and correctional settings. *Journal of Offender Rehabilitation, 35*(2), 1–17.

Graham, J. R., & Barter, K. (1999). Collaboration: A social work practice method. *Families in Society, 80*(1), 6–13.

Green, G., Thorpe, J., & Traupmann, M. (2005). The sprawling thicket: Knowledge and specialisation in forensic social work. *Australian Social Work, 58*, 142–153.

Guin, C. C., Noble, D. N., & Merrill, T. S. (2003). From misery to mission: Forensic social workers on multidisciplinary mitigation teams. *Social Work, 48*, 362–371.

Hufft, A., & Kite, M. M. (2003). Vulnerable and cultural perspectives for nursing care in correctional systems. *Journal of Multicultural Nursing & Health, 9*(1), 18–26.

Hughes, D. S., & O'Neal, B. C. (1983). A survey of current forensic social work. *Social Work, 32*, 393–394.

International Federation of Social Work. (2000). *Definition of social work*. Retrieved May 9, 2007, from http://www.ifsw.org/en/p38000208.html

James, J. (2000). The dysfunctional and the disappearing: Democracy, race and imprisonment. *Social Identities, 6*, 483–492.

Jansson, B. S., & Simmons, J. (1986). The survival of social work units in host organizations. *Social Work, 35*, 339–343.

Kafele, K. (2005, March 3). *Understanding cultural competence. Fourth colloquium on the legal profession.* University of Windsor. Retrieved August 10, 2008, from http://www.lsuc.on.ca/media/fourthcolloquiumkafele.pdf

Logan, S. M. L. (2003). Issues of multiculturalism: Multicultural practice, cultural diversity, and competency. In R. A. English (Ed.), *Encyclopedia of social work* (19th ed., 2003 supplement, pp. 95–105). Washington, DC: NASW Press.

National Organization of Forensic Social Work. (1997). *What is forensic social work?* Retrieved on May 9, 2007, from http://www.nofsw.org/

Payne, M. (2000). *Teamwork in multiprofessional care.* Chicago: Lyceum Books.

Roberts, A. R., & Brownell, P. (1999). A century of forensic social work: Bridging the past to the present. *Social Work, 44*, 359–369.

Tseng, W.-S., Matthews, D., & Elwyn, T. S. (2004). *Cultural competence in forensic mental health.* New York: Brunner-Routledge.

Van Wormer, K. (2001). *Counseling female offenders and victims: A strengths-restorative approach.* New York: Springer Publishing Company.

A History of Forensic Social Work in the United States

2

Mary Lou Killian
Tina Maschi

Social workers respond to individuals in the criminal justice system, and work to change the system in which such individuals find themselves. Moreover, social workers not only respond to individuals affected by state and federal laws, but also work to change those laws. Forensic social work is as old as social work itself, and it represents the full diversity of our profession, which includes advocating for those accused or convicted of a crime; standing up for victims; responding to youth in juvenile justice systems; testifying in court on behalf of both litigants and defendants; supporting and working alongside law enforcement professionals; and working to improve or change the processes and policies of the U.S. justice system.

How could social work not be present in all these arenas? Our profession revolves around social justice and human rights. Throughout U.S. history, social justice (and in later years, global and universal human rights) has been the core of the theory and practice of social work. Social workers stand for those who cannot; speak for those who have been silenced; and seek to create conditions of empowerment for individuals, families, and communities.

In this light, the history of forensic social work is hard to separate from the history of social work. In fact, one of social work's first professional societies was the National

Conference of Charities and Corrections, formed in 1879—pioneer social worker Jane Addams became the leader of the organization in 1909. This suggests the importance given to corrections, both in early conceptualizations of social services formed over a century ago and in today's understanding of the proper venues for social workers as actors and advocates. To trace the history of forensic social work, we first need to look at the history of forensic policy in the North American colonies and then at the creation of social work and the introduction of social workers to carry out or change those policies. Exhibit 2.1 lists major historical events in the history of forensic social work in the United States.

The History of Forensic Policy

The Colonial Era

No history of social work can be written without reference to the English Poor Laws of 1601. One reason they are significant is that they represent a merging of law and social policy, a codification of society's responses to individuals in distress with an emphasis on government as the entity in charge of those responses. The laws responded to people in poverty, dividing them into three categories: deserving, undeserving, and children (Day, 2006). The Poor Laws are also significant because they represent the first opportunity for intervention by individuals who would later create the field of social work: advocates for those on the receiving end of the law.

Later, early English colonists were influenced by the laws and systems of England. Legally, this meant they also codified responses to the impoverished members of their settlements: individuals were divided up and then either shuffled to almshouses (for those who could not work) or workhouses (for the able-bodied). They were reluctant, however, to turn to government as the appropriate and responsible institution for maintaining law and order (perhaps exhibiting what might now be understood as communal posttraumatic stress disorder from their experiences living under a monarch perceived to be overly rigid and tyrannical). As a result, early police forces were made up of men patrolling neighborhood streets, first at night, later during the day as well (Blakely & Bumphus, 1999). If a "criminal" were caught, the colonists sought swift punishment, usually of a corporal nature (Popple & Leighninger, 2002). Concepts of right and wrong—and views of human nature at the time—did not suggest that criminals would benefit from rehabilitation or that their victims needed support and advocacy.

The first institutions associated with crime and punishment were jails, which were simple holding cells for individuals, both children and adults, awaiting trial or punishment.[1] The ensuing political break from England and concomitant development of Enlightenment philosophies, however, popularized a valuing of rationality that in many ways survives today. "Rational man" was thought to be changeable if shown the error of his ways; extrapolated to corrections, this gave rise to "proportional" punishments rather than "punitive" ones and engendered early concepts of rehabilitation. After the Revolutionary War, the first prison in the United States—"Walnut Street Jail"—was constructed in Philadelphia in 1790 (Popple & Leighninger, 2002). Because at that time crime was seen as arising from disorder, prison staff imposed strict discipline, schedules, and order on incarcerated individuals. This philosophy often

Exhibit 2.1

Major Events in the History of Forensic Social Work in the United States

General U. S. History

Europeans leave European continent, settle in North America. Enslavement of Africans, Native Americans, and later the Irish, begins.

1766—North American colonies become independent from England, create the United States

1787—An Age of Rationality spreads through Europe and influences the writers of the U.S. Constitution

1812–1814—U.S. and Great Britain at war

1845—Portions of Mexico are annexed as Texas, setting off the Mexican–American war from 1846–1848

1861–1865—U.S. Civil War

Late 1800s—Varieties of internal combustion engines are perfected, setting the stage in the U.S. for the Industrial Revolution

1920—U.S. women gain the right to vote

1929—U.S. stock market crash sets off the Great Depression

1939–1945—Portions of the world fight in World War II

1950s—U.S. policy encourages White women to leave work and return home for the sake of their womanhood and their families

1961—Eleanor Roosevelt is appointed chair of President Kennedy's Commission on the Status of Women; its 1963 report documents discrimination in the workplace

1960s/1970s—Social movements in the U.S. bring focus on women's rights, civil rights for African Americans, and gay and lesbian rights

2001—On Sept. 11 the U.S. is hit by three simultaneous crimes of terrorism

Social Work History

1700s—*Men on patrol looked for "criminals"; punishment was usually corporal.*

1790—Concepts of prisons as rehabilitative grow; the first prison in the U.S. opens in Philadelphia: the "Walnut Street Jail."

Conceptualizations of corrections develop to include proportionate sentencing and programs encouraging reform.

1800s—*Theorists note that determinate sentences undermine efforts at individual reformation.*

1875—The Society for Prevention of Cruelty to Children is created

1876—The concept of parole is born; the first parolee is released from the Elmira Reformatory in New York.

1879—National Conference of Charities and Corrections is formed

1898—The first social work training school opens

1899—Illinois opens the first juvenile court

1900s

1907—The National Council on Crime and Delinquency was formed

1920—Two thirds of U.S. states institute procedures for probation, a concept originated in Massachusetts.

1921—The American Association of Social Workers is formed

1925—Forty-six states now have juvenile courts

Forensic social workers advocate for social, political, and economic reforms

1940s—Police social workers return to prominence in forensics

1960s—Federal social policies begin to emphasize social responsibility and deinstitutionalization of prisoners and the mentally ill

1973—First shelter for female victims of battering opens in Arizona

1974—The Juvenile Justice and Delinquency Prevention Act passes; The Child Abuse Prevention and Treatment Act passes

U.S. society sours on rehabilitation and begins to "get tough on crime"

1984—Victims of Crime Act passes

2001—On Oct. 26 the U.S. Congress passes the Patriot Act, establishing new executive branch powers for certain crimes carried over to almshouses and workhouses, which by definition were not correctional institutions, but whose operation was often indistinguishable from prisons. More opportunities for social work collaborative intervention were thus being created.

The 1800s

The 19th century saw a vigorous application of new legal and correctional policies. By midcentury, however, many were questioning if the philosophy was effective. If prisoners were sentenced to a fixed length of time, and if they were going to be incarcerated until their sentence was completed, regardless of their behavior, what incentive did they have to participate in the rigors of rehabilitative programs? Thus, the concept of early release as a reward for "good behavior" was created: Persons under incarceration began to be released early through parole. The first such individual was set free from the Elmira Reformatory in New York in 1876.

John Augustus, a wealthy shoe manufacturer in Boston, began social reform in the early 1840s when he started the practice of interviewing adults awaiting incarceration, personally posting their bail, and taking responsibility for their reformation, a pattern that was later instituted by Massachusetts as the process of probation. The practice spread to two thirds of the states by 1920 (Popple & Leighninger, 2002). Probation extended the concept of rehabilitation: those committing crimes could change their ways, either through discipline and programs in prison that could lead to early release, or through strict supervision and reform that could prevent incarceration completely. Though we cannot claim Augustus was a social worker, his actions foreshadowed those of the pioneers in forensic social work and helped solidify approaches to human nature that emphasized a person's ability to change and grow. Such views would soon extend to those in other "legal" institutions, such as almshouses and workhouses.

The 20th Century and the Birth of Social Work

National Conference of Charities and Corrections

Having declared independence, fought two wars with Britain, another between its own citizens, and experienced many social upheavals, the United States was grappling with a myriad of social issues. It was in this climate that social work as a profession began to develop. The first social work training school opened in 1898. Earlier, in 1879, the National Conference of Charities and Corrections (formerly the Conference of Boards of Public Charities) was created, becoming the National Conference of Social Work in 1917, and joining a collaborative to become the National Association of Social Workers in 1955 (Zenderland, 1998). Trailblazing social workers were concerned with social reform, and law and justice issues were a primary focus (Barker & Branson, 2000; Roberts & Brownell, 1999). The plight of the poor was a major concern of Mary Richmond, a pioneer in social work and the founding mother of casework (Colcard & Mann, 1930). Jane Addams, a Nobel Prize-winning social work pioneer, targeted the systems and policies that affected the poor of her day. Addams was also the founder of settlement houses (Day, 2006).

The Creation of Juvenile Courts

A key accomplishment of early social workers was to change the policy regarding young persons charged with criminal offenses (Platt, 1969, 1977). Julia Lathrop, Jane

Addams, and Lucy Flower pushed to get children out of penal institutions, where individuals as young as 5 were incarcerated with adults. Their efforts led to the birth of the juvenile justice system in 1899 (Center on Juvenile & Criminal Justice, 1999). The new system saw several innovations. The Juvenile Psychopathic Institute, founded as a result of advocacy by several residents of Hull House, including Florence Kelley, Alice Hamilton, Julia Lathrop, Ellen Gates Starr, Sophonisba Breckinridge, and Grace and Edith Abbott, began to conduct psychosocial assessments of children in the justice system (Open Collections Program, Harvard University Library, n.d.). Again, many collaborators came together—this time to create separate juvenile courts, the first seated in Illinois in 1899. By 1925, 46 states and the District of Columbia had created juvenile courts, where hearings considered delinquency as well as the needs of abused and neglected children. The Society for Prevention of Cruelty to Children (NYSPCC), founded in New York in 1875 and modeled after the early Societies for Prevention of Cruelty to Animals, presaged these later juvenile justice reforms (NYSPCC, n.d.).

These institutional changes were both fueled by and gave birth to new theories of human nature and childhood. Mary Richmond's efforts, first in Baltimore's Charity Organization Society and later as the director of the Russell Sage Foundation, argued for private social work practice, and for creating a system of social work education for "recognizing human differences and adjusting our systems of…law, of reformation and of industry to those differences" (quoted in Colcard & Mann, 1930, p, 5). Jane Addams's efforts called for structuring policies that saw children not as "mini-adults" but as developmentally different, young individuals needing guidance and care who could not be expected to see the world or make decisions as adults do. Children were thus afforded closed hearings and, eventually, confidentiality of their court records and limitations of the records' availability once the children attained adulthood (Center on Juvenile and Criminal Justice, 1999).[2]

Collaborative Reforms in Adult Courts

At the same time that juvenile courts were being created, U.S. policies regarding the larger criminal justice system were also in flux. With the advent of parole in the mid- to late 1800s and the creation of juvenile courts at the end of the century, reformers gained a renewed commitment to rehabilitation, a concept that had found itself on shaky ground prior to these changes. Prisons were renamed "penitentiaries," and their goals included repentance (hence the name) and reform of the individual (Blakely & Bumphus, 1999). These goals fit well with the dual aims of social work: changing social systems and changing the individuals who have strayed from those systems. For the latter, social casework was the proper response and individuals in penitentiaries were appropriate recipients. With the creation of the American Association of Social Workers in 1921 (forerunner to the National Association of Social Workers) casework became the central focus, and services focused on offenders made "correctional treatment specialists" of social workers (Roberts & Brownell, 1999).

Social Workers Call for Social Change

Social work swung back to an emphasis on social change, however, when the Great Depression began in 1929. Providing services for the "new poor" (i.e., individuals in poverty who were formerly working class or middle class) helped social workers realize that policy change was often the proper arena for their profession. Social workers testified before Congressional committees calling for policy revisions, and many New Deal programs were influenced by their expertise. As Secretary of Labor, Frances Perkins, who had been trained by Mary Richmond, was instrumental in creating reforms, including regulations ensuring safe conditions for American workers and the design and establishment of Social Security (Day, 2002; Frances Perkins Center, 2008). Social worker Harry Hopkins, appointed by President Hoover and again by President Franklin Roosevelt, oversaw new initiatives in the Works Projects Administration, which focused on youth; these were the forerunners of today's delinquency-prevention programs (Roberts & Brownell, 1999).

In the early 1920s, police social workers were common: they were women who provided social work advocacy as members of groups called Women's Bureaus, which functioned as divisions within local police departments. These positions were cut following the Great Depression, but returned to prominence in the 1940s. At that time, youth gangs were growing in number, and hundreds of child guidance clinics opened that employed social workers as court liaisons. Community-based councils and delinquency-prevention programs were created; these focused on supporting and intervening with individuals, including children who had dropped out of school, and members of what the courts labeled "problem families" (Roberts & Brownell, 1999).

Government Policy Includes Forensic Social Work

As great social change unfolded in the United States over the coming decades, changes in policies and approaches to criminal justice also evolved. Within the context of a new emphasis on reform and social responsibility (Sullivan, 2007), Presidents Kennedy and Johnson expanded federal policy and funding aimed at preventing or addressing juvenile delinquency. The prototype initiative was the New York City Mobilization for Youth. Created by a federal grant to the Columbia University School of Social Work, it laid the groundwork for a multitude of similar programs to follow (Sullivan, 2007). Forensic social workers also increased their role in juvenile and adult probation services. The executive director of the National Council on Crime and Delinquency was social worker Milton Rector, who felt that probation officers should hold master of social work degrees. At the same time, federal dollars were allocated for correctional treatment programs for adults, pretrial diversion programs, and 262 youth service bureaus. During this decade, social workers worked in police departments, psychiatric settings, juvenile justice programs, and at probation offices (Haynes, 1998; Roberts & Brownell, 1999).

In the early 1970s, Massachusetts social worker Jerome Miller created the soon-copied policy of moving youth in juvenile justice systems from institutions to smaller, community-based group homes. In 1974, the passage of the federal Juvenile Justice and Delinquency Prevention Act intensified the focus on deinstitutionalization (Nelson, 1984). At the same time, forensic social workers and child welfare reformers collaborated to highlight the incidence of child maltreatment and to create programmatic responses, first at the state and later at the federal level. This led to the passage of the Child Abuse Prevention and Treatment Act (1974), which appropriated funds for child abuse assessment and treatment teams, which were usually led by medical social workers (Day, 2006).

In 1973, the first shelter for women battered by their husbands opened in Arizona; later in the decade, shelters for female victims and services for male perpetrators of family violence begin to proliferate. Thus the focus on social responsibility that grew in the 1960s in the United States led to the institutionalization of certain initial reforms in the rights of women and children at the federal level. These initiatives brought a renewed focus on victims' needs and rights to the forensic social work arena.

A Shift From Social Reform to Individual Responsibility

Corrections policies began to focus on "get tough on crime" initiatives in the 1980s. Prison populations grew rapidly, and program dollars were stretched thin. Many correctional administrators spent the majority of their budgets on maintaining order and security in their institutions, leaving little funding for services. Feminists brought the impact of crime on survivors of domestic violence and rape to the national spotlight, highlighted by the landmark Victims of Crime Act (1984). The American public was not convinced that prisons were meeting the goal of reforming individuals and debated what to do in response to violent crime. Some have called what followed a "rage to punish," as harsher sentences and mandatory sentencing laws proliferated (Haney & Zimbardo, 1998). Though treatment services for perpetrators of domestic violence continued to be available, they were in outpatient settings, and the correctional goal of rehabilitation for incarcerated persons began to wane (Haney & Zimbardo, 1998).

The United States was struggling to determine a philosophy for correctional work (Gebelein, 2000). Was it truly "correctional"? Or was the point of prison systems to protect the public from the violent offenders locked inside? Was it to deter those who might otherwise commit violent crime? Was the point of prison simply for members of society to feel better because the "bad guys" were punished?

Faith in the possibility of rehabilitation was dealt a severe blow with the publication—and some would say the misinterpretation—of Robert Martinson's evaluation of reform programs, "What Works?" Martinson was one of three researchers, the last to join the project; he published the results early and without his colleagues, stating that little proof exists to suggest that rehabilitative programs are successful (Martinson, 1974; Wilks, 2004). When the full article was published, the conclusions were not as dramatic, suggesting that some efforts were effective under some conditions with some subsets of incarcerated persons (Lipton, Martinson, & Wilks, 1975). However, it was the first article to make such a claim and its strong questioning of the efficacy of rehabilitation had an impact.

In this climate, collaborative forensic social work opportunities shifted from prison-based rehabilitation to community-based victim/witness assistance programs, where it is estimated that approximately one third of the staff are social workers (Barker & Branson, 2000; Roberts & Brownell, 1999). Community-based corrections initiatives, such as halfway programs and community courts, also turned to social workers for expertise. In the mid-1980s, federal monies were appropriated for the RESTTA initiative: Restitution Education, Specialized Training, and Technical Assistance. This program of the federal Office of Juvenile Justice and Delinquency Prevention (OJJDP) offered local probation departments and courts the resources to hold juvenile offenders accountable, either through monetary compensation, community service, or direct victim services (Roberts & Brownell, 1999). Currently such programs can be found in OJJDP Juvenile Accountability Block Grants. Related to these approaches are the youth-focused "boot camp" or "tough love" projects that seek accountability by mandating early intervention for high-risk young offenders. The success of these programs is unclear, and some high-profile failures have affected their support.[3]

Social Work Post 9-11

The horrific crimes that occurred in the United States on September 11, 2001, and the myriad of local, state, and federal law and justice policies that have followed are creating a new chapter in forensic policy and changing social workers' roles. President George W. Bush's "War on Terror" led to many new laws, perhaps most significant of which was the Patriot Act: Uniting and Strengthening America by Providing Appropriate Tools Required to Intercept and Obstruct Terrorism, passed on October 26, 2001, and revised and reauthorized in March 2006. The Act heightened the role of governmental intervention to anticipate and prevent specific crimes and alters the protections provided for those accused. Although much of the Act focuses on international security concerns, domestic polices have shifted in its wake, affecting immigrants and those seeking refuge or asylum. In this unfolding arena, collaborative forensic social workers again face a continuum of tasks and challenges, from individual casework and intervention to policy advocacy and social change.

Summary and Conclusions

Over 100 years ago, social workers understood that government, as author and institutor of policy, can and should be an arena for reform. Their efforts in the justice system set a high standard for forensic social workers of today. Our foremothers saw that advocating for their "clients" meant advocating for systemic reform, as they collaborated to apply a two-pronged approach to social welfare: individual and social change. This bifurcation of social action weaves throughout the history of forensic social work. In today's sociolegal environment, the duality becomes a continuum of options for intervention, as social workers offer an integrated approach for clients across diverse settings. Chapter 3 assists social workers with conceptualizing their practice within and across multiple service systems.

Notes

1. This is well before several professions, such as psychology, helped to develop conceptions of childhood and children as developmentally different from adults.
2. Though see Platt's (1977) seminal work critiquing these reforms as ultimately hurting youth, pathologizing them, and institutionalizing their subservient social position.
3. For a famous example, consider the case of 14-year-old Martin Anderson, who died in custody in a "boot camp" in Florida in 2006. See www.MartinLeeAnderson.com Accessed September 2, 2008.

References

Barker, R. L., & Branson, D. M. (2000). *Forensic social work: Legal aspects of professional practice* (2nd ed.). New York: Haworth Press.

Blakely, C. R., & Bumphus, V. W. (1999). American criminal justice philosophy: What's old—What's new? *Federal Probation: A Journal of Correctional Philosophy and Practice, 63*(1), 62–66.

Center on Juvenile & Criminal Justice. (1999). *Second chances: Giving kids a chance to make a better choice.* Retrieved on July 27, 2007, from http://www.cjcj. org/pubs/archive.php

Colcard, J. C., & Mann, R. Z. S. (Eds.). (1930). *The long view: Papers and addresses of Mary E. Richmond.* New York: Russell Sage Foundation.

Day, P. J. (2006). *A new history of social welfare* (5th ed.). New York: Allyn & Bacon.

Frances Perkins Center. (2008). *Homepage.* Retrieved September 2, 2008, at http://www.frances perkins-center.org/history.html

Gebelein, R. S. (2000). The rebirth of rehabilitation: Promise and perils of drug courts. In *Sentencing and corrections: Issues for the 21st century.* Washington, DC: National Institute of Justice.

Haney, C., & Zimbardo, P. (1998). The past and future of U.S. prison policy: Twenty-five years after the Stanford Prison Experiment. *American Psychologist, 53,* 709–727.

Harvard University Library. (n.d.). *Open Collections Program: Working women: Jane Addams.* Retrieved September 2, 2008, at http://ocp.hul.harvard.edu/ww/people_addams.html

Haynes, K. S. (1998). The one hundred-year debate: Social reform versus individual treatment. *Social Work, 43,* 501–509.

Lipton, D., Martinson, R., & Wilks, J. (1975). *The effectiveness of correctional treatment: A survey of treatment evaluation studies.* New York: Praeger.

Martinson, R. (1974). What works? Questions and answers about prison reform. *Public Interest, 35,* 22–54.

New York Society for the Prevention of Cruelty to Children. (n.d.). *Our 129 year commitment to the safety and well being of children.* Retrieved on July 27, 2007, from http://www.nyspcc.org/beta_history/index_history.htm

Nelson, B. J. (1984). *Making an issue of child abuse: Political agenda setting for social problems.* Chicago: University of Chicago Press.

Platt, A. M. (1969). The rise of the child-saving movement: A study in social policy and correctional reform. *Annals of the American Academy of Political & Social Science, 381,* 21–38.

Platt, A. M. (1977). *The child savers: The invention of delinquency* (2nd ed.). Chicago: University of Chicago Press.

Popple, P. R., & Leighninger, L. (2002). *Social work, social welfare, and American society* (5th ed.). Boston: Allyn & Bacon.

Roberts, A. R., & Brownell, P. (1999). A century of forensic social work: Bridging the past to the present. *Social Work, 44,* 359–369.

Sullivan, P. (2007). *A selected history of juvenile justice facilities.* Retrieved on September 2, 2007, from http://www.aia.org/SiteObjects/files/ caj_a_20070323_juvenile_history.pdf

Wilks, J. (2004). Revisiting Martinson: Has corrections made progress in the past 30 years? *Corrections Today, 66,* 108–111.

Zenderland, L. (1998). *Measuring minds.* New York: Cambridge University Press.

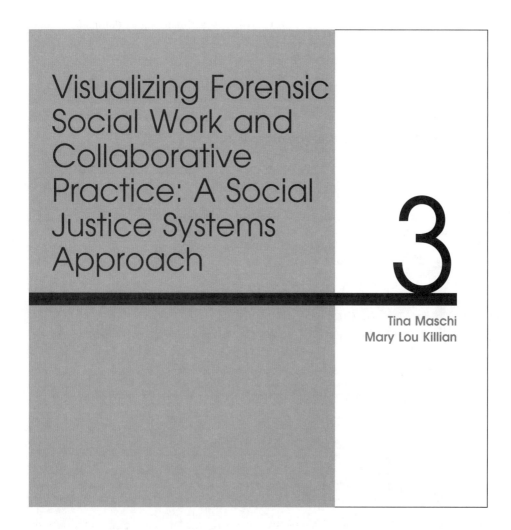

Visualizing Forensic Social Work and Collaborative Practice: A Social Justice Systems Approach

3

Tina Maschi
Mary Lou Killian

Social work can be characterized as an enduring and dynamic force whose presence has helped improve individual and societal conditions. Born out of early-20th-century efforts of charity workers or "friendly visitors," social work has grown from being a loose-knit group of community volunteers who were "doing good" to an internationally recognized profession endowed with the responsibility of providing social welfare services and advocating for social change (Addams, 1910; Ehrenreich; 1985; Richmond, 1917). However, contemporary social work practice finds itself in a complex and interactive global society fraught with social problems and has arrived at a critical crossroad in which advancing the mission of social work involves equipping practitioners with additional skills. Today, social workers must also navigate the legal system, collaborating from within to create change. Madden (2003) stresses the point: "If the social work profession is to be in control of its future, it must become committed to the role of exerting influence on the legal system through education, advocacy and proactive legal policy development" (pp. 3–4). To this end, this chapter frames forensic social work and collaboration through the lens of central guiding theories of social work practice: the person-in-environment perspective, social justice, and social systems theory. We propose an integrated theoretical perspective that we refer to as a *social*

3.1

A conceptual diagram of the social justice systems approach.

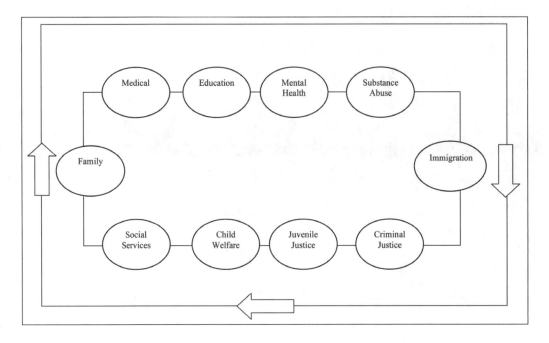

justice systems (SJS) approach. This perspective is useful for visualizing practice with clients influenced by social and legal issues. Figure 3.1 presents a conceptual diagram of the social justice systems approach.

This approach helps to visualize collaborative forensic social work practice in any practice setting. As illustrated, social workers working with individuals and families involved in the service systems are affected by social issues as well as laws, legal issues, and policies. As the arrows indicate, social workers can be involved with clients sequentially or concurrently, and be affected by civil law (e.g., going through a divorce, death of a loved one, sexual harassment on the job) or criminal law (e.g., victim of a violent crime, arrested for a criminal offense).

Collaborative forensic social work is an ideal vehicle for navigating the sociolegal environment. It integrates generalist and specialist practice with knowledge and skills of law, policy practice, and interdisciplinary collaboration. In fact, a commitment to practice that involves social and legal interventions is consistent with the historic two-pronged approach to social work practice.

The Two-Pronged Approach to Social Work Practice

Social work has long used a two-pronged approach to facilitate change: (a) assisting individuals and families to improve functioning and (b) combating unjust and unfair societal conditions through strategies of social reform (Bartlett, 1958; see Figure 3.2). These strategies are explained in the mission statement of the National Association of Social Workers *Code of Ethics* (1996):

> *The mission of social work is to enhance human well-being and help meet the basic human needs of all people, with particular attention to the needs and empowerment of people who are vulnerable, oppressed, and living in society. A historic and defining feature of social work is the profession's focus on individual well-being in a social context and the well-being of society. Fundamental to social work is attention to the environmental forces that create, contribute, and address problems in living. (p. 1)*

The two-pronged approach also is echoed in this definition of social work. The *Social Work Dictionary* defines social work as an "applied science of helping people achieve an effective level of psychosocial functioning and effecting societal changes to enhance the well-being of all people" (Barker, 2003, p. 408). Consequently, social work practitioners target their interventions at the micro level (e.g., individuals), the mezzo level (e.g., families and groups), and/or the macro level (e.g., institutions, organizations, cultures, and communities) (Zastrow & Kirst-Ashman, 2004). Miley, O'Meila, and Dubois (2007) outlined four major goals for practice addressing multilevel assessment and intervention strategies. These four goals are:

1. enhancing people's individual functioning, problem-solving, and coping abilities;
2. linking clients to needed resources;
3. working to develop and improve the social-service delivery network;
4. promoting social justice through the development of social policy.

It is interesting that the seemingly opposite roles of helper and advocate have both unified the profession (a common person-in-environment perspective) and divided it (Should the primary target of change be the individual or the environment?) (Bartlett, 1970). In social work literature, the environment is commonly referred to as the "social environment." We argue that expanding the definition of a "social environment" to include a "justice environment" is necessary for achieving positive outcomes consistent with the dual mission of social work.

Advancing a Social Justice Systems Perspective

The Social and Justice Environments

The social environment is often viewed as the place in which person-in-environment interactions occur (Zastrow & Kirst-Ashman, 2004). However, although the social environment is commonly viewed as omnipresent, the justice environment is equally present. The justice environment consists of individuals, families, and communities seeking fairness, equality, and the balance of power, as well as the laws, policies, and legal system that affect the social environment (Barker, 2003).

The presence of justice is implicit in the descriptions of the social environment. The social environment may range from an individual's interactions with social or organizational settings (e.g., home, school, society, work, agency, and neighborhood), social systems (e.g., individuals, groups, families, friends, and work groups), attributes

Part I Overview of Collaborative Forensic Practice

3.2

A two-pronged approach to practice in a sociolegal environment that influences social workers' activities across the field of practice.

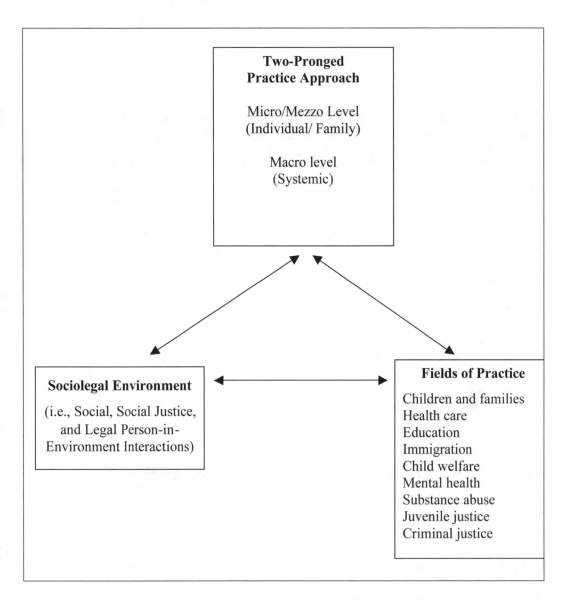

of society (e.g., laws and social norms and rules), social institutions (e.g., health care, social welfare, education, juvenile and criminal justice, and governmental systems), to social forces (e.g., political, economic, cultural, environmental, and ideological forces) (DuBois & Miley, 2003; Johnson & Yanca, 2004; Zastrow & Kirst-Ashman, 2004). Although person-in-environment interactions describe social settings and interactions, they are also suggestive of justice situations (e.g., denied employment because of a disability or history of incarceration) or settings (e.g., involvement in juvenile and criminal justice settings) and justice-oriented interactions (e.g., associating with delinquent peers, being arrested by the police for driving while intoxicated, being a victim of a bias crime, or losing one's home to eminent domain).

Envisioning Social Work Practice in a Sociolegal Environment

Most clients are affected by some type of legal issue, such as divorce, custody of children, accessing civil rights, death and inheritance, or being convicted of a felony (Madden & Wayne, 2003; Saltzman & Furman, 1999; Schroeder, 1997). In the United States, it is critical that social workers be aware of how our federal legal system operates. The U.S. legal system is made up of different branches, levels, and types of government. Laws range from the federal level—governing the entire United States—to individual state laws and local ordinances and regulations from municipalities, counties, and quasi-public agencies (Saltzman & Furman, 1999). Madden (2003) argued that law, with its legal rules and mandates, should be viewed as a mechanism that frames social work practice.

A Social Justice Systems Perspective

We propose a social justice systems perspective that conceptualizes the interaction of persons within a "social justice" environment. The core social work value of social justice is a central aspect of this perspective. Barker (2003) defined social justice as "an ideal condition in which all societal members have the same rights, protection, opportunities, obligations, and social benefits" (p. 404). The sociolegal environment represents a combination of social justice (person-in-environment interactions that seek a balance towards social justice or fairness) and the legal environment (which represents the law, the legal process, and institutions that seek individual and community protection). Thus, the SJS perspective allows social workers to pursue optimal social and justice outcomes for their clients across all fields of practice.

Figure 3.3 depicts a social justice systems map that shows the different pathways individuals and families may travel across the social service and/or justice systems of care. These service trajectories may span a continuum from the least to most restrictive service environments. The social justice system is comprised of an individual's proximal social system and the "social justice sectors of care." Each sector of care represents a service subsystem in which individuals are affected by this sector's laws and policies. Although health and education are universal services, the other subsystems are specifically designed to provide services for individuals and/or families at risk. Individuals and families may have varied patterns of system bias and discrimination, unmet service needs, and/or concurrent and/or sequential service-use patterns that include health, education, social services, child welfare, mental health, substance abuse, and juvenile justice and criminal justice service sectors of care.

The SJS framework builds on social systems theory. Social systems theory focuses on "the relationships that exist among members of human systems and between these

3.3

A conceptual diagram of the different systems that individuals and families may use in the social and justice sectors of care.

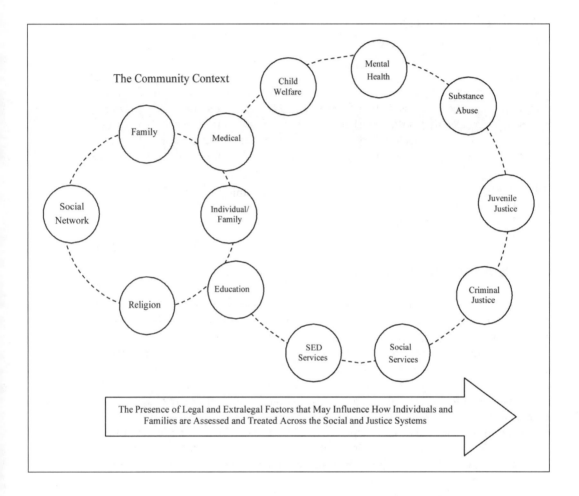

systems and their impinging environments" (Dubois & Miley, 2003, p. 59). Within each larger system are smaller nested subsystems. A change in one part of a system affects other parts of the system (Johnson & Yanca, 2004). Social work practitioners commonly assess and intervene in the subsystems of family, health care, education, social service, as well as political and legal systems.

In an ideal world, these social systems would function at their optimum potential. Families would be able to care for the physical, emotional, and social development of young and elderly family members; health and mental health institutions would assist all individuals in achieving and maintaining optimal physical, mental, emotional, and spiritual health; educational institutions would help all individuals to achieve the knowledge and skills needed to excel in society; social service systems would be able to help all individuals in need; and the political and legal system would provide protection, safety, and human rights to all individuals and families by developing or implementing laws, maintaining order, and fostering their creativity and potential.

However, the reality of our global society does not match this ideal. The interaction between and among systems is often conflicted because of social tension, service barriers, missed opportunities, power struggles, oppression, and other social injustices. Johnson and Yanca (2004) argue that when applying social systems theory, individuals' needs and rights must be considered in the context of larger systems because of these divergent environmental demands.

When applying an SJS approach, social interactions among individuals and their environment also are viewed as dynamic and multidimensional. The interaction between individuals and the different systems in their environment may significantly affect their level of functioning. For example, a single mother with four children who has no mode of transportation will be unable to get public assistance or food stamps. Because social workers "strive to ensure access to needed information, services, and resources; equality of opportunity; and meaningful participation in decision making for all people" (NASW, 1996, p. 1), a social worker for this family can apply a two-pronged approach to intervention: He or she may provide resource links to public assistance and employment services as well as advocating for the development of shuttle services for social service recipients.

Social workers also must recognize that individuals and families may be involved in multiple systems concurrently or sequentially (Garland, Hough, Landsverk, & Brown, 2001). For example, a child with emotional and behavioral problems may simultaneously be involved in special education services, community mental health services, and probation. Another child may have initially entered the child welfare system and then later gone through the juvenile justice system. The role of the social worker will include identifying obstacles, making resource linkages, or advocating for needed resources across these social institutions (Finn & Jacobson, 2003).

An SJS approach balances the goal of maximizing outcomes on both individual and societal levels. It also emphasizes the need for the knowledge and skills in forensic or legal issues, interdisciplinary collaboration, and generalist social work that integrates policy and practice. The SJS approach helps to frame social workers' efforts in pursuing social change, especially for vulnerable and oppressed populations affected by systemic issues (e.g., poverty, discrimination). Consistent with the NASW *Code of Ethics* (NASW, 1996), assessing for social and justice outcomes can "ensure access to needed information, services, and resources; equality of opportunity; and meaningful participation in decision making for all people" (p. 1). Thus, the jurisprudent social worker who is savvy with both policy and the law can more competently engage in multilevel intervention strategies that include direct practice, community organizing, supervision, consultation, administration, advocacy, social and political action, policy development and implementation, education, and research and evaluation (NASW, 1996).

Therapeutic Jurisprudence

An important element of the SJS approach is viewing law as an intervention. This principle is derived from the therapeutic jurisprudence literature, which examines the therapeutic (i.e., positive) and antitherapeutic (i.e., negative) consequences of legal rules, procedures, and actions (Madden & Wayne, 2003). According to Madden and Wayne (2003), "at the heart of therapeutic jurisprudence is the concept that law, consistent with justice, due process, and other relevant normative values, can and should function as a therapeutic agent" (p. 339). Thus, the impact of the law on a client may have positive or negative effects. For example, an individual with disabilities may win a court case for job discrimination based on legal protections inherent in the Americans with Disabilities Act. This is an example of how a law provided positive protections for this individual. In contrast, a single mother being released from prison on a controlled-dangerous-substance offense is denied public assistance based on a law that denies benefits to individuals with prior drug charges. This is an example of how a law provided negative or antitherapeutic effects on this mother's ability to receive needed services for herself and her family. Therefore, social workers must evaluate the intervention effects of the legal process and the outcomes on individuals, families, and communities. Based on this evaluation, an intervention strategy that incorporates a two-pronged approach that enhances social functioning and improves social justice outcomes can be devised.

Social workers who adopt principles of therapeutic jurisprudence will also be positioned to create conditions that empower clients or influence the development of laws and the ways current laws and policies can be applied most beneficially. Therapeutic jurisprudence is a useful perspective for social workers in interdisciplinary settings, working with professionals such as medical providers, psychologists, psychiatrists, police officers, probation officers, or attorneys. This perspective crosses professional boundaries and incorporates another important element, *interdisciplinary collaboration*, which is particularly concerned with creative problem solving in which the combined knowledge, skills, and techniques of multiple professionals seek to achieve social and justice outcomes (Madden, 2003; Madden & Wayne, 2003; Petrucci, 2007). A professional specialty, forensic social work, which focuses on equipping social workers with additional legal knowledge, is particularly well suited to take a leading role in the rapidly growing sociolegal environment.

Case Study: The Vera Institute of Justice

Mission and Method

The Vera Institute of Justice in New York City is a prime example of an organization that adopted a two-pronged approach in making the "justice system fairer, more humane, and more effective for everyone" (Vera Institute, n.d., para 3). In fact, it has a long history of doing so. Vera Institute is a nongovernmental criminal justice research and policy organization that has been an active participant in national and international justice-system reforms since 1961. The mission of Vera Institute is to combine expertise in "research, demonstration projects, and technical assistance to help leaders in government and civil society improve the systems that people rely on for justice and safety" (Vera Institute, n.d., para 1). Vera staff members actively help government and community partners achieve measurable improvements in "delivery of justice" policies and programs. They then share those innovations with the national and international community.

History

The Vera Institute was born out of the efforts of two concerned New Yorkers, Louis Schweitzer and Herb Sturz. In 1961, Schweitzer and Sturz perceived class bias in the New York City bail system. At that time, judges required virtually everyone to post a money bail to be released from jail while their case was pending. As a result, wealthier people got out of jail, whether they were likely to appear in court or not, whereas people who could not afford to post bail stayed in jail. Schweitzer and Sturz collaborated with New York criminal justice officials to identify the problem of inequitable bail policies. They then developed a set of criteria that were good indicators of a person's likeliness to appear in court as required and persuaded the court system to release people who met those criteria "on their own recognizance"—with no bail money. The demonstration project showed that a high number of individuals with little or no money who had strong ties to the community would still attend their scheduled court hearing if released on bail. The fact that Schweitzer and Sturz carefully documented the project's results provided systematic evidence for a viable alternative to an income-based bail policy, which protected all individuals' rights to freedom equally. In turn, this small demonstration project was widely adopted by national and international criminal courts and enabled judges to make fairer decisions about bail.

A Multidimensional Approach

Since this initial effort, the Vera Institute expanded its efforts and boasts an impressive track record of improving conditions for individuals at risk of unjust treatment. As of 2007, the Vera Institute coordinates at least two dozen justice-related projects. Consistent with evidence-based practices, the Vera Institute uses a multidimensional approach to problem solving that includes research, demonstration projects, and technical assistance.

Demonstration projects commonly begin with a close examination of the targeted justice system. The assessment is then used to create a practical "experiment" or strategy for reform. For example, to address adolescents' barriers to substance abuse and mental health treatment, Vera Institute staff members developed "adolescent portable therapy" in which a counselor would travel to youth in need of services. Often the innovations developed from the demonstration projects have developed into independent agencies that contract with the justice system to provide important services. Through 2007, at least 17 Vera demonstration projects have become independent nonprofit organizations (Goldstein, Jones, Pena, & Rai, 2007). For example, *Esperenza, NY* began as a demonstration project and is now an independent agency that intersects with the justice system. *Esperanza* is a multifaceted organization that works in collaboration with the New York City Department of Probation and other community agencies to help divert youth from juvenile justice or out-of-home residential placement.

The Structure: Centers, Program, and Demonstration Projects

The Centers

The Vera Institute's reform efforts are organized under three main centers. The first, the Center on Sentencing and Corrections, collaborates with criminal justice and government officials to develop and implement cost-effective public safety strategies. One recent project was designed to improve and expand community corrections programs in Alabama. Another project developed appropriate guidelines for sentencing felony drug offenders in Nebraska.

The second, the Center on Youth Justice, strives to improve social justice outcomes for youth, especially for those most at risk of juvenile justice involvement. This center uses data to inform decision making and improve program and policy development. Their staff has developed diversion programs designed to place justice-involved youth in the least restrictive settings possible. For example, one of the Center's recent projects was a collaborative effort with Connecticut legislators to transfer juveniles aged 16–17 from the adult correctional system back to the juvenile justice system.

The third, the Center on Immigration and Justice, targets reform at the intersection of the criminal-justice and immigration systems. This center seeks evidence-based justice solutions for laws and policies affecting immigrants and their families. Recent initiatives include reducing language and cultural barriers in the criminal justice system, increasing legal access for adults and juvenile immigration detainees, and using rigorous research methods to determine the nature and extent of human trafficking.

Recent Programs

Vera Institute has a series of initiative and stand-alone programs that operate outside the center structure. These programs include the Accessing Safety Initiative; the Child Welfare, Health, and Justice Program; the Substance Use and Mental Health Program; the Prosecution and Racial Justice Project; and the Commission on Safety and Abuse in Prisons.

The Accessing Safety Initiative attempts to address the needs of women with disabilities who have experienced sexual assault or domestic violence. The goal is to deliver more effective services to this population by promoting collaboration between local government and social service agencies. The program is currently operating in multiple locations across the United States.

The Child Welfare, Health, and Justice Program targets children's needs and rights, especially children placed in foster care. Program staff collaborate with child welfare, public health, and other government agencies to evaluate, improve, and increase the coordination of services for foster children and their families.

The Substance Use and Mental Health Program targets the rights and needs of individuals with mental health and/or substance-abuse problems. Using applied research, program staff help public officials, community organizations, and other important stakeholders understand the special needs of this population as well as develop effective responses to those needs in community and institutional settings.

Other programs directly target bias and neglect in criminal justice policy and programming. For example, the Prosecution and Racial Justice Project is a new initiative designed to reduce racial bias and discrimination in the criminal justice system. For example, the project staff help prosecutors track their decision-making processes to unearth racial/ethnic bias in the prosecutors' decisions or at work within the system. If sources of bias are detected, an intervention to reduce bias is planned, implemented, and then evaluated.

Another Vera program, the Commission on Safety and Abuse in Prisons, examines important issues affecting inmates and employees in U.S. jails and prisons. These issues include prison violence and inadequate medical and mental health care. This program is known for a national study that led to the landmark report, *Confronting Confinement* (Gibbons & Katzenbach, 2006). The information generated in this report was used to develop practical recommendations for improving the safety and health of prison employees and prisoners.

Demonstration Projects

Vera has also developed innovative projects to address injustices in the criminal justice system. These projects assist vulnerable populations, such as older adults, youth, and immigrant asylum seekers and include the Guardianship Project, Adolescent Portable Therapy, and the Appearance Assistance Project (Goldstein et al., 2007).

The Guardianship Project serves people who cannot care for themselves because of old age or illness. The program uses a support model that preserves the client's right to self-determination. Thus, the model provides assistance where needed yet allows clients to continue to make important decisions, lead fulfilling lives, and avoid unnecessary institutionalization.

A project targeting youth, Adolescent Portable Therapy, provides mental health and substance-abuse treatment for youths in the juvenile justice and child-welfare systems. The program provides a "mobile" counselor who can follow youth from community to institutional settings.

Another notable project was the New York City-based Appearance Assistance Project, which helped people seeking asylum and other noncitizens facing deportation. The program became widely known for spearheading a supervised release program (rather than placing people in detention for deportation proceedings). Because the Project's results demonstrated a high rate of attendance at hearings as well as lowered human suffering and financial cost, the U.S. Department of Homeland Security implemented an Intensive Supervision Appearance Program that has been adopted in at least eight U.S. cities (Goldstein et al., 2007).

Conclusion and Future Directions

The Vera Institute offers examples of how a group of individuals can create and implement innovate programming to help increase social functioning and improve social justice outcomes. The organization also continues to grow in size and influence. In 2007 Vera expanded its efforts by opening an additional office in Washington, DC. This will enable the Vera Institute's efforts to be a resource for policymakers, elected officials, and other stakeholders. Their new location should allow them to become even more involved in national debates around the administration of justice.[1]

Summary and Conclusions

This chapter reviewed the essential concepts and definitions of social work practice in a sociolegal context. It presented an SJS model in which the "environment" of the person-in-environment perspective represents social and justice issues. The need for forensic social work to integrate a two-pronged approach to practice, in which practitioners seek to empower individuals within sociolegal environments as well as changing those environments directly, was reinforced. Given the complexity of social problems in contemporary societies, adopting a two-pronged approach is one way to uphold U.S. (NASW, 1996) and international (International Federation of Social Work, 2000) mandates for social work practice.

Note

1. For more detailed information about Vera Institute's centers, programs, and demonstration projects or to review their downloadable publications, visit their Web site at http://www.vera.org/. If you are looking to start an organization or spin off a program from an existing organization, contact Vera Institute for a copy of their Spin-Off Tool Kit (Goldstein et al., 2007) at contactvera@vera.org. The tool kit can also be used for a class exercise in program development.

References

Addams, J. (1910). *Twenty years at Hull house.* New York: Macmillan.
Barker, R. L. (2003). *The social work dictionary* (2nd ed.). Washington, DC: NASW Press.
Barker, R. L., & Branson, D. M. (2003). *Forensic social work: Legal aspects of professional practice* (2nd ed.). Binghamton, NY: Haworth Press.
Bartlett, H. M. (1958). Working definition of social work practice. *Social Work, 3*(2), 5–8.
Bartlett, H. M. (1970). *The common base of social work practice.* Silver Spring, MD: NASW Press.
DuBois, B., & Miley, K. K. (2003). *Social work: An empowering profession* (5th ed.). Boston: Allyn & Bacon.
Ehrenreich, J. H. (1985). *The altruistic imagination: A history of social work and social policy in the United States.* Ithaca, NY: Cornell University Press.
Finn, H. L., & Jacobson, M. (2003). *Just practice: A social justice approach to social work.* Peosta, IA: Eddie Bowers.
Garland, A. F., Hough, R. L., Landsverk, J. A., & Brown, S. A. (2001). Multi-sector complexity of systems of care for youth with mental health needs. *Children's Services: Social Policy, Research, and Practice, 4*, 123–140.
Gibbons, J. J., & Katzenbach, N. B. (2006). *Confronting confinement: A report of the Commission on Safety and Abuse in America's Prisons.* New York: Vera Institute. Retrieved May 15, 2008, from http://www.prisoncommission.org/pdfs/Confronting_Confinement.pdf
Goldstein, K., Jones, B., Pena, J., & Rai, S. (2007). *Vera Institute of Justice: Spin-off tool kit.* New York: Vera Institute of Justice.
International Federation of Social Work. (2000). *Definition of social work.* Retrieved May 9, 2007, from http://www.ifsw.org/en/p38000208.html

Johnson, L. C., & Yanca, S. J. (2004). *Social work practice: A generalist approach* (8th ed.). Boston: Pearson Education.

Madden, R. (2000). Legal content in social work education: Preparing students for interprofessional practice. *Journal of Teaching in Social Work, 20*(1/2), 3–17.

Madden, R., & Wayne, R. H. (2003). Social work and the law: A therapeutic jurisprudence perspective. *Social Work, 48*, 338–347.

Madden, R. G. (2003). *Essential law for social workers.* New York: Columbia University Press.

Miley, K. K., O'Melia, M. O., & DuBois, B. (2007). *Generalist social work practice: An empowering approach* (5th ed.). Boston: Pearson Education.

National Association of Social Workers. (1996). *Code of ethics of the National Association of Social Workers.* Washington, DC: NASW Press.

Petrucci, C. (2007). Therapeutic jurisprudence in social work and criminal justice. In A. R. Roberts & D. W. Springer (Eds.), *Social work in juvenile and criminal justice settings* (3rd ed., pp. 287–299). Springfield, IL: Charles C Thomas.

Richmond, M. (1917). *Social diagnosis.* Philadelphia: Russell Sage Foundation.

Saltzman, A., & Furman, R. (1999). *Law in social work practice* (2nd ed.). Belmont, CA: Wadsworth.

Schroeder, L. O. (1997). *The legal environment of social work* (2nd ed.). Washington, DC: NASW Press.

Vera Institute of Justice. (n.d.). *Vera Institute of Justice: Making justice systems fairer and more effective through research and innovation.* New York: Author.

Zastrow, C. H., & Kirst-Ashman, K. K. (2004). *Understanding human behavior and the social environment* (6th ed.). Belmont, CA: Brooks/Cole-Thompson Learning.

Understanding Civil and Criminal Law

4

Christine Heer

Forensic social workers are required to interface with the legal system at various stages of the legal process and in different court settings (National Association of Social Workers [NASW], 2008). The NASW *Code of Ethics* (NASW, 1999) cautions social workers of their duty to be competent. Competence in legal systems requires a thorough knowledge of the substantive and procedural laws in their respective area of expertise. For example, custody evaluators need to know about the family and civil court systems. Social workers who are doing competency or mitigation work for those accused of a crime will need to understand substantive and procedural criminal law (NASW, 2003). Social workers who testify on behalf of injured patients need to know about tort law and criminal legal systems (Siegel, 2008). Social workers who work with the mentally and terminally ill should be familiar with probate law and the civil commitment system.

The law can be a complicated mix of statutes, rules, case law, and constitutional law. It changes frequently, and the forensic social worker must keep abreast of those changes. The social worker must also remember that each state has different laws and the federal system is different from state systems. This chapter offers a broad overview of criminal and civil legal systems. Space does not allow for a detailed analysis of each state or of the federal system. Therefore, the reader is advised to become familiar with the laws in her or his jurisdiction.

Finally, the reader must note that nothing in this chapter should be construed as legal advice; the social worker should contact a competent attorney whenever questions regarding legal rights and obligations arise.

Law for Social Work Practice: Civil and Criminal Law

This section provides a general overview of the law and legal procedures. The forensic social worker must be familiar with the law and procedures that are relevant to her or his case. The social worker will then be able to prepare her or his report/evaluation and testimony in the context of the system and ideally become a part of the quest for justice.

What Is "Law"?

What is the purpose of the law? Why do we have laws and where do they originate? The first question can be answered in many different ways but generally we have laws to provide order and avoid chaos. Much of the law we have today is based on English Common Law, some of which is written and some unwritten. Today our law comes from three main sources: (a) *Constitutions*, both the U.S. Constitution and individual state constitutions; (b) *statutes*, which are legislative laws voted on by the state's legislature and approved by the state's governor; and (c) *case laws*, which are judge-made laws or cases that have been decided by a court, either at the trial or the appellate level, and have been "published" by a designated judicial committee.

Civil and Criminal Law Systems: Definitions and Explanations

Many cases in which forensic social workers will become involved are conducted in either the criminal law or the civil law systems in their state. Note that states may have differing names for these systems, but for the purposes of this chapter the general terms *civil law* and *criminal law* shall be used.

Civil Law Procedure

Case Study

Tom is a social worker in private practice. He previously worked for 15 years in a trauma unit at a hospital. He has taught many classes on physical and emotional trauma and has published several journal articles. Tom has been contacted by an attorney who wants to hire him to evaluate her client, Wanda. Wanda was in a terrible car accident and suffered numerous injuries. Wanda is now afraid to leave the house, and when she does, she cannot get into a car without tremendous anxiety.

This example illustrates a matter of civil law. A civil matter is usually a dispute between two or more parties in which the plaintiff(s) (the party(s) who initiates the lawsuit) is alleging a "cause of action" against a defendant (or defendants). The "cause of action" is based on something the defendant did or did not do or it may be based in the plaintiff asserting a particular "right." Civil matters can be understood by looking at the "who," "what," "where," "how," and "when" of civil litigation.

Who Are the Participants?

It is best to start with the "who." Who participates in a civil action is defined by *standing*. Standing may be determined by whether or not the person has a real interest in the outcome of the matter. In other words, a person has standing if the matter at issue affects them directly.

There may be several parties involved in a matter. The plaintiff may sue one or more defendants. Sometimes the plaintiff does not even need to know who all of the defendants are at the time of the complaint's filing. The plaintiff can sue several "John Does" or the ABC Corporation if he or she is unable to ascertain the names of all of the defendants at the time the complaint is filed. Suits against numerous defendants are common in product-liability cases.

The defendant may also decide that he or she is not the only one liable for a cause of action so he or she may file a *cross claim* against another party to share the burden. A defendant may also file a counterclaim against a plaintiff. (This is common in divorces.) Needless to say, keeping track of plaintiffs and defendants can be a challenge.

In the case example, Wanda is the plaintiff. She will be naming the driver of the other car as a defendant. However, she will also be naming the car manufacturer (because her antilock brakes did not work correctly), the air bag manufacturer (because the air bag did not stop her from hitting the windshield), and the doctor at the hospital (because he did not check her foot to see if she had circulation problems). Wanda alleges she also has permanent nerve damage.

What Is the Cause of Action?

The *cause of action* refers to what was done and what remedies are available. Not all issues or disputes have a legal cause of action for which a party can file a complaint. In the civil realm, a cause of action could be malpractice, intentional infliction of emotional distress, negligence, or divorce. Many causes of action in civil cases were established by common law and case law. However, a new cause of action may be established by need, a court decision, or a state legislature. In the case example, Wanda will be citing *negligence* on the part of the driver, *products liability* (i.e., defective products on the part of the brake and airbag manufacturer), and *medical malpractice* on the part of the doctor. Other claims may arise as her lawyer investigates the case.

Filing the Complaint

A complaint is filed in a particular location based on jurisdiction and venue. *Jurisdiction* refers to which court has the authority to hear a particular matter. Jurisdiction may be based on the *subject matter* of the litigation and/or the *location or domicile* of the parties to the litigation or where the action took place. Jurisdiction can be a question of whether the case should be heard in a state or federal court, but the question of which state may be more complicated in other types of cases. It could also be an issue of which type of court the matter is heard in, for example, should the matter be heard in a criminal court or in a family court?

Subject Matter

In general, the state courts are defined by the type of subject matter with which they deal. Family courts address family matters, civil courts address civil matters, and criminal courts address criminal matters. A court's jurisdiction will be defined in rules, statutes, or constitutions. However, the question is not always so clear-cut. For example, a social worker may work with a gay couple who is splitting up and needs to be made aware of the legal process. This couple has been together for 20 years and has accumulated a lot of property. Several factors, including the state's legal stance on same-sex relationships, may effect which court has jurisdiction: Are they married, in a domestic partnership, civil union, or other reciprocal benefits relationship? Do they have children? Do they have an agreement? In some cases, the family court has jurisdiction. In other cases, civil court jurisdiction may be invoked for a partition action or to enforce a contract. A partition action occurs when the court is asked to divide the property interests held by two or more persons. The actual property can be divided or the property can be sold and the proceeds divided.

Location or Domicile

The physical location or citizenship of the plaintiff may define where the complaint is filed and heard. The venue of state courts may be divided by county, district, or parish. They may be further divided jurisdictionally by subject matter. Each state has its own court structure. The court may take into consideration where someone has to go to file or answer a pleading: Is the location overly inconvenient or does the person have little or no contact with that forum or geographic area? However, sometimes litigants must travel a distance to participate in our system of justice.

State Versus Federal Jurisdiction

Historically, this country placed great value on states being able to govern themselves without interference from the federal government. The U.S. Constitution determines when the federal government has jurisdiction over a matter. Most family law and criminal cases are heard in state courts and these cases can be very important when financial penalties or imprisonment are possible consequences.

When does a case belong in the federal courts? First, when issues involving federal law are implicated, for example, bankruptcies, federal civil rights actions, appeals and claims under the American with Disabilities Act or the Social Security Act, or the constitutionality of a law.

There are two other areas in which the federal court has jurisdiction: First, when there is diversity among the parties, for example, when none of the defendants share the same domicile as the plaintiff(s). In diversity jurisdiction matters there is also a requirement that the amount in controversy is greater than $75,000. (Amount in controversy means the value of the loss or anticipated judgment if the plaintiff is successful.) Second, federal jurisdiction is implicated when the matter involves a constitutional question. Constitutional-question jurisdiction usually comes up when a party claims that a law, rule, or policy; the enforcement of a law, rule, or policy; or the lack of enforcement of a particular rule is in violation of the U.S. Constitution. Civil rights claims, for example, often cite a violation of the Due Process Clause and/ or the Equal Protection Clause of the 14th Amendment of the U.S. Constitution as well as the federal Civil Rights Act of 1964.

In the case example, Wanda may need to file her claim in federal court if it turns out that none of the defendants shares the same state citizenship as Wanda. In other words, Wanda is a resident of State A and State A is where the accident occurred. The other driver, however, is a citizen of State B and was just driving through State A. In addition, the automobile company was incorporated in State C, and the airbag company was incorporated in State D. Because there is diversity of citizenship, the case may be heard in federal court. However, if both drivers were citizens of state A, then Wanda would file in State A's court.

Wanda subsequently learned that she had been fired from her state job because she is now permanently disabled as a result of the accident. Her manager told her that they do not employee disabled employees because it does not look good and costs the company too much money. Wanda then might then file a claim in federal court for a violation of the Americans with Disabilities Act.

Venue

Once jurisdiction is established there must then be a determination of the appropriate venue. *Venue* determines what county or parish or circuit the case will be heard in. Sometimes venue may be changed because of a party's connections to court personnel or because of the publicity a case has received in a particular venue, which may make it impossible to seat an unbiased jury.

Courts in both federal and state jurisdictions usually follow a three-tiered system: the trial courts; the appellate courts, which review trial court decisions; and the court of final appeals. In the federal system, for example, the U.S. District Courts are the trial-level courts. Each state has at least one district court. The U.S. Circuit Court serves as the federal court of appeals. There are 13 circuits in the United States. Several states may share a circuit court. For example, the 1st Circuit has jurisdiction over federal appeals cases in Maine, Massachusetts, New Hampshire, Puerto Rico, and Rhode Island. The final court of appeals in the federal system is the U.S. Supreme Court, which is the highest court in the land. Although the Supreme Court is usually considered an appellate court, it does have original jurisdiction in some cases, such as cases involving ambassadors and consulates and cases between a state and the U.S. government.[1]

State courts may use different language to describe their courts and social workers need to be to be familiar with their state systems (NASW, 2003). A social worker in New York, for example, who attends the New York Supreme Court, should be prepared to participate in a trial, as opposed to a final court of appeals. Note also that courts of final appeal require a party to petition the court to hear their appeal and the party can be turned away. In the U.S. Supreme Court and the state's highest courts, this petition is known as a *writ of certiorari*. Only 1–2% of cases filed with the United States Supreme Court are granted *certiorari*.

In Wanda's case, we will assume that both Wanda and the driver live in the same state and the accident occurred in Anytown County. Therefore, Wanda will file her complaint with the clerk of the trial-level court in Anytown, County, State of A. The members of the jury in Wanda's case will be residents of Anytown County.

How Does a Civil Case Begin?

Civil litigation starts with a written complaint that is filed with the court. Prior to filing, however, there are often attempts, and in some cases it is a requirement, to give notice of the complaint and settlement terms to the defendant(s). In certain cases, the plaintiff's attorney will send a demand letter to the defendant letting him or her know of the plaintiff's intent to file litigation and what it would take to settle the matter. For lawsuits against the government, specific notice may be required. The complaint must only give the other side *notice* about what the claim (or cause of action) is and what relief is being requested. Each state has its own requirements concerning how detailed the complaint must be. In most cases great detail is not required.

In the case example, in conversations with Wanda's attorney, Tom finds out that the attorney sent a letter to all of the defendants telling them that Wanda has suffered considerable mental and physical injury and that he plans on naming each of them in a lawsuit. He provides the potential defendants with a dollar figure to consider for settlement. The car and airbag company each responded that their products were not the cause of Wanda's injury. The other driver claims that the accident was Wanda's fault and that she should be paying him money. (Note that the insurance companies will be making many of these decisions.)

Upon receiving Tom's report that Wanda does meet the criteria for a diagnosis of posttraumatic stress disorder, the attorney drafts a complaint. In the complaint, the attorney details each count of negligence a well as all the injuries that Wanda suffered. He writes that each defendant should be responsible for paying $1 million in actual and punitive damages.

When to File the Complaint

The plaintiff must file his or her complaint within the *statute of limitations* set forth in the law. The statutes define the time frame for when a complaint must be filed; the clock begins on the date of the wrongful act that is the basis for the lawsuit. The time frame may vary, depending on state law and the nature of the case. Some statutes take into consideration the competency of the plaintiff in certain litigation. For example, the statute of limitations for childhood sexual abuse may begin when the child turns 18.[2]

In the case example, Wanda's attorney informs Tom that Wanda's accident happened 21 months ago. In State A, the statute of limitations in these kinds of cases is 2 years. The attorney tells Tom he would like an evaluation done before he files the complaint. Therefore, Tom must have his report submitted to the attorney within 3 months. Tom must seriously consider whether he can take this case because a delay might mean that Wanda loses her chance to file her lawsuit.

When the defendant *answers* the complaint, he or she must file a paper in which she/he admits or denies the allegations made and states any specific defenses he or she may have to the claims. The defenses are either procedural or substantive in nature, for example, stating that the complaint should be dismissed because the time of the statute of limitations has passed or the complaint was improperly served. Other defenses will address the merits, for example, the plaintiff has failed to state a claim on which relief can be granted. If a counterclaim is made, the plaintiff has a right to answer the counterclaim.

Case Study

The other driver files a counterclaim accusing Wanda of negligence. The claim alleges that Wanda caused the accident because she was texting on her cell phone. The counterclaim also alleges that Wanda was negligent because she did not have her car properly inspected. The car company and the airbag company both file answers in which they deny that their products malfunctioned. The airbag company also states a defense demanding the complaint be dismissed because the statute of limitations on this case ran out; the statute of limitations in their state is only 1 year.

Discovery Phase of Litigation

The lawsuit now proceeds to the discovery phase of litigation. *Discovery* is the process whereby information is shared and obtained between the parties. The most common forms of discovery are interrogatories and depositions. *Interrogatories* are questions that must be answered in writing and under oath. *Depositions* are proceedings in which a party or a witness is examined under oath in an out-of-court setting, for example, an attorney's office. Discovery is an information-gathering process and questions may be asked and must be answered even though they may not be allowable at trial. It is often hard for deponents (i.e., persons testifying at a disposition) to understand what to do when they are asked a question and the lawyer objects, and then tells the person he or she can answer. The objection must be made to preserve the objection for the trial. The social worker called for deposition should become familiar with the proceedings and rules and know what to expect before the deposition. Other forms of discovery include production of documents, requests for admissions to specific facts, and submission to expert evaluations.

Social workers acting in the role of a forensic expert will often be called to submit to depositions and/or complete interrogatories. Once the expert has completed her or his evaluation or report, that document will have been submitted to the other side (or both sides if the expert is court appointed). The purpose of this discovery is to gather more information about the report and the process taken by the expert to come to her or his conclusions and recommendations.

In Wanda's case, Tom received a *notice of deposition*. He arrives at the other driver's attorney's office. There is a court reporter present, along with attorneys for the car and airbag manufacturers. Tom has already notified Wanda in writing that nothing

Wanda told him during the evaluation process is confidential. Tom will have to answer all questions. One of the defense attorneys asks Tom what Wanda stated about her previous experiences with trauma. Tom immediately feels resistant to discuss the fact that Wanda told him she had been abused by her brother. However, Tom must answer the question. Tom then testifies to that history but quickly states he did not believe it was relevant.

During, and especially after the discovery process, the parties will be considering settlement of their disputes. The courts have a big stake in encouraging parties to settle, as do the parties. A recent study found that in civil matters both parties did better at trial than they would have had they settled in only 15% of cases (Kiser, Asher, & McShane, 2008). The court will use case management conferences and various alternative dispute-resolution processes—such as mediation—to promote settlement. The court's stake in settlement is so great that evidence rules disallow the admission of statements made in settlement proceedings. This encourages parties to be open participants in settlement processes.

Motions may be filed with the court during the pretrial period. A motion is a written request asking the court to take an action or to order a party to do something. The defendant may make several motions to dismiss the complaint altogether. A party may allege that the pleadings or complaint in and of itself does not support a cause of action; that is, even if everything the plaintiff claims is true, there is no cause of action for relief.

One may also argue that there are no material facts in dispute and, therefore, one party is entitled to immediate judgment (known as a motion for *summary judgment*). There may also be motions for pretrial injunctions requiring or preventing a party from performing a particular act (e.g., selling property), or a motion for *pendente lite* relief, setting forth temporary relief. For example, a court may order temporary support and custody in a divorce action.

The Trial

If the parties do not settle their differences, a trial is held. The trial will be overseen by a judge. The decision maker on the issue central to the litigation will either be the judge (this is known as a *bench trial*) or a jury. Jury service is familiar to many because juries are selected from the general population. The courts use public records (e.g., driver's licenses and voter records) to assemble a jury pool. The pool is then narrowed down by the *voir dire* or questioning process. The initial requirements for being a juror include being over the age of majority, being a U.S. citizen, and being a citizen in the jurisdiction where the trial is being heard. The prospective juror should not have personal knowledge or acquaintance with either the parties or their attorneys. A jury is picked via a process whereby the judge and the lawyers ask questions. The lawyers exclude potential jurors based on *cause* or based on *peremptory challenges.* Cause challenges are based on obvious biases. Peremptory challenges require no reason. However, potential jurors cannot be excluded solely on the basis of race [see *Batson v. Kentucky* (1986)]. A final jury may consist of 12 jurors (or fewer, depending on the state rules).

At trial, the plaintiff must present his or her case first. The plaintiff and his or her witnesses will be questioned by the plaintiff's attorney under direct examination. The attorney may not lead witnesses on direct examination but may elicit testimony through who, what, where, how, why, and when questions. The defense counsel will have the opportunity to cross-examine each witness and may use leading questions. A *leading question* suggests the answer within the question, for example, "Isn't it true, Ms. Smith, that you crossed against the light at the intersection?" Witnesses may only testify to information of which they have personal knowledge. Witnesses cannot testify to what someone else said. That is called *hearsay*. Witnesses cannot testify to their opinion about something unless it is about a matter of general understanding. For example, a witness may state, "Based on the smell of alcohol and his slurred words, in my opinion, the defendant was drunk."

When a forensic expert testifies, she or he may provide an opinion based on her or his evaluation to a degree of scientific or medical certainty. The expert never gives an opinion as to the ultimate issue, for example, "It is my opinion that the defendant is not liable." That is for the judge or jury to decide.

In Wanda's trial, Tom is asked by defense counsel on cross-examination whether he determined that Wanda's texting on the cell phone caused the accident. Wanda's attorney objects saying the question is not relevant to the subject matter of his expertise and that Tom is an expert on damages, not causation.

The plaintiff has the burden of proving his case by a preponderance of the evidence. This means that the trier of fact (judge or jury) must be surer than not as to liability. Some have referred to this as the 51–49% balancing test. Some civil matters (e.g., termination of parental rights) require a higher standard of clear and convincing evidence (see *Santosky v. Kramer*, 1982).

At the end of the plaintiff's case, the defendant may move for dismissal if the plaintiff's case did not meet its burden of proof. If the trial continues, the defense will present its case. The rules for direct examination and cross-examination remain. The defendant will present his or her side of the issue and continue to try to dismantle the plaintiff's claims. When the case is completed, each side gets the opportunity to present a *closing argument*, in which each side will summarize the evidence in their favor to try to persuade the trier of fact to produce a verdict for their side. The lawyers will likely discuss the credibility of witnesses. In most cases, credibility of witnesses is the key to winning. This is why the forensic expert must be well prepared before walking into the courtroom. The verdict will be rendered in the form of a finding of liability on each count in the complaint, followed by an assessment of damages. Damages may be assessed for actual losses, (i.e., what the plaintiff requires to make her whole) and punitive damages (i.e., an amount necessary to deter future wrongdoing).

Criminal Procedure

Case Study

Margaret, a social worker, has been hired by the defense in a case in which a wife, Beverly C., shot her husband, Ronnie. Beverly told the police she shot her husband because they had been fighting a lot and he told her that when he was finished with paying off his truck he was going to get rid of her once and for all. He did not need her any more for her money. She also said that her husband beat her many times over the years, yet the police were called only a couple of times more than 5 years ago. She went to court once but the judge said she was lying and dismissed the case. Beverly's attorney needs an expert to help the jury understand why Beverly did not just leave.

The procedures used in criminal matters are similar to civil procedures in some ways but are different in others.

Who Are the Parties in Criminal Matters?

The parties in criminal cases are the complainant and the defendant. The *complainant* is usually the government: either state or federal government. The caption of the case will be "The State of X versus John Smith." In the federal courts the caption may read "The United States of America versus Jane Smith." The government will be represented by district attorneys in some states, prosecutors in others. In a federal criminal case, the government is represented by the U.S. Attorney's Office.

In the case example, the matter will be captioned as the State of X v. Beverly Miller. John Corcoran is the district attorney for the County of Z in the State of X. He will be prosecuting the case on behalf of the State of X. Jerri Spencer is Beverly's attorney and the one who hired Margaret. Margaret will be listed as a defense expert.

What Is a Criminal Cause of Action or Violation?

Acts that are criminally unlawful are divided into two categories: those that are considered *malum in se* (i.e., those that are wrong in and of themselves) and those that are *malum prohibitum* (i.e., those that are prohibited by the will of the people). Criminal acts are codified in statutory codes along with the gradation and penalties for such acts. Crimes that are deemed *malum in se* are criminalized in all states. The intentional taking of a life of a human being falls into this category. These are usually acts for which there is universal acceptance that the behavior is wrong.[3]

In the case example, Beverly is initially being charged with first-degree murder. The prosecutor is charging that Beverly planned to kill her husband so that she could get the insurance money and get out of a bad marriage. Beverly is also being charged with unlawful possession of a weapon and resisting arrest. When the police came to the home one officer grabbed her arms to place her in handcuffs, Beverly became hysterical and began flailing her arms screaming, "Don't! Don't!" The case has gotten a lot of media attention and many in the community think Beverly should be punished because there is no excuse for taking a life. The defense's plan is to claim self-defense.

Prosecuting a Criminal Case

When prosecuting a criminal case, the government must prove all aspects of a criminal statute. Statutes are written to describe not only the prohibited act but the state of mind of the actor when he or she was committing the act. This is known as the *mens rea* (guilty mind). The state of mind may be characterized as one or all of the following: "Knowingly," "intentionally," "purposely," or "recklessly." The state must prove that the defendant "knew what he or she was doing," "intended to do what he or she was doing," did something with "a purpose to cause fear," or "did something recklessly without regard for the danger." The state of mind may be the difference between first-degree murder and second-degree murder or manslaughter. It could also make the difference between a guilty verdict and an acquittal.

In Beverly's case, Beverly's attorney, Jerri, has explained to both Beverly and Margaret that the state must prove under the law that Beverly knowingly, purposefully, and intentionally shot Ronnie. That is, she intended to kill him that day and had thought about it in advance and thought about how she was going to do it.

There are a few exceptions to the requirement of showing intent. In matters of strict liability, the act and the voluntary nature of the act are all that is required. For example, not "knowing" that a person was underage is not a defense to a statutory-rape charge.

Criminal acts are also distinguished between *felonies* (the more serious crimes) and *misdemeanors* (less serious crimes). Some states may use different terms for distinguishing the seriousness of a crime or offense. A person can be charged with several counts, depending on what took place. Beverly is being charged with a felony.

Where Criminal Matters Are Heard

As with civil matters, where criminal matters are heard depends on what the criminal act was and where it happened. An act that violates a federal law, such as failure to pay federal taxes or participating in insider trading, will be prosecuted in federal court in the district to which that the state belongs. An act that is not a violation of the federal law will be prosecuted in the particular state and county in which it occurred. An act that is committed on federal property, regardless of the state, will usually be prosecuted in federal court.

How Criminal Matters Proceed

Another significant difference between civil and criminal matters is how the matter proceeds through the system. Because of the severity of the penalties in criminal matters and the crowding of court calendars, criminal matters go through a number of steps before going to trial. When a person is first arrested, he or she will be initially charged in a complaint with a violation of the criminal code. The person will be brought before a judge, in person or by phone, to have bail set. *Bail* is a sum of money that the defendant must provide to the court. Bail can also be property, a surety bond, or a combination thereof. The amount of a cash requirement may either be the full amount or a percentage of the amount, which in many states is about 10%. The bail may need to be backed up with collateral property. A person may also be released on his/her own recognizance. The purpose of bail is to make sure the person appears for further court proceedings. Because of the commonly accepted legal maxim that a person is innocent until proven guilty, bail is not to be used for punishment or incapacitation. However, the nature of the crime the person is accused of committing can be used to determine flight risk. There are exceptions in which bail may be used to incapacitate the accused but such procedures are used only in extreme circumstances. Unfortunately, bail requirements lead to a disproportionate number of poor defendants, who do not have money or property to put up, remaining confined in jail until their trial is scheduled or until they can get a bail-reduction hearing.

In the case example, when Beverly was initially charged the judge set bail at $100,000. The prosecutor argued for a higher bail because Beverly had no family in state X and was considered a flight risk. The prosecutor argued that Beverly was a risk because of the seriousness of her crime. Although the judge was concerned about the flight risk, he did not agree that she would be a danger to others so he set the bail and will allow Beverly to place a 10% bond.

The bail may have provisions to it such as a "no contact with the victim" provision. Any violation of the terms of the bail can result in revocation of the bail and incarceration until trial.

Court Appearance and Plea

When the charge is a felony, the accused shall be called for a first appearance or arraignment, which is a formal notification of the charges against him or her. The accused is asked to plead guilty or not guilty. The accused may also plead *no contest*, which is an admission of the facts of the allegation but not an admission of guilt. A preliminary hearing may also be set at this time. At the preliminary hearing, which is sometimes called a *probable cause* hearing, evidence will be heard regarding whether there was probable cause to arrest and charge the accused. If the court determines that the evidence is sufficient, a *bill of information* is presented. However, a court could also dismiss the charges if there is a lack of evidence or probable cause. Beverly pled not guilty and plans to claim self-defense in that she reasonably believed that Ronnie was going to kill her.

Federal and Grand Juries

In the federal courts and many states, a grand jury may review the criminal charges. The prosecutor will present the evidence and witnesses to the grand jury. Although the grand jury is drawn from the same public pool as *petit* jurors, the grand jury is different. The attorneys have no say in choosing grand-jury participants. The grand-jury members can play an active role in the process and can even ask questions. The defendant does not present a case but may testify on request. The grand jury's role is to decide if there is enough evidence to proceed with an *indictment*. If the evidence is insufficient the grand jury can issue a "no bill." Although the matter is dismissed at this point, the prosecution can reintroduce the case in the future with new or better evidence. Double jeopardy, which is a 5th Amendment protection that stipulates that a person cannot be tried twice for the same crime, does not apply at this stage. The defendant may decide to enter a different plea based on the decisions of a grand jury.

Because the courts and correctional systems are so overcrowded, most defendants are offered the opportunity to plead guilty, usually to a lesser charge. Many defendants enter into plea agreements rather than risk going to trial, being convicted, and sentenced to a significant term of incarceration or the death penalty. Although deemed to be controversial in some law enforcement circles, plea-bargaining is an approved practice so long as the plea is voluntary and understood by the accused.[4] Whenever the accused pleads guilty, either at the arraignment or later in the process as a result of a plea bargain, the accused must explain in detail what he is admitting to and what he did. The court must be sure that the person knowingly and without coercion admitted to the crimes.

In the case example, Beverly was indicted on first-degree murder charges. The prosecutor approached Jerri Spencer and made an offer for a plea bargain. The prosecution wants Jerri to plead guilty to second-degree murder. Beverly could still face significant jail time even though the charge would be downgraded. Jerri is concerned about how the jury will view Beverly and does not want her to risk a trial. She asks Margaret what she thinks. Margaret explains to Jerri that there is a significant history of violence in this case and anyone in her Beverly's position would have believed Ronnie was going to kill her sooner rather than later. Beverly decides she wants to go to trial.

The Process After the Arraignment

Once the arraignment has occurred, the process is similar to a civil proceeding. A matter may be downgraded or remanded to the local or municipal courts.[5] There will be pretrial motions for dismissal or to clarify witness and evidence issues. There will be pretrial conferences to set the parameters of the case and the discovery calendar. The discovery calendar sets the time frames within which discovery (e.g., review of documents) must be completed. These time frames may be set forth in the statutes. For example, interrogatories must be answered within 10 days of service.

The discovery processes are also different in criminal cases. At the request of the defendant, the prosecutors must disclose any evidence that could exculpate the defendant or show that the accused may be innocent. However, depending on the state, the defendant may have an obligation for reciprocal discovery. Since the mid-1990s, more and more states have expanded the reciprocal-discovery rules for defendants in the belief that it helps trial move forward (American Bar Association, 2006).

Pretrial Intervention

Some defendants may be given the opportunity to participate in a *pretrial intervention* program. Pretrial intervention is a diversionary program limited to certain offenders. Usually habitual offenders or offenders accused of violent crimes are not eligible. The court will typically suspend the charges for a set period of time and ultimately dismiss the charges if the defendant complies with the terms of the program.

Right to a Speedy and Public Trial

The 6th Amendment of the U.S. Constitution guarantees the right to a speedy and public trial. However, neither the U.S. Constitution nor the Speedy Trial Act (18 U.S.C. § 3161–3174) (American Bar Association, 2006) have prevented defendants from sometimes waiting years before the trial is heard (American Bar Association, 2006). In the federal system, the courts will determine whether a delay has been unreasonable, based on the length of time and reason(s) for the delay, the prejudice to the defendant that is caused by the delay, and whether the defendant demanded a speedy trial (*Barker v. Wingo*, 1972).

The Constitution also guarantees the right to a jury trial in criminal matters in which the accused faces 6 months or more of incarceration. The jury will be picked by the same *voir dire* process used in the civil trial. Juries in criminal trials usually consist of 12 members. However, some states have allowed juries of only six members. A case in which the penalty on conviction is death must have a 12-member jury.

The penalties on conviction will vary according to state law. The options available are incarceration for a set or minimum period of time and/or a fine or a fine and a term of supervised probation. Some state sentencing structures impose increasing penalties for multiple offenses.

At Beverly's trial, Jerri puts Margaret on the stand to explain to the jury and the judge about battered woman's syndrome. Margaret explains about the long history of domestic violence and how things had gotten worse over time. Margaret explains why Beverly did not just leave Ronnie and how she was afraid that nobody would believe her. Margaret testifies that the judge's previous handling of Beverly's case confirmed what Ronnie always told her: that everyone would think she was a liar. Margaret told the jury that although most people would think it was easy to just leave an abusive partner, Beverly reasonably feared for her life. In the end, Beverly was found not guilty.

Summary and Conclusions

The social worker's role in civil or criminal proceedings may be that of an expert, custody evaluator, mediator, substance-abuse evaluator, domestic violence counselor, probation officer, child protective services worker, court worker who assesses a defendant for diversionary programs, or corrections-facility counselor. The social worker can bring his or her understanding of human behavior in individuals, groups, and systems to the legal process (Polowy & Gilbertson, 1997). The social worker can help the judge and/or jury fully understand behavior that may seem aberrant under normal circumstances but that is reasonable under stressful and traumatic circumstances. The social worker can help find solutions to long-term problems faced by courts and criminal justice organizations. The social worker is uniquely trained to perform these functions in these complex and important systems.[6]

Notes

1. 28 U.S.C. §1251
2. See, for example, Section 5533(b)(2) of Title 42 of the Pennsylvania Consolidated Statutes, or when the victim remembers the abuse occurring (N.J.S.A §2A:61B-1(b)), or both (5/13-202.2(b)).
3. Assisted suicide is criminally prohibited in all but one state. The U.S. Supreme Court left this up to the states. See *Gonzales v. Oregon*, 546 U.S. 243 (2006): Oregon is the only state that allows doctor-assisted suicide.
4. See *Brady v. United States*, 397 U.S. 742 (1970) and *Santobello v. New York*, 404 U.S. 257 (1971).
5. Again, the name of the court may vary by state. In Maryland, for example, these courts are known as "district courts."
6. Many schools now provide a joint degree program in law and social work. The following is a list of universities that provide either a dual law and social work degree, a forensic social work program, or both:

Boston College

Boston University

Brandeis University

California State University at Los Angeles

Florida State University

Fordham University

Gonzaga University

Loyola University

New York University

Rutgers University, Camden and Newark, NJ campuses

Southern University at New Orleans

Tulane University

University of Nevada—Las Vegas

University of Alabama at Birmingham and Cumberland Law School of Samford University

University of Illinois

University of Iowa

University of Kansas

University of Maryland, Baltimore, MD

University of Michigan

University of North Carolina Chapel Hill, NC

University of Pennsylvania

University of Toronto

Washington University of St. Louis

References

American Bar Association. (2006). *Standards for criminal justice: Speedy trial and timely resolution of cases* (3rd ed.). Washington, DC: Author. Accessed September 21, 2008, from http://www.abanet.org/ crimjust/standards/speedytrialtext.pdf

Barker v. Wingo, 407 US 514 (1972).

Batson v. Kentucky, 476 US 79 (1986).

Kiser, R. L., Asher, M. A., & McShane, B. B. (2008). Let's not make a deal: An empirical study of decision making in unsuccessful litigation. *Journal of Empirical Legal Studies, 5,* 551–591.

National Association of Social Workers. (1999). *Code of ethics of the National Association of Social Workers* (Section 4.08 & Section 4.04). Retrieved April 2, 2007, from https://www.socialworkers.org/pubs/code/code.asp

National Association of Social Workers. (2003). *Social workers as death penalty mitigation specialists.* Washington, DC: NASW Press. Available: https://www.socialworkers.org/ldf/legal_issue/200309.asp

National Association of Social Workers. (2008). *Legal and ethical issues in social worker—Lawyer collaborations.* Washington, DC: NASW Press. Accessed September 21, 2008, from https://www.socialworkers.org/ldf/legal_issue/200801.asp?back=yes

Polowy, C. I., & Gilbertson, J. (1997). *Social workers as expert witnesses.* Washington, DC: National Association of Social Workers, Legal Defense Fund. Available: http://www.socialworkers.org/ldf/lawnotes/LDFMemberPubs.pd

Santosky v. Kramer, 455 US 745, 1982. Retrieved August, 1, 2008, from http://supreme.justia.com/us/455/745/

Siegel, D. M. (2008). The growing admissibility of expert testimony by clinical social workers on competence to stand trial. *Social Work, 53,* 153–163.

Suggested Readings

American Academy of Psychiatry & the Law. (1989). *Ethical guidelines for the practice of forensic psychiatry.* Retrieved February 2008, at http://www.forensic-psych.com/articles/artEthics.php

Barker, R. L., & Branson, D. M. (2000). *Forensic social work: Legal aspects of professional practice* (2nd ed.). Binghamton, NY: Haworth Press.

Bowers, W. J., Givelber, D. J., & Blitch, C. L. (1986) How did Tarasoff affect clinical practice? *Annals of the Academy of Political & Social Science, 584,* 70–85.

Committee on Ethical Guidelines for Forensic Psychologists. (1991). Specialty guidelines for forensic psychology practice. *Law & Human Behavior, 15,* 655–665.

Cournoyer, B. R. (2005). *The social work skills workbook* (4th ed.). Belmont, CA: Brooks/Cole.

Herbert, P. B., & Young, K. A. (2002). Tarasoff at twenty-five. *Journal of the American Academy of Psychiatry & the Law, 30,* 275–281.

Hess, A. K. (2006). Practicing principled forensic psychology: Legal, ethical and moral considerations. In I. B. Weinere & A. K. Hess (Eds.), *The handbook of forensic psychology* (3rd ed., pp. 821–850). Hoboken, NJ: Wiley.

Kane, M. J. (1998). *Psychological experts in divorce actions* (3rd ed.) New York: Aspen.

Madden, R. G. (2003). *Essential law for social workers.* New York: Columbia University Press.

Pasewick, R. A. (1986). A review of research on the insanity defense. *Law & Mental Health: Research & Policy, 484,* 70–85.

Reamer, F. G. (2006). *Ethical standards in social work: A review of the NASW code of ethics* (2nd ed.). Washington, DC: NASW Press.

Stahl, P. M. (1994). *Conducting child custody evaluations: A comprehensive guide.* Thousand Oaks, CA: Sage.

From Intervention Roles to Multidisciplinary Practice

5

Laura Kelly
Nora Smith
Sandy Gibson

Social workers often encounter catastrophic circumstances of the human condition. Interpersonal violence, child abuse, sexual molestation, abuse and maltreatment of the elderly, suicide and attempted suicide, homicide, and addictive disorders might all be part of the daily experiences of the social work client. In forensic practice, social workers will interact with a wide variety of professionals and share responsibility to provide the client with needed services.

This chapter identifies roles of forensic professionals across and within a wide range of disciplines. It introduces potential conflicts that might arise among forensic professionals, describes the skills set necessary to successfully negotiate the conflicts, and offers an example of a successful forensic project highlighting interdisciplinary team collaboration.

Common Issues Among Professionals

In forensic practice, professionals can work on either side—prosecution or defense in criminal matters, and plaintiff or defendant in civil matters (see chapter 4 for more information). Professionals will also work within the criminal justice system. This might include jails, prisons, courts, half-way houses, and rehabilitation facilities for offenders. Forensic practitioners are also scientists, medical professionals, and mental health professionals and may be found in hospitals, laboratories, and clinics. "There is literally no end to the number of disciplines that become 'forensic' by definition. Nor is there an end in sight to the number of present or future specialties that may become forensic" (Longhetti, 1983, p. 3).

Collaboration With Other Professionals

Interdisciplinary team practice systems can be complex, especially when the philosophical beliefs of members of different disciplines conflict. These philosophical differences may include how team members define a problem and the strategies they use to solve it. As social workers, we should respect our colleagues, especially as collaboration is needed and is embedded in our National Association of Social Workers (NASW) *Code of Ethics* (NASW, 2005).

When there is a lack of respect in interdisciplinary practice, conflict and a lack of collaboration often results. For example, the systems dealing with child welfare and substance abuse differ in terms of primary interventions and have been known to have difficulty with collaboration in their interdisciplinary work. Their difficulty in collaboration has been described as "turf wars," protecting and defending their own positions and purpose. The end result of this conflict is not positive for clients. Ending the "turf wars" between agencies is necessary so that community partnerships of agencies can come together as one. Interagency disputes and resistance toward collaboration only slow down the process and any likely success for the client system involved (Azzi-Lessing & Olsen, 1996; Ellertson, 1994; Salmon & Farris, 2006; Smith, 2002). The social justice system needs strong interdisciplinary team practice and collaboration with competent, value-oriented professionals who focus on successful community-development tactics and techniques (Rodgers, 2000; Smith & Rodgers, 2002).

Collaboration With Clients

Social workers are well equipped through experience and education to work with clients. They offer expertise in researching and completing life histories, providing for people under stress, and helping individuals cope (Guin, Noble, & Merrill, 2003). Social workers can also educate law professionals about social welfare issues (Barker & Branson, 2000). Whether the client is the victim or perpetrator, guilty or innocent, incarcerated or otherwise institutionalized, or living within the community, the social worker might be part of a multidisciplinary team that includes (but is not limited to) lawyers, police, doctors, nurses, judges, corrections officers, and parole or probation officers. Collaborative forensic social work incorporates collaboration and legal knowledge and skills with a generalist social work practice across diverse populations and settings. This includes awareness of ethical principles such as protection, confidentiality, and self-determination.

Ethical Principles

Protection is central to all forensic issues; to protect the public is why laws are created. However, there are many circumstances in which laws produce outcomes for individuals that are harmful or anti-therapeutic, even when the intent was to produce a positive outcome (Wexler, 1996). Clients interacting with the legal system (whether they are victims or perpetrators) often find the system painful, invasive, and out of their control (Weinstein, 1997). These clients will interact with a number of professionals and they may not be able to differentiate easily what role each professional is supposed to play. It is important that each role be defined and distinguished by the professional. It is also important to explicate what information will and will not be shared among the forensic team members. Professionals must understand the obligations and constraints of the different professions, including confidentiality (Holdman, 2000). Rather than relying on informal systems of interaction between clinicians and other professionals, a more fully integrated system should be created and the client must understand the boundaries of each relationship.

For example, as indicated in the literature (Brownell & Roberts, 2002), even if a social worker is not directly employed by the social and criminal justice system that required the client to seek services, many clients will nevertheless view the social worker as a part of the system. It is critical that when a social worker initiates contact with a client in the social justice system (SJS) the social work makes it clear that although the client may be required to receive social work services, the social worker is not personally requiring it: If the client chooses to terminate services the social worker will not personally bring any sanctions against the client. However, it is also important that the client be aware that others may bring sanctions against him/her as a result of the termination of services.

In addition, clients may also experience frustration because they are often required to participate in a myriad of services as a result of their involvement with the criminal justice system, such as drug and alcohol treatment, anger management, parenting skills courses, or mental health services (Ryan, Hatfield, & Sharma, 2007). Overburdening a client with services, particularly those in which the client has no personal investment, may overwhelm the client and introduce a sense of powerlessness. Personal powerlessness over what services are received, how they are received, and for how long can often create defense mechanisms in clients that resist the potential value of services. Resistance to services may also arise as a result of the number of services being mandated.

Confidentiality

When working collaboratively with other SJS workers, it is important to remember the legal limitations placed on confidentiality with shared clients. As a social worker, you are very aware of the concept of confidentiality. However, when you are involved with the criminal justice system, certain exceptions to client confidentiality come into play. It is important to recognize that many such exemptions to confidentiality only exist with the permission of the client, and those that do not must be disclosed clearly to the client before services begin. For example, if a client is referred to services through probation, and the probation office wishes to be kept informed of the client's attendance, a social worker may only provide this information with the signed release-of-information form provided by the client. It is critical to inform clients that social work services will continue, even if they choose not to sign the release form; however, it is equally important that the social worker inform the client of the possible repercussions of not signing the form, such as having her/his probation violated and returning to jail (National Association of Forensic Social Workers, 1987).

Forming positive and respectful relationships with colleagues promotes a collaborative spirit in the provision of client services, but the social worker should remember that colleagues are not clients. They are serving as a referral source and that does not entitle them to more information than is allowed by the client's release-of-information form (NASW, 2005).

There are various exemptions to confidentiality in forensic social work that go beyond traditional exemptions, such as the social worker who is employed in a prison and is called to testify on a client's behalf at the client's parole hearing. It is critical that social workers clearly communicate all exemptions to confidentiality to clients (Evans, 2007). Failure to do so can profoundly damage a worker–client relationship, as a client will likely feel betrayed if the social worker discloses information to others, particularly to those who can respond in a punitive manner, when the client was under the impression that such information would be kept confidential.

Self-Determination

A key tenet of social work practice is the client's right to self-determination. Clients have a right to information about the type of treatment they are going to receive and the efficacy of that treatment in addressing their particular problem(s). Social workers have a legal and ethical responsibility to provide this information (NASW, 2005). When dealing with clients, the interests of individuals often must be weighed in relation to the needs of the larger community; thus social workers must consider individual intervention and social justice. The client should be made aware of these dual roles and the legal issues that create them.

Friction frequently develops between forensic professionals who fail to recognize their responsibilities to the client. For example, probation or parole officers may become frustrated with the perceived lack of progress of their clients in, for example, court-ordered treatment for substance abuse, domestic violence, or child abuse, but the social worker understands that a court-ordered client may need more time to ready him or herself for change before the "real work" of treatment can begin.

Law enforcement professionals may also feel that the helping professionals are "obstructing justice" when advocating for a client (e.g., perhaps to remove handcuffs during health care procedures), whereas social workers, nurses, and other health care workers might believe that police officers are using unnecessary force in the treatment of the client (Friedman, 1978). Because forensic situations rarely have an easy answer, professionals should consult honestly with one another to resolve dilemmas—"dilemmas that often go beyond the cursory ethics education presented in much of graduate education" (Guin et al., 2003, p. 371). There must be an understanding among professionals of the duties and responsibilities of each profession. This can only be accomplished through education and collaboration, and should be done in an organized way.

Dilemmas might also occur within one's own discipline. For example, one social worker might be working with the victim of a sexual assault. Another social worker might be working in the prison system with the accused perpetrator of the crime. Each professional may have a different belief about the outcome of such offenses and the appropriate intervention for her or his client. Collaborative forensic social workers must be prepared to deal with these conflicts.

A clear understanding of each discipline's role in each case will assist professionals in ensuring the best care for clients. The collaborative forensic social worker needs to possess a specific skill set to successfully negotiate this field of practice.

Skills Needed for Collaborative Forensic Social Work

There are a multitude of agencies and organizations in which social workers are employed that will require collaborative forensic social work services. It is critical that social workers understand the importance of these collaborative relationships in their practice to best serve the clients, including the clients' right to self-determination and their dignity and worth as persons. The following skills are of particular importance for the social worker working within the social justice system such as negotiating, sharing power, knowing your role, using a strengths-based perspective, client empowerment, advocacy, and communication.

Negotiating

The clinical relationship between social workers and their clients can be challenging because of the adversarial nature of the judicial system. Because of quasi-coercive situations in the forensic setting, the traditional social work attributes, such as empathy, warmth, and genuineness, which are essential components of therapeutic alliance, can be difficult to attain (Odiah, 2004). As indicated by Odiah (2004), social workers' fiduciary responsibilities become more complex when clients' rights to self-determination and informed consent are disregarded by psychiatric hospitals, probation/parole officers, doctors, and judges. When considering the dignity and worth of the person, the NASW *Code of Ethics* indicates that it is the social workers' obligation to "promote clients' socially responsible self-determination" (NASW, 2005, p. 5). This is particularly challenging for collaborative forensic social workers because clients often lose the right to a substantial degree of their self-determination. It is often the role of the social worker to serve as a negotiator on behalf of the client, always remembering the importance of both the clients' interests and the broader society's interests, while keeping social work values and ethical principles in mind.

Sharing Power

Social workers develop a shared power in partnership with clients, helping them to cultivate a greater sense of personal power to participate in, share control of, and influence events that affect their lives (Poorman, 2003). It is critical for collaborative forensic social workers to understand the significance of power in SJS relationships, particularly the innate power imbalance among the client, the collaborative forensic social worker, and the legal system. The legal system mandates what is to occur as a result of the offense, whereas the client attempts to satisfy those mandates. The collaborative forensic social worker helps the client navigate the legal system while fulfilling her/his own mandate as a social worker, all the while understanding the unique limitations and obligations of this role because of the forensic nature of the relationship.

Role Awareness

It is crucial to have a clear understanding of one's role as a social worker, particularly if the social worker is not an employee of the legal system, but s source of assistance to which the client is to referred by the legal system. There are many challenges to maintaining a therapeutic alliance in forensic settings, because, as noted earlier, social workers cannot offer clients the same confidences provided to nonclients. Odiah (2004) captured this struggle when she wrote: "Social work ethical precepts have little relevance in an environment where the information obtained during the therapeutic process may be used in an adversarial setting" (p. 30).

It important that your role as a social worker is clear to both your client and social justice colleagues, and that you educate them about your role. When everyone involved with the client and the SJS understands that you are an advocate for the human rights of the client, with the goal of a successful relationship between the client and the SJS, you will be well on your way to fulfilling your role. One significant component of this collaborative relationship is the need for all stakeholders to fully understand the legal implications of their relationship with the client.

Adapting and Maintaining a Strengths-Based Perspective

Studies show that the characteristics a person brings with him/her into a treatment setting play the most significant role in effective behavior change. Unfortunately, the criminal justice system tends to be more causation focused (e.g., Why did you do what you did? What is wrong with you?) than strengths focused, which can result in missed opportunities to create the greatest amount of behavioral change (Clark, 2005). An important skill when working with SJS clients is to use a strengths-based focus with the client while the client advances the identification of her/his goals. Using a strengths-based perspective the social worker assumes client competence and therefore provides for a leveling of the power relationship between social workers and clients (Cowger & Snively, 2002). The strengths-based perspective increases the possibility of liberating people from stigmatizing diagnostic classifications, such as that of "felon" or "addict," which promote sickness and weakness (Cowger & Snively, 2002), and developing personally empowered positive views of one's self. One major goal of almost every SJS client is to remove himself/herself from the system altogether, such as through regaining custody of his/her children or being removed from probation/parole entirely. Once this is the client-established goal, and the person's personal strengths have been identified, the forensic social worker can support the client in using his/her strengths to progress.

Empowering the Client

Involvement in the social justice system will affect an individual's sense of personal power, especially if the involvement results in mandated services and/or incarceration. Whether or not the social worker is employed as a part of the legal system (e.g., as a child protective services worker), the client may use defense mechanisms, such as projection, to claim that their SJS system workers are intentionally making life difficult with their requirements and monitoring. Although it is important to recognize how the loss of autonomy creates a sense of powerlessness for clients, it is also important not to allow defense mechanisms to blind the client from understanding that these consequences are the results of her/his own behavior. Allowing a client to continually blame the SJS for his or her woes will only serve to perpetuate a feeling of powerlessness and of being victimized by the legal system (Bradley, 2003; Carlin, Gudjonsson, & Rutter, 2005). To advance a sense of personal power with clients, it is important to recognize that the client's own behavior is what can reclaim her/his autonomy and personal power. This is not to suggest that clients should be confronted in a blaming manner, but clients should be helped to understand and accept that they are involved with the SJS as a result of their actions, and it is their actions (i.e., working toward their goals) that will enable them to ultimately end their relationship with the SJS.

Advocating

Signing consent forms could be considered as a type of coercion within a criminal justice setting. Refusal to sign such a form may lead them to believe they would be viewed negatively by persons such as probation officers and parole boards. Occasionally, SJS providers may ask for an open release form, which puts no limitations on what information can be disclosed to them about a shared client. Clients have indicated that they have been told that they must sign the form. It is critical that the social worker serve as an advocate for the client in these situations, because the client does not have equal power in the SJS relationship and may feel powerless to defend him- or herself. The social worker cannot ask a client to complete an open release-of-information form that leaves little information confidential and expect to have an open and honest relationship with the client (Leukefeld, 1991; Simon & Shuman, 2007). The social worker may refuse to participate with an open release-of-information form if the social worker feels that it is not in the best interest of the client.

Communicating

Communication is essential to collaboration. Yet, communication is challenging because the differences in professional training across disciplines may be a source of conflict. It is crucial for collaborative forensic social workers to realize that other professionals are probably not trained in the strengths-based perspective, and may often be frustrated by a substantial rate of client recidivism. Individuals who are personally responsible for the client's involvement with the justice system, such as child protective services and probation/parole workers, are commonly overworked with unrealistic caseloads that cannot possibly permit them the time necessary to become more personally involved with their clients' lives.

Interdisciplinary Team Practice: The Importance of Collaboration

Interdisciplinary team practice is often used when dealing with complex social problems, for example, gangs, substance abuse, child welfare, and domestic violence. Practitioners often need to form interagency partnerships to create a core plan, with the goal of having each professional "on board" with the intervention needed for the client system. Better outcomes for individuals and families have been observed through the use of more community- and neighborhood-based programs that work to collaborate in partnerships. Collaborative efforts are often needed for offenders and crime victims as well as for crime and other types of prevention efforts, such as substance abuse and mental health for individuals and families at risk (Pecora, Whittaker, Maluccio, & Barth, 2000; Recupero, 2008; Smith & Rodgers, 2002).

Case Study: The Mercy Center

The professional literature has emphasized the need for stronger coordination of services and the strengthening of communities to both prevent and treat crime, such as child maltreatment (Azzi-Lessing & Olsen, 1996; Ellertson, 1994; Smith, 2002). The Mercy Center in Asbury Park, New Jersey, has been recognized for its efforts in building a stronger community for families at risk, aimed at crime prevention and system re-entry ("Mercy Center expands," 2002; Smith & Rodgers, 2002). The Family Resource Center program of the Mercy Center works in collaboration with the child welfare and the criminal justice systems in providing services for both youth and adults. Through its after-school programming, the Youth with a Purpose (YWP) program provides positive role models and activities aimed at the enhancement of self-esteem and peer support. The YWP program works toward the prevention of crime and youth-gang involvement. It is intended to provide positive life choices and allows the children to participate in cultural, social, and recreational activities.

The Mercy Center houses 50 volunteers and 25 staff members who provide assistance to more than 7,000 Asbury Park residents each year. Executive Director, Veronica Gilbert Tyson, said, "What we try to do is really empower individuals so that they can become self-sufficient. ...We don't want to be a revolving door" ("Mercy Center expands," 2002, p. 2).

Among community members, the Center is known for its nonthreatening environment in which individuals feel comfortable to come and receive resources, counseling, and support. Collaborative forensic social workers at the Center work hard to develop a therapeutic alliance with their clients, while still needing to report on progress to mandated referral sources (e.g., probation and parole). The program is known for having staff members who have mastered the skills of sharing power and negotiating while working to empower each client.

The Center created a network with other community agencies and offers a "one-stop" approach to community practice. Services include family preservation services, family reunification services, mentoring, after-school programming, parenting education, substance-abuse services, the Women's Wellness Conference, a food pantry, and referral services. Referrals from the criminal justice system (e.g., probation, parole, and child protective agencies) are made on a daily basis.

Forensic social workers often find themselves at the core of the SJS when working with clients at the Mercy Center. This section of the chapter focuses on the social worker's integration of intervention roles and levels of practice into different disciplines (e.g., medical, education, child welfare, and substance abuse). A key component of this interdisciplinary work is collaboration. Negotiation is a skill that is necessary in working with the many different professionals involved with each client's case.

The Women's Wellness Conference is a well-known local community-partnership event. This conference is facilitated by program consumers, community members, and professionals, including social workers, nurses, lawyers, and teachers, who provide information on child rearing, women's health, and family relationships.

The Mercy Center model reflects what is captured in the literature regarding how to better serve agencies: an emphasis on community collaboration and partnership, using a strengths-based perspective aimed toward empowerment, self-sufficiency, and the prevention of recidivism (Manalo & Meezen, 2000; Pecora et al., 2000). The model reflects an SJS framework in which participants work to empower the client within her or his environment, linking the client to resources within the community.

In addition, this program is sensitive to the needs of each individual or family who uses their services and treats them as partners in a nonthreatening manner. The friendly, nonbiased, client-centered services have been noted as necessary for consumer satisfaction, service retention, and overall success. This also corresponds to the principles of therapeutic jurisprudence (Corse, McHugh, & Gordon, 1995; Pecora et al., 2000; Smith, 2002).

Summary and Conclusions

Although social workers are often well trained in specializations (e.g., mental health), it is essential that they are also effective when collaborating with criminal justice stakeholders. This requires social workers to be able to maintain strict boundaries of confidentiality and yet collaborate with others on behalf of their clients. Interdisciplinary collaboration allows for a unified set of goals that are both client-driven and yet compliant with criminal justice system mandates.

References

Azzi-Lessing, L., & Olsen, L. (1996). Substance abuse impacted families in the child welfare system. *Social Work, 41*, 15–24.

Barker, R., & Branson, D. M. (2000). *Forensic social work.* New York: Haworth Press.

Bradley, G. (2003). Praise and blame and Robinson. *Journal of Theoretical & Philosophical Psychology, 23*, 8–21.

Brownell, P., & Roberts, A. (2002). A century of social work in criminal justice and correctional settings. *Journal of Offender Counseling, Services Rehabilitation, 35*, 1–17.

Carlin, P., Gudjonsson, G., & Rutter, S. (2005). Persecutory delusions and attributions for real negative events: A study in a forensic sample. *Journal of Forensic Psychiatry & Psychology, 16*, 139–148.

Clark, M. (2005). Are clients, not treatment methods, the key to creating lasting behavior change? *ATTC Networker, 7*, 10–15.

Corse, S., McHugh, M., & Gordon, S. M. (1995). Enhancing provider effectiveness in treating pregnant women with addictions. *Journal of Substance Abuse Treatment, 12*(1), 26–41.

Cowger, C., & Snively, C. (2002). Assessing client strengths: Individual, family and community empowerment. In D. Saleebey (Ed.), *The strengths perspective in social work practice* (3rd ed., pp. 106–123). Boston: Allyn & Bacon.

Ellertson, C. (1994). The Department of Health and Human Services needs a major overhaul. *Children & Youth Review, 16*(5/6), 21–30.

Evans, T. (2007). Confidentiality in mental health services: A negotiated order? *Qualitative Social Work: Research & Practice, 6,* 213–229.

Friedman, E. (1978). The men in blue pair up with the people in white. *Hospitals, 52,* 153–163.

Gilbert-Tyson, V. (2001, Summer). Family resource center: A program of Mercy Center. *Mercy Center Newsletter.*

Guin, C., Noble, D., & Merrill, T. (2003). From misery to mission: Forensic social workers on multidisciplinary mitigation teams. *Social Work, 48,* 362–374.

Holdman, S. (2000, September). *Mitigation, investigation and jury selection in capital cases.* Paper presented at the Making the Cases for Life Conference, National Legal Aid and Defender Association, Houston, TX.

Leukefeld, C. (1991). Coordinating probation/parole services with community drug abuse treatment. *Perspectives, 3,* 40–44.

Longhetti, A. (1983). Editorial. *Journal of Forensic Sciences, 28,* 3–5.

Manalo, V., & Meezen, W. (2000). Towards building a typology for the evaluation of family support services. *Child Welfare, 79,* 420–422.

Mercy Center expands scope of helping those in need. (2002, August 14). *Asbury Park Press,* C11.

National Association of Forensic Social Workers. (1987). *Code of ethics.* Retrieved November 26, 2007, from http://www.nofsw.org/NOFSW_Code_of_Ethics.doc

National Association of Social Workers. (2005). *NASW standards for clinical social work in social work practice.* Washington, DC: NASW Press.

Odiah, C. (2004). Impact of the adversary system on forensic social work practices: Threat to therapeutic alliance and fiduciary relation. *Journal of Forensic Psychology Practice, 4,* 3–33.

Pecora, P. J., Whittaker, J. K., Maluccio, A. N., & Barth, R. P. (2000). *The child welfare challenge: Policy, practice and research.* New York: Aldine de Gruyter.

Poorman, P. (2003). *Microskills and theoretical foundations for professional helpers.* New York: Allyn & Bacon.

Recupero, P. (2008). Ethics of medical records and professional communications. *Child & Adolescent Psychiatric Clinics of North America, 17,* 37–51.

Rodgers, M. (2000, April). *Community development practice in Latvia: Implications for empowerment.* Proceedings of 7th Biannual European IUCISD Conference, Riga, Latvia.

Ryan, T., Hatfield, B., & Sharma, I. (2007). Outcomes of referrals over a six-month period to a mental health gateway team. *Journal of Psychiatric & Mental Health Nursing, 14,* 527–534.

Salmon, G., & Farris, J. (2006). Multiagency collaboration, multiple levels of meaning: Social constructionism and the CMM model as tools to further our understanding. *Journal of Family Therapy, 28,* 272–292.

Simon, R., & Shuman, D. (2007). *Clinical manual of psychiatry and law.* Washington, DC: American Psychiatric Press.

Smith, N. (2002). Reunifying families affected by maternal substance abuse: Consumer and service provider perspectives on the obstacles and the need for change. *Journal of Social Work Practice in the Addictions, 2*(1), 33–53.

Smith, N., & Rodgers, M. (2002). Community partnerships for children at risk: Examples from Latvia and America. *Social Worker, 4,* 121–125.

Springer, D., & Roberts, A. (2007). *Handbook of forensic mental health with victims and offenders: Assessment, treatment, and research.* New York: Springer Publishing Company.

Weinstein, J. (1997). And never the twain shall meet: The best interests of children and the adversary system. *University of Miami Law Review, 52,* 152–176.

Wexler, D. (1996). Therapeutic jurisprudence in clinical practice. *American Journal of Psychiatry, 153,* 453–456.

Part II

Forensic Practice in Family and Social Services

The Family and Social Work Practice

6

Nancy J. Mezey
Rebecca Sanford

Social workers will probably find it necessary to interact with, assess, and develop intervention plans for families and their individual members in a variety of settings. Although many of us talk about "the family," families in the United States exist in a variety of structures and have very different needs. Single-parent families, divorced families, lesbian and gay and transgendered families, blended families, dual-income-earning families, and a host of other "nontraditional" families make up approximately 90% of U.S. families today (Ameristat, 2003). Although families have been changing significantly over the past several decades, laws are still based on the notion that most families are, or should be, made up of an economically secure husband married to a home-making wife and their genetically connected children. As a result, many families not only bear the brunt of political and social prejudice, but can be left without the necessary economic and social support necessary to maintain healthy families; that is, quality relationships, access to important resources (e.g., adequate education, jobs, housing, food, and health care), and the ability to negotiate other systems (e.g., education, work, health care, and criminal justice).

Although many factors shape the development of quality family life, family laws and policies that directly affect the formation, support, and experiences of families are a major player in determining which families will gain the support they need to become or remain healthy. Laws that address intimate partner violence, marriage, divorce, custody and adoption, reproductive rights, and policies intended to help families balance work and home responsibilities are among those that greatly affect the health of families. However, these laws have different effects on different types of families, depending on a given family's economic, racial, sexual, and gender status. This chapter offers a framework to help social workers think critically about families in the United States: the needs of families, the laws that directly affect families, and the effectiveness of those laws in helping to develop and maintain healthy families. The chapter describes the tools necessary for assessing and intervening on behalf of families, keeping in mind that family needs often develop from the social and economic context in which each family is situated.

Overview of Field of Practice

To understand the diversity of families, their needs, and how to help create healthy families, we must first understand why diverse families have historically developed in the United States, what families look like today, what laws exist regarding families, and what social and economic issues families are facing.

History of the Family

The main reason family diversity exists today is because historic economic and social factors have privileged and oppressed different groups of people in ways that have encouraged and/or forced them to create a variety of family forms. Despite beliefs that there is some form of "traditional" family that creates social and economic stability (Baca Zinn, Eitzen, & Wells, 2007), no such family ever existed. The diversity of families we see today comes out of a varied past based on the class, race, gender, and sexual inequalities that different groups of people have historically faced. Because wealthy, White, heterosexual families have held most economic, social, and political power throughout U.S. history, their families have been, and remain, the model by which all other families are judged. However, "The Family" that Americans now view as the "best" (i.e., the "traditional" family) only existed for a select group of people during a short historical period in the mid-1900s (Coontz, 1993).

Prior to the Industrial Revolution, and particularly during the premodern Colonial period (1600s through 1800), when there were few established social institutions and early settlers lived in an agrarian economy, White English migrants created a family that helped them adapt to the New World. Following a Puritan model, the father exercised authority over his wife, children, and servants (if wealthy enough to afford them). "Family" was equivalent to social life; there was no separation between "public" and "private" life. People lived in a "family-based economy" in which women, men, and children worked in concert at different tasks based on age and gender to produce the food and goods they needed (Mintz & Kellogg, 1988).

During this premodern time, wealthy White families had servants or slaves who performed their daily tasks. Slaves were largely denied the right to form permanent family relationships and had little access to marriage. To marry would have suggested the social and legal expectations of remaining together, which was not possible for slaves, who were often sold and traded by White slave owners. Creating permanent families would have also granted "human" status to slaves, something slave owners did not want. Whites further denigrated Blacks by viewing them as immoral because they engaged in sexual relations outside of marriage. By creating a legal barrier to marriage and family, and developing a cultural view of Blacks as sexually immoral, as well as denying Blacks the opportunity to accumulate or inherit wealth, Whites created a historical legacy that continues to shape African American families today.

In the early 1800s, the U.S. economy began to move from an agrarian model to an industrial one. Production of material goods moved from the home to factories, creating a physical division between where one worked and where one lived, thus giving rise to a "modern" age that revolved around a "family-wage economy." Rather than producing their own goods, families began purchasing goods based on the income of the male wage earner (Mintz & Kellogg, 1988). As the U.S. became industrialized, the structure and function of many families changed to meet the needs of the new economy. For middle-class White families, the home became a woman's world and work moved outside the home to become a man's world (Mintz & Kellogg, 1988).

Unlike their middle-class White counterparts, women from working-class and poor families, as well as from families of color, had to work outside the home. Therefore, they developed a culture of dual-income earners rather than the breadwinner–homemaker model that existed among middle-class White families. Because Blacks were continually denied access to education, jobs, and land ownership, Black men's ability to become sole breadwinners was thwarted, leading Black women to continue their roles in the workforce (Wilson, 1987). Because of the economic and social mandate of slavery, followed by continued racial discrimination, the middle-class White notion of women's dependence on men has existed outside the framework of African American experiences and beliefs (Blum & Deussen, 1996; Jarrett, 1994).

The 1930s brought the Great Depression, which forced middle-class families to pool their resources—something lower-class families and families of color had been doing for years. The family became less private because of the need to bond together. Although divorce rates declined, rates of desertion soared. Because families could not afford to support many children, public opposition to birth control began to ease. The New Deal came into effect, the first time the government regulated family welfare (Mintz & Kellogg, 1988).

World War II brought the United States out of economic depression and had a great impact on families. As men were shipped off to serve in the war, middle-class White women entered the workforce in record numbers, which caused child care to became a problem. Because of the disruptions of the war and the attempt to recover from the Depression, there was also a high level of instability in society and families.

After World War II, during the late 1940s and throughout the 1950s, middle-class Whites felt the need to create stability in their lives. Women who had worked in factories returned home to perform their housewife and mothering duties full time. White middle-class men resumed their roles as head of household and breadwinner. Families returned to strict gender roles that existed during the early 1900s. It was during this 10- to 15-year period that the "golden age" of the "traditional" nuclear family took root in the United States (Coontz, 1993).

The "golden age" was short-lived, however. The 1960s and 1970s brought new social turmoil. Not only did we begin to see a shift from a manufacturing to a service economy, but the Civil Rights, Women's Rights, and Gay Liberation movements took root and allowed people to recognize diverse interests and needs in the United States.

Birth rates decreased, divorce rates increased, and White middle-class women reentered the work force.

Social turmoil continued throughout the 1980s and 1990s, but in a different form from preceding decades. Instead of focusing on progressive social movements, the late 1900s saw both conservative and progressive change in which the public began debating topics such as "diversity," "family values," and "same-sex marriage." These debates have continued into the the 21st century. In the changing landscape of the past 30 to 40 years, we are finding that family forms continue to change dramatically. Families with two breadwinners, single mothers, divorced parents, nonmarried cohabitators, and lesbian and gay partnerships are now the norm.

As this brief history shows, the structure of families is race and class specific. Historically, families of color and working-class families were not able to form the idealized middle-class White family form, even though they knew it existed and often strived to achieve it. This history also shows that what most people consider the "traditional" family is not traditional at all. Arising out of the modern era, the "traditional" family only existed for a small group of people and for a short period of time. Yet it is the model by which all other families are judged, and on which many of our family laws are based. As a social worker working with families, assuming there is one correct and predominant family form can lead to mistaken assessments and harmful interventions. It is important to understand the historical reasons why certain families have developed as they have. It is equally important to remember that many families are healthy even though they do not have a "traditional" structure; many families with a "traditional" structure may face multiple problems.

Recent Demographics

According to the U.S. Census Bureau, a household "includes all the people who occupy a housing unit as their usual place of residence," whereas a family consists of "a group of two or more people who reside together and who are related by birth, marriage, or adoption" (U.S. Census Bureau, 2007). Because the governmental definition of "family" is more limited than our own definition, we will use the data on households in the United States to review demographic trends.

Of the 181,171,000 total household groups counted by the 2006 Census, 42.7% of those groups are classified as "family households." Nearly 77% of family households consist of married partners with both spouses present; the largest age group comprises those aged 55–64 years, and makes up 21.2% of family households with married partners. According to the Federal Interagency Forum on Child and Family Statistics (Forum, 2008), 67% of children aged 0–17 lived with two married parents, which represents a decline from the 1980 data, which indicates that 77% of children lived with two married parents (Forum, 2008). The majority of family households include at least one income earner.

Statistics reveal that contemporary family size varies by culture. The mean household size for all households is 2.57 people. According to 2006 Census data (U.S. Census Bureau, 2006), Hispanic households tend to be the largest, with a mean of 3.34 people; Asian households have a mean of 2.93 people per household, Black households have a mean of 2.62 people per household, and White households have a mean of 2.54 people per household.

Poverty and access to health care affect contemporary families. Approximately 18% of children aged 0–17 live at or below the poverty level as of 2005. Although the rates of children living in poverty have oscillated in the past two decades, ranging from 22% in 1993 to 16% in 2000 (Forum, 2008). In 2002, 40% of children living with single mothers lived in poverty (Lichter & Qian, 2007). Statistics also show that about 11% of children in the United States aged 0–17 are not covered by some type of health insurance and nearly 19% of children have not received the usual infant and early-childhood vaccines (Lichter & Qian).

Regarding family planning, access to abortion is restricted in many states. Forty-six states allow health care providers to refuse to perform abortion services and 43 permit entire institutions to refuse to perform abortion services. Twenty-four states require waiting periods for women seeking abortions, generally set at 24 hours, and 36 states explicitly prohibit abortion, sometimes with the exception that the procedure may be performed when it is necessary to protect the women's life (Guttmacher Institute, 2007).

As family planning often includes the choice to have children, it is important to consider the many family configurations in which children will be raised. The institution of marriage in the United States has weakened in recent history (National Marriage Project, 2007). Historically marriage has been the only socially acceptable form of living arrangement for couples and families, but today this is no longer the case. Family form diversity abounds: "Fewer adults are married, more are divorced or remaining single, and more are living together outside of marriage or living alone. Today, more children are born out-of-wedlock (now almost four out of ten), and more are living in stepfamilies, with cohabiting but unmarried adults, or with a single parent" (National Marriage Project, p. 6). Despite such trends, 85% of American people expect to marry at some point in their lifetimes (National Marriage Project).

In addition to changing trends in marriage, data suggest that not all families function in healthy ways. Child abuse and neglect affect approximately 12 of every 1,000 American children (Forum, 2008). Many women in families also face the threat of violence and are nearly nine times as likely as men to experience intimate-partner violence. In addition, 7.7% of women are raped by an intimate partner each year (Tjaden & Thoennes, 2000). Battering also exists within same-sex relationships, although rarely are the needs of those women and men met by social services or public policy (Renzetti, 2007). These data suggest that social workers must pay attention to many different aspects of family life, particularly as they relate to issues of gender inequality and age-specific problems.

Current Trends

In legal terms, courts and policymakers have traditionally viewed families as having the responsibility for raising children, and due-process protection for families is expected under the law (Saltzman & Furman, 1999). However, such protection does not extend beyond regulation of that which would also be in the public's best interest. Although social workers have limited roles in some family/legal settings (e.g., divorce without children in the union), they have more significant roles in other legal arenas. Because most family law is based at the state level, social workers will need to be familiar with laws and regulations in the states in which they practice.

Social workers may work in a variety of family-related settings in which they must help family members negotiate unhealthy family relationships. In the case of suspected child abuse, neglect, and/or endangerment, social workers are mandated reporters. They may also have encounters with children through adoption or foster-placement work, divorce proceedings involving children, and in interventions with survivors of domestic violence (Saltzman & Furman, 1999). Social workers may also assist in finding safe housing for survivors, especially elderly survivors, of family violence (Saltzman & Furman).

Social workers working in prison settings will need to be familiar with the 1997 Adoption and Safe Families Act (ASFA). ASFA mandates that a state initiate termination of parental rights if that person's child or children have "been in foster care for 15 out of the past 22 months—6 months if the child is younger than [3] years old" (Bernstein, 2000, p. 2). Often the parents whose rights are being terminated are incarcerated. Because most parents who are in prison have mandatory minimum sentences longer than ASFA time limits, they often lose parental rights (Saltzman & Furman, 1999).

Additional issues complicate reunification between an incarcerated parent and child. Nearly every parole and child reunification plan requires that the ex-offender or parolee have gainful employment within days or weeks of release. In the United States, women earn an average 38% less than men, even for the same work. Moreover, having served time in prison restricts the type of work an ex-offender may find and dramatically reduces the number of companies willing to hire her or him. Many of the "pink-collar" employment opportunities requiring limited training or education that would be a mainstay of low-income or working-on-advancement women, such as child-care positions, teacher's aid, nursing assistant, and recreation aides in nursing homes are unavailable. In addition, because an ex-offender usually cannot be bonded except by a state program, other entry-level jobs such as bank teller or even cleaning personnel at companies that bond their employees, are unattainable.

An additional complication is that even if the ex-offender finds gainful employment, she may find her wages garnished under child-support enforcement laws (Bernstein, 2000, p. 5). To complicate matters, if addiction was part of the problem that initially led to involvement with the criminal justice system, getting clean and staying sober may require in-patient treatment, making parental responsibilities more difficult to maintain.

Given that over 1.5 million minors have a parent in a state or federal prison, ASFA has the potential to affect many of our nation's children (Mumola, 2000). Although many of these children faced family instability prior to their parent's incarceration (Johnston, 2001), research suggests that children are greatly affected by parental incarceration. Children experience their parent's incarceration as a traumatic event, thus redirecting children's energy away from developmental tasks. The uncertainty in their lives raises children's stress levels. Because schools and communities have few, if any, programs to help children of incarcerated parents, such children face a number of barriers to successfully completing the tasks that school and home demand (Travis & Waul, 2003).

Understanding the laws affecting a wide range of families equips social workers with the knowledge and skills needed to help families overcome the difficulties they face and to build healthy families. This area of family practice is in significant need of policy reform and program development to assist these families in need.

Scope of the Problem

Social science research suggests that there is a general misconception of what families are, what goals they can attain, and how they can accomplish those goals (Dill,

Baca Zinn, & Patton, 1998). As discussed previously, many Americans use a narrow definition of what constitutes a healthy family. In addition, they tend to believe that healthy families are the key to a healthy society. Although we, as family scholars, are certain that without healthy families, we cannot have a fully healthy society, we are also certain that to be healthy, the social environment, including laws, must support all families in a variety of ways.

To be "healthy," families must meet three criteria. First, they must have quality relationships between and among family members. Second, they must be able to access important material resources, for example, schooling, jobs, health care, housing, safe environments, drug and alcohol treatment, family planning, marriage, divorce, child care, legal counseling, and psychological counseling. Third, families must be able to negotiate the different systems through which those resources are obtained. Families must have the ability to speak and cooperate with educators, workers, and medical, financial, and legal officials to fully access and benefit from the resources these people provide within their specific institutions.

Although most problems that families encounter manifest themselves within the family (e.g., drug or alcohol abuse, intimate partner violence, child abuse, abandonment), many of those problems arise out of a context that exists external to the family. It is the social worker's job to help families become healthy by addressing their internal concerns, connecting them to external resources, and helping them negotiate external systems. Because many issues that affect the health of families are shaped by a variety of laws (both directly and indirectly aimed at families), social workers must be aware of those laws and their impact on families.

For families to successfully navigate and access resources, there must be legal policies in place to make doing so possible. Families need safe housing, adequate medical care, reproductive health services, sufficient nutritional food, education, and support services. Because of the bureaucratic nature of many of the systems offering assistance to families, family members must have a fair level of sophistication to navigate the systems and access such assistance. Centralization of services and a holistic, team-oriented approach that views the entire family's needs together and in relationship to influences external to the family are vital to ensure continued access to family-sustaining services (Dewees, 2006).

Relevant Theoretical Frameworks

Theory in its simplest form answers the question, "Why?" Why are some families healthier than others? Why do some family members engage in risky or harmful behavior? Why do laws support some families and constrain others? Different theories prompt us to ask different questions and help us answer questions in different ways. Because the questions we ask and the answers we get are critical to assessment and intervention, social workers must understand a variety of theoretical frameworks to help guide their work. There are many theories pertaining to families that are relevant to social workers and we highlight two of them in the section that follows.

Multiracial Feminism

Overview

Multiracial feminism is important because it provides a useful framework from which to consider how power, privilege, and oppression shape families and their interpersonal relations. Multiracial feminism is a social structural and constructionist approach that places difference at the center of its analysis to examine how women are dissimilar from one another based on race, class, and sexuality (Baca Zinn & Dill, 1996). The theory focuses on power structures that exist both within and external to families and that help families survive, pull families apart, and/or change families in general.

Issues Addressed

Multiracial feminism addresses three main issues that can help social workers think about the families and family members they counsel. First, the theory recognizes that there is no "normal" family; rather, it is critical to understand the social context in which each family exists. Second, multiracial feminism understands power as being central to human relations, and race, class, gender, and sexuality as fundamental organizing principles that distribute rewards and resources in unequal ways to different groups of people. Third, multiracial feminism recognizes that people within families negotiate, challenge, and/or capitalize on social inequality. Social workers can greatly benefit from understanding how multiracial feminism examines the relationship between social forces and people's negotiations of these forces in shaping family experiences.

Life-Course Perspective

Overview

The *life-course perspective* (also known as the *family life cycle framework*) examines how "most families, regardless of structure or composition, progress through certain predictable marker events or phases (such as marriage, the birth of a first child, children leaving home, the death of grandparents)" (Goldenberg & Goldenberg, 2000, p. 23). The family is a developmental system, one that changes with the events that occur over the course of the family's lifetime. The life-course theory maps out eight common transition points through the life cycle: married couple, childbearing family, preschool children, school children, teenagers, launching children into adulthood, middle-aged parents, and aging family members. Social workers should be cautioned, however, that because of changing factors outside of families, these transitional points are often complicated by external factors (Goldenberg & Goldenberg, 2000).

Issues Addressed

A main issue that life-course theorists examine is the conditions under which families cope with life changes, and the conditions under which life changes cause families to become unstable. The social worker's concern is to help families remain stable, or regain stability, particularly because destabilized families tend to move away from being healthy families. Another issue is how families might lack the flexibility or ability to effectively make the transition through an event. To address such issues, social workers must look at a variety of factors, including those outside families (e.g., social, cultural, political, economic, and community-related factors), as well as those within families (e.g., family structure and interpersonal family dynamics) (Goldenberg & Goldenberg, 2000).

Common Practice Settings

Social workers who deal with families may find themselves in a variety of work settings completing many different tasks. For example, they may be involved in public and/or private human service agencies in the planning and implementation of services to single women who become pregnant (i.e., single-parent services). These services typically include counseling about the choices surrounding continuing the pregnancy, childbirth preparation, legal counseling regarding parental rights, family planning, education and employment counseling, money-management counseling, and child-care and child-development counseling (Zastrow, 2004).

Social workers involved in family issues may have a place in the courtroom, testifying about the best custody situation for a child whose parents are separating, divorcing, or in a custody dispute. Such testimony would be based on the prescribed involvement with family members in interview settings, home visits, and review of materials. In supervised custody arrangements, social workers may find themselves supervising visitation between parents and children. In cases of family violence, social workers may provide crisis intervention and long-term counseling to the adult, child, or elderly survivors. They may also serve as legal advocates who accompany survivors of violence to court-related appointments. In addition, social workers may provide safety planning to children and families who are attempting reunification into a previously violent home.

Should a parent relinquish parental rights and a child be placed in foster care, pending adoption social workers may be involved in recruitment, selection, and training of foster parents as well as in counseling parents who are considering placing their children for adoption. In certain adoptions, social workers may make home visits and file reports regarding the home environment into which a potential adopted child would be placed. They also may work with a variety of parents, including single and same-sex parents.

VOICES FROM THE FIELD

Ken Lewis, EdS, PhD
Director, Child Custody Evaluation Services of Philadelphia, Inc.

Agency Setting

Although my home office is in Philadelphia, I accept court appointments around the country. Some appointments are for joint- or sole-custody evaluations; some are for custody modifications; and some are for specific problems like Parental Alienation, Separation of Siblings, Parentification, Vulnerable Child Syndrome, and so on.

Practice Responsibilities

Imagine you are a forensic social worker in the area of child custody. A family court judge appoints you to recommend the best custody arrangement for a child whose parents are divorcing. Your responsibility includes deciding where the child should go to school, how often the child should spend time with each parent, what telephone contacts should be allowed with the other parent, who should be the child's primary doctor, what religious activities should be allowed, how and where the child should spend summers...and a variety of other things that relate to the child's life. Wouldn't this be awesome responsibility! This is the job of a Child Custody Evaluator. It is child advocacy in domestic relations litigation.

Expertise Required

Knowledge of social work and the social sciences in general are required. An advanced degree in any social science (social work, psychology, sociology, anthropology) is important when you need to interview parents and other references from different ethnic and cultural backgrounds. Additionally, one must have good observation and interviewing abilities, clear report-writing skills, and cross-examination experience in court. Social work skills are important for comprehensive child-centered evaluations and home studies.

Here are more details about the skills required for this work:

1. Observations. Observe children in their home environments. Spend equal time observing the children in the presence of each parent. During these observations, collect data that portrays each parent's parenting style. Organize the data to identify each parent's strengths and weaknesses. Although it is usually not wise to ask children directly about parental preference, listening to their experiences will often provide clues about which residence will serve their best interests.

2. Interviews. Interview the parents and collaterals (teachers, ministers, doctors, family members, neighbors, godparents, and others) to learn about the child's history. Collaterals can provide relevant data that either confirms or denies the allegations that one parent may make against the other parent. Spend private time with the child to understand his or her feelings.

3. Listening Skills. The social work skill of listening is unquestionably a requirement for custody-evaluation work. Sometimes what is behind the words is more important than what is actually said. Data derives from what is said and what is observed, not from what you think a person feels when that person is talking.

4. Evaluating Documents. Review legal documents presented by the attorneys and review other documents provided by the parents (such as diaries, photographs, letters, etc.) These documents will help you develop questions for your interviews. Be careful about self-serving documents because often the parents (and lawyers) attempt to persuade you through their maneuvers.

Practice Challenges

When I accepted my first case as a Custody Evaluator, I spent 10 hours on it. I spoke with both parents, family members, neighbors, and school teachers; and I spent private time with the two children. When I wrote my report, I recommended custody and visitation based on what I *felt* was best for those children. But one parent did not agree with my conclusions, and the case went to court. At trial, the disagreeable parent's attorney tore me apart. When the attorney asked me if I could support my conclusions with data, I was stumped. I learned from that experience that effective expert testimony requires evidence, not feelings and emotions. I learned that evaluators should collect data; then organize that data, and draw conclusions from it. The conclusions arrived at should form the basis of the recommendations.

Sensitivity to racial, ethnic, and cultural activities within the family of the child whom you are evaluating can be a challenging but important dimension of a comprehensive custody evaluation. This is particularly true when the contesting parents themselves hold divergent views on how their child should be reared. Likewise, gender differences can be equally challenging. What do you do when one parent insists that he or she can raise the couple's child better than the other parent *solely* because of gender similarity? A well-trained social worker should be able to look beyond stereotypes and focus on the child's history, the child's current situation, and the child's future. For me, these issues have been the most challenging because they have caused me to inquire deeper into the child's needs.

Professional Involvement

Because social workers will find themselves in a variety of settings, and administrating different types of services, they may be completing their job duties in concert with other human service, medical, educational, and governmental agents. For example, their supervisors may include school personnel (in an educational setting) or hospital administrators (in a health care setting). In addition, although social workers may have a set of assigned tasks as part of their job descriptions, informal assessment and referral to additional services may become part of the scope of effective job completion. For example, in the educational setting, the social worker's job may include interventions targeted toward a child in the school setting. However, to more effectively meet the needs of the child, referrals for additional human services, health care, or counseling may be needed for the entire family.

Roles of Collaborative Teams in System

Nearly every social worker is working in *social welfare*, a broad term that comprehensively explains social workers' duties, and indicates that their involvement can be with any or all of the following professionals: psychiatrists, psychologists, nurses, attorneys, recreational therapists, teachers, physicians, urban planners, prison administrators, legal system representatives, and caregivers (Zastrow, 2004, p. 7). Because the services provided to families are potentially broad in scope, the social worker may provide a number of services to family members, including personal, protective, informational and/or advisory, and maintenance services (Zastrow, 2004, p. 10). The collaborative team would be made up of the appropriate individuals, based on the setting in which the social worker encounters the family in need of services. To help lead all families toward health, social workers may need to help members of their collaborative team gain a broader understanding of families and their needs.

Assessment, Prevention, and Intervention

Assessment and intervention in the family setting may involve different types of assessment instruments. Acquiring background information on family functioning and the provision of basic human needs would be an initial assessment completed by a social worker. Social workers would need to assess basic human needs (e.g., access to safe housing, nutritional food, and basic health care) before they perform more in-depth assessments. Although a detailed explanation of specific assessment and treatment tools is beyond the scope of this chapter, many valuable tools are available. Assessments used with families may include instruments such as the Family Support Scale (Dunst, Trivette, & Deal, 1988) and the Social Support Inventory (Timmerman, Emanuels-Zuurveen, & Emmelkamp, 2000). Setting-specific assessments may include the School Functioning Assessment for a child in a school setting, or any of the U.S. Department of Labor Work Force Readiness Credential for someone seeking employment services to support her or his family (Coster, Deeney, Haltiwanger, & Haley, 2008; National Workforce Readiness Council, 2007). Other assessments, such as for a domestic violence situation, may involve determining the current safety of the family and the acquisition of necessary housing, food, and educational resources in the event of the removal of one or more family members from their home.

Regarding intervention, multiple therapies have been shown to be effective in a variety of ways. For example, multisystemic therapy is an effective intervention for those working with juvenile offenders and youth with serious antisocial behavior (Henggeler, 1997). Other therapies include Brief Strategic Family Therapy, Family Behavior Therapy, Functional Family Therapy, and Multidimensional Family Therapy. (For additional information on these therapies and their effectiveness, see Austin, MacGowen, & Wagner, 2005.) Knowing which assessment tool and intervention strategy is appropriate for a given family situation is important in helping to create healthy families.

Skills, Stories, and Case Studies

To help build healthy families, social workers in family services must guard against potential biases toward what constitutes a "good" or "normal" family, based on their own experiences. There is some evidence, for example, that social workers prefer—and therefore recommend to the court—a continuing placement with a middle-class foster family as opposed to reunification with a child's working-class family, even if the reasons for foster placement have been resolved, simply because the social worker feels that the child would have better opportunities with the middle-class family (Saltzman & Furman, 1999). Advocacy for the child's best interest is paramount, but social workers must carefully consider their own prejudices when they consider what constitutes the "best" placement.

Cultural understanding across a spectrum of family types, family rituals, and family expectations is also a key skill in effective family practice. Culture includes more than ethnicity or geographic nationality. It also includes levels of group identification, heritage, history, norms, and values passed down across generations. As discussed earlier, for example, some family groups have always required dual wage-earners to work outside the home, thus relegating child-care or home-care responsibilities to younger members of the family. Such a configuration may be perfectly functional and healthy for all participants, and must be judged according to the norms of that family, not the "ideal" family a social worker may think "should" exist.

VOICES FROM THE FIELD

Ruth S. Angaran, MEd, MSW, LCSW
Owner, Counseling Associates, P.A.

Field of Practice

I am in private clinical practice. My connection to forensic work is through custody evaluations, parenting coordination, and divorce coaching on a collaborative divorce team.

Position

I own Counseling Associates, P.A., a private for-profit counseling practice with six other practitioners in the office.

Agency Setting

Counseling Associates has been around in Gainesville, Florida, for approximately 30 years. We conduct the usual therapies, and about half of our practice is involved with divorcing couples and their children.

Practice Responsibilities

I conduct a team-custody evaluation with Dr. Thomas N. Dikel, a very talented neuropsychologist in my practice. I manage the office, pay the bills, and answer the phones! And I see the normal caseload of clients' problems: depression, anxiety, some who are very seriously ill referred directly from the local mental health inpatient facility. The rest of the time I deal with high-conflict divorcing parents, assisting them with their communication and acceptance issues; with collaborating couples seeking a collaborative divorce; and with couples and their children post-divorce as a parenting coordinator. I also evaluate couples as to their suitability for a rotating custody. Occasionally I have done adoption home-studies for private adoptions. And the court sometimes appoints me to supervise reconciling parents and children following allegations of abuse (where the accused parent has been ordered to see the child at the Visitation Center only). In these cases I get to know all the parties, observe them together, and facilitate more and more time unsupervised when I deem it is warranted.

Expertise Required

I have a master's degree in clinical social work and did doctoral training in a dual master's/PhD program at Ohio State in clinical social work. I have also trained in family mediation, (40 hrs.) parenting coordinator training (20 hrs.), divorce-coaching for collaborative divorce cases (16 hrs.), plus countless continuing education units (CEU) in custody evaluation issues. I learned to testify in court from my mentor in the practice, Dr. Mary Horn, who did this for years and years. She wanted to let it go and to pass it on.

I observed her in interviews, I observed her in court. She asked the judges to allow me to sit in just to hear her part of the testimony. Invaluable experience! Then I read and read everything I could get my hands on about evaluation procedures and guidelines and conducting a balanced investigation into allegations from the partners involved in the divorce.

Practice Challenges

The challenges are making sure that I stay abreast of laws and rules in family law, and concepts in mediation and collaboration; finding the most effective way to facilitate agreement or cooperation between co-parents who loathe each other for the sake of the children in the middle, and simply maintaining my cool.

Common Legal and/or Ethical Issues

Recently, I was faced with having to reexamine my informed-consent procedures. I read in the most recent literature on the subject that working with the attorneys involved to cover all the issues, both legal and mental health, is probably the most advised way to go. The clients need to understand what my role is, what the process is and is not, and what the result will be. Often they have misunderstood that the custody-evaluation process is not confidential. I find that I am a lioness protecting her cubs when it comes to protecting the children from their angry parents, so I do a really thorough job explaining the process to them and how they should answer if they feel that I have asked a question that is going to put them on the hot seat. We also encountered a father who was angry after the report was complete; he felt that the children's counselor was unethical in speaking with me based solely on the authorization of their mother. We researched it, while consulting experts, to explain that if he had refused permission we would have just taken it to the judge to decide…which she would have granted more than likely, and he would have appeared to be obstructionist.

Brief Description of Collaborative Activities
With Professionals and/or Other Stakeholders

I am a member of Association of Family and Conciliation Courts (AFCC) and the Florida Chapter of that national organization. It is a collaboration that occurs across professional lines. Most of what I do every day is about working to cooperate or collaborate: on a collaborative divorce team, on an assignment to facilitate reconciliation of a parent with a child (working with agencies, attorneys, parents and judges).

I am also an active member of the local Family Law Advisory Group (FLAG) whose membership includes professionals across the professions.

Additional Information

I encourage social workers in training to get all the experience they can in the forensic arena. If they are willing to put their belief in themselves on the line—by testifying in court—this is a very rewarding arena. It takes courage; it takes training; it takes being very thorough and very honest. Otherwise, you will never gain the respect of the attorneys and the judges without whom you will not be able to do the work!

Case Study: The Need for Cultural Understanding

The case of Theresa B., a White, 26-year-old mother of a biracial 7-year-old daughter, demonstrates some ways social workers may become involved with a family in need of services in which they need to show not only cultural understanding, but also an understanding of structural forces and constraints. Theresa was convicted of attempted murder when she was 24 years old. Under the influence of drugs and alcohol, and possibly based on unaddressed psychiatric problems, Theresa stabbed her father repeatedly at their home, thinking he was attacking her. Her father, though he required prolonged medical care, survived the attack and eventually resumed a normal life. A social worker was involved with the family while the father was hospitalized because the family had no health care coverage and required access to in-home nursing care that they could not afford. The social worker helped the family access the required health care and other agencies that provided medical assistance to the father. The social worker also assisted with child care for their granddaughter during the convalescence and recovery period.

Once arrested, Theresa was consumed with remorse and became suicidal; she was consequently placed on suicide watch awaiting her trial. Social workers visited her at the county jail where she was held without bond until her trial. The testimony and assessments of the social workers and psychiatrists who interviewed her were part of the legal process that determined Theresa should serve a 10-year term for her actions. Once incarcerated, social workers at the prison assessed her again, and developed a treatment plan for Theresa's addiction and anger issues. Her long-time boyfriend, an IV-drug user, died of an overdose shortly after she was incarcerated and, because he was not immediate family, there was no provision for her to be able to attend a private viewing of his remains or to attend the funeral. Social workers ran the grief management support group and saw Theresa individually as she coped with this loss. She became suicidal again at this time, and remained under the care of counselors and a psychiatrist, who prescribed psychotropic medication.

Because Theresa's sentence was long, and because social workers for the child-welfare services organization in her state determined Theresa's parents' home not to be the best placement for her daughter's long-term best interests, they started the process of terminating Theresa's parental rights, which ultimately were terminated. Social workers were part of the process as they worked on her daughter's behalf, assessing the girl's performance in school and at home, as well as her current and projected relationship with her mother and extended family, and making recommendations to the court as to what placement would suit her needs most effectively in the long term. Rather than the same social worker completing all the phases of intervention in this case, many social workers were involved in the various needs this family presented. Theresa's case illustrates the need for social workers to carefully assess each person's life circumstances, needs, and limitations. Because many factors shape people's lives in a variety of ways, social workers must be careful to assess many issues that may force them to reconsider their own definitions and assumptions about what makes for a healthy family.

Summary and Conclusions

In the United States, we have diverse families who face a multitude of issues, concerns, and problems. Family is only one social institution, but it intersects with many other institutions such as work, education, health care, and criminal justice. This intersection means that what happens in one institution often affects families as well. In addition, families, like all social institutions, are shaped by structures of race, class, gender, and sexuality that socially locate families in different ways and offer unequal access to economic, social, and cultural resources that families need to remain healthy. Family structure does not determine the health of a family. Families of all shapes and sizes—single-parent families, divorced families, lesbian and gay families, blended families, dual-income-earning families, and many other "nontraditional" families—form quality interpersonal family relationships, have access to important resources, and can negotiate other social systems and institutions. However, many families, regardless of structure, are not healthy. The following list offers a summary of points we suggest will help social workers become more successful in helping families move toward good health:

- External structures of race, class, gender, and sexuality shape family experiences in many different and unequal ways.
- Historical and social factors shape family structures in different ways, but this does not mean that some family structures are better than others.
- Family law is often based on the assumption that a specific family structure (e.g., the "traditional" nuclear family) has always and should always exist, even though 80–90% of our families are not structured that way. Policymakers often assume that having such a structure makes families healthy, despite social science data that directly challenge this assumption.
- Families are interconnected to many other social institutions. Therefore, laws that are meant to affect other institutions often greatly affect families.

We encourage social workers to incorporate a critical perspective that questions the structures, laws, institutions, and access to resources that shape families and interpersonal relationships within families. We also encourage social workers to use a critical perspective to help families become healthy in the broadest sense: to form quality interpersonal family relationships, have access to important resources, and negotiate other social systems and institutions.

References

Ameristat. (2003). *Traditional families account for only 7 percent of U.S. households.* Population Reference Bureau. Retrieved on May 9, 2007, from http://www.prb.org/AmeristatTemplate.cfm?Section=

MarriageandFamily&template=/ContentManagement/ContentDisplay.cfm&ContentID=8288 [1996, 1/05/06]

Austin, A. M., MacGowan, M. J., & Wagner, E. F. (2005). Effective family-based interventions for adolescents with substance use problems: A systematic review. *Research on Social Work Practice, 15*(2), 67–83.

Baca Zinn, M., & Dill, B. T. (1996). Theorizing difference from multiracial feminism. *Feminist Studies, 22*, 321–331.

Baca Zinn, M., Eitzen, D. S., & Wells, B. (2007). *Diversity in families* (8th ed.). Upper Saddle River, NJ: Pearson.

Bernstein, N. (2000, October 25). Motherless children: The drug war has stamped an entire class of parents as permanently unfit. *Salon.com.* Accessed October 18, 2002, from http: archive.salon.com/ mwt/feature/2000/10/25/drug_families/print.html

Blum, L., & Deussen, T. (1996). Negotiating independent motherhood: Working class African American women talk about marriage and motherhood. *Gender & Society, 10*, 199–211.

Coontz, S. (1993). *The way we never were: American families and the nostalgia trap.* New York: HarperCollins.

Coster, W., Deeney, T., Haltiwanger, J., & Haley, S. (2008). *School function assessment.* New York: Pearson Associates.

Dewees, M. (2006). *Contemporary social work practice.* Boston: McGraw-Hill.

Dill, B. T., Baca Zinn, M., & Patton, S. (1998). Valuing families differently: Race, poverty and welfare reform. *Sage Race Relations Abstracts, 23*(3), 4–30.

Dunst, C. J., Trivette, C. M., & Deal, A. G. (1988). *Enabling and empowering families: Principles and guidelines for practice.* Cambridge, MA: Brookline Books.

Forum. (2008). *Forum on family and child statistics.* Retrieved April 25, 2009, from http://www.childstats.gov/

Goldenberg, I., & Goldenberg, H. (2000). *Family therapy: An overview* (5th ed.). Belmont, CA: Wadsworth/Thomson Learning.

Guttmacher Institute. (2007). *State policies in brief: An overview of abortion laws.* New York: Author.

Henggeler, S. W. (1997, May). Treating serious antisocial behavior in youth: The MST approach. *Juvenile Justice Bulletin.* Washington, DC: U.S. Department of Justice, Office of Juvenile Justice & Delinquency Prevention.

Jarrett, R. (1994). Living poor: Family life among single parent, African-American women. *Social Problems, 41*(1), 30–49.

Johnston, D. (2001, May). *Incarceration of women and effects on parenting.* Paper presented at the meeting, "Effects of Incarceration on Children and Families," sponsored by Northwestern University, Evanston, IL.

Lichtner, D. T., & Qian, Z. (2007). Marriage and family in a multicultural society. In S. J. Ferguson (Ed.), *Shifting the center: Understanding contemporary families* (pp. 42–58). Boston: McGraw-Hill Higher Education.

Mintz, S., & Kellogg, S. (1988). *Domestic revolutions: A social history of American family life.* New York: Free Press.

Mumola, C. J. (2000). *Incarcerated parents and their children.* Bureau of Statistics Special Report. Washington, DC: U.S. Department of Justice.

National Marriage Project. (2007). *The state of our unions 2007: The social health of marriage in America.* Piscataway, NJ: Rutgers University Press.

National Workforce Readiness Council. (2007). *National Workforce Readiness Credential: Candidate handbook.* Washington, DC: US Chamber of Commerce, Institute of Competitive Workforce.

Renzetti, C. M. (2007). Toward a better understanding of lesbian battering. In S. J. Ferguson (Ed.), *Shifting the center: Understanding contemporary families* (pp. 635–647). Boston: McGraw-Hill Higher Education.

Saltzman, A., & Furman, D. M. (1999). *Law in social work practice* (2nd ed.). Chicago: Nelson-Hall.

Tjaden, P., & Thoennes, N. (2000). *Full report of the prevalence, incidence, and consequences of violence against women: Findings from the National Violence Against Women Survey.* Washington, DC: U.S. Department of Justice, National Institute of Justice and Centers for Disease Control and Prevention.

Timmerman, I. G. H., Emanuels-Zuurveen, E. S., & Emmelkamp, P. M. G. (2000). Assessment of social support inventory (SSI): A brief scale to assess perceived adequacy of social support. *Clinical Psychology & Psychotherapy, 7*, 401–410.

Travis, J., & Waul, M. (2003). Prisoners once removed: The children and families of prisoners. In J. Travis & M. Waul (Eds.), *Prisoners once removed: The impact of incarceration and reentry on children, families, and communities* (pp. 1–28). Washington, DC: Urban Institute Press.

U.S. Census Bureau. (2006). *Table AVG1. Average number of people per household, by race and Hispanic origin, marital status, age, and education of householder: 2006.* Washington, DC: Author. Retrieved September 2008, from http://www.census.gov/population/www/socdemo/hh-fam/cps2006.html

U.S. Census Bureau. (2007). *American factfinder glossary. U.S. Census Bureau.* Retrieved September 24, 2008, from http://factfinder.census.gov/home/en/epss/glossary_h.html and http://factfinder.census.gov/home/en/epss/glossary_f.html

Wilson, W. J. (1987). *The truly disadvantaged.* Chicago: University of Chicago Press.

Zastrow, C. (2004). *Introduction to social work and social welfare: Empowering people* (8th ed.). Belmont, CA: Brooks/Cole-Thompson Learning.

Social Services: Meeting Basic Human Needs of Income, Food, and Shelter

7

Anne Sparks

Through the passage of the Social Security Act of 1935, the United States made a commitment to provide a national safety net for poor and vulnerable populations. The Act established a social justice framework that includes governmental and societal responsibility for assisting individuals and families who have difficulty meeting their basic human needs. This chapter focuses on the key role of social work professionals in establishing, maintaining, and improving programs needed to ensure a basic level of income for families with children (i.e., income security), access to adequate nutrition (i.e., food security), and access to adequate shelter (i.e., housing security). The activities of social workers in legal arenas affecting basic human needs include influencing the passage and implementation of laws that establish programs (and standards of eligibility) and advocating for clients' rights to access programs, as well as directly serving clients involved with the criminal justice system (both offenders and victims).

The general category of people whose basic needs have not been, or may not be, adequately met includes those considered poor (i.e., living at or below the poverty level), those living in economically distressed communities that lack adequate resources, and those who are vulnerable due to as a result of factors such as age and discrimination based on gender or race/ethnicity. Women have been considered vulnerable because of barriers to employment, lower earnings in comparison to similarly employed men, and (for mothers) the responsibilities of caring for children. Women subjected to violence and abuse are considered particularly vulnerable, and social work has provided leadership in advocating and developing specialized services for battered women and their children. Children are vulnerable because of their dependence on others and their environment for healthy development. In 2006, 17% of children in the United States lived in families officially considered poor, and African American and Latino families with children were more than twice as likely as White families with children to experience economic hardships (National Center for Children in Poverty, 2007).

As part of our ethical duty to promote the general welfare of society, social workers contribute to the ongoing debate about how to create and maintain "living conditions conducive to the fulfillment of basic human needs" (National Association of Social Workers [NASW], 1999, pp. 26–27); as practitioners we use our professional knowledge and skill to connect individual clients with basic resources. Social workers collaborate with other professions and interest groups to establish programs and services at local, state, and national levels and to monitor programs' responsiveness and adequacy. The fact that people who grow up in poverty face a greater likelihood of experiencing incarceration makes it especially important to focus on the needs of offenders who reenter poor communities after serving their sentences. Some victims of crime, particularly women with children who attempt to leave a domestic violence situation, are also at high risk for poverty.

Social work has long been involved with public welfare agencies and their income-maintenance function. The profession's advocacy role is evident in the strong opposition it mobilized to the initiative known as "welfare reform" that ended Aid to Families with Dependent Children (AFDC) in 1996 and replaced it with Temporary Assistance to Needy Families (TANF). The profession has supported expansion of national programs to prevent hunger such as as the Food Stamps Program and the National School Lunch Program, and social workers at the local level play key roles in developing and maintaining emergency food resources such as community meals, soup kitchens, and food pantries. The profession's involvement in the housing arena includes advocating for subsidized housing for people with low and moderate incomes; at local and state levels, social workers have helped create residential programs to meet the needs of specific groups such as offenders reentering the community who need treatment for substance abuse.

This chapter provides a brief overview of these arenas of basic human needs (public assistance, food insecurity, and housing) and discusses describes the challenges faced by social workers who serve populations with these needs, including offenders and victims of crime. The chapter draws particular attention to the current increase in vulnerability to homelessness caused by the housing-foreclosure crisis and suggests that to contribute to the establishment of a more effective "safety net," social workers must develop expertise in analyzing and influencing economic policy.

Public Assistance or "Welfare"

The Social Security Act of 1935 established Aid to Dependent Children (later known as AFDC). The program provided assistance to children in poor families without a male breadwinner, based on the rationale that mothers were needed by their children

and should not be forced to work outside the home. During the 1970s, as role expectations based on gender changed and more mothers entered the labor market, public
debate began to focus on the increase in the number of female-headed households
that received public assistance. During the 1980s, criticisms of AFDC were bolstered
by concerns that childbearing among unmarried adolescents had increased, and many
unmarried fathers took no financial responsibility for their children. The push for
welfare reform gained momentum from the argument that welfare dependency was
becoming a way of life for some families and from recognition that the bureaucratic
culture of AFDC did not provide resources, nor encourage development of skills that
would enable recipients to become self-sufficient. Although research did not support
claims that poverty was caused by the childbearing of unmarried women, such ideas
continued to influence the public. Qualitative researchers found that although AFDC
recipients often sought employment, low-wage jobs did not provide the income or
stability they needed in order to care for their children adequately (Edin & Lein, 1997).
Nevertheless, the Personal Responsibility and Work Opportunity Act (PRWOA) of 1996
became law, ending AFDC and establishing Temporary Assistance for Needy Families.

Fundamental changes in public assistance as a result of PRWOA include the
limiting of receipt of cash assistance to a maximum of five 5 years in a person's
lifetime, the requirement that recipients must participate in work or work-related
activities, and new latitude for each state in deciding how to spend TANF funds
(which are now received as a Block Grant). During the first five 5 years of welfare
reform, a strong economy and the increased earned-income tax credit (EITC) made it
possible for many TANF recipients (primarily single mothers) to transition successfully
from welfare to work. Some in this group received training that enabled them to
obtain jobs with benefits and the possibility of advancement; others, however, obtained
low-wage positions without benefits or job security. A study of the impact of welfare
reform that focused on the income of former recipients found that one group had
increased their income since leaving TANF, whereas another group had dropped into
deeper poverty (Acs & Loprest, 2007). Some recipients who haven't benefited from
work-preparation programs have been permitted to continue as TANF recipients as
a result of documented hardships (e.g., severe health problems or caring for family
members with disabilities). Allard (2002) found that 42 states were enforcing a lifetime
ban preventing felony drug offenders from ever receiving welfare.

Regulations in the most recent reauthorization of TANF place more requirements
on the states, including new restrictions on what states are allowed to count as work
or work-related activities for current recipients. The National Association of Social
Workers (NASW) and the Child Welfare League of America (CWLA) unsuccessfully
campaigned against the new rules (CWLA, 2006; NASW, 2006a). In testimony to the
House Committee on Ways and Means, NASW (2006b) pointed out that meeting the
new rules would increase recipients' needs for child care, although no additional
funding for child care was being provided. The Center for Law and Social Policy
(2007) recommended to the House Ways and Means Committee that Congress remove
arbitrary limits on education and training for TANF recipients, allow modifications
of participation requirements for individuals with disabilities, and restore cuts in
funding for child-support enforcement.

The limitations of the assumptions underlying TANF and the inability of the
program to respond to the recent sharp increases in costs of food and fuel (while
homelessness and unemployment rise) raise profound concerns (Dillon, 2008). Social
workers as individual professionals and as members of organizations and coalitions

are encouraged to use advocacy skills to strengthen the safety-net function of TANF and improve its ability to lead to stable, decently paying employment. Social workers providing services to potential, current, or former TANF recipients should familiarize themselves with NASW's policy statement on TANF (NASW, 2006c) and obtain guidance from their state NASW chapter as well as the national NASW office in order to advocate effectively (NASW, 2007).

Because of variations among the states in regulations and the amount of cash assistance a family may receive per month, there is no manual that can be used in every state to inform TANF applicants and recipients of all relevant procedures, available benefits, and eligibility requirements. The eligibility of ex-offenders for TANF also varies from state to state. However, in all states, applicants and recipients do have the right to request a Fair Hearing when they believe that an adverse decision affecting their status was incorrect. Such decisions include denying benefits, sanctioning a client, and terminating benefits. Besides setting the individual maximum lifetime limit of five 5 years on receiving TANF (although permitting states to grant some exemptions), federal regulations require that states sanction recipients by decreasing their cash assistance when recipients fail to comply with work requirements. Social workers serving low-income families need to be aware of the hardships that sanctioning causes (Reichman, Teitler, & Curtis, 2005) and the rights of recipients to appeal the decision to impose sanctions (as well as decisions to deny and terminate benefits) through the Fair Hearing procedure (U.S. Department of Public Health and Human Services, 2007a). Lens (2006) analyzed administrative data from Fair Hearing decisions in Texas and found that 49% of the hearings resulted in reversing the action that had been taken by the welfare office. The Fair Hearing records showed that the most frequent reasons for reversing decisions were that welfare workers had failed to provide or obtain necessary information, had applied the rules too rigidly without considering the goals of the program, or had entered case information incorrectly (Lens, 2006). Social workers should obtain information about the policies and procedures of the welfare offices serving their clients. If a client receives a notice of denial, sanction, or termination from TANF, the social worker should explore with the client whether grounds may exist for appealing this decision (e.g., the possibility of administrative error or documented conditions that interfere with the clients' ability to understand and comply with requirements). If such grounds exist, the client may decide to request a Fair Hearing. Social workers also need to be aware of TANF's Family Violence Option (FVO), which gives states the flexibility to exempt victims of domestic violence from certain program requirements and to extend the time limits on benefits so they can obtain safety for themselves and their children (Postmus & Ah Hahn, 2007).

Food Insecurity

To indicate the degree to which people lack adequate means of obtaining food and risk malnourishment, the U.S. Department of Agriculture (USDA) has replaced the term "hunger" with two categories of "food insecurity": *Low* food security means that people have a reduced quality or quantity of food because of budget limitations; *very* low food security means that people have to cut back on eating or they skip meals on a frequent basis. In 2006, 35.5 million people in the United States lived in households considered to be "food insecure" (Food Research & Action Center, n.d.a).

The main safety net provided by the federal government for people experiencing food insecurity is the Food Stamp Program, which subsidizes the purchase of food by low-income individuals and families through an electronic benefit transfer system. In 2003, 55% of households using food stamps contained children, 18% contained an elderly person, and 23% contained a disabled person (Food Research & Action Center, n.d.b). Eligibility requirements vary somewhat from state to state, but, in general, households with a net income equal to or less than 100% of the poverty guidelines are eligible (U.S. Department of Agriculture, 2007). Poverty-level income for a household of four in 2007 was $20,650 (United States Department of Health & Human Services, 2007b). Food stamps, combined with unemployment insurance, help prevent hunger in communities facing the loss of jobs. However, only 57% of the working-poor families that are eligible for food stamps receive them (America's Second Harvest, 2007).

A survey of 23 U.S. cities found that the needs for emergency food assistance were not adequately met in 2007, and 19 of the 23 cities expected the demand for food assistance to increase in 2008 (U.S. Conference of Mayors, 2007). The survey found that, in addition to factors of poverty, unemployment, and high housing costs, the recent jump in foreclosures on mortgages and increases in the cost of living, including food costs, exacerbated the current "hunger crisis" (p. i). Cities reported that, because the Food Stamp Program benefit levels have not kept up with the increasing price of food, some families use up their monthly allotment of food stamps before the month ends and then seek emergency food assistance (U.S. Conference of Mayors). However, the quantity of food available for distribution on an emergency basis has decreased because of a drop both in donations from supermarkets (as inventory tracking has improved) and in supplies coming from the federal Agriculture Department's Bonus Commodity Program. Food banks across the country are currently reporting critical shortages (America's Second Harvest, 2007). Social workers are involved in local campaigns to collect money and food in response to these shortages, but in order to meet needs on a national level, local efforts need have to join larger scale efforts such as the Food Research and Action Center's Campaign to End Childhood Hunger (Food Research & Action Center, n.d.c).

Homelessness

National policy began to address the needs of homeless people in 1987 through the Stewart B. McKinney Homeless Assistance Act. During the 1990s, shelter services expanded throughout the United States, and increased numbers of people sought these services. According to Burt (2001, p. 1), "On any given day, at least 800,000 people are homeless in the United States, including about 200,000 children in homeless families." Social workers provide a variety of services to individuals and families who are homeless (or in danger of becoming homeless) and also work at local, state, and national levels to improve these services and address the causes of homelessness. The groups at greatest risk of becoming homeless are those with incomes below the poverty level who cannot afford housing (Burt, 2001). Physical disabilities and health and mental health problems (including substance abuse) are risk factors, as are limited education or skills training, and the gap between wages for unskilled work and the cost of housing (Burt, 2001). For youth, experiences of physical and sexual abuse, foster home placement, and incarceration (for males) are predictors of homelessness. Children who experience homelessness have more cognitive and emotional difficulties than other children and are also at greater risk for homelessness in adulthood (Burt, 2001). The experience of even a brief period of homelessness, for children or adults, is stressful and disruptive.

In a 2007 survey of 23 major cities, the U.S. Conference of Mayors (2007) found that 23% of those using emergency shelters and transitional housing programs were members of homeless families, whereas 76% were single adults, and 1% were unaccompanied youth. Six cities reported an increase in the overall number of people, and 10 cities reported an increase in the number of households with children who used shelters and transitional housing services in 2007. Twelve cities reported that they were not able to serve everyone who requested shelter. Cities in 2007 identified the lack of affordable housing, poverty, and domestic violence as common causes of homelessness for households with children; for single individuals, the most common causes were mental illness and substance abuse. Fifteen of the surveyed cities predicted that there will be an increase in requests for emergency shelter among households with children in 2008 as a result of the foreclosure crisis and increases in poverty. The most common response of officials surveyed to the question of what their city needed to do to reduce homelessness given by officials surveyed was to provide more permanent housing (U.S. Conference of Mayors, 2007). Although generally critical of federal housing policy, social work analysts support programs such as Section 8 housing vouchers, which expand opportunities for the poor to obtain decent housing in economically stable communities (Gilbert & Terrell, 2005). The Violence Against Women Act includes funding for emergency shelters, transitional housing, and permanent housing for victims of domestic violence (National Low Income Housing Coalition, 2007).

Stable housing is frequently mentioned as one of the major needs of offenders upon their release from jail and prison (see chapter 20, "Reentry in the 21st Century"). Programs that involve key stakeholders in the community and provide a structured transitional experience for offenders leaving jail or prison report a below-average rate of recidivism among their clients (Yamatani, 2008). A recent federal law (The Second Chance Act of 2007) authorizes funding to promote this type of comprehensive planning and collaboration in the provision of services to former prisoners reentering the community (Nelson & Turetsky, 2008). A model that may be more feasible in smaller communities is the inclusion of the housing needs of ex-offenders in the agenda of the local housing coalition (Coming Home, n.d.).

Because economic policy directly affects housing policy (as well as the design of public assistance and food supplement programs), social workers who want to join efforts to prevent homelessness and develop strategies to meet the housing needs of their clients and communities should become familiar with NASW's statement on economic policy as well as its statement on housing policy (NASW, 2006c). In addition, the foreclosure crisis mentioned above earlier is a recent national development that requires social workers to become more familiar with the impact of predatory lending practices on vulnerable populations and on the public in general.

VOICES FROM THE FIELD

Jeff Yungman, MSW, LISW-CP, MPH, JD
Clinical Director of Crisis Ministries
Director of Crisis Ministries Homeless Justice Project

Agency Setting

Crisis Ministries, located in Charleston, South Carolina, provides social services, primary care, and mental health care and counseling in addition to the basic needs of food and shelter to over 150 homeless men, women, and children every night. In January 2006 the Crisis Ministries Homeless Justice Project was created as a partnership among Crisis Ministries, the Charleston School of Law, Nelson Mullins Law Firm, and Pro Bono Legal Services. It is designed to help homeless individuals and families by removing obstacles, both legal and social, which prevent homeless men and women from regaining self-sufficiency. The Crisis Ministries Homeless Justice Project is one of therapeutic jurisprudence designed to be client-centered in that services are provided to the client on site; and it is holistic in that it assesses all the needs of the individual to provide not only legal services, but social services as well.

Practice Responsibilities

As the Clinical Director I am responsible for supervision of the eight case managers in addition to carrying a caseload composed of individuals with mental health issues and/ or legal issues. As Director of the Crisis Ministries Homeless Justice Project I take the initial referrals for any individual with a legal issue (primarily civil issues). Each referral is then forwarded to the Nelson Mullins Law Firm and Pro Bono Legal Services for assignment. At the monthly legal clinic the client meets with his/her attorney and a law student to discuss their her/his case. I then provide follow-up on identified legal and social issues with the assistance of the law student assigned to the case, an MSW intern, and the Crisis Ministries case management staff. In addition, I assume responsibility for some cases, primarily disability cases.

Expertise Required

The position requires an MSW with extensive knowledge of the legal system and legal issues. I started in the position prior to receiving my law degree and except for representing individuals in court, a legal degree is not absolutely necessary.

Practice Challenges

The greatest practice challenges for working with the homeless in general are lack of affordable housing, lack of universal health care, and lack of a living minimum wage. The greatest practice challenges as Director of the Homeless Justice Project are the increasing criminalization of homelessness, the snail-paced disability process, and the difficulty recruiting volunteer attorneys.

Common Legal and/or Ethical Issues

The common legal issues handled by the Crisis Ministries Homeless Justice Project include disability claims, family law, including divorce, child custody, and child support, landlord/tenant issues, wills and power of attorney, expungements and pardons, employment claims, and some municipal criminal charges. Although not an ethical issue per se, I have found it difficult at times to reconcile my veteran social work approach to a problem with my new legal approach to that same problem.

Brief Description of Collaborative Activities
With Professionals and/or Other Stakeholders

I am a member of the Crisis Ministries Homeless Justice Project advisory board that is tasked with developing the project to its maximum potential and with recruitment of both attorney and law students. In that regard, I have presented at information sessions and continuing legal education (CLEs) at the Charleston School of Law. In addition I am a member of the South Carolina Re-entry Initiative program, a group of community members and professionals who help individuals released from prison reintegrate themselves into society.

Housing Crisis and Predatory Lending

Two striking phenomena that occurred in 2007 indicated that the affordable housing shortage in the United States had reached a critical point and needed immediate attention. First, large populations of homeless people became visible in major cities where housing policies did not address housing needs. For example, as a result of a decision by a federal court of appeals, Los Angeles agreed to stop enforcing an ordinance used by police to arrest homeless people sleeping on sidewalks until 1,250 units of low-cost housing are built, which will take about three 3 years (Archibold, 2007). In New Orleans, demonstrators protested as the federal government began tearing down the city's largest public housing projects without providing any housing for the displaced residents (Eaton, 2007). A spokesperson from the Advancement Project, which initiated legal action to stop the demolition, said that residents who were forced to evacuate New Orleans because of Hurricane Katrina wanted an interim-housing plan that would allow them to return (Advancement Project, n.d.; Eaton, 2007).

Second, beginning early in 2007, the percentage of home mortgages going into default began to rise as homeowners faced steep increases in the monthly payments due. More than 635,000 foreclosure notices were filed in the United States between August and November 2007 (Stabenow, 2007). Increases in monthly mortgage payments stem from variable interest rates and other features of subprime lending, in which lenders are not held to the same regulations as traditional banks (Wharton School of the University of Pennsylvania, 2007). In subprime lending, borrowers whose income levels and credit histories would not normally qualify them for loans are offered loans at higher interest rates and with higher fees than those offered by traditional lenders. The term "predatory lending" is used when borrowers are not knowledgeable about the actual terms of the agreement or clearly lack the means to meet the terms of repayment, and deceptive promotional offers may be involved (Association of Community Organizations for Reform Now, n.d.). In some cases, the brokers who arranged the loans may face criminal charges (Hirsh, 2008).

Many of the practices of predatory lending can be considered violations of the Fair Housing Act and the Equal Credit Opportunity Act (Grow & Epstein, 2007; Miami Valley Fair Housing Center [MVFHC], n.d.). Social workers need to be aware of the consumer rights of vulnerable groups (National Consumer Law Center, n.d.) and may collaborate with nonprofit attorneys taking legal action against predatory lenders (MVFHC, 2008). One model is provided by Metropolitan Family Services, a comprehensive social service agency in Chicago that campaigns for regulation of predatory lending (Metropolitan Family Services, 2008). Social work agencies should have resources available to help clients develop financial literacy and avoid inappropriate loans (Federal Housing Administration, n.d.). While working to strengthen consumer protection regulations and enforcement, social workers also need to provide consumers with information and skills that will enable them to manage debt when necessary (Sheafor & Horejsi, 2006). NASW supports a coalition that promotes long-term financial stability (Stoesen, 2007) and financial-literacy training (Divided We Fail, n.d.). Programs that provide financial education to youth through interaction with financial institutions have shown promise (Johnson & Sherraden, 2007) and programs that promote asset accumulation have reported some success in going beyond the notion of the "safety net" to address the causes of poverty (McKernan, Ratcliffe, & Nam, 2007; Sherraden, 2007).

Applying Social Work Theories and Skills

Systems theory is helpful when working with client populations who struggle to meet basic human needs, and especially those with legal and criminal justice involvement, because it enables social workers to understand how clients are affected by a range of institutions and systems. The social worker needs to provide a way of linking clients to necessary resources, using "resource consultation or case management" (Greene, 1999, p. 240), and often must help to develop or strengthen those resources as well. Social workers use systems theory to understand structural aspects of organizations and programs that control resources; they use systems theory together with ecological theory to assess the needs in a given community and develop and implement strategies to address those needs. In the criminal justice arena, social workers must translate their knowledge of the system's requirements and available resources into information that clients can comprehend and use. Following is a description of situations in which a social worker in a shelter for the homeless uses the skills of case management, collaboration, advocacy, and education to provide ways for people to access resources and establish stable living situations.

The agency is a faith-based organization and the shelter serves several counties in rural Appalachia. The social worker initially meets with each homeless individual and family staying in the shelter to conduct an assessment and develop a service plan. The homeless clients come from many backgrounds: Some have experienced personal difficulties that have made them particularly vulnerable, whereas others have lived for long periods in extreme poverty without heat and running water. Some people have lived in rental storage units; others have "coasted from couch to couch."

Youth no longer eligible for foster care services upon reaching legal adulthood at the age of 18 often become homeless. It is vital for the social worker to coordinate services and communicate regularly with other organizations that also serve the shelter residents and/or have authority in their lives, such as probation officers and child protective services.

Clients have the opportunity to receive a positive reference from the shelter staff, based on following their case plan and demonstrating their willingness and ability to keep their living area clean and interact appropriately with staff and other residents. This reference has a positive impact because the shelter is a respected agency with a history of collaborating effectively with other institutions within the community. The reference may help the client obtain an apartment or open a bank account without providing a credit check; it may persuade a judge to sentence the client to community service instead of a term in jail. The social worker advocates on behalf of clients with other agencies, for example, clients may have been unaware of requirements they were expected to meet, perhaps in order to continue to receive food stamps, because they had no residence where they could receive mail. The shelter allows clients to use its address and makes it possible for them to accomplish basic tasks that are taken for granted by people with housing, for example, making phone calls, obtaining identification, and traveling to health care services and agencies where they can apply for permanent housing or disability benefits. The social worker educates the clients about the systems that affect their current and future ability to reach their goals. She/he also educates people in the community about the causes and prevalence of homelessness and involves them in the program as volunteers. The social worker is currently facing an ethical dilemma because of federal funding requirements. To maintain its funding, the shelter is required to collect extensive personal information from every shelter resident and enter it into an online database. Respecting clients' rights to privacy and informed consent, the social worker informs new residents of the information system and asks if they are willing to give the information and have it entered into the database. Clients' wishes have been respected, and usually a minimal amount of information is entered; however, pressure to obtain complete data from every resident has recently increased.

VOICES FROM THE FIELD

Bradley J. Schaffer, LMSW, BCD
Division Director, Community Psychiatry & Supervisory, Social Worker, VA Medical Center

Agency Setting

I have been employed by the VA Medical Center for nearly 22 years. The VA Medical Center, Cincinnati, Ohio, is a multisite medical system with an academic teaching mission that includes medical centers, rehabilitation facilities, and Community-Based Outpatient Clinics (CBOCs). Services include mental health, primary care, domestic abuse, substance abuse, homeless, housing, specialized OEF/OIF (Operation Enduring Freedom and Operation Iraqi Freedom), incarcerated veteran outreach, and emergency care. My Community

Psychiatry Division (CPD) staff is assigned to clinical services at all campuses and CBOC's of the facilities and participate in the mission of the VAMC. The Mental Health Care Line (MHCL) has an academic affiliation with the University of Cincinnati, Department of Psychiatry and other professional schools (e.g., Social Work, Psychology, and Nursing) and participates in the VHA-supported training programs. Staff are called on to provide services at multiple sites in the organization, conduct outreach to the community, and at times provide home visits to veterans. The CPD offers a full spectrum of homeless outpatient programs, community outreach, and mental health/primary care CBOC services. The staff assigned within the CPD provides direct clinical care and are administratively and clinically responsible to the supervisory social worker.

Practice Responsibilities

The primary purpose of my role as a supervisory social worker is to provide leadership, budgetary oversight, and programmatic management to programs, such as: Health Care for Homeless Veterans (HCHV), Homeless Women Veterans (HWV), Housing and Urban Development/VA Supportive Housing (HUD/VASH), Grant & Per Diem (G&PD), Homeless Dental, Domestic Violence, Prison/Jail Outreach, Special Projects, and CBOC Mental Health. I provide the same type of leadership and oversight to staff: social workers, psychiatrists, psychologists, nurses and support personnel assigned to the MHCL, CPD of the VA Medical Center, Cincinnati, Ohio. I provide line supervision to all assigned staff within the CPD; administrative, budgetary and clinical consultation to MHCL management; fiscal, clinical staff, and direct clinical care. I am a member of the MHCL Behavioral Health & Sciences Committee (BH&SC) and the MHCL Partnership Committee. I participate in all management-level decisions and am directly responsible for the administrative, clinical, budgetary, space, personnel, and professional activities related to the CPD. I serve on various professional, MHCL, CPD, VA Healthcare System of Ohio and Mental Healthcare System of Ohio, and VISN 10 committees, task forces, work groups and community. I report directly to the Director, MHCL, Cincinnati, Ohio.

Expertise Required

Currently, I am a supervisory social worker, GS-0185 (Social Work series), Grade GS-13. You need to be a social worker, GS-12 at least 1 year to qualify, have a master's of social work degree, and have an independent license in any state.

Practice Challenges

I have provided clinical services 2 days per week since 2003 (prison/jail outreach and domestic violence). I have encountered over 300 veterans during prison/jail outreach and nearly 800 in the DV program. These are unique forensic and diversion-style programs not typically found at VA medical centers. The challenges are staffing, budget, follow-up, and sustained support.

Common Legal and/or Ethical Issues

Some of the more common issues are domestic-abuse recidivism, substance-abuse relapses, witnessing veterans being mandated to local programs while VA services are available, sex-offender housing, coping with postprison release to homelessness so VA eligibility requirements can be met, not being able to place a person under age 18 in a government vehicle, and so on.

Brief Description of Collaborative Activities
With Professionals and/or Other Stakeholders

1. Collaborated with the University of Cincinnati, School of Social Work on two studies: Homeless Veterans & Domestic Abuse (n = 706) to conduct a program evaluation and Veterans Fatherhood Study (in-progress) to local Internal Review board (IRB).
2. Facilitated a 13-week domestic-violence prevention program for veterans with a community partner. This program is an approved reentry portal by the Ohio Department of Rehabilitation & Corrections (ODRC). Nearly 800 veterans have been screened using a Domestic Violence/Abuse Screen (DV/AS) tool with nearly 200 successful outcomes.

Summary and Conclusions

Social work has historically focused on basic human needs and society's responsibility to provide a safety net for vulnerable populations. The profession's work in legal arenas related to meeting basic human needs includes influencing the passage and implementation of laws that establish programs (and standards of eligibility) and advocating for clients' rights to access programs, as well as directly serving groups with criminal justice system involvement (both offenders and victims). The current slowing of the economy in the United States makes the inadequacies of current public assistance programs, emergency food programs, and housing resources matters of great public as well as professional concern. Social workers are beginning to mobilize in response to the housing crisis brought on by massive foreclosures and will be involved in trying to meet the emerging needs of struggling communities as the crisis continues. In response to the damaging effects of predatory lending, the profession must focus advocacy efforts on consumer protection and accountability in the home-mortgage and banking industries. To contribute to creation of a more effective "safety net," social workers are strongly urged to increase their expertise in analyzing and influencing economic policy.

References

Acs, G., & Loprest, P. (2007). *TANF caseload composition and leavers synthesis report.* Washington, DC: The Urban Institute. Retrieved December 27, 2007, from http://www.urban.org/UploadedPDF/411553_tanf_caseload.pdf

Association of Community Organizations for Reform Now. (n.d.). *Predatory lending.* Retrieved September 28, 2008, from http://www.acorn.org/index.php?id=2626

Advancement Project. (n.d.) *Hurricane Katrina.* Retrieved January 1, 2008, from http://www.advancementproject.org

Allard, P. (2002). *Life sentences: Denying welfare benefits to women convicted of drug offenses.* Washington, DC: The Sentencing Project: Research and Advocacy for Reform. Retrieved August 29, 2008, from http://www.sentencingproject.org/PublicationDetails.aspx?PublicationID=484

America's Second Harvest. (2007). *America's Second Harvest—The nation's food bank network.* Retrieved December 31, 2007, from http://www.secondharvest.org

Archibold, R. (2007). Los Angeles to permit sleeping on sidewalks. *The New York Times,* October 11, p. A21.

Association of Community Organizations for Reform Now. (n.d.). *Predatory lending.* Retrieved September 28, 2008, from http://www.acorn.org/index.php?id=2626

Burt, M. (2001). *What will it take to end homelessness?* Washington, DC: The Urban Institute. Retrieved September 1, 2005, from http://www.urban.org/url.cfm?ID=310305

Center for Law & Social Policy. (2007). *Congress should take action to restore flexibility and funding lost in 2006 welfare reauthorization and HHS regulations.* Retrieved December 27, 2007, from http://www.clasp.org/publications/flexibility_2006_tanf_testimony.pdf

Child Welfare League of America. (2006). *Letter from CWLA to the Office of Family Assistance, U.S. Administration for Children and Families regarding TANF interim final rule.* Retrieved December 26, 2007, from http://www.cwla.org/advocacy/tanf.htm

Coming Home. (n.d.) *Coming home: Athens county plan to end homelessness.* Retrieved August 30, 2008, from www.endhomelessness.org/files/1733_file_AthensOH.pdf

Dillon, S. (2008). Hard times hitting students and schools. *The New York Times.* Retrieved September 28, 2008, from http://www.nytimes.com/2008/09/01/education/01school.html?hp

Divided We Fail. (n.d.) *Managing finances.* Retrieved January 2, 2007, from http://www.aarp.org/issues/dividedwefail/about_issues/divided_we _fail_platform_managing_finances.html

Eaton, L. (2007). In New Orleans, plan to raze low-income housing draws protest. *The New York Times.* Retrieved December 31, 2007, from http://www.nytimes.com/2007/12/14/us/nationalspecial/14orleans.html?fta=y

Edin, K., & Lein, L. (1997). *Making ends meet: How single mothers survive welfare and low-wage work.* New York: Russell Sage Foundation.

Federal Housing Administration. (n.d.). *Resources for homebuyers.* Retrieved January 2, 2007, from http://www.fha.gov/buyer/resources.cfm#4

Food Research & Action Center. (n.d.a). *Hunger and food insecurity in the United States.* Retrieved on December 30, 2007, from http://www.frac.org/html/hunger_in_the_us/hunger_index.html

Food Research & Action Center. (n.d.b). *Food stamp program.* Retrieved December 30, 2007, from http://www.frac.org/html/federal_food_programs/programs/fsp.html

Food Research & Action Center. (n.d.c). *Campaign to end childhood hunger.* Retrieved December 31, 2007, from http://www.frac.org/html/ctech/ctech_index.html

Gilbert, N., & Terrell, P. (2005). *Dimensions of social welfare policy.* Boston: Allyn & Bacon.

Greene, R. (1999). *Human behavior theory and social work practice* (2nd ed.). Hawthorne, NY: Aldine de Gruyter.

Grow, B., & Epstein, K. (2007, May 21). The poverty business. *Business Week,* pp. 57–67.

Hirsh, M. (2008, June 2). *Mortgages and madness: Questionable lending practices turned a peaceful Cleveland neighborhood into a blighted slum.* Retrieved August 29, 2008, from http://www.newsweek.com/id/138503

Johnson, E., & Sherraden, M. (2007). From financial literacy to financial capability among youth. *Journal of Sociology & Social Welfare, 34,* 119–146.

Lens, V. (2006). Examining the administration of work sanctions on the frontlines of the welfare system. *Social Science Quarterly, 87,* 573–590.

McKernan, S., Ratcliffe, C., & Nam, Y. (2007). *The effects of welfare and IDA program rules on the asset holdings of low-income families.* Retrieved January 2, 2008, from http://www.urban.org/UploadedPDF/411558_ida_program.pdf

Metropolitan Family Services. (2008). *Metropolitan family services moves beyond payday loan reform.* Retrieved September 28, 2008, from http://www.metrofamily.org/articleDetail.asp?objectID=1957

Miami Valley Fair Housing Center. (2008). *Client services.* Retrieved February 7, 2008, from http://www.mvfairhousing.com/client_services.php

Miami Valley Fair Housing Center. (n.d.). *Why is predatory lending a fair housing issue?* Retrieved February 7, 2008, from http://www.dontriskyourhome.com/fair_housing.htm

National Association of Social Workers. (1999). *Code of ethics of the National Association of Social Workers.* Washington, DC: NASW Press.

National Association of Social Workers. (2006a). *Oppose the temporary assistance for needy families (TANF) interim final rule.* Retrieved December 26,2007, from http://www.socialworkers.org/advocacy/alerts/2006/082106.asp

National Association of Social Workers. (2006b). *Written testimony of Elizabeth J. Clark, Hearing to "Review outcomes of 1996 Welfare reform."* Retrieved December 26, 2007, from http://www.socialworkers.org/advocacy/letters/2006/072406.asp

National Association of Social Workers. (2006c). *Social work speaks: National Association of Social Workers policy statements, 2006–2009.* Washington, DC: NASW Press.

National Association of Social Workers. (2007). *PACE: Building political power for social workers.* Retrieved December 29, 2007, from http://www.naswdc.org/pace/default.asp

National Center for Children in Poverty. (2007). *Who are America's poor children? The official story.* Retrieved February 8, 2008, from http://www.nccp.org/publications/pub_787.html

National Consumer Law Center. (n.d.). *Distinct populations.* Retrieved February 7, 2008, from http://www.consumerlaw.org/issues/distinct_populations/index.shtml

National Low Income Housing Coalition. (2007). *Violence against women act.* Retrieved December 27, 2007, from http://www.nlihc.org/detail/article.cfm?article_id=2809&id=46

Nelson, A., & Turetsky, V. (2008). *Second Chance Act of 2007: Community safety through recidivism prevention.* Center for Law & Social Policy Legislation in Brief. Washington, DC: Retrieved August 29, 2008, from http://www.clasp.org/publications.php?id=10&year=2008#0

Postmus, J., & Ah Hahn, S. (2007). The collaboration between welfare and advocacy organizations: Learning from the experiences of domestic violence survivors. *Families in Society: The Journal for Contemporary Services, 88,* 475–484.

Reichman, N., Teitler, J., & Curtis, M. (2005). TANF sanctioning and hardship. *Social Service Review, 79,* 215–236.

Sheafor, B., & Horejsi, C. (2006). *Techniques and guidelines for social work practice.* Boston: Allyn & Bacon.

Sherraden, M. (2007). Assets for all: Toward universal, progressive, lifelong accounts. In J. Edwards, M. Crain, & A. L. Kalleberg (Eds.), *Ending poverty in America: How to restore the American dream* (pp. 151–163). New York: New Press.

Stabenow, D. (2007). *Stabenow, housing industry and advocates meet to address foreclosure crisis in America.* Retrieved January 2, 2007, from http://www.stabenow.senate.gov/press/2007/110707Mortgage presser.htm

Stoesen, L. (2007). " 'Divided we fail' " supported. *NASW News, 52*(9), 6.

U.S. Conference of Mayors. (2007). *Hunger and homelessness survey: A status report on hunger and homelessness in America's cities.* Retrieved December 31, 2007, from http://www.usmayors.org/HHSurvey2007/hhsurvey07.pdf

U.S. Department of Agriculture. (2007). *USDA food stamp program: Food stamps make America stronger.* Retrieved December 31, 2007, from http://aspe.hhs.gov/poverty/07poverty.shtml

U.S. Department of Public Health & Human Services. (2007a). *TANF program policy manual, section 1500, case management, subsections 1506–1, 1506–2 and 1506-3.* Retrieved December 29, 2007, from http://www.dphhs.mt.gov/hcsd/tanfmanual

U.S. Department of Health & Human Services. (2007b). *The 2007 HHS poverty guidelines.* Retrieved December 31, 2007, from http://aspe.hhs.gov/poverty/07poverty.shtml

Wharton School of the University of Pennsylvania. (2007). *How we got into the subprime lending mess.* Knowledge @ Wharton. Retrieved September 28, 2008, from http://knowledge.wharton.upenn.edu/article.cfm?articleid=1812#

Yamatani, H. (2008). *Overview report of Allegheny county jail collaborative evaluation findings.* Center on Race & Social Problems, School of Social Work, University of Pittsburgh. Retrieved August 29, 2008, from http://www.crsp.pitt.edu/downloads/JailStudy.pdf

Assisting Female Victims of Intimate Partner Violence: The Role of Victim Advocates

8

Marie Mele

Working with victims of intimate partner violence can be both a rewarding and challenging job. The rewards come from helping people who are in need of information, assistance, and advocacy. The challenges come from navigating an unorganized, fragmented, and underfunded criminal justice system that often fails to meet the needs of crime victims. This chapter addresses the experiences and needs of female victims of intimate partner violence. It examines common practices used and issues faced by victim advocates—who are often trained social workers—who work with women who have been victimized by a male intimate partner. The first-hand experiences of a victim advocate for female victims of intimate partner violence are highlighted.

Scope of the Problem

Although men are victims of intimate partner violence and there are cases of mutual violence, women are much more likely than men to be victimized by an intimate partner. Women account for 9 out of 10 victims of intimate partner violence (Bureau of Justice Statistics, 2000). Each year, roughly 2 million women are physically assaulted by their intimate partners, and 52% of women report that they have been physically assaulted by an intimate partner at some point in their lives (Tjaden & Thoennes, 2000). Roughly, 4 out of 10 women who are assaulted by an intimate partner seek medical treatment for their injuries (Bureau of Justice Statistics, 2000). In addition, battered women are four to five times as likely than nonbattered women to require psychiatric treatment, and five times as likely to attempt suicide (Heise, 1993)

Although women of all races, ethnicities, and income levels may suffer violence at the hands of their intimate partners, some women are at greater risk of victimization than others. African American and Native American Indian women have the greatest risk of victimization by an intimate partner (Tjaden & Thoennes, 2000). Also, lower income women often experience higher rates of intimate partner violence than higher income women (Bachman & Saltzman, 1995). The relationship between race and risk of victimization may be confounded by income, because African American women generally have lower incomes than non-African American women (DeNavas-Walt, Proctor, & Lee, 2005). Women of low income often have few resources to escape abusive relationships and may be financially dependent on their abusive partner. As a result, their risk of victimization (and revictimization) is higher than that of women who are financially independent. Research also suggests that Native American couples are more likely than couples of other races to use violence (Bachman, 1992); however, more research is needed to determine the extent to which intimate partner violence among this population can be explained by social and environmental factors. This is an area in which social workers who work with victims and/or offenders could contribute to our understanding of these relationships.

Relevant Theoretical Frameworks

Intimate partner violence has been described as a pattern of coercive control (Pence & Paymar, 1986), in which the abusive partner asserts his power over the victim through the use of verbal threats and physical violence. Within this framework, violence and the threat of violence are seen as tools that the abusive partner uses to gain greater power in the relationship (Dobash, Dobash, Wilson, & Daly, 1992). Intimate partner violence has also been described as "instrumental aggression," whereby acts of aggression and violence are intended to control the victim's behavior and demonstrate dominance (Frieze & McHugh, 1992).

Johnson (1995) suggested that intimate partner violence could not be understood as a single phenomenon, and offered two typologies: *common couple violence*, which is characterized by mutual low-level physical aggression; and *patriarchal intimate terrorism*, in which men batter female partners to maintain coercive control. These typologies highlight the importance of understanding the context within which violent acts occur, because a single act of violence can take on different meanings in different contexts. Dutton and Goodman (2005) likewise suggested that social context gives meaning to the abuser's behavior and the victim's response, emphasizing the importance of examining the social context within which coercion, acts of aggression, and violence are used in intimate relationships. Although research suggests that women do use violence against their intimate partners (Archer, 2000), women's use of violence is often committed in response to male violence or in self-defense (Dekeseredy & Schwartz, 1998). In addition, women are more likely than men to experience severe violence at higher frequencies and to experience negative consequences (e.g., poor mental health) as a result of violence (Anderson, 2002; Archer, 2000).

Understanding intimate partner violence as a pattern of coercive control and instrumental aggression can help advocates and social service providers assist victims (and offenders) in understanding the complex dynamics of abusive intimate partner relationships. Interventions can be tailored to address the systemic use of coercion and control to help batterers reform their behavior, alter their way of thinking, and protect victims from further victimization. Knowledge of the dynamics of intimate partner violence can also assist criminal justice practitioners (e.g., police, prosecutors, judges) to understand the pattern of abuse within which individual acts of violence occur, and make more informed decisions about case disposition and victim safety.

The Rise of Victim Advocacy

For many years, social workers and activists have advocated for the rights of crime victims and assisted with their needs, especially during the criminal justice process. Efforts to help victims were formalized in the early 1970s, when the first victim-assistance programs were established in San Francisco and Washington, DC (Wallace, 1998). Over the next 2 decades, victim-assistance programs were created throughout the United States. These programs were designed to serve as a resource for crime victims and provided services, for example, support groups, counseling, and accompaniment to criminal justice proceedings.

Among the first adult victims to receive special attention from advocates were victims of sexual assault and intimate partner violence. This was largely to the result of the efforts of the National Organization for Women (NOW), which formed a task force in 1976 to examine the problem of intimate partner violence, and the National Coalition Against Sexual Assault (NCASA), which was established in 1978 to promote services for sexual-assault victims (Wallace, 1998).

As public knowledge of and attention to violence against women increased throughout the 1970s and 1980s, more programs and services were created to assist victims and help protect them from further victimization. During this time, police departments and prosecutor's offices began hiring victim advocates, also known as victim/witness coordinators, to assist victims of intimate partner violence whose cases were being processed in the criminal justice system. This assistance usually came in the form of trial preparation and referral to social services (e.g., victim compensation and counseling). Over time, the role of victim advocates for this population has remained largely the same, although the numbers of advocates working in the criminal justice system and the types of services available to victims have increased significantly. Today, advocates can offer victims of intimate partner violence a variety of services, including access to legal aid, short-term financial assistance, safe housing, individual and family counseling, and assistance in obtaining a restraining order.

The Role of Victim Advocates

Victim advocates are typically employed by a prosecutor's office or victim service agency, although some are employed by a police department. Advocates who work within a police department are usually counselors or social workers who are called to the scene of an incident of intimate partner violence by police to assist the victim and provide her with information on available social services (e.g., counseling and safe housing). Advocates who work within a prosecutor's office usually do not make contact with the victim until a criminal case has been filed by police and the case is transferred to the prosecutor's office (usually a day or 2 after the incident is reported to police). The first meeting between an advocate and a victim typically takes place at the courthouse where the defendant is being arraigned or the victim is filing for a restraining order against the defendant. Advocates who work for a victim service agency might not make contact with a victim until she calls the agency for assistance.

Advocates who work with victims of intimate partner violence have numerous responsibilities and work with a number of different professionals, including police officers, prosecutors, judges, case workers, probation officers, and social service providers. The advocate's primary responsibility is to make sure the victim's immediate needs are met. These needs often include information on her case (e.g., day, time, and location of the next court hearing) and the victim's role in the criminal justice process, as well as access to legal aid, financial assistance, and safe housing.

Legal aid is most often needed by victims who wish to file a petition in civil court (e.g., restraining order, child custody). Advocates can provide information on local attorneys who represent victims of intimate partner violence either pro bono or for reduced fees. Financial assistance usually comes in the form of victim compensation, which is often allocated to victims by a state compensation board. Advocates usually make victims aware that these funds exist and help them fill out the paperwork to apply for needed assistance. Safe housing is mostly a concern for victims who believe they are in physical danger and cannot return home. Battered women's shelters and safe houses are usually able to accommodate short-term housing needs. Advocates often make victims aware of these services and arrange for transportation if victims cannot get to safe housing on their own.

Another common need among victims of intimate partner violence is professional counseling. Counselors can help victims begin to process their experiences of abuse and help them understand that they are not to blame for their partner's actions. This is especially important for victims who have endured chronic or long-term abuse, because they are at the greatest risk of further victimization and are most likely to return to their abusive partner. Although some police officers provide counseling information to victims when they respond to a call for service, advocates are usually the first to disseminate this information to victims.

If a criminal case goes to trial, advocates often assist in preparing the victim for her role in the trial process. This role typically entails testifying in court on behalf of the state. Most criminal cases, however, are resolved through a plea bargain and do not result in a trial. In plea bargaining, advocates make the victim's wishes known to the prosecutor so that an appropriate resolution to the case can be decided. Advocates may also assist victims in writing a *victim impact statement*, which is usually read to the court (or by the judge) at the defendant's sentencing hearing. A victim impact statement can be a powerful tool for victims to express how their partner's abuse has affected them personally. It also allows the victim to express her opinion on how the defendant should be punished and/or how the case should be resolved. In some cases, a victim advocate may also serve as an expert witness to provide testimony on the dynamics and implications of intimate partner violence. (For more information on expert testimony, see chapter 4.)

Depending on the outcome of the criminal case, the victim may decide to file a petition in civil court. Victims of intimate partner violence often use civil courts to obtain restraining orders, seek child support and custody, and initiate divorce proceedings. It is common for victims to feel overwhelmed by the prospect of navigating the civil justice system, especially if they have never done so before. Victim advocates play a key role in helping victims understand and access the services available to them in civil court.

In my practice as a victim's advocate, the service most commonly sought has been obtaining a _civil restraining order_, also known as a _protection order_ or _protection from abuse order_, which is a civil court order that instructs the defendant not to harm or have contact with the victim. A restraining order may also prohibit the defendant from having contact with the victim's children or family members. Advocates often explain to victims the process of obtaining a restraining order and assist them with the necessary paperwork. Advocates may also accompany victims to restraining order hearings and help them understand the outcome of proceedings, including the judge's final ruling and the provisions of the order.

Common Practice Settings

Although most victim advocates are employed by a prosecutor's office or victim service agency, a great deal of their time is spent in courthouses, where most criminal justice proceedings take place. Accompanying victims to court hearings and explaining the proceedings requires advocates to be familiar with the functions and operations of both criminal and civil courts. This also requires advocates to have close working relationships with court administrators, prosecutors, and judges, as well as case workers and social service providers.

These relationships are often fostered by the existence of multidisciplinary teams. Multidisciplinary teams are groups of professionals from diverse disciplines who come together to provide comprehensive assessment and consultation on specific cases. In cases of intimate partner violence, multidisciplinary teams usually consist of victim advocates, police officers, prosecutors, court administrators, probation officers, child protection workers, and victim service providers. Teams promote coordination and communication among agencies by bringing agency representatives together on a regular basis to share information and expertise. This coordination often helps to identify service gaps and ensure that the needs and interests of all parties involved (i.e., victims, offenders, children) are addressed. The primary purpose of a multidisciplinary team is typically to help resolve difficult cases, including those that involve repeat victims and those with children at risk of harm. Because children often witness intimate partner violence, and may also be victims of abuse, these cases usually receive greater attention from team members. Cases that involve elderly victims may also be given priority. (For more information on the victimization of children and the elderly, see chapters 9 and 13.)

Domain-Specific Legal and Ethical Issues

There are several laws that seek to protect victims of intimate partner violence from their abusive partners. Laws regarding mandatory (or presumptive) arrest are the most notable and perhaps most controversial. Mandatory-arrest laws were largely a result of academic research (e.g., Sherman & Berk, 1984), and civil liability lawsuits (e.g., *Thurman v. City of Torrington* [1984]), which called into question the widespread practice of nonarrest in cases of intimate partner violence and led to significant changes in public policy.

Mandatory Arrest

The single most influential piece of research regarding mandatory arrest was conducted by Sherman and Berk (1984), who found that arresting batterers was associated with a reduction in subsequent intimate partner violence. The results of their research led to the creation of mandatory-arrest policies by police agencies throughout the country. These policies require officers to arrest a batterer when probable cause exists to believe that a crime occurred, regardless of the victim's consent or preference. Despite the lack of consensus on the utility (i.e., deterrent effect) of mandatory arrest, most police departments in the United States have a policy that encourages police officers to arrest in cases of intimate partner violence.

The civil court case of *Thurman v. City of Torrington* (1984) also had a significant impact on the way police respond to intimate partner violence. Tracy Thurman was a battered woman from the city of Torrington, Connecticut, who repeatedly sought and did not receive police protection from the violent attacks of her estranged husband. She subsequently filed a civil lawsuit against the City of Torrington, challenging police policies that treated intimate partner violence differently from other assault cases as a denial of equal protection under the law. She won the lawsuit and was awarded $1.9 million dollars in damages. This case was an important part of the momentum to change the way police respond to intimate partner violence, and challenged police administrators to create policies that would better protect victims from their abusive partners.

Restraining Orders

Laws regarding restraining orders also seek to protect victims of intimate partner violence from subsequent victimization. Although restraining orders are issued typically by civil courts, violating the conditions of a restraining order may result in criminal penalties. In most states, violation of a restraining order is considered a misdemeanor offense and is punishable by jail time and/or a monetary fine. The primary purpose of these penalties is to protect victims by deterring defendants from violating the conditions of a restraining order.

Every state also has what are called "full faith and credit" laws. The full faith and credit provision of the Violence Against Women Act of 1994 requires that every restraining order issued by a state court be given full faith and credit by courts in other states. This means that the conditions of a restraining order should be enforced regardless of what state the victim is in, as long as the order is valid (i.e., has not expired).

When advocating for victims of intimate partner violence, the legal document that victim advocates work with most often is a restraining order. Although every state has a slightly different process for obtaining a restraining order, it usually starts with the victim (plaintiff) filing a petition in a civil court (e.g., Court of Common

Pleas or Family Court) that describes the abuse she has suffered and the protection she is seeking. Next, an emergency or *ex parte* hearing is held, at which a judge will either grant the plaintiff a temporary restraining order and set a date for a final hearing (usually held within 10 days of the initial hearing) or deny the temporary order. At the final hearing, a judge decides whether to grant a final order and rules on the conditions of the order. Depending on state statute, a final restraining order can be effective for any length of time. In the state of New Jersey, for example, final restraining orders do not expire unless the victim requests a withdrawal hearing, at which a judge will decide whether to vacate the order.

The process of obtaining a restraining order can be confusing and overwhelming to victims, especially those who are reluctant to follow through with the process. Because the majority of victims who seek a restraining order do not have an attorney, many of them rely on advocates to explain the process and prepare them for court hearings. Advocates also help victims understand the protections offered by a restraining order and how the provisions of the order will affect their lives. Advocates may also have to convince victims of the importance of obtaining a restraining order and the importance of notifying the police if the defendant violates the order. This is especially true for victims whose partners pose a continuing threat to their safety.

Ethical Principles

The primary mission of victim advocates is to assist victims by protecting their rights, assessing their needs, and referring them to the appropriate social services. Although advocates are not necessarily bound by a formal set of ethical principles, they adhere to many of the principles set forth by the National Association of Social Workers' *Code of Ethics* (NASW, 1999).

To assist victims of intimate partner violence, advocates must treat each person in a caring and respectful manner. This is especially true for victims who are reluctant to accept help or who may not recognize the potential danger their partner poses to them. Advocates often must convince victims of what is in their best interest while respecting their right to self-determination. If a victim refuses to accept necessary services (e.g., safe housing), the advocate must respect her decision. This requires advocates to walk a fine line between insisting on necessary help and honoring the victim's choices. Advocates must also respect a victim's right to privacy. Although there is no legal expectation of privacy between an advocate and a victim, advocates may refer victims to a professional (e.g., counselor) who can promise confidentiality if that is something the victim requests. As a general rule, however, advocates only disclose information shared by a victim if it is necessary to protect her safety or for the purpose of legal proceedings (i.e., to prosecute a criminal case).

Assessment, Prevention, and Intervention

To assess victims' needs and refer them to the appropriate social services, advocates often complete an intake or screening form for each victim with whom they come in contact. These forms record the victim's personal and demographic information, including her name, age, race, sex, marital status, occupation, address, and phone number. Advocates may also collect information on the victim's experiences of abuse (e.g., type of abuse suffered) and the length and status of the victim/offender relationship. This information is collected and maintained by advocates for the purposes of needs assessment and service referral, but may also be shared with other professionals, including members of a multidisciplinary team.

Although biopsychosocial assessment tools, such as the Rapid Psychosocial Assessment Checklist for Juvenile and Criminal Justice Settings (Maschi, 2009) (see Appendix B), are not routinely used by victim advocates, elements of such tools may be used, including the reason for referral and relevant history. The psychosocial areas of family, medical/mental health, legal issues, and environmental conditions (e.g., safe housing) are often affected by intimate partner violence. For this reason, advocates may collect information on these areas to make appropriate decisions regarding service referral. The following is a list of questions often asked by victim advocates to develop a better understanding of a victim's experiences and needs:

- Describe the most recent incidents of abuse or threats of abuse you have experienced.
- Were children involved in these incidents?
- Were there any witnesses or evidence (e.g., letters, phone messages)?
- Did you call the police? Did the police take any actions? What was the outcome?
- Has your partner used or threatened to use a firearm against you?
- Does your partner have access to a firearm?
- Do you have a safety plan?
- Do you feel safe returning to your home?
- What are your immediate needs (e.g., shelter, money, legal aid)?

Practitioner Skill Set

Advocates who work with victims of intimate partner violence must draw on a number of professional and personal skills. Among the most important are oral and written communication, interpersonal skills, professionalism, networking, and collaboration. Advocates must be able to communicate with victims face-to-face and in writing. This requires an understanding of the victim's plight and knowledge that the victim may be overwhelmed by (or disappointed in) the amount of information she has received from criminal justice professionals and social service providers. Advocates often help victims sort through the information they have received and assist them in obtaining information they still need. Obtaining this information usually requires advocates to network with other actors in the criminal and civil justice systems. Thus, networking skills are crucial for advocates to do their job effectively. Equally important is the ability to collaborate with professionals from a wide range of agencies (e.g., law enforcement, social services, court administration) to help victims navigate the system. Collaborating with people of different backgrounds and expertise requires advocates to have a sense of professionalism. This includes properly addressing people of standing (e.g., judges) and behaving appropriately in situations that require reverence (e.g., courtroom). Professionalism also requires credibility and follow-through, as well as setting boundaries with victims who may ask more of advocates than the advocate can deliver.

For advocates who work with victims of intimate partner violence, communicating empowerment to victims is an important aspect of advocacy. Empowerment is communicated to victims not only by providing them with necessary information and referring them to appropriate services, but also by helping victims take control of their situation and giving them a sense of self-worth. This entails normalizing their feelings of shame or embarrassment and letting them know that they are not alone in their efforts to free themselves from abuse. Empowerment is especially important for victims who may feel powerless to escape abusive relationships. Advocates, in a sense, help victims find their voice and encourage them to do what is in their best interest and the interest of their children. This may entail helping a victim prepare a victim impact statement to be read in court or to organize a safety plan for the next time she encounters violence at the hands of her abusive partner.

Case Study

As a victim advocate who works primarily with victims of intimate partner violence, I have met many women who found themselves in terribly abusive relationships that were difficult for them to escape. Many of these women had children in common with their abusive partners, were financially dependent on their partners, and hoped that their partners would change. These characteristics applied to one woman in particular, who I met after her husband beat her so badly she needed to be hospitalized to receive medical treatment for her injuries. The day after her attack, I went to the hospital to try to convince her to come to a battered women's shelter, because her husband had still not been caught by the police and I was concerned about her safety. Despite her extensive physical and emotional trauma, she refused to go to a shelter and was convinced that her husband did not intend to harm her as badly as he did. She wished to return home once she was released from the hospital. Although I was disappointed in her decision not to seek shelter, I respected her decision and informed her of other options she could take to protect herself and her children, including obtaining a restraining order and pursuing criminal charges against her husband. Ultimately, she did obtain a restraining order and assisted in the prosecution of her husband on charges of aggravated assault.

As an advocate, my job was to educate her on the services available and allow her to make her own decision as to what she believed she needed. Although I did not agree with all of her decisions, I respected her right to self-determination and I did my best to empower her to take control of her situation. It was also my responsibility to help her navigate the criminal justice system, which required me to collaborate with prosecutors, police officers, court personnel, and service providers. Collaborating with people of various backgrounds and disciplines called for professionalism and a commitment to protecting the rights and interests of a woman who was in desperate need of advocacy and support. Advocating for this woman taught me the importance of "starting where the client is" and viewing a complex situation from the client's perspective, which is often very different from the perspective of a professional seeking to help.

Summary and Conclusions

As the information provided in this chapter suggests, many women continue to be victims of intimate partner violence, and the work of victim advocates who serve these women is challenging. Advocates must be able to assess the needs of victims, refer them to appropriate services, protect their rights, empower them, and help them navigate the criminal and civil justice systems. These responsibilities require advocates to possess various personal and professional skills and to collaborate with many different professionals. Unfortunately, there is never a shortage of victims in need of assistance; however, advocates are often motivated by the knowledge that they have made a difference in someone's life and can effect change by helping one person at a time.

Online Resources for Victim Advocates

National Center for Victims of Crime—provides a digest of recent news articles and notices about professional meetings and conferences: www.ncvc.org

National Coalition Against Domestic Violence—provides links to research, resources and hotlines: www.ncadv.org

National Crime Victims Research and Treatment Center—supports research on the impact of victimization and the effectiveness of treatment: www.musc.edu/cvc

National Organization for Victim Assistance—provides information on training programs and professional conferences: www.try-nova.org

Office for Victims of Crime—provides links to resources, state compensation programs, and training opportunities: www.ojp.usdoj.gov/ovc

Office on Violence Against Women—provides links to groups that assist victims of domestic violence, sexual assault and stalking: www.ojp.usdoj.gov/vawo

References

Anderson, K. (2002). Perpetrator or victim? Relationships between intimate partner violence and well-being. *Journal of Marriage & Family, 64*, 851–865.

Archer, J. (2000). Sex differences in physical aggression to partners: A reply to Frieze (2000), O'Leary (2000), and White, Smith, Koss & Figueredo (2000). *Psychological Bulletin, 126*, 697–702.

Bachman, R. (1992). *Death and violence on the reservation: Homicide, family violence and suicide in American Indian populations.* Westport, CT: Auburn House.

Bachman, R., & Saltzman, L. (1995). *Violence against women: Estimates from the redesigned survey.* U.S. Department of Justice, Bureau of Justice Statistics. Washington, DC: U.S. Government Printing Office.

Bureau of Justice Statistics. (2000). *National crime victimization survey.* Washington, DC: U.S. Government Printing Office.

Dekeseredy, W., & Schwartz, M. (1998). Male peer support and woman abuse in postsecondary school courtship: Suggestions for new directions in sociological research. In R. Bergen (Ed.), *Issues in intimate violence* (pp. 83–96). Thousand Oaks, CA: Sage.

DeNavas-Walt, C., Proctor, B., & Lee, C. (2005). *Income, poverty and health insurance coverage in the United States.* Washington, DC: U.S. Government Printing Office.

Dobash, R., Dobash, R., Wilson, M., & Daly, M. (1992). The myth of sexual symmetry in marital violence. *Social Problems, 39*, 71–91.

Dutton, M., & Goodman, L. (2005). Coercive control and intimate partner violence: Toward a new conceptualization. *Sex Roles, 52,* 743–756.

Frieze, I., & McHugh, M. (1992). Power and influence strategies in violent and non-violent marriages. *Psychology of Women Quarterly Special Issue: Women & Power, 16,* 449–465.

Heise, L. (1993). Violence against women. *World Health, 46,* 21–35.

Johnson, M. (1995). Patriarchal terrorism and common couple violence: Two forms of violence against women. *Journal of Marriage & the Family, 57,* 283–294.

Maschi, T. (2009). Rapid psychosocial assessment checklist for juvenile and criminal justice settings. In T. Maschi, C. Bradley, & K. Ward (Eds.). *Forensic social work: Psychosocial and legal issues in diverse practice settings* (pp. 367–372). New York: Springer Publishing Company.

National Association of Social Workers. (1999). *Code of ethics.* Washington, DC: NASW Press.

Pence, E., & Paymar, M. (1986). *Power and control: Tactics of men who batter.* Duluth, MN: Minnesota Program Development.

Sherman, L., & Berk, R. (1984). The specific deterrent effects of arrest for domestic assault. *American Sociological Review, 49,* 261–272.

Thurman v. City of Torrington (1984). United States District Court, D. Connecticut, October 23, 1984 (595 F. Supp. 1521).

Tjaden, P., & Thoennes, N. (2000). *Full report of the prevalence, incidence, and consequences of violence against women: Findings from the national violence against women survey.* Washington, DC: U.S. Department of Justice, Office of Justice Programs.

Violence Against Women Act of 1994. Pub. L. No. 103–322, Title IV, 108 Stat. 1902.

Wallace, H. (1998). *Victimology: Legal, psychological, and social perspectives.* Needham Heights, MA: Allyn & Bacon.

Forensic Practice With Older Adult Victims of Abuse

9

Janet Mahoney
Morris Saldov

When one thinks about abuse and exploitation in families, the first thing that often comes to mind is spousal or child abuse. Elder abuse has been one of the last forms of family violence to receive societal attention and is the least reported form of domestic violence. Elder abuse was barely known in the United States until 1978 (Bonnie & Wallace, 2003). Elder abuse continues to be a topic of secrecy and remains hidden in many U.S. families. Unfortunately, unless there are obvious signs of mistreatment, elder abuse may be difficult to detect.

In this chapter, elder abuse will be discussed in a framework that includes both interpersonal and institutional types of abuse. *Interpersonal abuse* includes physical, psychological, and sexual abuse. *Institutional abuse* entails systemic violations of rights, exploitation, and factors affecting the ability to give informed consent for treatment. Social workers, nurses, and other health care personnel need to address the problem of elder abuse by developing skills to assess, treat, and help prevent it in both community and institutional settings.

Background

Nearly 566,000 reports of elder abuse were made nationally in 2003, almost 20% more than in 2000 (Gearon, 2007). With the elderly being the fastest growing segment of the U.S. population, the problem of elder abuse is expected to escalate (Bell, Wade, & Goss, 1992). In 2000, 35 million people were older than age 60 in the United States. By 2030 the numbers of older people will more than double to 70 million. People age 85 and older will increase from 4.2 million in 2000 to 8.9 in 2030 (U.S. Census Bureau, 2004). Advances in health care treatments, medical research, and better nutrition are just a few of the reasons people are living longer.

Elder abuse can happen anywhere, at any time, and may be committed by almost anyone. Abuse may take place in the home or in nursing homes and health care facilities by loved ones, caregivers, or strangers (Eliopoulos, 2005). Occurrences of elder abuse will continue to increase as Americans live longer. From 1986 to 1996 there was an increase in the number of reported cases of domestic elder and vulnerable adult abuse nationwide, from 117,000 reports in 1986 to 293,000 reports in 1996. This is an increase of 150% since 1986 (National Center on Elder Abuse, 1998). It is important to remember that this number only reflects the "reported" cases. The actual number is probably larger. Society's negative attitudes toward older people are often based on misinformation and stereotyping. Ageism is one such stereotype. Ageism may be compounded by discrimination based on gender, culture, religion, or lower socioeconomic status. Unfortunately, until society changes its views toward older people and in reporting abuse, no one escapes ageism.

In response to the underreporting of elder abuse, Congress in 1974 called for Adult Protective Services (APS) programs to be formed in every state. The American Association of Retired Persons (AARP) Web site has a state-by-state Elder Abuse Resource List that includes Adult Protective Services, ombudsmen and attorneys general for each state (Gearon, 2007). All 50 states now have Adult Protective Services agencies. In some states, failure of professionals to report suspected cases of abuse results in misdemeanors, punishable by receiving a fine or imprisonment (Capezuit, Brush, & Lawson, 1997).

Recent Trends

As is frequently the case with other crimes, elder abuse victims are often violated by someone known to them. Thirty-six thousand nonfatal offenses and 500 homicides are committed on elders by friends and family members annually (Klaus, 2000). According to the National Center on Elder Abuse (1998), as many as 84% of elder abuse cases go unreported. Other studies have suggested that only 1 in 14 incidences of elder abuse cases is ever reported (Pillemer & Finkelhor, 1989). Currently there is no nationwide tracking system to study elder abuse, although the National Center on Elder Abuse does monitor cases reported from Adult Protective Services. State statistics on elder abuse vary widely. McNamee and Murphy (2006) reveal numerous factors that impede investigations, including physical conditions that may be caused by abuse, illness, or accidents, ageist attitudes by investigators, elders' trauma, and fear of reprisal.

Definitions of Elder Abuse

Definitions of elder abuse vary. Indeed, some underreporting may be attributed to the lack of clarity and consistency as to what constitutes elder abuse. The National Center on Elder Abuse divides elder abuse into seven categories: physical, emotional, sexual abuse, financial exploitation, neglect, self-neglect, and miscellaneous (Tatara & Kuzmekus, 1997). Lau and Kosberg (1979) describe four different types of abuse. The first deals with *physical abuse*, which includes beating, withholding personal or medical care, and failure to supervise an impaired person so as to present a risk of injury. The second type is *psychological abuse*. This form of abuse is less objective, but nonetheless harmful. Psychological abuse occurs by instilling fear through verbal assaults, threats, or isolating the person. The third type is *material abuse*. Material abuse occurs through theft or mismanagement of money or personal belongings. Finally, there is a *violation of the elder's rights to self-determination*, as prescribed by federal legislation (Patient Self-Determination Act, 1990). In these situations older people may be deprived of their rights as adults to provide informed consent for interventions taken on their behalf (Lau & Kosberg, 1979).

In addition to abuse inflicted by another person, self-neglecting behaviors that are ignored or even encouraged need to be examined as another possible form of elder abuse. Self-neglect occurs when older adults engage in behaviors that threaten their health and safety. Some cases of self-neglect involve unhealthy living conditions, lack of awareness that a problem exists, and hoarding behaviors (Hooyman & Kiyak, 2005). In these situations there is no outsider purposely offending the older person. Professional interventions are aimed at building trust to allow the introduction of some services to reduce dangerously unhealthy living conditions (Hooyman & Kiyak, 2005).

In addition, just as younger individuals fall prey to sexual violence, older people can be victims of sexual abuse. Sexual predators may see older people as easy prey. The physical and cognitive impairments that can be part of aging make older people more vulnerable (Dugan, 2004). An older person is more likely to have a serious injury that may not fully heal owing to their frail and vulnerable biopsychosocial systems. In addition, older people are less likely to report abuse by caregivers because of their dependency on others, use of threats about nursing home placement to keep victims silent, or generational beliefs about sex and morality that create feelings of shame and guilt (Dugan, 2004).

Assessment and Physical Indicators of Abuse

The assessment of elder abuse includes the use of physical indicators. Physical abuse is more objective than other types, such as sexual and emotional abuse. When it comes to physical abuse, injured older people present varying conditions and changed appearance. Bruises on the forearms may indicate that victims were trying to defend themselves (Pyrek, 2006). Twelve to 36 hours after blunt trauma bruises will appear reddish purple. The color of bruises generally progresses from purple-blue to bluish-green to greenish-brown to brownish-yellow before fading away. Forensic science can estimate a bruise's age more precisely. Physical signs of sexual abuse may include bruising on the inner thighs, sexually transmitted diseases, and/or pain or itching in the genital area. Emotional signs may include depressed behavior, fear of certain people, and changes in personality (Dugan, 2004). Health professionals can use the Danger Assessment Instrument (Campbell, Sharps, & Glass, 1995) or the Elder Assessment Instrument (Fulmer, Street, & Carr, 1984) to measure elder abuse. Both are easy to use and reliable.

Knowing how to recognize the signs of sexual abuse is important for nurses and social workers. The John A. Hartford Foundation has played a leading role in promoting elder abuse detection and prevention into social work education. The National Committee for the Prevention of Elder Abuse also provides training and resources to help nursing and social work professionals address issues of elder abuse. The Web addresses for both of these organizations are located at the end of this chapter.

Sexual Assault Nurse Examiners (SANE) are specially trained registered nurses who use sensitivity throughout the examination and interview process of sexual assaulted individuals (Pyrek, 2006). SANE nurses play a key role in assessing, treating, and providing resources for people who have been sexually abused. Social workers may work on multidisciplinary teams that include SANE nurses. Social workers and SANE nurses collaborate to promote patient care and safety. Therefore, it is important for social workers to know the SANE protocols.

Relevant Theoretical Frameworks

There is no single theory that explains elder abuse. The literature suggests a number of frameworks in the etiology of abuse. Kosberg and Garcia (1995) formulated a list of six attitudes that promote elder abuse: ageism, sexism, pro-violence attitudes, reactions to abuse, negative attitudes toward people with disabilities, and family care giving imperatives.

The three theories most widely used in the United States to explain elder abuse are *social learning theory, social exchange theory* (which encompasses situation stress and dependency), and the *psychopathology of the abuser* (Fulmer, 1991; Tomita, 1990). Social learning theory views abuse as something that is learned. The theory holds that children exposed to violence are likely to grow up to adopt proabuse norms that eventually contribute to abusing their own parents or grandparents (Fulmer & O'Malley, 1987).

Social exchange theory, in regard to elder abuse, refers to rewards and punishments. This theory postulates that interacting with elders has little to offer in the way of rewards, so engaging with them is time-consuming, costly, and does not reap benefits, therefore it is considered a punishment (Barnett, Miller-Perrin, & Perrin, 2005). The theory presumes that the high costs of assuming responsibility for elder care, in combination with few extrinsic rewards (except, perhaps, an intrinsic benefit derived from the discovery of new personal strengths), can result in abuse (Barnett et al., 2005). Stress and dependency theories suggest that elders who are abused are those who create inordinate levels of stress for family caregivers. These types of theories, however, are inaccurate through their suggestion of "blaming the victim." Elders who are dependent on caregivers for physical, financial, or emotional support may experience a high level of stress. Vulnerable elders—those with a medical, psychiatric, or social problem that makes them vulnerable—are considered to be at higher risk of abuse (Wilber & Reynolds, 1996).

Some experts believe that caregiver stress may be the major source of elder abuse (Steinmertz, 1983). Hwalek, Neale, Goodrich, and Quinn (1996) found that substance

<table>

9.1	An Ecological Systems Approach to the Prevention of Elder Abuse			
Prevention	Ecological Systems			
	Micro	Meso	Exo	Macro
Primary	Informing seniors of their human rights and of elder abuse prevention services	Community education	Interagency cooperation	Media campaigns
Secondary	Treatment for abuse	Community participation in offering support to the abused	Coordination of intervention and treatment among agencies	Laws requiring treatment for abusers
Tertiary	Counseling and empowering at-risk elderly to avert abuse	Community-based initiatives	Coordination of prevention programs in health, mental health, services to the aged, etc.	APS research on vulnerable elderly

</table>

abuse by the caregiver or the patient significantly increases the risk of physical violence and neglect, and that psychological and character pathology in the caregiver and patient are also major risk factors.

Intervention, Solutions, and Current Trends

The social justice systems model presented in chapter 2 is a framework that can be applied to elder abuse because it conceptualizes the connection between persons in a "social justice" environment. Using a combined prevention and ecosystems model, nurses, doctors, and social workers can collaborate and intervene to prevent or treat elder abuse at all levels of the ecosystem (see Table 9.1).

Nurses, doctors, and social workers typically respond to or report cases of abuse, assess and treat the victim (e.g., micro assessment and secondary prevention) to prevent further abuse. A comprehensive social–legal approach to the prevention of elder abuse must also seek primary and tertiary prevention at all levels of the ecosystem. For example, primary prevention at the micro level might consist of informing seniors about their right not to be abused and educating the children of elderly parents about their obligations not to abuse or neglect them. Primary prevention might entail community programs aimed at educating communities about the topic of abuse to prevent a first occurrence. Likewise, interagency cooperation among health care, housing, and social service agencies can be coordinated to educate providers for primary prevention of elder abuse.

At the macro level, laws can be toughened to require treatment for abusers; educational and media campaigns focusing on treating elders with respect and support

9.2   Systems of Support to Prevent Abuse*

System	Instrumental	Affective
Formal	APS, NGOs, government services	Nursing homes, assisted living, hospice, palliative care, community centers, hospitals
Informal	Family, friends, neighbors, and colleagues	Family, friends, neighbors, and colleagues

*Based on Lockery (1991, p. 5).

may be undertaken. In tertiary prevention, frail or vulnerable elders who are identified as being at higher risk for abuse, such as living with adult children who are known abusers or have addiction problems, should be targeted for intervention to prevent abuse before it occurs. Tertiary prevention can be practiced at all levels of the ecological system as well to avert abuse in high-risk populations. Tertiary prevention at the macro level might consist of changing APS policies, so that they conduct more research to identify higher risk populations for abuse, which can then be used to help prevent abuse with similar populations. Lockery's (1991) model for formal and informal sources of support is useful for assessing and intervening with elderly who are at risk of abuse (see Table 9.2).

Primary, secondary, and tertiary prevention of elder abuse at all levels of the ecosystem will require an assessment of the systems of support that help to avert and/or respond to abuse. Formal systems of support include APS, nongovernmental organizations, and other government programs intended to prevent abuse. On an informal level, family members, friends, neighbors, and work colleagues may also be effective in preventing abuse (i.e., community-based models of prevention). Emotional (affective) support or abuse of the elderly can occur at formal levels when elders are abused or supported in institutions, for example, nursing homes, assisted living facilities, hospice, palliative care units, community centers, or hospitals.

Unified efforts to prevent, identify, and intervene in elder abuse cases are of great importance. As the population of the aged grows, unless changes occur that aid in the prevention of elder abuse, it is likely that there will be an increase in the numbers of older people who are abused and an increase in the number of cases reported to the authorities.

The Vulnerable Adult Specialist Team (VAST) is a model for the integration of medical and social services (Mosqueda, Burnight, Liao, & Kemp, 2004). The VAST provides the APS and criminal justice agencies with access to medical experts who examine medical and psychological injuries of elder abuse victims. Collaboration among the health team and criminal justice members will lead to improved coordination of resources for the victims of elder abuse.

Role of Collaborative Team Members

The purpose of collaborative teams is to coordinate the care and prevention of abuse of the elderly. Many facilities use multidisciplinary teams that specialize in caring for older people who have been abused in some way. Both formal initiatives (e.g., multidisciplinary teams, interdisciplinary/I-Teams) and informal resources (e.g., caregiving relatives, friends, and neighbors) hold promise for helping to intervene and prevent elder abuse. These collaborative approaches enlist doctors, nurses, social workers, and psychologists with the help of law enforcement, criminal justice systems, domestic violence programs, clergy, ombudsmen, and volunteers to identify, treat, and prevent abuse.

Each member of an interdisciplinary team will have a role to play in the care of the older person and detection and prevention of elder abuse. Physicians and nurses play a key role in assessing the risks for physical elder abuse. Social workers and psychologists can help to assess the psychological, social, and financial aspects of abuse. Gray-Vickery (2004) wrote that with careful assessment, documentation, and reporting, health care professionals can make a critical difference in the welfare of older people.

Ethical and Legal Issues

The Older Americans Act has expressed the nation's commitment to protecting vulnerable older Americans at risk. Title VII (Vulnerable Elder Rights Protection), chapter 3 was created to promote abuse prevention and avert neglect and exploitation. Title VII has provisions for ombudsman programs and state legal assistance development that help older adults in long-term care and was designed to serve as an advocacy tool (National Center on Elder Abuse, 1998).

Again, it is important for social workers to be aware that laws differ from state to state, but most states require professionals to report all suspected cases of elder abuse to the proper authorities, usually through Adult Protective Services (APS). Once elder abuse is suspected, a report should be made to APS. Because reporting requirements do vary, health professionals need to know their own state's reporting laws. The Legal Counsel for the Elderly (LCE) provides technical assistance, publications, training, and referrals (some for no fee). A hotline connects callers with an attorney who will try to resolve the issues or advise the caller where to obtain help.

Ethical and legal dilemmas may arise over differences in cultural groups' norms in defining "qualify of life," "survival needs," and "self-being." The Self-Determination Act (SDA, 1990) protects the rights of elders to personal autonomy in medical decision making. Unfortunately, the lack of a culturally adaptive definition of "self" has led to complications and delays in obtaining informed consent and therefore in treating the patient by medical practitioners in multicultural settings (Saldov & Kakai, 1998). The concept of "self" in many Asian, African, and southern European cultures is communal. Therefore medical decision making needs to take these differences into account. Cultural competence is needed to assess styles of decision making by patients and their families or significant others (Saldov & Kakai, 2004). The failure of health care organizations to promote culturally competent practices has serious health and biopsychosocial consequences, including death and physical complications for the elderly (Saldov, 1994). This failure can be considered a form of institutional abuse or neglect. The legal requirement to seek individual consent by adhering to the SDA definition of self as individual, can and does come into conflict with the ethical obligation to practice in a culturally competent manner. Safety and security measures for one person may represent incarceration for another. Therefore there is no single universal cross-cultural definition of abuse.

Case Study

As a social worker, you and a nurse practitioner working in a major medical center have been assigned to an 81-year-old widow named Grace. She was brought to the emergency department for shortness of breath by her 72-year-old female roommate, Gertrude. The two have been living together for the past 10 years, after Grace's husband of 50 years passed away.

You and the nurse notice that Grace is very quiet as she sits in the emergency waiting room. She looks untidy and has bruises on both arms in various stages of healing. In addition to conducting a focused respiratory assessment the nurse practitioner uses the Abuse Assessment Screen (AAS) to assess for abuse. A "yes" answer warrants that a careful assessment follow to ascertain how recent and serious the abuse. Not surprisingly, Grace answers "no" to all the AAS questions. The nurse practitioner and social worker suspect abuse.

Over the course of Grace's visit to the emergency room, what medical care needs should be addressed? In addition to her medical treatment, what are the social services interventions, legal advice regarding orders of protection, housing and home-care needs of this patient? Are there caregiver concerns that should be addressed? If so, what are they?

Keep in mind that the answers to the questions above may vary depending on state laws and circumstances. A thorough respiratory assessment should be conducted by the nurse practitioner. Information about safety issues regarding physical, emotional, sexual, and financial abuse are most often collected by the nurse and shared with the social worker. It is important for social workers to understand the abuse assessment conducted by the nurse and the results obtained by the assessment. Nonjudgmental and nonthreatening statements should be used to elicit answers from the patient. For example, "I have seen bruises like the ones on your forearms in patients who have been abused. Do you feel safe?" Depending on the answers, the social worker will provide the necessary help and resources. Information about caregiver stress should be provided to the caregiver. The short-term goal is Grace's immediate safety. Long-term goals include providing Grace with legal advice, safe housing, and home-care needs.

Summary and Conclusions

Health professional working with an interdisciplinary team must be aware of the values that underlie each definition of abuse and be prepared to use principles of ethical decision making to guide intervention (Matteson & McConnell, 1988). A multifaceted strategic plan needs to be developed to address the problem of abuse. Initiatives need to come from the local, state, and federal levels. More research is required to guide prevention programs and education approaches. The media must keep the public aware of the incidences of abuse as well as resources to go to for help. Web sites depicting the signs, symptoms, and reporting mechanisms need to be developed and shared with the public. Finally, funding is needed for all these efforts to decrease the incidence of elder abuse. Social workers, nurses, and members of the criminal justice system working together play a pivotal role is advocating for their patients/clients through direct assessment and treatment, getting involved with legislative action, conducting and using research, taking part in community involvement, and increasing awareness. Working collaboratively will lead to "quality care"—the only kind of care that human beings deserve.

Resources

■ To find the local Adult Protective Services administrator in your state, contact the National Association of Adult Protective Services Administrators, 1900 13th St., Suite 303, Boulder, CO 80302; (720) 565–0906; http://www.apsnetwork.org
■ To find the State's Attorney General's Office, contact the National Association of Attorneys General, 750 First Street NE, Suite 1100, Washington, DC 20002; (202) 326–6000

The following Web sites are resources about aging topics and elder abuse:

■ **American Association of Retired Persons** 7601 E. Street NW, Washington, DC 20049; (800) 424–3410; http://http://www.aarp.org
■ **Administration on Aging** U.S. Department of Health and Human Services, Washington, DC 20201; (202) 619 0724; http://www.aoa.gov/eldfam/ Elder_Rights/Elder_Abuse/Elder_Abuse.asp
■ **American Bar Association Commission on Law and Aging** 740 15th Street NW, Washington, DC 20005; (202) 662–8690; http://wwwabanet.org/elderly
■ **American Society on Aging** http://www.asaging.org
■ **Danger Assessment Instrument** by Campbell (1988); (410) 955–2778; e-mail: jcampbel@son.jhmi.edu; http:www.nvaw.org/research/instrument.shtml.
■ **Elder Abuse and Neglect Assessment** by Fulmer (1984, 1986, 2000); New York University, (212) 998–9018; http://www.medscape.com/viewarticle/ 493951
■ **John Hartford Foundation** http://www.jhartfound.org
■ **Legal Counsel for the Elderly** P.O. Box 96474, Washington, DC 20090; (202) 434–2152, (800) 424–3410 : http://www.aarp.org/aarp/lce/
■ **Meals on Wheels Association of America** http://www.mowaa.org
■ **Medicare Hotline** (800) 638–6833; http://www.medicare.gov
■ **National Adult Protective Services Association** 1900 13th Street, Suite 303, Boulder, CO 80302; (720) 565–0906; http://www.aspsnetwork.org
■ **National Center on Elder Abuse** 1202 15th Street NW, Suite 350, Washington, DC 20005; (202) 898–0578; http://elderabusecenter.org
■ **National Committee for the Prevention of Elder Abuse** http:// www.preventelderabuse.org/

■ **National Council on Aging** http://www.ncoa.org
■ **National Fraud Information Center** (800) 372–8347

References

Barnett, O., Miller-Perrin, C. L., & Perrin, R. D. (2005). *Family violence across the lifespan: An introduction* (2nd ed.). London: Sage.

Bell, F., Wade, A. H., & Goss, S. C. (1992). *Life tables for the United States Social Security Area 1900–2080.* Actuarial study No. 107. Sponsored by the U.S. DHHS, Social Security Administration, Office of the Actuary. Washington, DC: Social Security Administration.

Bonnie, R. J., & Wallace, R. B. (Eds.). (2003). *Elder mistreatment: Abuse, neglect and exploitation in an aging America.* Washington, DC: National Academies Press.

Campbell, J. C., Sharps, P., & Glass, N. (1995). Risk assessment for intimate partner violence. In P. Georges-Franck & L. Pagani (Eds.), *Clinical assessment of dangerousness: Empirical contributions* (pp. 136–157). New York: Cambridge University Press.

Capezuit, E., Brush, B. L., & Lawson, W. T. (1997). Reporting elder mistreatment. *Journal of Gerontological Nursing, 23,* 24–32.

Dugan, K. (2004). *Signs of abuse: Elderly often unrecognized victims of sexual abuse.* Retrieved on December 10, 2007, from http://www.seniorjournal.com

Eliopoulos, C. (2005). *Gerontological nursing* (6th ed.). Philadelphia: Lippincott, Williams & Wilkins.

Fulmer, T. T. (1991). Elder mistreatment: Progress in community detection and intervention. *Family & Community Health, 14*(2), 26–34.

Fulmer, T., Street, S., & Carr, K. (1984). Abuse of the elderly: Screening and detection. *Journal of Emergency Nursing, 10,* 131–140.

Fulmer, T. T., & O'Malley, T. A. (1987). *Inadequate care of the elderly.* New York: Springer Publishing Company.

Gearon, C. J. (2007). *State-by-state elder abuse resource list.* Retrieved on July 30, 2007, from http://www.aarp.org/bulletin/yourlife/statbystate_elder_abuse_resourcelist.html

Gray-Vickery, P. (2004). Combating elder abuse. *Nursing, 34*(10), 47–51.

Hooyman, N., & Kiyak, H. A. (2005). *Social gerontology: A multidisciplinary perspective* (7th ed.). Boston: Pearson Allyn & Bacon.

Hwalek, M. A., Neale, A. V., Goodrich, C. S., & Quinn, K. (1996). The association of elder abuse and substance abuse in the Illinois elder abuse system. *The Gerontologist, 36,* 694–700.

Klaus, P. A. (2000) *Crimes against persons age 65 or older, 1992–1997.* Bureau of Justice Statistics, U.S. Department of Justice. Washington. DC: U.S. Government Printing Office.

Kosberg, J. I., & Garcia, J. L. (1995). Introduction. In J. I. Kosberg & J. L. Garcia (Eds.), *Elder abuse: International and cross cultural perspectives* (pp. 1–12). Binghamton, NY: Haworth.

Lau, E. E., & Kosberg, J. L. (1979). Abuse of the elderly by informal care providers. *Aging, 299,* 10–15.

Lockery, S. A. (1991). Care giving among racial and ethnic minority elders. *Generations, 15*(4), 58–62.

Matteson, M., & McConnell, E. S. (1988). *Gerontological nursing concepts and practice.* Philadelphia: Saunders.

McNamee, C. C., & Murphy, M. B. (2006). Elder abuse in the United States. *National Institute of Justice Journal, 255.* Retrieved November 15, 2007, from http://www.ojp.usdoj.gov/nij/journals/255/elder_abuse.html

Mosqueda, L., Burnight, K., Liao, S., & Kemp, B. (2004). Advancing the field of elder mistreatment: A new model for integration of social and medical services. *The Gerontologist, 44,* 703–708.

National Center on Elder Abuse. (1998). *Elder abuse incidence study.* Retrieved July 17, 2008, from http://elderabusecenter.org

Patient Self-Determination Act (1990). Sections 4206 and 4751 of Omnibus Reconciliation Act of 1990, Pub L No. 101-508 (November 5, 1990).

Pillemer, K., & Finkelhor, D. (1989). The prevalence of elder abuse: A random sample survey. *The erontologist 28,* 51–57.

Pyrek, K. M. (2006). *Forensic nursing.* Boca Raton, FL: CRC Press.

Saldov, M. (1994). The ethnic elderly in Metro Toronto hospitals, nursing homes and homes for the aged: Communication and health care. *International Journal of Aging & Human Development, 38,* 117–135.

Saldov, M., & Kakai, H. (1998). Cultural barriers in oncology: Issues in obtaining medical informed consent from Japanese-American elders in Hawaii. *Journal of Cross-Cultural Gerontology, 13*, 265–279.

Saldov, M., & Kakai, H. (2004). The ethics of medical decision-making with Japanese-American elders in Hawaii: Signing informed consent documents without understanding them. *Journal of Human Behavior and the Social Environment Special Issue on Aging in the Social Environment*, 10, 113–130.

Steinmertz, S. K. (1993). The abused elderly are dependent: Abuse is caused by the perception of stress associated with providing. In R. J. Gelles & D. R. Loseke (Eds.), *Current controversies on family violence* (pp. 222–236). Newbury Park, CA: Sage.

Tatara, T., & Kuzmekus, L. B. (1997). *Elder abuse information series No. 2 Summaries of statistical data on elder abuse in domestic setting for FY 95 and FY 96*. Washington, DC: National Center on Elder Abuse.

Tomita, S. K. (1990). The denial of elder mistreatment by victims and abusers: The application of neutralization theory. *Violence & Victims, 5*, 171–184.

U. S. Census Bureau. (2004). *Demographic data 2000*. Retrieved July 17, 2008, from http://www.2010census.biz/prod/cen2000/dp1/2kh00.pdf

Wilber, K. H., & Reynolds, S. L. (1996). Introducing a framework for defining financial abuse of the elderly. *Journal of Elder Abuse and Neglect, 8*, 51–60.

Part III

Forensic Practice in Education

Education, Social Work, and the Law 10

Carolyn Bradley
Rosemary Richards
Regina Doyle

Social workers working in educational settings strive to ensure that children develop intellectually, socially, and emotionally. Struggling families often, either willingly or unknowingly, bring their problems with their children to social workers in the schools.

A school social worker must have knowledge, skills, and expertise to be able to successfully negotiate multiple systems on behalf of the client. The school, which so often serves not only as an educational setting but also as a community resource center, deals with health care agencies, law enforcement, the courts, probation, corrections, and child protective services. The effective school social worker must be knowledgeable about community resources as well as be up to date regarding the numerous federal and state laws concerning services within the public school.

This chapter provides a brief history of social work services in schools. It addresses recent demographics and trends and the scope of the problems in this specialty area. Relevant theoretical frameworks are examined from the perspective of the varied roles of the school social worker. Common issues requiring social work services in a school setting, as well as common practice settings and collaborative practice with other professionals are also addressed. Specific legal and ethical issues of concern in the practice of school social work are reviewed and issues of assessment, prevention, and intervention are discussed. Finally, cases are reviewed that exemplify the issues, skills, and collaborative aspects of social work practice in the schools.

Overview of Field of Practice

History

Early 1900s

Social work services in U.S. schools began in 1906, primarily out of concern for the needs of urban students. Services began with "visiting teachers," employed by private agencies and civic organizations, whose primary role was to improve attendance and to foster understanding and communication between the school and the community. Coinciding with the development of "visiting teachers" and attention to attendance was the enactment of compulsory education laws (National Conference of State Legislatures [NCSL], n.d.). These laws, developed on a state-by-state basis between 1852 and 1918, mandated that children attend school between certain ages and for a minimum number of days per year. These initial school social work services began in New York City, Boston, and Hartford. In 1913, the first school social workers were employed by the Board of Education in the city of Rochester, New York (Constable, Massat, McDonald, & Flynn, 2006).

In 1916, at the National Conference of Charities and Corrections, a presentation given by Jane Culbert defined the role of the school social worker (Constable et al., 2006). Culbert's description of the work of the "visiting teacher" detailed the need for respect for differences, inclusion, focus on the child in his or her environment at home and in school, and recognition of education as a relational process. Almost 100 years later, this description still applies.

The early years of social work services in the schools focused on family and neighborhood conditions that interfered with attendance and helping the teacher understand the home conditions of the child. By the 1920s concerns with delinquency and the influence of the mental hygiene movement moved the focus of school social workers away from community issues and more on individual psychological concerns. Social workers were called on to assist in understanding the emotional needs of children and how these needs, left unmet, could lead to social maladjustment (Huxtable, 1998).

The 1940s–1960s

The 1940s through the 1960s saw the role of the school social worker become even more focused on working with socially and/or emotionally maladjusted children. Services during this period primarily involved casework with individual students and their families, consultation with teachers, and referrals to community agencies (Huxtable, 1998).

However, by the late 1960s, recognition of increasing problems within the schools and the communities in which they were located caused another shift in focus in school social work. The struggle for social and economic equality created an awareness of the disparity in the quality of education provided to children based on their race, economic status, and geographic location. Remedies were sought through the development of programs such as Head Start, a federally funded program created in 1965 to promote school readiness through services to low-income children and their families (Administration of Children and Families [ACF], n.d.). In response to issues such as these, social workers began to move away from the traditional focus on individual casework and began to engage in more advocacy (Huxtable, 1998).

The 1970s and 1980s

Since the 1970s, the role of the school social worker has changed in response to the mandates of specific legislation. In 1975 schools were affected by the enactment of the Education for All Handicapped Children Act of 1975 (PL 94-142). This federal law created a new role for social workers: They were part of a *child study team* (CST), an interdisciplinary team responsible for specific services and focused primarily on the identification of children with learning disabilities within the school setting.

The 1990s to the Present Day

In March 1994, the Goals 2000: Educate America Act (1994) was enacted. This federal legislation recognized the personal and social factors that affect a child's ability to learn. Issues such as substance abuse; behavioral difficulties; and the complex interaction of emotional, family, and social factors were acknowledged as impeding academic achievement. The law recognized the need for specialized help with problems of this type. Such specialized help could be provided through social work services. Amendments in 1997 to the Individuals with Disabilities Education Act (IDEA) of 1997 (PL 105-17) provided additional social work services in the schools, including more traditional casework and counseling services, especially for children with behavioral and attention-deficit problems. This legislation also strengthened the rights and the involvement of parents, which, as always, strengthened the social work liaison and advocacy function (Constable et al., 2006).

Focus of School Social Work

The primary focus of school social work is the resolution of issues that children bring from their families and their communities into the schools. Through the resolution of such sociolegal issues, social workers hope to assist the students they serve in improving attendance, raising academic achievement, and reducing violence in schools and neighborhoods. How this work is done is shaped in part by federal and state legislation and regulations, by local resources, and by the definition of the role of the social worker within each individual school district.

Recent Demographics

In the United States it is difficult to estimate the number of social workers working in schools. Services provided by social workers are often done under different titles, for example "crisis intervention counselor," "behavioral counselor," or "student assistance counselor." In 1996, it was estimated that there were over 9,000 school social workers in the United States (Torres, 1996).

In the 2007–2008 academic year, it is estimated that there are 49.6 million students in public elementary and secondary schools in the United States (National Center for Education Statistics [NCES], 2007). The types of services provided through social work in schools, ranging from traditional CST work to reentry services for students returning from correctional and/or treatment facilities, varies based on funding, the number of staff members, and the ages of the students.

Current Trends

The practice of school social work as a specialty area has gained legitimacy. This is evidenced in several ways: professional journals devoted to the topic, professional organizations dealing solely with the area, legislation mandating such services, states requiring licensing or credentialing, and the National Association of Social Workers (NASW) creating a national specialty credential. Despite these gains and the specialized sociolegal expertise offered by school social workers, school social work in its many manifestations is often one of the first services to be reduced when school budget constraints are encountered.

The primary tasks of the school social worker are casework with students and their parents and collaboration with staff. Issues addressed are broad and multifaceted, ranging from completion of required documentation for special education services to child abuse, attendance, and family issues, for example, death, separation or divorce, health issues, pregnancy, substance abuse, suicide, and homelessness (Constable et al., 2006).

Scope of Problems

The need for school social work is easily documented when one reviews national trends concerning truancy, dropout rates, violence, and other social problems (NCES, 2007). The development of prevention and intervention programs to address such issues is uniquely suited to the skills and training of the professional social worker. Counseling and advocacy services for students with learning problems and/or family problems are also areas in which social work services have been demonstrated to make noticeable and sustainable change (Usaj, Shine, & Mandlawits, n.d.). Therefore, social work services should be available to students, families, and staff from preschool through high school. Such services should be provided at a reasonable student to worker ratio.

Relevant Theoretical Frameworks

The social worker providing services in a school needs to be aware of a variety of theories, depending on the function she or he performs. Social workers providing traditional CST services must be familiar with learning theories as well as counseling approaches.

In general, school social workers do not provide therapy. Short-term, problem-focused counseling as well as crisis intervention may be provided. Approaches such as *reality therapy* (Glasser, 1965) or *motivational interviewing* (Miller & Rollnick, 2002) are often used. *Family systems theory* (Nichols & Schwartz, 2005) is a useful approach in the school setting because the concepts can be applied when working with students or in understanding the organizational context.

An understanding of *organizational theory* (Bolman & Deal, 1991) is also useful within the school setting when negotiating the school system's hierarchy as well with interagency collaboration such as law enforcement and/or corrections.

Common Issues

Myriad issues are referred to the services of the school social worker. The exact role and responsibility of the worker is often dictated by the title under which the worker functions, relevant federal and state laws and regulations that mandate functions, and the local school governing body that employs the social worker.

Functions of the school social worker—for example, CST assessments, attendance and truancy interventions, collaboration with child welfare services, bullying and violence prevention services, crisis counseling, and other mental health services—are mandated or suggested by specific legislation (Constable et al., 2006). Other functions are determined by the specific district. The best summary of the scope and function of the school social worker is to improve attendance; reduce violence; and address emotional, social, and/or family problems and to assist with raising academic achievement. In addition, the social worker may also be responsible for providing consultation services to school personnel. The manner in which these tasks are envisioned and carried out varies widely.

Common Practice Settings

Settings/Jobs

The most common setting for a social worker in a school is as a member of a CST. As a member of a CST, the social worker assists in the identification, evaluation, and remediation of students with learning disabilities. This function is the same whether the service is provided at the elementary or high school level. CST members are required to be knowledgeable of federal legislation such as the Individuals with Disabilities Act (IDEA) (PL 105-117) and federal and state codes regarding the provision of special education services (Constable et al., 2006).

Social workers may also work in schools under a variety of titles providing crisis intervention services, specialized counseling services (e.g., substance-abuse prevention and intervention, truancy intervention, conflict resolution), and as supervisors of specific programs. When providing these types of services, the worker also must be knowledgeable of the specific laws and regulations that govern the provision of these services.

Each of these positions may require specific educational licenses or certifications issued by the department of education of the state in which the school is located. Information regarding licensure and/or certification may be obtained through the department of education Web site in the state in which a person intends to practice.

School social work services are provided in public and private schools. Some private schools do not require the social worker to have a state license and/or an educational credential.

Professionals Involved

School social workers interact with a variety of professionals within and outside of the school. As previously noted, within the school, social workers often function as part of an interdisciplinary CST. The other members of the CST may include a school psychologist, a learning consultant, a speech therapist, a school nurse, as well as other consultants and specialists as needed. The social worker will also interact with guidance counselors, teachers, and administrators within the school.

The social worker as a CST member or under another title providing services within the school may also be involved with juvenile officers, probation officers, hospital personnel, and mental health and addiction professionals. Social workers will often be the contact person in the school for child protective service workers with whom students and their families are involved. Because of the likelihood of the need for collaboration with outside systems, it is necessary for the worker to be aware of the regulations regarding how the school may interact with them. Although professional social workers must always function within the guidelines for practice specified within the NASW *Code of Ethics* (NASW, 1999, 2002) school social workers must also consider the confidentiality guidelines of the School Social Work Association of America (2001) and comply with laws such as the Family Educational Rights and Privacy Act (FERPA) (PL 93-380) of 1974, which governs the dissemination of school records, and the federal confidentiality regulations regarding the release of substance-abuse information (42 CFR-2 [Section 42 of the Code of Federal Regulations, Part 2] and the Health Insurance Portability and Accountability Act of 1996 [HIPPA]) (Constable et al., 2006).

The Role and Function of Social Workers in Schools

School social workers have varying and multifaceted roles and functions, which is the result of federal and state legislation, legal decisions, the characteristic focus of social work, and how the school district understands and values social work services. The social worker's role is often formed by the interaction of the professional and personal focus of the individual worker with the structure and expectations of the particular school (Constable et al., 2006). The school social worker is responsible to multiple constituencies: students and their families, faculty, school administrators, local school governing bodies (e.g., Boards of Education), and the community. Therefore, the school social worker performs all the functions associated with professional social work, for example, counselor, advocate, developer of linkages, policy analyst, and researcher.

One of the most common roles for a school social worker is as part of a CST often comprised of a school psychologist and a learning consultant. This team is responsible for identifying, assessing, and providing remediation plans for students with learning disabilities. In this capacity, the school social worker is responsible for the social assessment of the student. This assessment is conducted by observing the child in school, meeting with the parent(s) to obtain a social and developmental history, talking with the teacher, and reviewing any available, pertinent school records.

If a child is found to have a learning disability a remediation plan is developed, known as the Individualized Educational Plan (IEP) as required by the IDEA (Constable et al., 2006), with the consultation and written consent of the parents. One of the

CST members will then be assigned to the student as a case manager. The case manager is responsible for monitoring the student's progress and determines any changes that might be needed to the student's remediation plan. The case manager must meet annually with the student, parents, and teacher to review and update this plan as long as the student is receiving special education remediation services. In addition to assessment and case manager responsibilities, school social workers may also provide counseling to special education students, either individually or in groups. Counseling may include social skills and behavioral management issues. Consultation services may also be provided to teachers working with special education students.

Within schools there will often be a team responsible for interventions with students with academic and/or behavioral problems but who are not eligible for special education services. These teams are often made up of a building administrator, a guidance counselor, a social worker, a teacher, and other appropriate school personnel. The social worker involved with such a team has the opportunity to provide prevention and/or early-intervention services. Students referred to this type of service are often involved in truancy or have other problems in the community that affect school performance. The social worker is often the most knowledgeable and appropriately trained among school personnel to intervene with students and their families in these types of situations.

Many schools have developed specific programs (often entitled *student assistance programs*) to identify and intervene with students with substance-abuse problems or who come from families with substance-abuse problems. These teams are often led by social workers with specialized training in addictions. When students are identified as using substances, the social worker is responsible for the initial assessment and determination of the need for referral for treatment services. This role requires interaction with parents, treatment providers, and often law enforcement and/or correctional personnel.

As federal mandates have been enacted to ensure that public schools are safe and drug free, violence prevention programming has been added to the duties of the student assistance counselor.

Social workers working in student assistance programs use advanced direct practice, policy, and community-organizing skills. In the role of the school substance-abuse and violence prevention specialist, the social worker is responsible for the development and implementation of prevention programs (Slovak, 2006), often delivered in the form of assembly programs and classroom presentations, faculty and parent education programs, and psychoeducational groups for students.

Crisis intervention teams are another service found within schools that requires social workers. These teams are set up to manage crisis such as the death of a student or a faculty member or any other type of traumatic event (Constable et al., 2006). A member of this team will most likely be called on to perform a threat assessment of a student presenting with either suicidal or violent thoughts or behavior. These teams, developed as a result of federal mandates for safe and disciplined schools, operate under specific local education governing body policies and procedures.

Specific Legal and Ethical Issues

All assessment and remediation services provided by CSTs require signed consent by a student's parent if that student is under 18 years of age. The provision of special education remediation services involves the completion of numerous legal and educational documents requiring the signatures of school personnel and parents. Failure to complete the required paperwork within specified timelines can result in legal action by the student's family. Cases of this nature are usually resolved in an administrative law or civil rights hearing.

Counseling services provided to a student under 18 other than crisis intervention requires parental notification and consent. The exception to this rule is services to a substance-abusing student provided through a student assistance counselor. The provision of such services is covered under 42 CFR-2. Parental notification of the provision of such services to students may be done only with the written consent of the student. Although adherence to this level of confidentiality is mandated by federal regulation, it often creates ethical dilemmas for the social worker regarding parental involvement, which may be necessary to obtain a higher level of care for an abusing student.

Assessment, Prevention, and Intervention

Assessment, prevention, and intervention services provided in a school setting by a social worker will vary, depending on the title and function of the social worker. Usually such services will entail assessment, remediation planning, and monitoring done by a social worker as part of a CST. In some school districts, the social worker may also be responsible for providing counseling services to students receiving special education services.

Social workers providing services through student assistance programs are responsible for prevention, education, identification, assessment, intervention, and referral services concerning substance abuse. Social workers may plan and provide programs for students, their families, and the community on prevention of substance abuse. In schools, social workers functioning as student-assistance counselors (SACs) may teach lessons on substance-abuse prevention in classrooms. SACs are also responsible for identification, assessment, intervention, and referral of students who are abusing substances or who come from homes where substance abuse is a problem. SACs are able to assess for substance abuse, refer for outside treatment services, and provide individual counseling and in-school support groups. Students who require inpatient services for substance use will, on return to school, have reentry plans developed with the SAC, the student, and rehabilitation center staff.

Schools are increasingly confronted with students who have a myriad of emotional and social issues that affect their academic performance. Social workers in the school are often seen as the experts called on to deal with students with such problems. Emotional and social issues presented in the school run the gamut from severe psychiatric problems (e.g., depression with suicidal ideation and/or gestures) to relationship problems, harassment, sexual-identity issues, attention-deficit/hyperactivity disorder (ADHD), eating disorders, parental divorce, physical and sexual abuse, aggression, and violence (National Center for Educational Statistics, 2007).

Given the wide range of possible issues presented by students, social workers need to have excellent assessment skills and knowledge of crisis-intervention strategies (Richmond, 1917). Assessments, regardless of the role of the social worker within the school, need to be multidimensional and address cultural considerations. The assessment process within the school can be complex, because of the various specialized tasks performed by the social worker. In general, a social work assessment covers problem identification, identification of the client system (i.e., who is asking for services), and the target system (i.e., what is expected to change). The assessment will cover multiple domains within the client's life and focuses on her or his strengths. Components to be addressed may include demographics and data source, referral source, presenting problem, family information, health/physical/intellectual/emotional functioning, interpersonal/social relationships, religion/spirituality, strengths/problem-solving capacity, economics/housing, impressions/assessment, and goals/interventions (Miley, O'Melia, & DuBois, 2007). The product of the assessment process—a social assessment report—is a written document that becomes part of the student's record. The format for the final report is usually determined by the school district.

Some districts will provide standardized assessment instruments for use by the social worker based on whatever service they are providing. School social workers working on CSTs will often use The *Child Development Inventory* (Ireton, 1990) or *The Behavior Assessment System for Children Structured Developmental History (BASC-SDH)* (Reynolds & Kamphaus, 1992). SACs have a variety of assessment instruments available based on the age of the student, for example, *Adolescent Substance Abuse Subtle Screening Inventory (SASSI)* (see chapter 14 on mental health and addictions for additional instruments). Crisis intervention or behavioral specialists may use standardized instruments specific to their services [e.g., *Beck Depression Inventory* (Beck, Steer, & Brown, 1996)]. A variety of assessment formats and instruments may be reviewed in the text *Clinical Assessment for Social Workers* (Jordan & Franklin, 2003).

Resources for social workers in schools are most frequently available through the professional associations specific to the title under which the social worker operates. Three national organizations providing resources are the NASW's School Social Work Section, the School Social Work Association of America, and the National Association of Student Assistance Programs. All three organizations provide resources and information about national/regional conferences.

Practitioner Skill Set

Social workers providing services in schools must possess a variety of skills. Excellent verbal and written language skills are necessary. The ability to communicate clearly and effectively with people from different socioeconomic and educational levels is a requisite for this work. School social workers must have knowledge of and the ability to interact with people from different racial, ethnic, and cultural backgrounds. Social workers in schools provide case management and advocacy services for the students and their families. Social workers will often assist students' families in identifying and applying for eligible services within the school and in the outside community.

As the liaison to the community, the school social worker needs to be able to interact with law enforcement, treatment providers, and, often, correctional personnel. In these interactions, the social worker must be cognizant of ethical and legal considerations in the disclosure of an exchange of information regarding students.

Case Studies

Given the breadth of services provided by social workers in schools, it would be difficult, if not impossible, to present one case that typifies what issues may be presented by students. Therefore, three cases will follow: one student with developmental/learning problems, another student with behavior problems, and a final case regarding sexual-orientation issues.

James

James is a 3-year-old African American male who resides with his maternal grand-mother, 14-year-old maternal aunt, and a 7-year-old cousin. The other two children are reported to do well in school and participate in general education classes. There are no other adults in the home.

James is referred for CST evaluation by his pediatrician because of delays in language development and difficulties with attention and behavior. James uses only single words and short phrases and has a vocabulary of approximately 50 words. He has problems following direction and staying on task. When frustrated or upset, James will scream, kick, bang his head, and/or throw objects. Grandmother uses "time-outs" for discipline.

James requires constant supervision, and he is described as impulsive and showing poor judgment. He is reported to dart into the street. When the family is outdoors, James requires his hand to be held by other family members at all times for safety reasons.

James is reported to be affectionate with his family but shy with strangers. The 14-year-old aunt, the grandmother's main support in caring for James, and the 7-year-old cousin are reported to be gentle and supportive with James.

The family is active in the Baptist church, where James participates in a child-care program during services. In that setting, James is reported to enjoy playing with cars and trucks, pushing vehicles back and forth with another boy. In this program, James's interest in activities is described as short lived.

James was born at 31 weeks' gestation, weighing 2 pounds, 4 ounces; he was 17 inches in length. Head circumference appeared smaller than normal. At birth, James experienced difficulty breathing and eating. He was placed in a neonatal care unit for 11 weeks. It is reported that James's mother used crack cocaine and marijuana throughout the pregnancy.

His grandmother brought James home upon his discharge. His mother lived in the home for a short period after James came home. The grandmother reports that currently the mother visits occasionally but is mostly absent from James's life. The mother is reported to continue to use drugs and to be "living on the streets." James's father is incarcerated for selling drugs. He has not developed a relationship with James. The grandmother has sole custody of the child.

James experienced a delay in attaining developmental milestones. He spoke his first word at $2^1/2$ years and continues to have speech difficulties. He walked without assistance at 17 months. James is mostly toilet-trained with occasional episodes of nocturnal enuresis. He is able to dress himself.

James is reported to be generally healthy. There is no history of head injuries, convulsions, or hospitalizations. He is reported to have a healthy appetite. He is a restless sleeper and snores. He has a history of ear infections.

James was evaluated by the CST and found to be eligible for services as a student with learning disabilities. He was enrolled in a preschool handicapped program in which he received speech services and occupational therapy services. A behavioral plan was developed to address time on task concerns and to help James develop more appropriate ways to deal with frustration.

Brian

Brian is a seventh-grade student who is failing several subjects, doing little homework, coming to school late, and presenting behavioral difficulties. Although appearing academically uninterested, he presents as sociable and enjoys the social aspects of school.

Brian began to experience academic problems during middle school. His standardized test scores are all in the average range. Although usually friendly and sociable, he becomes sullen and uncommunicative when discussion focuses on academic problems. Brian does not received special education services.

The school has attempted to address Brian's declining academic performance through conferences with his parent. Brian resides with his biological mother, her boyfriend, and a younger female sibling. His mother often does not attend scheduled conferences.

Brian came to the attention of the student-assistance counselor after an incident with a teacher in which he was verbally disrespectful and insubordinate. After being referred to the assistant principal for this behavior, Brian was noted to be unusually tired, irritable, and red-eyed. Brian was then asked to submit to a drug test, which he refused. As required, Brian's mother was contacted regarding the behavior and the request for a drug test.

On notification of the request for the drug test, Brian's mother did come to school. Brian and his mother conferred regarding the drug test. The mother seemed unusually concerned about the outcome of such a test.

The student-assistance counselor, Brian, and his mother met. From this discussion, it became known that the family was using marijuana together and that the parental figures and Brian were selling marijuana as well. Brian and his mother agreed to the drug test, which came back positive for high levels of THC, the chemical in marijuana. The level was indicative of someone who smoked marijuana daily.

The family was referred to child protective services (CPS) and the police. The mother denied dealing as did Brian. Police involvement ended as dealing could not be proven. CPS continued to support the mother's recovery.

Brian's behavior continued to deteriorate in school and resulted in a CST referral. He was determined to be eligible for special education services as a student with severe behavioral difficulties.

Brian became known to the juvenile court as a result of incidents in the community. The SAC advocated with the court to order Brian into rehabilitation rather than a correctional facility. The court accepted the recommendation of the SAC and Brian was sent to an inpatient rehab facility.

Brian successfully completed inpatient treatment for substance abuse. He returned to the school with a recommendation for outpatient treatment and in-school support services provided by the SAC.

Brian's mother relapsed and did not follow through with Brian's aftercare program. Brian began using again and was involved in a series of burglaries in the community. Brian was caught, convicted, and sent to a juvenile correctional facility.

Irina

Irina is a 14-year-old ninth-grade student. She immigrated to the United States from Russia with her family when she was 12 years old. She does well academically and maintains a "B" average. There are no attendance problems. Although she speaks perfect English, Irina remains isolated socially. She presents some discipline problems for teachers.

Irina is rejected socially by the other girls. They report that she tells "outrageous stories" regarding going to bars in a large city within access to the school district through public transportation. Although a fairly good soccer player, Irina refuses to be involved with organized sports. Teachers report problems with verbal exchanges with Irina and other students. When requested to cease the exchange, Irina will disregard the teacher's directives resulting in a referral for insubordination to the main office.

Irina's parents have participated in conferences at school regarding discipline problems. They report that they are experiencing similar problems at home. They express concern that Irina often stays out late on the weekends and that they do not always know her whereabouts. They report that she is sullen and withdrawn at home. Attempts by school personnel to engage Irina in discussions about problems with other girls have been unsuccessful.

Over the course of Irina's ninth-grade school year, her appearance changed. She began wearing more dark-colored clothing and appeared to take less interest in her hair. She stopped using any make-up and wore no jewelry other than a watch. Her jackets and backpack were covered with buttons with slogans and rainbow flags.

After wearing a t-shirt to school with a slogan regarding dating women, Irina was referred to the SAC for an interview. Although affirming Irina's right to wear the t-shirt, the SAC tried to open a conversation with the student regarding why that t-shirt and what the student was trying to tell everyone. With much support and gentle probing, Irina was able to disclose the questions that she was beginning to have regarding her sexual orientation. Irina was able to disclose her anger and frustration at feeling that she did not fit in with girls her own age, her increasing depression, and a somewhat detailed plan for suicide. The t-shirt provided a vehicle for someone to ask Irina a direct question regarding her sexual orientation.

Irina met with her parents and the SAC. A referral was made to a local therapist comfortable with dealing with adolescent sexual-orientation issues.

Discussion

James's case highlights the skills required of a social worker on a CST. In this capacity, the worker must be able to establish rapport so as to obtain a detailed history and to provide a biopsychosocial assessment of the student and his family. The ability to engage the student and family at this level may allow for the provision of services at an early age to remediate the learning problem. Often, early remediation can prevent school dissatisfaction, which can lead to social and behavioral problems.

Brian's case demonstrates the function of the SAC in the school setting. The knowledge base of the SAC, the ability to handle crises, and the strategies that need to be employed to obtain treatment for the student is highlighted in this case.

Irina's case highlights an emerging issue regarding sexual orientation in adolescents and the need for the school social worker to be knowledgeable and aware of such issues. The case highlights the clinical skills that are often needed in the school setting to be able to deal effectively with adolescents.

In all of the cases presented, the social worker had to be aware of and adhere to all federal and state laws and regulations and local governing board policies and procedures as well as to follow the appropriate confidentiality regulations.

Summary and Conclusions

This chapter presented an overview of social work services in the school. It examined the origin and development of such services in the United States. Contemporary functions of the school social worker and the various legal, academic, and social emotional issues addressed were presented. In chapter 11, the special considerations for the educational needs of students returning to school postincarceration are reviewed.

References

Administration of Children and Families [ACF]. (n.d.). *Office of Head Start*. Retrieved August 29th, 2007, from http://eclkc.ohs.acf.hhs.gov/hslc/About%20Head%20Start

Beck, A. T., Steer, R. A., & Brown, G. K. (1996). *Manual for Beck Depression Inventory II (BDI-II)*. San Antonio, TX: Psychology Corporation.

Bolman, L. G., & Deal, T. E. (1991). *Reframing organizations*. San Francisco: Jossey-Bass.

Constable, R., Massat, C. R., McDonald, S., & Flynn, J. P. (2006). *School social work*. Chicago: Lyceum Books.

Education for All Handicapped Children Act. (1975). Pub. L. No. 94-142. Retrieved October 4, 2006, from http://users.rcn.com/peregrin.enteract/add/94-142.txt

Family Educational Rights and Privacy Act (FERPA). (1974). 20 U.S.C.S.§1232 Retrieved October 1, 2008, from http://www.ed.gov/policy/gen/guid/fpco/ferpa/leg-history.html

Glasser, W. (1965). *Reality therapy*. New York: Harper & Row.

Goals 2000: Educate America Act. (1994). (H.R. 804). Retrieved October 4, 2006, from http://www.ed.gov/legislation/GOALS2000/TheAct/index.html

Health Insurance Portability and Accountability Act of 1996 (HIPPA). (1996). Pub. L. No. 104-191. Retrieved October 4, 2006, from http://www.cms.hhs.gov/HIPAAGenInfo/Downloads/HIPAALaw.pdf

Huxtable, M. (1998). School social work: An international profession. *Social Work in Education, 20*(2), 95–109.

Individuals with Disabilities Education Act Amendments of 1997. (1997). Pub. L. No. 105-17, 20 U.S.C.

Ireton, H. R. (1990). *Child development inventory assessment of children's development, symptoms, and behavior problems*. Retrieved August 29th, 2007, from http://eric.ed.gov/ERICDocs/data/ericdocs2sql/content_storage_01/ 0000019b/80/13/b1/56.pdf

Jordan, C., & Franklin, C. (2003). *Clinical assessment for social workers.* Chicago: Lyceum Books.

Miley, K. K., O'Melia, M., & DuBois, B. (2007). *Generalist social work practice.* Boston: Pearson.

Miller, W. R., & Rollnick, S. (2002). *Motivational interviewing.* New York: Guilford Press.

National Association of Social Workers. (1999). *Code of ethics.* Washington, DC: NASW Press.

National Association of Social Workers. (2002). *NASW Standards for school social work services.* Washington, DC: NASW Press.

National Conference of State Legislatures [NCSL]. (n.d.) *Compulsory education.* Retrieved August 29, 2008, from http://www.ncsl.org/programs/educ/CompulsoryEd.htm

National Center for Educational Statistics (NCES). (2007). *Overview of public elementary secondary schools and districts.* Retrieved July 15, 2007, from http://nces.ed.gov/index.asp

Nichols, M. P., & Schwartz, R. C. (2005). *The essentials of family therapy.* Boston: Allyn & Bacon.

Richmond, M. (1917). *Social diagnosis.* New York: Russell Sage Foundation.

Reynolds, C. R., & Kamphaus, R. W. (1992). *BASC—behavioral assessment system for children: Manual.* Circle Pines, MN: American Guidance Service.

School Social Work Association of America. (n.d.). *School Social Work Association of America.* Retrieved May 1, 2007, from http://www.sswaa.org/

School Social Work Association of America. (2001, March 15). *School social workers and confidentiality.* Retrieved August 27, 2008, from www.sswaa.org/members/confidentiality.html

Slovak, K. (2006). School social workers' perceptions of student violence and prevention programming. *School Social Work Journal, 31*(1), 30–42.

Usaj, K., Shine, J., & Mandlawitz, M. (n.d.). *Response to intervention: New roles for school social workers.* Retrieved August 27, 2007, from http://www.sswaa.org/index.php?option=com_content&view=article&id=112:response-to-intervention-new-roles-for-school-social-workers&catid=35:resources-publications&Itemid=80

Torres, S. (1996). The status of school social workers in America. *Social Work in Education, 18,* 8–18.

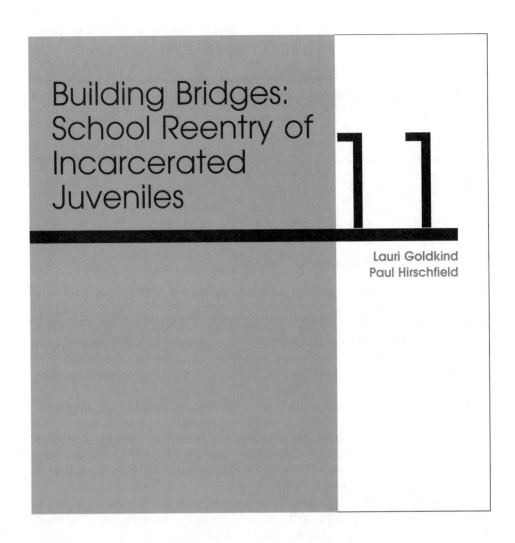

Building Bridges: School Reentry of Incarcerated Juveniles

11

Lauri Goldkind
Paul Hirschfield

Many at-risk youth and their families must navigate multiple service systems—educational, child welfare, juvenile justice, and/or mental health. Consequently, to be effective, social workers inside and outside of these settings must help youth and their families negotiate and accommodate the often-conflicting schedules, policies, and expectations of multiple bureaucratic institutions. This is especially true for social workers in the public education and juvenile justice arenas. Since the late 19th and early 20th century, fields of social work practice in both sectors have emphasized advocacy and interorganizational communication and cooperation (Constable, Flynn, & McDonald, 2002; Reamer, 2004). Recent decades have witnessed an invigorated emphasis on information sharing and cross-agency collaboration between these institutional domains (Stephens & Arnette, 2000). In this chapter, we focus on services that aim to facilitate the successful return of youth from custodial settings to community educational settings.

Facilitating a smooth transition for school-aged ex-offenders may be of vital importance. Educational and juvenile justice scholars and policymakers often view schooling as the most accessible and reliable pathway toward a healthy and productive future for youth released from secure custody. Without a high school diploma or some other meaningful educational certification, young ex-offenders, particularly those of African American descent, face a bleak future. A recent federal report finds that only 39% of Black high school dropouts are employed at age 19 compared to about 60% of White dropouts (Bureau of Labor Statistics, 2007). Likewise, nearly 60% of Black male dropouts are imprisoned by the age of 30 to 34 compared to 11% of non-Hispanic White dropouts (Pettit & Western, 2004). Clearly the life chances and social outcomes of disadvantaged youth are a function of their educational experiences and opportunities (Arum & Beattie, 1999).

Scope of the Problem

The need for postrelease social and education services may be greater than ever. Nearly 100,000 people under age 21 are released each year from correctional facilities in the United States (Snyder, 2004). More often than not, freedom is short-lived. A recent study finds that 81% of male offenders 17 and under in New York City were rearrested within 36 months of their release from state custody (Frederick, 1999). Similarly alarming rates of juvenile reoffending have been reported nationally, ranging from 50% (Lipsey, 1999) to 71% (Wiebush, McNulty, Wagner, Wang, & Le, 2005). Further, research suggests that youth involved in the justice system exact high economic costs for the United States. Cohen (1998) estimates the costs to society of a single youth leaving school and turning to drugs and crime as a way of life as between $1.7 and $2.3 million. A high rate of dropout among delinquent youth may help account for the fact that states with higher numbers of high school dropouts tend to have higher rates of violent crime (Page, Petteruti, Walsh, & Zeidenberg, 2007).

The burning questions regarding policy and programs are not *whether* young ex-offenders should get back into school following release but rather *how* to most effectively facilitate sustained school reenrollment and *which* types of educational settings are the strongest, most reliable bridges to social opportunity. Social workers often play important roles on both ends of the bridge. On the corrections side, they may be responsible for prerelease assessments, planning, and coordination with outside systems as well as securing postrelease placements. And on the community side, they may be responsible for coordinating reentry services, including those that pertain to educational reintegration. In the text that follows we outline the barriers to school reentry, discuss the strengths and weaknesses of various interventions, and provide some general guidelines for the design and evaluation of these programs.

Youth emerging from secure confinement have a slim chance of reenrolling in school and an even slimmer chance of advancing. An early study found that among 487 school-eligible youth released from Wisconsin juvenile correctional facilities in 1979, only 2.5% earned a high school diploma by 1982, whereas 16.5% received a general equivalency diploma (GED) (Habermann & Quinn, 1986). A more recent study found that 95% of youth released to jurisdictions across Kentucky were unable to make a successful transition into either a mainstream or transitional school setting (Stephens & Arnette, 2000). Such patterns typically signal a *resumption* of the persistent school disengagement, failure, and avoidance that young offenders often exhibit prior to their incarceration. And such academic difficulties, in turn, are often a product of serious deficits in reading and quantitative skills as well as emotional and behavioral problems. At least 45% of incarcerated youth suffer from a learning disability (U.S. Department of Education, 1999).

School Reenrollment Hurdles

The obstacles that released youth face in reintegrating into school go far beyond the internal. The hurdles youth face include midsemester reenrollment, inadequate intake screenings, and a frequent lack of credits or transferable schoolwork between correctional institution and school. As a former administrator at a specialized school admission program for court-involved youth (the School Connection Center of New York City; see below), the lead author experienced firsthand the issues and challenges associated with helping adjudicated youth re-enter school in an urban setting. Youth in most jurisdictions across the country are legally entitled to public education services at least until the age of 18. But, without adequate information and advocacy, juveniles returning from custodial facilities often have a hard time even getting past the reenrollment stage.

Youth released during the middle of the semester may be told that they have to wait to enroll until the next semester, as Giles (2003) observed in New Jersey. The logistics of admitting students midsemester often involve a complicated process for both the youth as well as the school. Workers at the School Connection Center (SCC) experienced this difficulty firsthand. They discovered that placing students midterm could lead to students feeling overwhelmed and lost in courses that were already many weeks into a semester's sequence. Because most schools operate under a traditional September enrollment model, school staff are often ill-equipped to issue partial or transfer credit and to match students released midsemester with appropriate course choices. In addition, Mayer (2005) observed that some Chicago schools are reluctant to admit students released from confinement either because of their tainted memories of individual students or because they are concerned that such students bring down their test scores and attendance and bring up their levels of crime and disorder.

The educational exclusion of young ex-offenders can also be indirect, subtle, and not necessarily intentional. For example, youth along with a very inconvenienced parent—who must take time off from work—may come to the enrollment meeting, only to discover that they lack the necessary paperwork to enroll (proof of address, past transcripts, health records), or that the credits the youth earned while incarcerated will not transfer, or that the school system insists that the student, owing to his or her special education or ex-offender status, needs to go to an alternative school or receive home-based instruction until he or she is ready to return to regular school (Stephens & Arnette, 2000). In New York State (NYS), young people under 16 years old placed in confinement in an NYS Office of Children and Family Services (OCFS) facility may experience high school for the first time within a correctional setting. Incarcerated youth receive student credit hours for each class completed. However, receiving schools in the community may not understand how to calculate their accumulated credits, because the New York City Department of Education (NYC DOE) is on a separate credit accumulation system. As a result, young releasees often lose hard-earned course credit and are scheduled for classes they have previously completed. These experiences, which reflect the absence of efficient, centralized, and standardized records transfer and reenrollment processes, may lead frustrated or ambivalent students to give up on school reenrollment.

Re-enrollment is only the first school reentry hurdle. Youth also face obstacles to staying enrolled and advancing educationally. For special education students, who comprise a large share of young releasees, success requires following through on an individualized education plan (IEP), which may include access to special education teachers and special services like tutoring and literacy enhancement. Giles noted that even special education students in New Jersey are often denied adequate education, as receiving schools are often unwilling or unable to follow mandated IEPs (Giles, 2003).

All of these problems can result from the failure of juvenile justice agencies and educational agencies to share information in a timely fashion. This leads to gaps and delays in services, inappropriate service placements, and duplications in services (Giles, 2003; Stephens & Arnette, 2000). Sensible models of closing these gaps will be discussed later. The response of many juvenile courts to the large number of court-involved youth who are unwilling or unable to return to or stay in school can, at times, make matters worse. Judges, probation, and parole departments increasingly enforce mandates that youth under juvenile justice supervision enroll and attend schools (or face sanctions), which put more pressure on school systems to find educational placements for these students. Several large jurisdictions like Chicago, and the states of Texas, Tennessee, and Washington, responded to this pressure by creating specialized, often mandatory, transitional school environments for offenders released from county or state custody (Bickerstaff, Leon, & Hudson, 1997; Brooks, Schiraldi, & Ziedenberg, 1999; Mayer, 2005). This may mean easier access to some school environments postrelease but harder access to desired schools or to the "least restrictive educational environments" mandated for special education students. On the other hand, some promising models of interagency collaboration and communication and transitional educational programming have emerged in recent years, for instance, a report from Just Children highlights a wide array of emergent programs and strategies from across the U.S. (Geddes & Keenan, 2004). Unfortunately, very little empirical research guides reform efforts and a veritable patchwork of services is the result.

Practical Approaches to School Reentry

Before reviewing the various models currently in use for school reenrollment, it is useful to discuss some of the broader characteristics of effective practice in school reentry that have been identified in the literature. For nearly 20 years, scholars and practitioners have been proposing successful transitional models to re-engage adjudicated youth with school. Key elements include prerelease transitional planning, interagency communication, and follow-up and evaluation posttransition.

School reentry planning should begin on entry to a correctional facility. To position custodial school educators to begin the prerelease transition process most efficiently, educational institutions need to transfer expeditiously student's transcripts, IEPs, and other academic documents on enrollment in a custodial school. Conversely, best practice suggests that the timely transfer of records at exit should be a priority for custodial school staff (Stephens & Arnette, 2000).

As much literature on school reenrollment for court-involved students recommends, open lines of communication among all organizations involved with juvenile offenders are necessary to establish a comprehensive treatment approach for offenders and their families (Stephens & Arnette, 2000). Open communication can prevent replication of services or, worse, lack of services. It can also expedite the reenrollment process creating seamless school transitions between custodial schools and community schools.

Among the models identified as successful programs for supporting youth transitioning from corrections facilities to community schools are specialized admissions centers that facilitate enrollment in a variety of educational settings, short-term transitional programs, and long-term transitional school programs.

Specialized Admissions Centers

Specialized admissions centers often make use of interagency collaboration and communication to expedite the school admissions process for youth involved with juvenile justice systems. Two such specialized admissions programs are the School Connection Center, which operated in Manhattan, and Philadelphia's RETI-Wrap program. Both programs use what is likely the most efficient means of interagency service coordination and information-sharing—housing staff from both justice agencies and local educational institutions under one roof.

School Connection Center

The School Connection Center (SCC) was designed to address the issues identified earlier. The lead author served as the associate director of SCC from the beginning of the program until it closed nearly 3 years later (and its functions transferred to a citywide centralized enrollment system). SCC was launched in June 2002 by the Center for Alternative Sentencing and Employment Services (CASES) as a response to the tremendous difficulty its case management staff had in getting youth returning from detention enrolled in school. Prior to launching the program, CASES met for 2 years with various institutional players in the local and state juvenile justice and education worlds to foster a collective understanding of the barriers to educational reintegration and to develop a coordinated response. CASES convened the Committee on Court Involved Students, a group that included representatives from the New York City Departments of Education, Probation and Juvenile Justice, the New York State Office of Children and Family Services, the Mayor's Office of the Criminal Justice Coordinator, as well as other nonprofit service providers to develop solutions to the reenrollment and school-retention challenges faced by youth returning from custody. Two programmatic recommendations arose from the work of the Committee, the School Connection Center, further described here, and Community Preparatory High School (Community Prep). SCC was designed as the exclusive admission center for Community Prep, and as a point of entry for school-enrollment services for all youth returning to Manhattan from detention. The Committee on Court Involved Students continued serving in an advisory capacity once the programs were operational. Several agencies also committed staff to the project from their home organizations.

From the beginning, the design of SCC included a social worker on staff. Although the role of the social worker evolved during the operation of the program, program administrators recognized early in the program's implementation that a social worker's ability to develop caring relationships and provide ongoing support would be helpful for students and their families. Additionally, social workers' specialized training in building relationships and forging open, nonjudgmental channels of communication were thought to be vital to the program's operational structure.

At the School Connection Center, staff from the diverse educational and justice agencies expedited the school admissions process. SCC staff represented all of the major institutions that affect a formerly incarcerated student's life; the Departments of Education and Probation as well as CASES staff were all housed at one site with access to all the relevant databases so as to serve youth and their families most expeditiously. Founded as a one-stop admissions hub, the Center placed young people returning from custody in a range of educational settings, including traditional middle and high schools and into Community Prep High School, a transitional school site established by CASES specifically serving youth returning from the justice system. Following school registration, the Center monitored students' school attendance for 3 months, and provided advocacy and mediation services to help parents obtain special education services and to help school staff deal with any challenges related to re-entering students. Youth were referred to SCC prior to their release from detention (or soon after release). Center staff conducted outreach to the family and the probation or aftercare worker to set up intake appointments. The intake process consisted of two interviews with Center staff. The first intake interview was conducted by either a social worker or probation officer and paralleled a traditional social work "bio-psycho-social" probing of all the relevant areas of a youth's home and family environment. The second intake interview was conducted by a Department of Education staff member and consisted of an academic review as well as an assessment of a youth's academic interests.

Case Study: Joseph M.

Joseph,* a 15-year-old Latino male, was referred to SCC by the transition planner at the Horizon Detention Center in the Bronx. Joseph was released from Horizon on January 15th, after spending 4 months in detention. The intake staff assigned to Joseph has been calling his aunt since before his release from Horizon, yet it still took the family over 3 weeks to make it to SCC for an intake interview. Joseph, his aunt, and the social worker finally meet for the interview on February 9th, approximately 15 school days after the start of the spring semester.

The social worker learns that Joseph repeated the third and fifth grades. She also notices that Joseph was arrested on his former middle school's property and his co-defendant (and former friend) was attending school with him at the time of Joseph's arrest. Joseph has never been to a public high school. In the chart prepared before Joseph's arrival are academic records that detail Joseph's academic history within the New York City public school system: all admissions and discharges, standardized test scores, and any special education information (including testing and assessment). A review of these records reveals that Joseph has not attended school for more than 2 consecutive years. In addition, he was recommended for a special education placement, but the assessments were never conducted.

The social worker meets with Joseph and his aunt together and then separately. She conducts a needs assessment with Joseph, focusing on his juvenile justice history,

---

*Please note that this case study is a composite of the common issues faced by many students and not just one specific youth.

his academic history, and his learning style. In addition, she assesses what other pursuits Joseph has to constructively occupy his time. Based on Joseph's interests and the shortage of opportunities to pursue them, she recommends potential extracurricular activities, which are forwarded to a CASES program staff member. Later, this staff member meets with Joseph to register him for enrichment programming, including boxing after school, as well as placing him on a list for an adult mentor through the nonprofit organization Big Brothers/Big Sisters.

After meeting with the social worker individually and with his aunt, Joseph and his aunt meet with a Department of Education School Placement Worker. The placement worker, an expert on NYC schools, works in consultation with the social worker to make a school placement recommendation for Joseph.

Joseph is placed at a high school specializing in science and environmental studies, areas in which Joseph demonstrates interest and some aptitude (evidenced by his detention transcripts and state assessment scores). The school placement worker coordinates Joseph's school registration with the school and Joseph's family and attends a registration appointment with Joseph and his aunt.

Joseph's attendance in school is monitored weekly by staff at SCC for the first 3 months of his enrollment. If he should miss more than 2 days of school in a given week, staff will contact both his home and the school to offer assistance and additional supports.

Philadelphia's Re-Entry Transition Initiative

Similar to the School Connection Center, Philadelphia's Re-Entry Transition Initiative—Welcome Return Assessment Process (RETI-WRAP), is a transition center sponsored by the various Philadelphia education, human services, and justice institutions. Adjudicated youth returning from a day treatment program, court-ordered placement, or incarceration are required to attend RETI-WRAP before transitioning back into the public school system (Socolor, 2005). Whereas participation in the School Connection Center's services was voluntary, youth in Philadelphia are court-mandated to participate in the RETI-WRAP assessment process. Students attend all day for 14 days following release from a custodial site. They spend their time taking academic assessments and attending life-skills and school-readiness training. Based on their transcripts and the 10-day assessment process, young people are assigned a school placement.

Other Transitional Services

Finally, Karcz (1996) evaluated the Youth Reentry Specialist Program (YRS) in 1996. Although YRS did not create a centralized admissions office, its approach is similar to the collaborative admissions models reviewed previously, except the YRS program operated at the state level. Youth Reentry Specialists worked to place special education youth leaving state facilities into 1 of 170 special education units in Wisconsin, which include vocational training centers. Evaluation results suggest social service professionals can effectively mediate between correctional facilities and community educational programs to secure appropriate school and curricular placements, albeit ones that tend to be outside of the educational mainstream. It is worth noting that Karcz's (1996) evaluation of the YRS program is one of the few quantitative studies assessing the effectiveness of school transition services. A rigorous outcome-based evaluation of School Connection Center and Community Prep High School (CPHS) by the second author is currently under way. It examines whether participants in SCC and CPHS reenroll in school and avoid further legal trouble more frequently and for longer periods than similar releasees who could not participate.

The three transition programs detailed earlier represent programming in New York City, Philadelphia, and Wisconsin. They are rare examples of programs that are both innovative and documented by researchers and the juvenile justice literature. Transitional education initiatives certainly exist elsewhere, and a more detailed and comprehensive review of these initiatives is sorely needed.

Specialized Schools and Alternative Education Programs

Specialized admissions centers and programs serve not only to facilitate reenrollment but also to steer youth into placements they deem appropriate. Placement options include mainstream school, transitional school programs, or enrolling in longer term alternative school programs. Although the default option for young people returning from custody is still mainstream public schools, many court-involved youth are deemed unsuitable for immediate reentry into a mainstream community school and are placed in a transitional or alternative educational environment instead.

The default option has its benefits. It does not necessarily require any new services and seems to offer the greatest chances of mainstream social reintegration. But mainstream schools also have their drawbacks. As mentioned earlier, mainstream school environments are not always hospitable to young ex-offenders and may be rife with negative social influences. Furthermore, returning directly to mainstream school may not be an option. Alternatives to mainstream schools include a variety of short and longer term transitional school and alternative school programs (Birnbaum, 2001). Some jurisdictions feature educational programs specifically tailored to the specialized needs of juvenile justice youth.

Example: Community Preparatory High School

Community Preparatory High School (CPHS) is an 18-month (i.e., 3 semesters) alternative school program for adjudicated youth. CPHS and the School Connection Center began as sister programs, with SCC serving as the sole referral point for CPHS. However, in November 2004, the Department of Education (DOE) replaced the SCC with a centralized, citywide system for returning released offenders to school. Accordingly, the DOE now places youth directly into CPHS. Administered jointly by CASES and the New York City Department of Education, the CPHS provides both academic and intensive social services. CPHS uniquely offers remedial reading and math classes as well as coursework that provides credits toward a high school diploma. The school also blends a competence-based youth development approach with restorative practices to encourage productive classroom participation and good citizenship. Students are assigned "Community Advisors" who help them identify strengths and realistic goals and develop constructive solutions to frustrating and challenging situations that arise. Discipline involves restorative interventions that aim to build emotional literacy and repair the harm done to individuals and to the school community. Staffing for the school includes traditional teachers, paid for by the New York City

Department of Education, a DOE school social worker, as well as the Community Advisors and a Co-Director, who are CASES employees. The CASES staff works closely with each student to identify and pursue realistic goals. The CASES Executive Director reports that alumni are provided 6 months of follow-up support (Copperman, 2004).

CPHS represents an alternative school option for juvenile justice youth. All school reentry programs featured here offer some degree of interagency collaboration; from the SCC specialists whose job it is to explicitly create mutual understanding and collaboration between correctional agencies and schools to the staff at Community Prep High School, who cooperate with probation and other aftercare providers to monitor students' attendance.

Policy Issues

Specialized admission centers and alternative schools purport to steer youth toward appropriate and beneficial placements that are designed to accommodate the special needs of the young-offender population. This generally means settings that provide individualized instruction and a highly structured, supportive environment. However, it is important to consider whether there are costs to segregating ex-offenders in specialized school settings that serve mainly ex-offenders. Transitional programs market themselves as a bridge—a transitional phase—from correctional institutions to mainstream education. But there is limited evidence that many students actually make this transition. One study of a state-funded and university-administered transitional school for juvenile parolees found that only 2 of 146 students enrolled during the 1994–1995 school year earned any high school credits (Smith, 2003).

Thus, rhetoric aside, students may understandably get the impression that the real purpose of some of these programs is to isolate them from the "normal population"—a daily reminder of their second-class citizenship status (Birnbaum, 2001). Such impressions are reinforced when placement in these programs is mandatory, for instance, among all youth released from secure settings. When youth are mandated to school settings lacking the amenities found in mainstream schools, schooling can become conflated with punishment. Birnbaum, who studied a transitional program for delinquents, observes, "when schooling becomes a feature of sentencing, the lines between education and punishment are ambiguous....What goes by the name education can itself seem like punishment" (p. 67). Mandatory placement of delinquents into specialized schools not only can affect the commitment on the part of students, but it can affect the perceptions of teachers and administrators. Teachers and administrators who operate, staff, and fund such segregated environments may come to define their purpose as the isolation and control (or even punishment) of a criminal population rather than the education of needy, marginalized students (Gregg, 1998).

Irrespective of whether school-aged releasees return directly to mainstream schools or to a transitional school environment, most commentators agree that additional services and interagency coordination are needed. But are the juvenile justice mandates, assessments, transition teams, monitoring, and labels that accompany this help an asset or a hindrance? The free exchange of information and personnel between schools and the justice system can help both institutions better understand and serve their clientele. However, information on the legal problems of students may also stigmatize students. Likewise, frequent interaction of school staff with police and probation officers in schools may lead school staff to view students through the lens of law enforcement and privilege penological imperatives over pedagogical ones. The blurring of the lines between schools and the justice system may be a double-edged sword.

Recommendations

Interagency communication, student choice, and entry into the education system (and away from the justice system) are three ideas significant to the success of court-involved students with regard to their successful school reentry. Interagency communication and coordination are critical to ensuring appropriate placements, the delivery of social and special education services, and the transfer of credits. However, once a student is enrolled in school, juvenile justice and school authorities must exercise appropriate discretion, so information-sharing is used for inclusionary rather than exclusionary purposes.

Second, students should have access to both mainstream and alternative placements with the choice informed by a careful assessment of students' needs and interests. Both types of placement should have rolling admissions and a wide array of curricula and services. Students for whom a high school diploma is no longer a realistic option should be offered classroom-based or tutoring-based preparation for the general equivalency diploma, preferably in conjunction with specific vocational training and job placement (Lipsey & Wilson, 1998).

Third, whenever possible ex-offenders should be integrated into effective alternative schools outside of the management of the justice system that also serve students displaced from mainstream schools for reasons others than justice system involvement. In this way, schools can accommodate their special needs without perpetuating their stigmatization as ex-offenders.

VOICES FROM THE FIELD

Laura A. Lowe, MSW, LCSW, PhD
Juvenile Probation/Parole Specialist

Agency Setting

(I am currently a social work educator, but for this profile I am responding about my most recent full-time forensic position.) As a full-time worker, I worked for a southeastern state with the community component of juvenile corrections. So in this case, we worked closely with the juvenile court, but I did not work for the juvenile court.

Practice Responsibilities

At this job I ran an Intensive Supervision Program (ISP) for juveniles on probation or aftercare and co-led a therapy group for adolescent males with sexually aggressive behaviors. The sex offender therapy program for male adolescents included ongoing weekly outpatient group therapy on relapse prevention, changing thought patterns, empathy building, appropriate behavior, communication skills, social skills, and sex education. This responsibility was not a regular component of this position with GA Department of Juvenile Justice (DJJ). The ISP program included providing counseling with youth and families (anger management, parenting skills, crisis counseling, and behavior management) and case management activities (monitoring behavior at home and school and coordinating treatment through other providers). I also supervised two staff members. Other responsibilities included maintaining case files, securing residential treatment for youth when necessary, and making reports for and providing testimony in juvenile court.

Expertise Required

Although a bachelor's degree (any) was required to qualify for this position with Georgia DJJ, I would say that a master's degree was needed for the ISP program and even more so for the additional therapy work, which most ISP workers did not provide.

Practice Challenges

Numerous practice challenges existed in this position; I will talk about a few. There was a serious lack of resources for this population of juvenile offenders. It was difficult to obtain good mental health treatment for youth, despite the fact we know that the majority of youth (and adults) in the criminal justice system have mental health issues. This was true whether you were talking about outpatient or residential programs.

Though I was blessed with a small caseload, most of our Juvenile Probation Officers (JPOs) worked on so many cases at one time that their efforts were largely aimed at dealing with crises, rather than providing maintenance services. More workers were badly needed; particularly workers who were well trained in how to work with people. Prevention efforts were largely unheard of in this system.

All types of juvenile offenders deal with the issue of being labeled by the system, which then leads to differential treatment in the community. For example, our youth often got targeted by the school they attended. Administration would look for excuses to kick them out of school or out of school-related activities. These youth definitely needed the structure that school provides; the last thing they needed was to be kicked out of school before they completed their education or be held back because of suspensions, and so on. Looking at the sexually aggressive youth, consider the community-notification laws that are growing in support across the country. Being labeled as a sex offender, sometimes for life, does not bode well for success for juveniles or adults; these practices set this population up to fail. Policy efforts provided challenges in this position.

Common Legal and/or Ethical Issues

As a social worker, there were some ethical challenges for me in this system. At this time the criminal justice system, even the juvenile system, is largely dominated by an expectation of punishment. This ran pretty contrary to my professional values. Dealing with value conflicts between my organization and my profession, or society and my profession could be fairly difficult at times. The ethical issues of consent (i.e., nonvoluntary clients) and confidentiality of course played a significant role in the conflicts I experienced. In my work with juveniles with sexual aggression, another particular issue was the balance between my responsibility to protect the community and my responsibility to my clients.

Brief Description of Collaborative Activities
With Professionals and/or Other Stakeholders

I worked with a variety of professionals from different disciplines. Other JPOs in my system were trained in "criminal justice"; their value orientation was significantly different than social work. Additionally, I worked with law enforcement, mental health providers (psychiatrists), health workers (doctors), school personnel (teachers, administrators), lawyers, and judges. A large part of my work with other disciplines involved advocacy—particularly of services for clients. However, I also brokered services, facilitated treatment and service, and provided consultation on client issues.

Additional Information

Professionals who work in this field (where they are sorely needed) need to have a good support system of other social workers. It is easy to feel swallowed by the system, feel very isolated, and stray from your value base. My advice is to find (a) good supervisor(s) within or outside your agency and talk with this person regularly. Also, go to conferences in social work that will reconnect you to other social workers, your own value base, and remind you why you are working.

Summary and Conclusions

For more than a century, social work has informed and guided practice and policy concerning at-risk children within the juvenile justice and public education realms. One important social work principle, according to The National Association of Social Work *Code of Ethics* (1999, p. 1, preamble), is that "fundamental to social work is attention to the environmental forces that create, contribute to and address the problems of living." In the case of youth returning from correctional settings to educational settings, it is clear that institutional policies and practices and judicial mandates are themselves "environmental forces" that often obstruct the pathway to success. For this reason, it is vital that social workers operating in both educational and juvenile justice institutions fully understand the possibilities for interagency collaboration and interinstitutional information sharing. Social workers are ideally suited to reaching across institutional barriers to effectively advocate and coordinate for youth and their families as well as advocate for policy changes and the development of programs through organizational collaboration. In this way, youth-serving institutions can work toward the common goal of returning court-involved youth to the mainstream rather than working at cross-purposes. Social workers are often the best equipped for these roles thanks to their grounding in a multisystemic, ecological perspective, as well as their advocacy and relationship-building skills. These skills can be a tremendous resource for clients exiting the justice system and seeking school reentry (Reamer, 2004). However, these skills may not be put to their best uses until more knowledge of "what works" in school reentry becomes available. We hope this chapter is an important step in expanding this knowledge.

References

Arum, R., & Beattie, I. R. (1999). High school experience and the risk of adult incarceration. *Criminology, 37*, 515–537.

Bickerstaff, S., Leon, S. H., & Hudson, J. G. (1997). Preserving the opportunity for education: Texas' alternative education programs for disruptive youth. *Journal of Law and Education, 26*(4), 1–39.

Birnbaum, S. (2001). *Law and order and school: Daily life in an educational program for juvenile delinquents.* Philadelphia: Temple University Press.

Brooks, K., Schiraldi, V., & Ziedenberg, J. (1999). *School house hype: Two years later.* San Francisco: Center on Juvenile and Criminal Justice.

Bureau of Labor Statistics. (2007). *America's youth at 19: School enrollment, training, and employment transitions between Ages 18 and 19 summary.* Washington, DC: U.S. Department of Labor. Available: http://www.bls.gov/news.release/pdf/nlsyth.pdf

Cohen, M. (1998). The monetary value of saving a high risk youth. *Journal of Quantitative Criminology, 14*(1), 5–33.

Constable, R., Flynn, J. P., & McDonald, S. (2002). *School social work: Practice, research and theory.* Homewood, IL: Dorsey Press.

Copperman, J. (2004, Dec.). *Testimony of Joel Copperman, Executive Director of CASES before the New York City Council Committee on Education. Regarding barriers to continuing education for youth released from juvenile detention facilities.* Available from http://council.nyc.gov/html/committees/education.shtml

Frederick, B. (1999). *Factors contributing to recidivism among youth placed with the New York State Division for Youth.* New York State Division of Criminal Justice Services, Office of Justice Systems Analysis Research Report: Albany, NY.

Geddes, S., & Keenan, K. M. (2004). *A summary of best practices in school reentry for incarcerated youth returning home.* Charlottesville, VA:

Giles, D. R. (2003). *School related problems confronting New Jersey youth returning to local communities and schools from juvenile detention facilities and juvenile justice commission programs.* Paper presented at The New Jersey Institute for Social Justice and the New Jersey Public Policy Research Institute's Re-Entry Roundtable Juvenile Reentry Session, Trenton, New Jersey.

Gregg, S. (1998). *Schools for disruptive students: A questionable alternative?* Charleston, WV: Appalachia Educational Laboratory.

Habermann, M., & Quinn, L. (1986). The high school re-entry myth: A follow-up study of juveniles released from two correctional high schools in Wisconsin. *Journal of Correctional Education, 37*, 114–117.

Karcz, S. (1996). An effectiveness study of the Youth Reentry Specialist (YRS) program for released incarcerated youth with handicapping conditions. *Journal of Correctional Education, 47*(1), 42–46.

Lipsey, M. (1999). Can intervention rehabilitate serious delinquents? *Annals of the American Academy of Political and Social Science, 564*, 142–166.

Lipsey, M. W., & Wilson, D. B. (1998). Effective intervention for serious juvenile offenders: A synthesis of research. In R. Loeber & D. P. Farrington (Eds.), *Serious and violent juvenile offenders: Risk factors and successful interventions.* Thousand Oaks, CA: Sage.

Mayer, S. (2005). *Educating Chicago's court-involved youth: Mission and policy in conflict.* Chicago: Chapin Hall Center for Children.

National Association of Social Workers. (1999). *Code of ethics.* Washington, DC: NASW Press.

Page, A., Petteruti, A., Walsh, N., & Zeidenberg, J. (2007). *Education and public safety.* Justice Policy Institute. Retrieved August 20, 2008, from: http://www. justicepolicy.org/images/upload/07-8_REP_EducationAndPublicSafety_PS-AC.pdf

Pettit, B., & Western, B. (2004). Mass imprisonment and the life course: Race and class inequality in U.S. incarceration. *American Sociological Review, 69*, 151–169.

Reamer, F. G. (2004). Social work and criminal justice: The uneasy alliance. *Journal of Religion and Spirituality in Social Work, 23*(1/2), 213–231.

Smith, B. J. (2003). Cultural curriculum and marginalized youth: An analysis of conflict at a school for juvenile parolees. *Urban Review, 35*, 253–280.

Snyder, H. N. (2004). An empirical portrait of the youth reentry population. *Youth Violence and Juvenile Justice, 2*(1), 39–55.

Socolar, P. (2005, fall). New efforts to stem flow of dropouts from Philadelphia schools. *Philadelphia Public School Notebook, 13*(1), 1.

Stephens, R. D., & Arnette, J. L. (2000). *From the courthouse to the schoolhouse: Making successful transitions.* Washington, DC: U.S. Department of Justice, Office of Justice Programs, Office of Juvenile Justice and Delinquency Prevention.

Wiebush, R. G., McNulty, B., Wagner, D., Wang, Y., & Le, T. N. (2005). *Implementation and outcome evaluation of the intensive aftercare program: Final report.* Office of Juvenile Justice and Delinquency Prevention. Washington, DC: U.S. Department of Justice.

U.S. Department of Education. (1999). *Twenty-first annual report to Congress on the implementation of Individuals with Disabilities Education Act.* Washington, DC: Author.

Part IV

Forensic Practice in Child Welfare

Child Welfare

Nora Smith

This chapter focuses on the child welfare system as an area of forensic social work practice. It provides an overview of the problem and major historical events related to the rise of child welfare services. Next, the common theories used, as well as the types of ethical and legal issues and practice settings involved in child welfare are reviewed. Lastly, recommendations for assessment, prevention, and treatment, including a case study, are presented.

Problem Overview

The child welfare system is a family-focused system. That is, the focus of child welfare in the United States is on the family unit because it is the most common place children are found to be at risk. Official statistics reveal that 80% of child maltreatment perpetrators are parents. Of the reported maltreatment, more than half (61%) were crimes of child neglect, with 58% caused by women (with 90.5% of parents being of biological status) and 42.2% by men (Children's Bureau, 2007).

Official statistics reveal that child maltreatment has affected many of our nation's children. According to these statistics, children are the subjects of child protective investigation at a rate of 48.3 per 1,000 children, with approximately 3.6 million cases investigated in the year 2005. Of the children investigated, approximately 25% (i.e., 899,000 children) of the cases were substantiated. This figure does not take into account the number of cases not reported and child abuse left undetected (Children's Bureau, 2007).

Children can be victims of different types of maltreatment, especially neglect. Of the 899,000 children abused, 62.8% experienced neglect, 16.6% were physically abused, 9.3% were sexually abused, 7.1% were psychologically maltreated, and 2% were medically neglected. The remaining 14.3% were victims of "other" types of maltreatment, for example, abandonment, threats of harm, or congenital drug addiction (Children's Bureau, 2007).

Child maltreatment also differs by gender and age. In 2005, girls made up 47.3% of those abused and boys 50.7%, with younger children more susceptible to abuse. Not included in these statistics are the number of children who died. During the year 2005, 1,460 children died from abuse or neglect. Of these children, 76.6% were under the age of 4 (Children's Bureau, 2007).

Children who come to the attention of child welfare services are at the risk of foster care placement. As of September 2005, there were 513,000 children residing in foster care in the United States. This number has more than doubled since 1982, when there were 243,000 children in care (Children's Bureau, 2007). Trends over the past 2 decades, including social and political trends, account for this dramatic increase and will be described in the text that follows.

System Overview

The Adoption and Safe Families Act (AFSA; 1997) encapsulates the U.S. policy for children in the United States who have experienced, or are at risk for, maltreatment in the form of abuse or neglect. This federal law guides each state in providing child welfare services, which refers to the specialized field of practice designed to prevent, protect, and care for children at risk or harmed, and for promoting their well-being and that of their families. AFSA identifies the goals of the child welfare system as (a) to protect children from harm, (b) to preserve existing families, and (c) to promote the development of children into adults who can live independently (Samantrai, 2004).

Child welfare services require a multidisciplinary system. As with many other service environments, various disciplines collaborate in child welfare, although there are often debates in terms of best practices. In child welfare, two schools of thought have developed based on the goals just mentioned. There are those who believe in child advocacy and those who work to strengthen and preserve the family. Child welfare specialists learn to find a middle ground; however, they are often presented with personal and professional value conflicts.

Overall, the field of child welfare demands that social workers have a strong sense of personal awareness. This awareness includes examining one's own beliefs while understanding the research on the price of child removal versus the provision of in-home services. This field of practice requires scholars to be open-minded and view both schools of thought, always striving for what Samantrai (2004) identified as the "goodness of fit" for the child and her or his family.

History of Child Welfare

The Rise of Child Welfare Services

Probably the best known case involving the welfare of a child that resulted in major system reform occurred at the turn of the 19th century. In the late 1800s, Mary Ellen Wilson was beaten repeatedly by her parents. At the time, there was no protective agency for children, therefore, concerned neighbors contacted the Society for the Prevention of Cruelty to Animals (SPCA). The efforts of the SPCA produced the Society for the Prevention of Cruelty to Children (SPCC), founded in 1874. By the beginning of the 20th century over 250 such agencies had developed across the country (Costin, 1985; Pecora, Whittaker, Maluccio, & Barth, 2000).

Our lack of a "service system in place" prior to the end of 19th century resulted in child welfare being the responsibility of community members. Abandoned and/ or abused children were commonly placed as agricultural laborers or domestic servants. For example, over 80,000 orphaned children were sent to Canada between 1828 and 1925 (Peikoff & Brickey, 1991; Samantrai, 2004). In essence, the practice of removing children from their families and communities stripped these youngsters of participating in society as a *child* but instead as a "worker" or "servant." The fate for children not yet old enough to work was equally dismal. Infants and toddlers were commonly placed in asylums. The conditions resulted in only a small percentage living beyond the first few weeks. For example, records indicate that 500 of 600 infants admitted to a Montreal foundling home in 1863 and 199 of 224 admitted to an asylum in Ottawa in 1883 died (Peikoff & Brickey, 1991).

The Roots of National and International Child Advocacy

The increased awareness of societal mistreatment of children in the early 20th century gave rise to the child advocacy movement. Child protection societies and SPCC chapters were sprouting across the country to protect children. Protection of the rights of children went beyond U.S. borders and became a globally recognized concern. In 1924, the League of Nations adopted the Declaration of the Rights of the Child. The principles set forth in the declaration set the stage for the conceptualization of child welfare policy in the United States: Children are to have a name and nationality at birth, adequate nutrition, housing, recreation, medical services, protection from all forms of neglect, abuse, and exploitation; children with physical, mental, or social handicaps have the right to special treatment, education, and care. This declaration also stresses that unless to the result of exceptional circumstances a child in her or his tender years shall not be separated from her or his mother. This declaration demands that children receive protection provided by the public authorities (Gross & Gross, 1977; Samantrai, 2004).

Protective Legislation for Children

This history of U.S. child welfare policy development includes the Social Security Act of 1935, the Child Abuse Prevention and Treatment Act of 1974 (CAPTA), the Adoption

Assistance and Child Welfare Act of 1980 (AACWA), and Adoption and Safe Families Act (ASFA) of 1997. The Social Security Act established that each state must have a plan for child protection; CAPTA set standards for prevention and treatment services. The AACWA worked to set standards for family preservation, reunification, foster care, and adoption; ASFA was enacted to further define and specify these standards, replacing the previous policy under the AACWA.

Current Trends in Foster Care Services

Since the 1980s, the foster care population has doubled in size, becoming a prominent part of child welfare service provision (Azzi-Lessing & Olsen, 1996; Carten, 1996; Pecora et al., 2000). Many families that come to the attention of child welfare present with a host of individual, family, and environmental factors, including poverty and homelessness, unstable housing, the lack of extended family and community support, limited role models for effective coping, and living in dangerous and crime-ridden neighborhoods (Carten, 1996; Tracy, 1994).

Inadequacies within the policy structure of the AACWA have been linked to the "oversizing" of the foster care system. AFSA was enacted in response to this crisis. Prior to AFSA, concerned citizens and policy advocates criticized child welfare policies that allowed children to "linger" in foster care. This was detrimental to children and their families because it impeded reunifications and adoptions (Azzi-Lessing & Olsen, 1996; Ellertson, 1994; Gustavsson & Rycraft, 1993).

Children from families at risk present a variety of issues. These families may have a host of needs that include family violence, sexual and physical abuse, and intergenerational patterns of involvement with social service systems (Bush & Sainz, 1997; Corse, McHugh, & Gordon, 1995; National Institute on Drug Abuse [NIDA], 1994). Children from substance-affected families are said to populate 80% of the child welfare system (Children's Bureau, 2007). The introduction of crack cocaine in the 1980s also had an impact in the increase of children in need of foster care (Azzi-Lessing & Olsen, 1996; Carten, 1996; Pecora et al., 2000). AFSA guides public policy for parents with substance-abuse issues and their children. Tighter legal restrictions have been enacted since the late 1990s regarding treatment and recovery. For example, parental rights are now terminated if a child is in foster care for longer than 15 months. Thus, practitioners treating families involved in the child welfare system must act quickly if efforts to reunify mother and child are to be made, considering the high rate of relapse and needs of women recovering from addictive drugs (Smith, 2006).

The Current Child Welfare Debate

Two important competing goals of child welfare policy, family preservation and child protection, continue to fuel the debate about child rights versus parental rights. Should efforts be made to preserve families, especially for mothers who use drugs? And, if so, where will these children go, who will adopt them? In an effort to help children who have been maltreated, U.S. laws also focus on permanence and the goal of finding stability and nurturance for each child (Samantrai, 2004). Therefore, this work begins with families who present at risk and the children who enter the system, and requires attention to both prevention and intervention efforts. With consideration of the major cause of child maltreatment and prevalence of relapse and difficult treatment processes, parental substance abuse must be a priority in this plan (Smith, 2002).

Research suggests there are obstacles for chemically dependent mothers, child welfare service providers, and substance abuse service providers regarding the obstacles within the child welfare system (Smith, 2002). In 1999, I conducted a qualitative study that examined the views of these participants regarding the obstacles for recovery and family reunification. Recommendations from these participants called for service improvement, including the infusion of a stronger family focus for family preservation services from the time of investigation through permanency planning. The participants also stressed the importance of specialized treatment for substance-affected families in the child welfare system. The importance of increased system coordination and communication between the child welfare and substance-abuse system was also strongly expressed by the mothers and service providers (Smith, 2002; Tracy, 1994).

The implications of this study support the use of family-centered theory in child welfare practice. Theories that explain child abuse and direct practice in child welfare are rooted in family-centered development and systemic intervention (Pecora et al., 2000; Rycus & Hughes, 1998; Samantrai, 2004). Service providers engaged in the child welfare system, whether directly or indirectly, must understand the importance of family-centered, culturally competent practice from investigation to the treatment and healing of the children and families served.

Relevant Theoretical Frameworks

Practice within child welfare occurs on a continuum from investigation to assessment to treatment. Because child welfare is a family-centered problem, a theoretical approach that often involves the family system is useful when examining the biological, psychological, social, environmental, and physical conditions of the child. There are many theories pertinent to each stage of the practice continuum with a family-centered, culturally competent lens needed to view the situation at all times (Pecora et al., 2000; Samantrai, 2004).

Systems theory, which is reviewed in chapter 3, is widely used in the practice and social planning of child welfare. Systems of care, and what are known as "wraparound services," work to address the biopsychosocial and cultural needs of children and families. Wraparound services link statewide services from medical assistance and mental health directly to child-service divisions and their specific populations. Moreover, wraparound services use collaborative treatment teams of professionals, caregivers, and community resources for each child and his or her family, working to meet their specific needs (Anderson, McIntyre, & Somers, 2004; Ferguson, 2007).

Attachment theory is another relevant theory for child welfare practice. The use of attachment theory, a developmental theory, is critical in the assessment of the child's current functioning, her/his development, and coping. Attachment theory also provides insight as to the bond and relationship between the child and his or her parent. Cultural competence in assessment is critical as the child's needs are determined, understanding the language and traditions of the child's life. Empowerment theory is another theoretical lens useful for practice in a child welfare setting. Kondrat (1995) described empowerment as a "metaframework," explaining how approaches and interventions work toward this goal. Solomon (1976) purported that empowerment-based approaches are useful toward reducing the effects of powerlessness that survivors of child maltreatment may experience.

Common Issues Across the System

The practice of child welfare includes many different service systems and professionals. Social workers, teachers, doctors, and lawyers are just some of the professionals who will have direct contact with children who are victims of abuse. Practice with families and children in the child welfare system necessitate a comprehensive plan of action. Resource accessibility to food, clothing, shelter, transportation, legal assistance, parenting training, medical care, and mental health services is needed in preparation for encounters with children and families in the child welfare system (NIDA, 1994).

A practitioner in this field can expect to have contact with several different types of social service organizations (e.g., legal and medical) in creating a comprehensive plan of action, once the safety of the child is established. When family preservation is the plan for the child and her or his family, the practitioner should become familiar with local resources for the family (e.g., 12-step meetings, other self-help programs, and outpatient counseling services).

Common Practice Settings

As previously stated, the child welfare system itself requires intervention along a continuum. Areas of practice along this continuum include prevention, protection, foster care, family reunification, adoption, family court, and treatment services for parent and child.

Types of Settings

Practitioners interested in the protection and healing process for maltreated children may begin with prevention work with "at-risk" children and families. Prevention can take place within a school-based or preschool program (e.g., Head Start). Practitioners may also work with young mothers in parenting-education programs toward the prevention of neglect, promoting healthy development for families with limited resources (Crosson-Tower, 2004; Pecora et al., 2000).

The most common practice setting in the child welfare system is protective services. Those working in child protection are case workers who investigate the first report of alleged child maltreatment, make permanency recommendations, and follow the case until, or if, closure takes place.

Types of Jobs

If a child is removed from his or her family's home, the child will be placed in temporary care, either foster care, kinship care, or residential care. (The latter is usually reserved for children with special needs or when foster care placements are not available.) Practitioners may work in these settings or work as the placement worker themselves. If the goal is to reunify the child with the family once the family has received treatment, practitioners may also work in the area of family reunification. Finally, there are settings for adoption specialists when reunification is not possible or parental rights are terminated (Rycus & Hughes, 1998).

Professionals Involved

The child welfare system is composed of many different types of professionals—from investigation and law enforcement officers, to protective caseworkers and social workers, to psychologists, and medical personnel. Other social work professionals working in substance-abuse treatment, domestic violence centers, public assistance, emergency rooms, and psychiatric hospitals will have frequent involvement with the child welfare system (Children's Bureau, 2007; Pecora et al., 2000). The system is complex and multidisciplinary—many fields of practice come together to assist children and their families.

Collaborative Teams

Purpose

Because of the enormous mix of disciplines involved, the level of complexity inherent in child welfare practice requires a strong collaborative team. The need for interagency coordination in child welfare has long been established and is now seen in the system of care and wraparound service model (Ferguson, 2007). It is crucial that all members of the treatment team work together from assessment to intervention. This collaboration is necessary whether working on family preservation, reunification, or the finalization of adoption proceedings (Azzi-Lessing & Olsen, 1996; Ellertson, 1994; Gustavsson & Rycraft, 1993; Pecora et al., 2000).

Team Members

State child welfare agencies have developed a system of care initiatives and wraparound service models using a team approach that includes family members, caregivers, community supports, and service professionals for each child and family. This system of care is built on the need for collaboration and interdisciplinary teamwork (Ferguson, 2007).

A model for collaboration and interdisciplinary teamwork for child welfare in our country is the National Children's Advocacy Center (NCAC). There are nearly 500 NCAC centers in the country, with more states working to develop county centers each year. The NCAC works to bring social service and criminal justice systems together under one roof to work with abused and neglected children. It houses most of the service continuum from investigation to counseling services. This type of center allows the child to have a safe and friendly environment to remain in while forensic and medical investigations take place, in addition to aftercare counseling and support. The center eliminates the need for the child to remain in police stations or emergency rooms during the investigation (NCAC, 2001).

The NCAC model adopts a "one place, one team, one coordinated response" plan (Monmouth County Child Advocacy Center, 2002, p.1). At the heart of the NCAC is a multidisciplinary team comprised of law enforcement, child protection, medicine, mental health, the prosecutor's office, and victim advocates (Kulman, 2001). The function of the multidisciplinary team is to provide the safest, most permanent plan for the child. The importance of coordinating one plan is critical for a successful outcome for the child.

Legal and Ethical Issues in Child Welfare Services

The child welfare system is driven by policy and procedure. The current policy that dictates practice is the ASFA. The steps toward legal action begin with the report of alleged abuse or neglect. Next, screening must be completed to determine the risk for the child. The family home or residential facility will receive a visit from the state child protective agency. During this stage, it is determined if the case needs investigation and assessment, or if the case should be closed. If the level of risk is justified to remove the child from the home, this may take place immediately (Olsen, 1996; Pecora et al., 2000).

Federal child welfare policy requires that each child have a uniform case record (UCR) that provides the investigative report, living conditions, and evaluation of the family's progress. This record is reviewed by a family court judge, who then makes a decision as to whether or not the family is ready to reunify, if foster care should continue, or if the child should be freed for adoption (Maluccio, Fein, & Olmstead, 1990).

ASFA worked to streamline this process so that more is required in the documentation of family progress, with tighter restrictions for families so that children do not languish in foster care. Elements of prior policy had been criticized for a lack of consistency and unclear guidelines for family-court judges, leaving children in foster care for long periods of time. States now have permission to enact termination of parental rights if a child is in foster care for more than 15 months.

The child welfare system has been in a state of reform over the past decade. For example, in New Jersey, after many years of heightened media attention, reform began with the death of 7-year-old Faheem Williams. A child familiar with the child welfare system, Faheem was found dead, stuffed in a plastic storage bin in Newark, New Jersey. A *New York Times* article written by Richard Lezin-Jones refers to Faheem's death as one that helped to point out the failures of New Jersey's Child Welfare System (Lezin-Jones, 2004).

It must be acknowledged that child welfare systems are always under scrutiny, where caseworkers are the ones who either "take children away" or don't and "cause their death." These are common, unfair critiques that make it hard to work directly in the system. Strong child advocates who remain and work in the system add to the success of positive outcomes for children. The temptation to leave this work because of the negative image is there, whereas the strength in those who remain proves their devotion and concern for the children in their care (Pecora et al., 2000; Rycus & Hughes, 1998).

Assessment, Prevention, and Intervention

Screening and Assessment Tools

Different states have different standardized measures for assessment. The core of assessment in child welfare practice is the federally mandated detailed UCR plan. This plan is based on the initial assessment for intervention and services to be provided for the child, the family, and, if necessary, the foster family if the child is removed (Samantrai, 2004).

The "goodness of fit" model presented by Samantrai (2004) covers the basis for how this assessment process is examined. As Samantrai indicates,

> What needs to be assessed then, is the "goodness of fit" between the child's needs and the parents' ability to meet those needs according to the prevailing norms of society at that particular point in their life. In each assessment, the questions the child welfare workers needs to ask himself/herself and answer are: "What does this child need—physically, emotionally, developmentally? Which of these needs can the parents meet adequately, which needs are they not able to meet adequately, and what kind of risk of harm does this pose for the child?" (p. 28)

The initial screening and interview of children who have been abused requires building safety and rapport. Bourg and colleagues (1999) recommended a neutral and friendly approach, in which the assessment avoids intense questioning and reactions that demonstrate shock and fear. Responses should be calm, nurturing, and supportive.

Resources

The "goodness of fit" model is an excellent resource for those working directly and indirectly in the child welfare system (Samantrai, 2004). Rycus and Hughes (1998) also provide excellent resources for screening and assessment. Their model emphasizes the investigation of the first report, visiting family homes, assessment of the home environment, establishing relationship, and what to look for in the provision of basic child-care skills, nurturing, discipline, and supervision. These authors communicate to first responders, such as the child protection workers, emergency medical professionals, and law enforcement officers. They also provide avenues of safety for the worker and considerations when visiting a home for the initial investigation. Included in these considerations are observation of the family member's demeanor, looking for substance abuse and behaviors of violence, positioning oneself for safety, including knowledge of exits in the home and anticipation of potential problems because family members usually are not welcoming and may display anger toward the investigator.

Psychosocial Assessment in Child Welfare

In addition to federally mandated child welfare investigations, child and family practice settings, whether privately contracted or community based, will also have their own models for intake and assessment. See examples of psychosocial assessments in

Appendices A and B. The Strengths-Based Psychosocial Assessment (Child Welfare and Community Populations and Settings) (Appendix A) is an example of a comprehensive assessment that can be used to assess children in their environment using a strengths-based empowerment approach. This model captures the direction of assessment, working toward empowerment in the intervention. The integration of theoretical approaches within the assessment and practice of child welfare previously described (e.g., family systems, attachment theory, and empowerment) are integrated within this psychosocial assessment (Bush & Smith, 2005). An example of a rapid psychosocial assessment that can be used with the offenders, such as the perpetrators of child maltreatment, is found in Appendix B.

Practitioner Skill Set

In an effort toward building competency in the practice of child welfare, several U.S. universities have partnered with each other toward the goal of building such competency, increasing the level of professionalism in the child welfare system. The emphasis on communication and skill sets revolves around competencies developed by evidence-based research models, for example, California Social Work Education Center (CalSWEC). The New Jersey Baccalaureate Child Welfare Education Program (BCWEP) (2006) is a consortium of undergraduate social work programs in New Jersey working in partnership with the New Jersey Department of Children and Families on enhancing recruitment and retention for caseworkers in public child welfare. Embedded in each student's learning plan are competencies that cover the cultural competence required in this field, as well as the necessary communication, practice, writing, and case management skills. This model also has a focus on advocacy and collaboration, in addition to components of legal and expert testimony necessary in forensic practice (Falk, 2005).

VOICES FROM THE FIELD

Raymond Olszewski, Jr.
Licensed Master of Social Work, Diplomate in Forensic Social Work, Forensic Evaluator

Agency Setting

I am employed at the Assessment and Resource Center (ARC) in Columbia, South Carolina. The ARC is a nationally accredited Child Advocacy Center (CAC) through the National Children's Alliance. We are an outpatient clinic specializing in child abuse evaluation and treatment. The ARC is funded and supported with cooperation from several public entities, including the South Carolina Department of Mental Health, the University of South Carolina Medical School–Department of Pediatrics, and the Children's Hospital of Palmetto Richland Memorial Hospital.

Practice Responsibilities

As a forensic evaluator I conduct forensic interviews of suspected child-abuse victims. Our referrals come exclusively from law enforcement and child protective services agencies in and around Columbia, SC. I conduct these interviews in response to allegations of all types of child maltreatment, including sexual abuse, physical abuse, neglect, and witness to all of the above. I also conduct other specialized forms of child interviewing, including witness to homicide and other violent acts. These interviews are conducted using a nationally recognized and defensible interviewing protocol known by its acronym, RATAC (Rapport, Anatomy identification, Touch inquiry, Abuse scenario, and Closure). Ideally interviews are observed by the specific case investigators assigned to that case and subsequently the cases are discussed at our regularly scheduled multidisciplinary team (MDT) case-review meetings. I am currently the MDT coordinator and have been in that capacity for 10 years. I have responsibility for putting together the meeting agenda and facilitating the meeting itself.

Expertise Required

There is no specific degree requirement for this job. In my agency alone, interviewers come from a variety of educational backgrounds, including psychology, social work, rehabilitation counseling, and drama therapy. Degrees in our office range from master's to doctoral. But I know of competent interviewers who have only a bachelor's degree. There is also no certification for this type of work. There are many week-long basic and advanced interview-training courses offered at the state and national level around the country. The majority of these courses are good and provide frontline professionals with the basic skills needed to conduct competent child forensic interviews. Much of what I learned was from on-the-job training, learning from other seasoned interviewers and from attending as many child-interview-related workshops and trainings as I could.

Practice Challenges

The field of child forensic interviewing is relatively new and is still evolving. Much has changed in the 10 years I have been working in this field. One of the biggest challenges is staying current in the field and paying attention to new and developing trends. We have recently identified a growing number of cases that fall under the maltreatment category of pediatric condition falsification (PCF). These are cases that involve a caregiver's intentional fabrication of child-abuse allegations to obtain some self-serving desired outcome (such as sole custody). What we are finding is that these cases are time intensive and require a sophisticated approach in both the child interview and in the rendering of opinion.

Another practice challenge faced by anyone in this field is burnout and the potential for vicarious trauma. The subject matter we deal with on a daily basis is difficult, depressing, and demoralizing. It is a real challenge to create an environment that allows and encourages well individuals to remain in the field. I have found that the use of humor is the main thing that sustains me in this profession. Without the sort of "MASH" mentality that exists in our clinic, for me the job would not be doable.

Common Legal and/or Ethical Issues

In my position I am frequently involved with legal professionals in the legal process. Our interviews are intended to assist in the investigation of some crime, so it follows then that we are often called as witnesses when these cases come to trial. I have testified as both an expert and lay witness in numerous family and criminal court proceedings, including a court martial. One of the challenges we face is the constant education of attorneys, judges, and juries in child-abuse issues. Much work can go into pretrial preparation and the filing of motions to make the child's courtroom experience less threatening and more beneficial to the tryer of fact.

Brief Description of Collaborative Activities With Professionals and/or Other Stakeholders

As described earlier I am the coordinator of our local multidisciplinary response team, which meets on a regular basis to conduct case reviews of cases currently under investigation in our local jurisdiction. The case reviews are attended by personnel from the core agencies involved in the investigative process. This includes the specially assigned prosecutor, the law enforcement detective assigned to the case, the child protective services worker assigned to the case, the forensic pediatrician, the forensic interviewer, and the victim advocate. We discuss the cases in detail, make plans for follow-up work, and track the cases until their dispositions.

I am also the co-author of our local MDT-response protocol, which outlines the procedures various agencies will follow in the investigation of a child-abuse complaint.

Additional Information

Individuals who are interested in this type of work should interact with children as much as possible. There is a great deal to learn from just being around children and learning about how they communicate and what they are capable of. Along with this experience, there is a need for some formal education about child development and the dynamics of child abuse and trauma in general. It is essential to have an interest in the legal system and a willingness to participate in both the investigation and prosecution of child abuse.

Case Study

Based on the models of assessment and intervention described here, the following case is presented for analysis and critical thinking. The setting of this case takes place in a substance-abuse treatment center that offered family-reunification services for mothers who were abusing substances and found to be neglecting and/or abusing their children. This is the case of Patty, whose name and identifying information have been changed for reasons of confidentiality.

Patty was referred to the Rensselaer Addiction Center (RAC) by the County Child Protective Service Agency (CPS). Patty was reported to CPS by a neighbor who noticed that she would leave her 16-month-old son alone in the evening. One early morning the neighbor broke into Patty's home after hearing the baby cry for hours. She immediately called the authorities who found the baby weighted down in his crib by a dirty diaper, unfed, and dehydrated. Drug paraphernalia was also found in the home, leading to the discovery of Patty's ongoing addiction to cocaine.

Patty's son (Jake) was removed from the home and Patty was charged with child maltreatment. She was mandated to substance-abuse treatment, weekly drug screening, and a mental health evaluation.

On admission to the RAC, a comprehensive psychosocial assessment was completed, evaluating her own family history, childhood development, and factors that led to her substance abuse. Jake entered a family foster home and remained with them throughout the investigation and reunification attempt. The goal for Patty and Jake was to work toward family reunification, which would entail recovery for Patty, parent–child visitation, and a plan for aftercare and support. Patty's recovery was extremely complex. In addition to her cocaine dependence, she was also diagnosed with borderline personality disorder and posttraumatic stress disorder.

Patty's treatment took place before New York state had enacted ASFA, so the timeframe for Patty to reunify was not limited to the 15-month restriction. Patty had several relapses, was referred to two different inpatient and detoxification centers, and aftercare back at the RAC. After 3 years, Patty was able to remain drug-free for 6 months and was ready for a dispositional hearing in the family court system to work toward a stronger plan for reunification. In the meantime, Jake had built a relationship with his foster family but still wanted to return to his mother. As Patty's primary counselor, the author worked to prepare a plan of aftercare and support for Patty that included employment and career planning, self-help meetings, housing, and parenting education. Patty was preparing for her hearing and displayed considerable anxiety as the date grew closer.

The hearing began at 9 a.m. with all of the collaborative teams present, including attorneys, the child-welfare caseworker, the foster parents, a representative from the substance-abuse treatment provider, the family court judge, and Jake. Patty was late. All parties, including Jake (now 5), were waiting in anticipation. A discussion between the foster parents and the attorneys took place, and they expressed their desire to adopt Jake. At 9:45, the judge announced that we would wait for an additional 15 minutes; however, because this was Patty's last hearing before termination of parental rights would be considered, he was not pleased. A few minutes later Patty arrived. It was apparent that she was in her clothes from the night before; she proceeded to sabotage the hearing. She was under the influence and as a result her parental rights were terminated.

Patty later revealed that she felt she could not be the parent Jake deserved but could not admit to this. Jake's foster parents adopted him and he was still able to visit with his mother. Patty returned to her recovery program and remained sober in an effort to continue her supervised visitation with Jake. One year later, Patty was discharged from the RAC and successfully reached her treatment goals.

Although this case appears to be a failure, there were many elements of success. This is typical of child-abuse cases, in which the course of intervention is complex. The policy components of ASFA now work to prevent ongoing long-term foster-care placements and would have worked to expedite this process for Patty and Jake. This case illustrates the ethical dilemmas and conflicts for parents in the system, in addition to the split loyalties for children who often want to be with their biological parents despite the crimes they have committed.

This case is an excellent example of how practice occurs on many different levels, across many different continuums and spectrums, with the knowledge of both policy and intervention skills crucial toward the success of such cases.

Acknowledgment

This chapter is dedicated to the lives and memories of the two children mentioned in this chapter, Eliza Izqueirdo and Faheem Williams. It is presented in celebration of those child welfare service providers who remain strong and devoted to the care of abused children, like Virginia Kenny, BSW, MSW, of New Jersey.

References

Adoption and Safe Families Act. (1997). Pub. L. No. 105-89, 111 Stat. 2115, codified as 42 USCA § 1305 note.

Adoption Assistance and Child Welfare Act. (1980). Pub. L. No. 96-272, 94 Stat. 500, codified as amended, 42 USCA § 670 et seq.

Anderson, J. A., McIntyre, J. S., & Somers, J. W. (2004). Exploring the experiences of successful completers of a system of care for children and their families through case narratives. *Journal of Family Social Work, 8*(1), 1–25.

Azzi-Lessing, L., & Olsen, L. (1996). Substance abuse impacted families in the child welfare system. *Social Work, 41,* 15–24.

Baccalaureate Child Welfare Education Program. (2006). *Competency based learning plan.* Retrieved May 9, 2007, from http://www.stockton.edu/~falkd/BCWEP.htm

Bourg, W., Broderick, R., Flagor, R., Kelly, D. M., Ervin, D. L., & Butler, J. (1999). *A child's interviewer's guidebook.* Thousand Oaks, CA: Sage.

Bush, I., & Sainz, A. (1997). Preventing substance abuse from undermining permanency planning: Competencies at the intersection of culture, chemical dependency and child welfare. *Journal of Multicultural Social Work, 5*(2), 78–97.

Bush, I., & Smith, N. (2005). The Monmouth University psychosocial. In K. Ward & R. Sakina-Mama (Eds.), *Breaking out of the box* (pp. 77–86). Chicago: Lyceum Books.

Carten, A. (1996). Mothers in recovery: Rebuilding families in the aftermath of addictions. *Social Work, 41,* 214–224.

Child Abuse Prevention and Treatment Act. (1974). Pub. L. No. 93-247, 88 Stat. 4 codified as amended, 42 USCA § 5101 et seq.

Corse, S., McHugh, M., & Gordon, S. M. (1995). Enhancing provider effectiveness in treating pregnant women with addictions. *Journal of Substance Abuse Treatment, 12*(1), 26–41.

Costin, L. B. (1985). The historical context of child welfare. In J. Laird & A. Hartman (Eds.), *A handbook of child welfare: Context, knowledge, and practice* (pp. 53–76). New York: Free Press.

Children's Bureau. (2007). *Child maltreatment 2005.* U.S. Department of Health & Human Services. Washington, DC: U.S. Government Printing Office.

Crosson-Tower, C. (2004). *Exploring child welfare: A practice perspective.* Boston: Allyn & Bacon.

Dickerson, J. (1995, May 10). Clintonites rescue drug addicted mothers. *Atlanta Journal,* Sec. A, p. 7.

Ellertson, C. (1994). The Department of Health and Human Services needs a major overhaul. *Children & Youth Review, 16*(5/6), 21–30.

Falk, D. (2005). *BCWEP competency based learning plan.* Retrieved on May 11, 2007, from http://www.stockton.edu/~falkd/BCWEP.htm

Ferguson, C. (2007). Wraparound: Definition, context for development, and emergence in child welfare. *Journal of Public Child Welfare, 1*(2), 91–113.

Gustavsson, N., & Rycraft, J. (1993). The multiple service needs of drug dependent mothers. *Child & Adolescent Social Work Journal, 10,* 84–106.

Gross, B., & Gross, R. (Eds.). (1977). *The children's rights movement*. New York: Anchor Press.

Kondrat, M. E. (1995). Concept, act, and interest in professional practice: Implications of an empowerment perspective. *Social Service Review, 5*, 405–428.

Kulman, D. (2001, May 18). Prosecutors to establish child advocacy center. *Two River Times*, p. 34.

Lezin-Jones, R. (2004, January 4). Child fatality and the New Jersey child welfare system. *The New York Times*, p. A34.

Maluccio, A. N., Fein, E., & Olmstead, K. A. (1990). *Permanency planning for children: Concepts and methods*. New York: Routledge, Chapman, & Hall.

Monmouth County Child Advocacy Center. (2002). *Brochure: Friends of the Monmouth County Child Advocacy Center, Inc*. Freehold, NJ: Author.

National Children's Advocacy Center. (2001). Retrieved May 16, 2007, from http://www.nationalcac.org

National Institute on Drug Abuse [NIDA]. (1994). *Women and drug abuse. NIDA Capsule Series* (C-94–02). Washington, DC: Author.

Olsen, L. J. (1996). Assessing risk in families affected by substance abuse. *Child Abuse & Neglect, 20,* 18–27.

Pecora, P. J., Whittaker, J. K., Maluccio, A. N., & Barth, R. P. (2000). *The child welfare challenge: Policy, practice and research*. New York: Aldine de Gruyter.

Peikoff, T., & Brickey, S. (1991). Creating precious children and glorified mothers: A theoretical assessment of the transformation of childhood. In R. Smandych, G. Dodds, G. Dodd, & A. Esau (Eds.), *Dimensions of childhood: Essays on the history of children and youth in Canada* (pp. 29–62). Winnipeg: University of Manitoba Legal Research Institute.

Rycus, J. S., & Hughes, R. C. (1998). *Field guide to child welfare*. Washington, DC: Child Welfare League of America.

Samantrai, K. (2004). *Culturally competent child welfare practice*. Pacific Grove, CA: Brooks/Cole.

Smith, N. (2002). Reunifying families affected by maternal substance abuse: Consumer and service provider perspectives on the obstacles and the need for change. *Journal of Social Work Practice in the Addictions, 2*, 33–53.

Smith, N. (2006). Empowering the "unfit" mother: Increasing empathy, redefining the label. *Affilia, 21*, 116–125.

Social Security Act. (1935). 49 Stat. 620.

Solomon, B. B. (1976). *Black empowerment: Social work in oppressed communities*. New York: Columbia University Press.

Tracy, E. M. (1994). Maternal substance abuse: Protecting the child, preserving the family. *Social Work, 39*, 117–131.

Forensic Interviewing for Child Sexual Abuse

13

Kenneth J. Lau
Eileen C. Treacy

This chapter focuses on a methodology for conducting forensic interviews for children who may have been sexually abused. The typical social work interview allows trained and licensed social workers to assess and identify a family member's strengths and needs as well as to develop a service plan with the family. This broad, versatile approach incorporates the use of a variety of interviewing techniques. Social work interviewing is used at every step of the child welfare process, from intake through case closure; it is used with individuals and groups as well as children and adults.

Although the forensic interview employs some of the same techniques as the social work interview, such as open-ended and multiple choice questions, the *forensic interview* is much more focused. Traumatization can occur each time a child relates an abuse incident he or she has experienced, or in false-allegation cases when a child is coached. This is why forensic interviewing is so appealing; it fits well with efforts to safeguard and enhance child well-being and the social work code of ethics, which prohibits social workers from causing harm to their clients. Because the social work profession often lacks education and training in investigative interviewing and legal prosecution in child-abuse cases, additional training is required for forensic interviewers in these areas.

Review of Literature on Forensic Interviewing

The goal of the forensic interview with children is to obtain a narrative of what the child heard and observed during alleged abuse (Gudjonsson, 1992). Since the 1980s, the child welfare system has embraced the forensic interview because it promised to be a tool that would help them investigate reports of child maltreatment and keep children and families safe. In child-sexual-abuse cases, skillful forensic interviews are important to ensure the protection of innocent individuals and the conviction of perpetrators of abuse. Studies have examined several factors that influence disclosure during interviews, including both interviewer and child characteristics (Lamb & Edgar-Smith, 1994; MacFarlane & Krebs, 1986). Numerous interviewing techniques have received attention in the literature, including allegation-blind interviews, open-ended questioning, and cognitive interviewing, the Touch Survey, truth–lie discussions, and use of anatomical dolls (Cronch, Viljoen, & Hansen, 2005).

Recent studies have examined instruction in forensic interviewing, such as structured-interview protocols and the extended forensic evaluation model (Carnes, Nelson-Gardell, Wilson, & Orgassa, 2001; Conte, Sorenson, Fogarty, & Rosa, 1991; Poole & Lamb, 1998). In addition, the Child Advocacy Center (CAC) model has been established as a strategy to prevent repeated child interviewing, as well as an effort to ensure that legitimate cases move forward for prosecution, whereas nonlegitimate cases do not. CACs provide a safe, child-friendly atmosphere for children and families to receive services (Cronch et al., 2005).

In its guidelines for investigative interviewing in cases of alleged child sexual abuse, the American Professional Society on the Abuse of Children (APSAC, 1997) stated that "Investigative interviewing in cases of alleged abuse requires specialized knowledge. This knowledge can be acquired in a variety of ways (e.g., formal course work, individual reading, workshops and conferences, professional experience and supervision), and should include familiarity with basic concepts of child development, communication abilities of children, dynamics of abuse and offenders, categories of information necessary for a thorough investigation, legally acceptable child interviewing techniques, and the use of interview aids (such as drawings or anatomical dolls). Specialized knowledge is especially important when young children are interviewed" (APSAC, 1997, p. 2).

The child welfare system's focus is on children's safety, well-being, and permanency, as well as supporting families. Although punishment of child abusers is not the primary goal, many people do view the conviction of offenders as a positive community outcome. Therefore, although it is reasonable to ask whether forensic interviewing results in more prosecutions and convictions of child abusers, there is not yet a sufficient amount of research to provide a clear answer to this inquiry (Cross, Jones, Walsh, Simone, & Kolko, 2007).

What Is Forensic Interviewing?

"The forensic interview is an essential component of the fact-finding process in cases of physical and sexual abuse. The goal of the interview should be to obtain a statement from a child in a developmentally sensitive, unbiased, and truth-seeking manner that will support accurate and fair decision-making in the criminal justice and child welfare systems" (New York State Children's Justice Task Force [NYSCJTF], 2002, p. 2). The forensic interview is not and should not be part of a treatment process. In fact, professionals who have an ongoing or a planned therapeutic or casework relationship with the child should not conduct the forensic interview or an extended forensic interview.

> *A forensic interview should be child-centered. Although the interviewer directs the flow of conversation through a series of phases or steps, the child's abilities should determine the vocabulary and specific content of the conversation as much as possible. The forensic interviewer must be alert to developmental differences in language and memory and never assume what a child means by the use of a particular word. For example, "oral sex" might mean talking about sex. Therefore, the interviewer should clarify potentially ambiguous words or phrases. Similarly, the interviewer must make certain to use words and concepts that the child understands. (NYSCJTF, 2002, p. 2)*

Reports or allegations of child physical and sexual abuse are reported to child protective and law enforcement agencies from many different sources. Reports can be generated from family, neighbors, and friends or they can be reported to the local agencies by mandated reporters. Once a report is accepted by the investigating agency, an investigator from law enforcement and, when appropriate, a child protective worker will be assigned to conduct the investigation. When more than one agency is involved, it is critical that the investigators work using a multidisciplinary team (MDT) approach when conducting forensic interviews. Both the law enforcement investigator and the child protective investigator need to be appropriately educated and trained in conducting joint forensic interviews. They need to understand each other's roles and responsibilities throughout the investigation.

If possible, before beginning a forensic interview, the investigators should speak with the reporting source. From that discussion, the investigators should determine the context and environment of the initial abuse concerns and verify the accuracy of the initial report. The source may also provide additional information not contained in the report. Prior to conducting the forensic interview, the investigators should identify other hypotheses that might explain the allegations. By doing this, the investigators maintain open minds throughout the investigation, including during the actual interview of the alleged victim. If the investigators explore a single hypothesis, they might only focus their efforts at "proving" that hypothesis. Not only is this a poor investigative technique, it is not in the best interest of the child if that hypothesis proves to be inaccurate.

During the actual forensic interview, the interviewer should attempt to rule in/out alternative explanations for the allegations that were identified after receiving the initial report. For example, when a child uses terms that may indicate sexual touching, the interviewer should assess the child's understanding of those terms and explore whether the touching might have occurred in the context of routine care-taking or medical treatment. When a child reports details that seem inconsistent, it is the interviewer's responsibility to clarify whether the events described could have occurred by exploring whether more than one event is being described or whether words are being used in an idiosyncratic way. For example, "Daddy touched my privates with his finger and it hurt" could have a number of explanations: the child complained of "pee pee" hurting and Daddy asked to see where it hurt and touched the area; Daddy was applying cream for a severe rash, or Daddy touched the child for sexual reasons.

The Forensic Interviewer

There are a number of methods used for child-abuse investigations, including: child-advocacy centers, formal multidisciplinary team investigations, informal multidisciplinary investigations, parallel investigations (i.e., when CPS and law enforcement conduct separate investigations), and individual agency investigations. Although the qualifications of potential interviewers in each setting may vary, there are some basic criteria to consider in choosing who should conduct child interviews. Social workers often play a key role whether they are practicing as a CPS investigator, CAC employee, or mental health expert. A key factor contributing to a successful forensic interview is the interviewer's comfort in interacting with children. Although this quality alone does not guarantee a successful interview, tension conveyed by an interviewer who is uncomfortable with children will be difficult to overcome and may impede the establishment of rapport and an open line of communication with the child. Training in social work provides many of the skills needed to successfully interview children who have been victims of serious abuse. The forensic interviewer should also have knowledge of the following: child-interviewing techniques, child development, child-abuse dynamics and effects, legal issues regarding child witnesses, and cultural issues affecting abuse interviews/investigations (APSAC, 1997; Bourg et al., 1999; Sattler, 1998; Sorenson, Bottoms, & Perona, 1997). The interviewer should be able to articulate the source(s) of that training, education, and experience because the professional's training education and experience will be introduced as part of the qualifications of the interview if the case goes to court. The forensic interviewer needs to be flexible to allow for differences across interviews, as well as behavioral and emotional changes that may occur during an interview. The interviewer needs to be patient and able to adapt to the child's pace. The interviewer also must be able to maintain objectivity, including the ability to prevent personal and professional biases from entering into or affecting the interview.

The forensic interviewer needs the skills to interview children in a nonleading and nonsuggestive fashion. The forensic interviewer must avoid introducing information or suggesting events that have not been mentioned by the child. In addition, the interviewer should not project adult interpretations onto situations and use comments such as "that must have been frightening." Many child sexual abuse cases have no medical evidence, no physical evidence, and no witnesses other than the child and the perpetrator of the abuse. Thus, decision making in these cases must, in part, depend on the child's disclosure, corroboration, and the fact pattern of the case. False disclosures or denials of child abuse may occur, and forensic interviewers require tools to help them distinguish false allegations from valid allegations of abuse (NYSCJTF, 2002).

Backgrounds and professions of the individuals who conduct forensic interviews vary from community to community, and from investigation to investigation. Sometimes, they are conducted only by child welfare workers in the field; sometimes an extended forensic interview is conducted by a therapist, or other specially trained professional, in a controlled, child-friendly environment.

Interview Location

The forensic interviewer often prefers to conduct these interviews in a neutral setting. Although expedient, "improvised" settings (e.g., the child's home or school) may not be ideal. A child's ability to recall past events is significantly influenced by his/her surroundings. The best practice in forensic interviewing is identifying a location that is neutral, reassuring, and child-friendly. Child advocacy centers (CACs) and child abuse assessment centers (CAACs) can be excellent locations for forensic interviewing. The CAC offers a comfortable room with children's furniture, toys, interviewing props, and other aids for observing and documenting interviews.

Research completed by Joa (2004) illustrated the benefits of using a CAAC when conducting forensic interviews. In the research project, 50 children who were seen at the CAAC were matched on age and relationship to the perpetrator with 51 children who were not evaluated at a CAAC to determine whether the groups differed in legal outcomes in cases of sexual abuse. The results indicated that the CAAC children were significantly more likely to have court cases filed, to have more overall counts charged, to have more counts charged against biological fathers and stepfathers who were alleged perpetrators, and to have a greater number of defendants pleading or being found guilty compared to cases involving children not seen at the CAAC. There were also significantly more cases filed for 4- to 6-year-olds and children at least 12 years old if they were seen at the CAAC.

The National Children's Advocacy Center (NCA) Guidelines for Interviewing Children in Cases of Alleged Sexual Abuse (Annon, 1994) recommends that only one person should interview the child. The only people in the room should be the child and the interviewer, unless there is a compelling need to do otherwise. There are advantages and disadvantages to both single-interviewer and team (e.g., child protection and law enforcement) approaches. On the one hand, children may find it easier to build rapport and talk about sensitive issues with a single interviewer. Other team members may ensure that a broad range of topics are covered, thus reducing the need for multiple interviews. When two professionals are present in the room, it is best to appoint one as the primary interviewer, with the second interviewer taking notes or suggesting additional questions as the interview is drawing to a close. Interviewers should not discuss the case in front of the child. Seating the second professional out of the line of sight of the child or in an observation room may make the interview seem less intrusive and confrontational.

At times, the presence of social support persons during forensic interviews might be necessary if the child is not willing to talk with the interviewer. Although it makes intuitive sense that children might be more relaxed with a support person present, studies have failed to find consistent or great benefits from allowing a support person in the room (Davis & Bottoms, 2002).

Purpose of a Forensic Interview

It is critical that the forensic interviewer talk with the child in a safe, child-focused environment to determine if he or she has been physically or sexually abused. In addition to yielding the information needed to make a determination about whether abuse has occurred, this approach produces evidence that will stand up in court if the investigation leads to civil (i.e., family) or criminal prosecution. Properly conducted forensic interviews are legally sound in part because they ensure the interviewer's objectivity, employ nonleading techniques, and emphasize careful documentation of the interview.

A goal of the forensic interview is to facilitate the child's accurate recall of events. Every opportunity is provided to obtain the child's account of what transpired. This is done by beginning with the most general, "open ended" phase of the interview and then proceeding to more narrow forms of questioning when required. The interviewer must demonstrate patience and allow the interview content to come from the child.

Why Are Forensic Interviews Needed?

Many perpetrators of sexual abuse deny the abuse when questioned by investigators. As a result, the alleged victim's statement is critical because, in many cases, there are no witnesses or physical evidence of abuse perpetrated on the child. Yet developmental issues, such as children's varying abilities to recall events and use language, as well as the trauma they may have experienced, complicate efforts to obtain information about the abuse. The forensic interview is designed to overcome these obstacles. Another goal of the forensic interview is to obtain a statement from a child in an objective, developmentally sensitive, and legally defensible manner (Davies et al., 1996). To ensure that facts are gathered in a way that will stand up in court, forensic interviews are carefully controlled: the interviewer's statements and body language must be neutral, alternative explanations for a child's statements are thoroughly explored, and the results of the interview are documented in such a way that they can bear legal scrutiny.

Most state laws require that, once child protective services accepts an allegation that a child has been physically or sexually abused, a child protective investigator must have timely face-to-face contact with the child. During this meeting, the investigator assesses safety and determines whether steps need to be taken to ensure the child's immediate well-being. Forensic interviewing can be quite useful at this juncture. It should be noted that law enforcement investigators do not have the same time-related mandates requiring that they must conduct timely interviews when it comes to interviewing the alleged victim of abuse. One of the objectives of forensic interviewing is to reduce the number of times that children are interviewed. The concern is the possible contamination of the child's memory of the alleged incident(s) being investigated. Research and clinical experience indicate that the more times a child— especially a young child—is interviewed about alleged abuse, the less reliable and legally defensible that child's testimony may become (Sattler, 1998).

Conducting the Forensic Interview

The forensic interview is a crucial tool in child welfare. Forensic interviewing is often the only way the authorities can learn enough to make a fact-based determination of whether child abuse has occurred. Forensic interviewing can also yield information child protective workers need to build a safety plan for a child and to support the child's family.

Forensic interviewing is important as it brings child welfare agencies together with other community and state agencies. Because forensic interviewing is often used in combination with a multidisciplinary response to child maltreatment, it helps professionals learn about each other's roles and how the larger system serving families and children operates. It enables these professionals to see that, despite differences in their missions, human services and law enforcement agencies share two common goals: fostering healthier, safer relationships for children and preventing further exploitation and harm. Because forensic interviews can play a pivotal role in investigations of sexual and severe physical abuse of children, social workers need to know how they are conducted.

Cultural Considerations

"Culture is one of the filters that people use to interpret life experiences. Culture is different from race or ethnicity. It is not based on the skin color, but accumulative life experiences" (NYSCJTF, 2002, p. 34). Culture encompasses many different factors: language, family structure, socioeconomic status, gender and gender roles, moral and religious values, traditions, history, parenting practices, sexual attitudes, tolerance level for emotionalism, and individual versus group orientation. Recent research indicates that members of different cultural groups may respond differently to children's disclosure of sexual abuse (Feiring, Coates, & Taska, 2001). A child's cultural background may also affect the child's appraisal of the abusive experiences (e.g., level of self-blame) and the level of social support that the child may receive. Furthermore, the manner in which emotionality may or may not be expressed is also related to culture and ethnicity.

In forensic interviewing, the interviewer should explore: family structure (e.g., extended, nuclear, single), gender-role expectations, child-care practices, financial management of the household, reasons for immigration, level of contact with family in the country of origin, religious belief systems, social networks, and attitudes about sexual violence (NYSCJTF, 2002). Interviewers need to integrate these cultural concerns into the interview process. Very often, the factors that make it more difficult for some children to disclose sexual abuse are culturally related (e.g., gender-role expectations). Cultural issues may also contribute to the likelihood of a recantation. Language proficiency is another important consideration for the interviewer. It should never be assumed that English is a universal language understood by all children. Ideally, children should be asked what language they speak at home, as well as what language they would prefer to use. In sex-abuse investigations, it would not be appropriate to use another family member or neighbor for the purpose of translation. Translation, in and of itself, raises additional considerations and therefore, the selection of an interpreter should be a thoughtful and deliberate process rather than a haphazard practice of simply finding someone who speaks the child's language.

Forensic Interview Models

There are many ways to conduct forensic interviews, and there is no single model or method endorsed unanimously by experts in the field. Some of the many forensic interviewing models in use today are the Child Cognitive Interview, Step-Wise Interview, Narrative Elaboration, A Model Child Abuse Protocol–Coordinated Investigative Team Approach developed by the State of Michigan's Children's Justice Task Force (Governor's Task Force, 1998), and the New York State Children's Justice Task Force Forensic Interviewing Best Practices Guidelines (NYSCJTF, 2002). Like many of the others in existence, these five interview models have been shown to be more effective in helping children recall information than standard interviewing techniques.

There are, however, some basic elements common to most forensic interviews, which usually include phases to the interview, such as an introduction, rapport-building, developmental assessment (including learning the child's names for different body parts), guidelines for the interview process, competency assessment (where, among other things, it is determined whether the child knows the difference between lying and telling the truth), narrative description of the event or events under investigation, follow-up questions, clarification, and closure (Cordisco & Carnes, 2002).

Sexual-Abuse Dynamics and the Accommodation Syndrome

The nature of the sexual abuse affects the manner in which the child relates the abuse. As mentioned previously in this chapter, the forensic interviewer needs to have a strong background in child development and an understanding of trauma in children. It is helpful if she or he has training and understanding of sexual-abuse dynamics (Sgroi, 1982) and the child sexual abuse accommodation syndrome (CSAAS; Summit, 1983). Understanding the sexual-abuse dynamics and the accommodation syndrome helps forensic interviewers to be attentive to the possible modus operandi of the offender and the impact of that modus operandi on the child (e.g., the differential impact of a sadist offender vs. a more seductive offender).

Although there is a great deal of consistency between the sexual-abuse dynamics and the CSAAS, understanding and integrating both constructs into the interview process is extremely helpful to the forensic interviewer. The dynamics are especially useful when exploring the child's relationship with the alleged perpetrator before/during/after the abusive relationship. The accommodation syndrome sensitizes the interviewer to the trauma a victim of abuse might experience and assists the interviewer in understanding delayed or conflicting disclosures, how children cope with ongoing abuse, and why they sometimes retract their allegations. It is also useful to prosecutors, who may wish to introduce expert testimony about the syndrome and to explain delayed disclosure or child behaviors that may be confusing (e.g., a false denial, which is a child who initially denies the allegations even though he was sexually abused).

Sex-Abuse Dynamics

There are five phases to sex-abuse dynamics: engagement, sexual interaction and progression, secrecy, disclosure, and suppression. Understanding these phases will help the forensic interviewer frame the interview with the alleged victim. It is important for the forensic interviewer to know that most often there is a preexisting relationship between perpetrator and victim. The offender could be a parent, relative, teacher, coach, or neighbor. As a result, the relationship between the child and the perpetrator may have developed over a period of time. This period is called the engagement phase.

Engagement Phase

This is a phase during which a perpetrator can manipulate the potential victim. In some instances, it may mean providing physical or emotional attention to a child who may otherwise not be receiving sufficient affection from other caretakers. The perpetrator may engage in nonsexual physical contacts, such as wrestling, horse-play, having child sit on his/her lap, or lying down with the child. The perpetrator can also misrepresent societal norms about physical contact (i.e., manipulates the child's own natural curiosity about sexual issues). Some perpetrator strategies during the engagement phase may include the use of pornography and erotica such as nudist magazines or computer-generated stimuli. In this phase, the offender must gain access and opportunity to the child, establish him/herself in a trusted authority position over the child, and begin the process of breaking down the child's inhibitors about sex.

Sexual Interaction/Progression Phase

When the interaction between the child and the perpetrator crosses the line into sexualized behavior, this is called the sexual interaction and progression phase. Often, perpetrators will start with hands-off behaviors using noncontact offenses (e.g., verbal comments about sex, pornography, exposure, masturbation). Then, the perpetrator may engage in minimally intrusive hands-on behaviors (e.g., touching or "accidental" touches, fondling, kissing) and, in some instances, the perpetrator may engage in oral contact. The rationale for this type of behavior is that they do not create physical trauma and the child does not have to disrobe. Many perpetrators want to believe that they are not hurting the child and have the distorted belief that the child wanted to engage in these sexual behaviors. The perpetrator may monitor the child's reactions making sure not to frighten the child and, as a result, the child may not resist.

It should be noted that, for some perpetrators, sexual gratification is achieved by the hands-off behaviors, including fondling and touching. For others, there may be further progression of sexual acts overtime. Sexual gratification may result in further progression of the sexual acts over time, depending on the perpetrator's access and opportunity to the child and the perpetrator's sexual interests. The perpetrator may initially progress into oral and/or anal penetration by using objects, fingers, or other body parts. Other perpetrators may vaginally penetrate the child. In terms of the longevity of the sexual progression, it may range from a short period of time to an extended time period.

Secrecy Phase

The perpetrator must rely on the child maintaining secrecy about the sexual behaviors. The secrecy phase often starts soon after, or overlaps with, the sexual-interaction phase. The perpetrator may use various strategies to ensure that the child keeps the "secret." With younger children, there is often less need for the perpetrator to use direct or overt threats. It may be just a simple statement like, "This is our little secret." In addition, victims often feel self-blame for the sexual abuse and this may make it more difficult for them to disclose.

With older children, especially if the abusive behavior has increased in frequency over time, there may be more direct threats (e.g., "if you tell, you will end up in foster care," or "no one will believe you," or "people will blame you and hold you responsible," or the perpetrator may use a direct threat of violence). There are many strategies that perpetrators use to get children to keep the secret. It is important for forensic interviewers to explore issues related to secrecy when interviewing a child. Many victims of sexual abuse never disclose their abuse (Finkelhor, 1984). Some may not label their experiences as "abuse," others may be too frightened to disclose, others blame themselves, whereas others may fear negative outcome for the offenders or other family members (Goodman-Brown, Edelstein, Goodman, & Jones, 2003).

Disclosure Phase

In the disclosures phase, it is important for the forensic interviewer to understand the different types of disclosures: (i.e., *purposeful* and *accidental*). A purposeful disclosure occurs when the victim specifically discloses to others information related to the abuse. The disclosure could be to a friend, family member, or a mandated reporter (e.g., therapist). In these cases, the interviewer should explore what motivated the child to disclose at this particular time. Some of the reasons for a purposeful disclosure include concern for a younger sibling, desire to escape from family pressure, not wanting to engage in the sexualized behavior any more (i.e., fear of getting pregnant), or an age-appropriate desire for increased independence. In purposeful disclosures, inquire about the reason(s) the child made the disclosure.

Accidental disclosures may arise in a number of ways, including observations of the actual sexual abuse by a third party, physical injury to the child, sexually transmitted disease and/or pregnancy, age-inappropriate sexual behavior, another child's disclosure, and a parent/caretaker may report suspicions of possible abuse by another party. In accidental disclosures, the child may be ambivalent about giving information and fearful of consequences of disclosure.

Suppression Phase

The final phase is the suppression phase. In light of the disruption that is often seen after the disclosure, the child may question whether it was wise to make the disclosure. The child may attempt to limit or retract the disclosure because of both *internal* and *external* pressure. The internal pressure may be demonstrated by the child's feelings of guilt, self-blame, disloyalty to family, fear of threats coming true (e.g., no food, financial problems, foster care), feelings of concern for the perpetrator, or fear of loss of love and family.

The external pressure for suppression may result from a number of different factors, including the anger and other emotions that siblings and family members express to the child, threats from the perpetrator, the child's perception that the perpetrator is no longer a threat, disbelief of the sexual abuse by family members, and/or the child being removed from the home and wanting to return to the family. Often, it is best to view the suppression as a wish by the child that the family could return to a prior level of functioning.

Child Sexual Abuse Accommodation Syndrome

There are also five phases to the accommodation syndrome: secrecy; helplessness; accommodation and entrapment; delayed, conflicted, or unconvincing disclosure; and retraction and recantation (Summit, 1983).

Secrecy

This is similar to the dynamics of secrecy previously described, but Summit (1983) explains how the perpetrator often develops strategies that promote some degree of responsibility in the child for the victimization, for example, "If you tell, *we* will get into trouble." The child may look to the trusted adult to label the sexual behavior, which results in the experience being both a source of fear and a promise of safety. The perpetrator may convince the child to believe that everything will be alright if the child does not talk about the sexual contact with anyone.

Helplessness

In society children are expected to listen to adults who have positions of authority. Research continues to indicate that a large percentage of children are abused by people with whom they have a preexisting relationship (USDHHS, 2007). Children who are abused may feel that they cannot do anything to break out of the pattern of ongoing abuse. It is important to note that children do not have equal power with the offender or adequate understanding of the consequences of the behavior. This is even true with adolescents. While the abuse is happening, some children become passive, nonresponsive, and depressed. They may not take advantage of opportunities that others view as chances for them to escape the abuse, because often children perceive the perpetrator as being all-knowing and all-powerful. The perpetrator, in turn, may see the uncomplaining or sexually curious child as consenting.

Accommodation and Entrapment

In the accommodation phase, a child learns strategies to cope with the repeated acts of abuse. These strategies often include isolation, promiscuity, suicidal thoughts, dissociation, substance abuse, multiple personalities, self-destruction, mutilation, and aggressive behavior (Summit, 1983). The child may adapt positive behaviors, such as excelling in school and receiving good grades. The child's safety is contingent on these strategies for maintaining some degree of mental health.

Delayed, Conflicted, or Unconvincing Disclosure

The child is often ambivalent about whether to disclose, perhaps out of confusion and/or fear. The child often perceives she or he has the responsibility to either destroy or preserve the family (Goodman-Brown et al., 2003). Children may "test the waters" by providing a partial disclosure, then give more information if s/he feels believed and safe. The child may give unconvincing disclosures by providing information in a "matter of fact" or conflicted manner. Children often delay disclosing until they feel ready and safe.

It is important for forensic interviewers to remember that disclosure is a process that often happens over time (Sorensen & Snow, 1991). Children may be more likely to disclose if they feel less loyalty to the offender (e.g., mom's boyfriend vs. biological father) (Elliot & Briere, 1994). Children in foster care may disclose prior sexual abuse in their family of origin because they feel safe and do not have ongoing contact with the perpetrators (Gries, Goh, & Cavanaugh, 1996).

Retraction and Recantation

Forensic interviewers need to be aware that some children will retract valid allegations for a number of different reasons. The child may feel that the perpetrator has "learned the lesson" and no longer poses a threat. The child may miss the perpetrator, who often is otherwise an active, supportive parent or parent figure. As a result, a child might see retraction as a way to return the family to a more comfortable lifestyle and end the emotional suffering of other family members. In some instances, a recantation may be valid, as the original allegations were untrue (i.e., a true recantation).

Summary and Conclusions

The forensic interview is a critical component of a child-abuse investigation. Forensic interviewers should have knowledge and training about child development, cultural considerations, the legal requirements of child protective services and law enforcement prosecutions, sexual-abuse dynamics, as well as being able to rule in/out other rival explanations for the child's statements and behaviors other than abuse. The Forensic Interviewing Best Practice Example provides a step-by-step methodology to conducting such interviews and can be found in Appendix D.

References

American Professional Society on the Abuse of Children. (1997). *Guidelines for practice.* North Charleston, SC: Sage.

Annon, S. J. (1994). Guidelines for interviewing children in cases of alleged sexual abuse. *Issues in Child Abuse Accusations, 6*(3). Retrieved February 16, 2007, from http://www.ipt-forensics.com/journal/volume6/j6_3_2.htm

Bourg, W., Broderick, R., Flagor, F., Kelly, D. M., Ervin, D. L., & Butler, J. (1999). *A child interviewer's guidebook.* Thousand Oaks, CA: Sage.

Carnes, C. N., Nelson-Gardell, D., Wilson, C., & Orgassa, U. C. (2001). Extending forensic evaluation when sexual abuse is suspected: A multisite field study. *Child Maltreatment, 6,* 230–242.

Conte, J. R., Sorenson, E., Fogarty, L., & Rosa, J. (1991). Evaluating children's reports of sexual abuse: Results from a survey of professionals. *American Journal of Orthopsychiatry, 61,* 428–437.

Cordisco, S. L., & Carnes, C. N. (2002). *Child centered forensic interviewing.* Retrieved May 1, 2005, from http://www.ispcan.org

Cronch, L. E., Viljoen, J. L., & Hansen, D. J. (2005). Forensic interviewing in child sexual abuse cases: Current techniques and future directions. *Aggression and Violent Behavior, 11,* 195–207.

Cross, P., Jones, L., Walsh, W., Simone, M., & Kolko, D. (2007). Child forensic interviewing in Children's Advocacy Centers: Empirical data on a practice model. *Child Abuse and Neglect, 31,* 1031–1052.

Davies, D., Cole, J., Albertella, G., McCulloch, L., Allen, K., & Kekevian, H. (1996). A model for conducting forensic interviews with child victims of abuse. *Child Maltreatment, 1,* 189–199.

Davis, S. L., & Bottoms, B. L. (2002). The effects of social support on the accuracy of children's reports: Implication for the forensic interview. In M. L. Eisen, J. A. Quas, & G. S. Goodman (Eds.), *Memory and suggestibility in forensic interview* (pp. 437–457). Mahwah, NJ: Lawrence Erlbaum.

Eliot, D., & Briere, J. (1994). Forensic sexual abuse evaluations of older children: Disclosures and symptomatology. *Behavior Science and the Law, 12,* 261–277.

Feiring, C., Coates, D. L., & Taska, L. S. (2001). Ethnic status, stigmatization, support, and symptom development following sexual abuse. *Journal of Interpersonal Violence, 16,* 1307–1329.

Finkelhor, D. (1984). *Child sexual abuse new theory & research.* New York: Free Press.

Goodman-Brown, T., Edelstein, R., Goodman, G., & Jones, D. (2003). Why children tell: A model of children's disclosure of sexual abuse. *Child Abuse & Neglect, 27,* 525–540.

Governor's Task Force on Children's Justice Subcommittee. (1998) *A model child abuse protocol.* State of Michigan, Department of Human Services DHS-Publication number 794. Retrieved February 15, 2008, from http://www.michigan.gov/documents/dhs/DHS-Pub-794_206830_7.pdf

Gries, L., Goh, D., & Cavanaugh, J. (1996). Factors associated with disclosure during child sexual abuse assessment. *Journal of Child Sexual Abuse, 5,* 1–20.

Gudjonsson, P. N. (1992). *The psychology of interrogation, confessions, and testimony.* West Sussex, UK: Wiley.

Joa, D. (2004). Legal outcomes for children who have been sexually abused: The impact of child abuse assessment center evaluations. *Child Maltreatment, 9,* 263–276.

Lamb, S., & Edgar-Smith, S. (1994). Aspects of disclosure: Mediators of outcome of childhood sexual abuse. *Journal of Interpersonal Violence, 9,* 307–326.

MacFarlane, K., & Krebs, S. (1986). Techniques for interviewing and evidence gathering. In K. MacFarlane & J. Waterman (Eds.), *Sexual abuse of young children* (pp. 67–100). New York: Guilford Press.

New York State Children's Justice Task Force. (2004). *Forensic interviewing best practices.* Albany, NY: New York State Office for Children and Families.

Poole, D., & Lamb. M. (1998). *Investigative interviews of children: A guide for helping professionals.* Washington, DC: American Psychological Association.

Sattler, J. M. (1998). *Clinical and forensic interviewing of children and families.* San Diego: Jerome M. Sattler Publishing.

Sgroi, S. (1982). *Handbook of clinical intervention in child sex abuse.* Lexington, MA: Lexington Books D.C. Heath.

Sorenson, E., Bottoms, B. L., & Perona, A. (1997). *Intake and forensic interviewing in the children's advocacy center setting: A handbook.* Washington, DC: National Network of Children's Advocacy Centers.

Sorensen, T., & Snow, B. (1991). How children tell: The process of disclosure in child sexual abuse. *Child Welfare League of America, 70,* 3–15.

Summit, R. (1983). The child sexual abuse accommodation syndrome. *Child Abuse and Neglect, 7,* 177–193.

United States Department of Health and Human Services. (2007). *Child maltreatment (2005).* Retrieved August 4, 2006, from http://www.acf.hhs.gov/programs/cb/pubs/cm04/index.htm

Part V

Forensic Practice in Mental Health and Substance Abuse

Mental Health and Addictions: Legal and Ethical Issues for Practice

14

Carolyn Bradley
Kelly Ward

Since the inception of the profession, social workers have been at the forefront of providing services to people with mental health and/or addiction problems and their families. Therefore, it is not surprising to find that in the 21st century, social workers are the major providers of mental health and addiction services in the United States. Thus, it is imperative that social workers be aware of the best practices, and, especially, the legal and ethical issues affecting this important and ever-growing practice area.

Scope of the Problem

Mental illness and addictive illness are nondiscriminatory diseases (Frances, Miller & Mack, 2005). Social workers working with individuals with mental health and/or addictions issues need to be cognizant that these illnesses may be present in persons regardless of age, sex, race, socioeconomic level, educational level, sexual orientation, or religion. The National Institute of Mental Health (NIMH; 2008) estimates that 26.2% of Americans over the age of 18 (approximately 58 million adults) are diagnosed with a mental illness every year. Although many people are diagnosed, only about 6% suffer from serious mental illness. In 2006, the Substance Abuse and Mental Health Services Administration (SAMHSA) estimated that 22.6 million Americans (9.2% of the population age 12 or older) were abusing or dependent on some type of substance (alcohol or drugs). In that same year, 2.5 million people received treatment for a substance-abuse illness (SAMHSA, 2006).

Overview of the Field of Practice

Social workers have been involved in the delivery of services to persons with mental illness and/or addictive illness and their families since the development of the profession at the turn of the 20th century. From the time of the friendly visitors and the settlement house movement (the very first social workers), social workers have provided prevention, education, identification, and intervention services to individuals dealing with these illnesses (Richmond, 1917). In addition, they have advocated for more humane treatment, parity of care with other medical illnesses, and guarantees of confidentiality regarding treatment to increase participation in rehabilitation.

Social workers participate in service delivery within this area across the fields of practice. From direct service as counselors to policymakers and researchers, the mental health/addictions field is an area in which social work is actively involved.

Since the late 1980s, the mental health/addictions area of social work practice has experienced a rapid growth in the demand for services and concomitant rapid changes in service delivery systems. With the increase of demand for services have come the advent of managed care and the development of many new powerful pharmacological interventions. Both of these changes have greatly affected the method of service delivery in both mental health and addictions.

Relevant Theoretical Frameworks

Many approaches may be used when working with persons with mental illness and/ or addictive illness and their families. For the purposes of this section, mental health approaches will be discussed first, then addictions, and finally approaches for working with co-occurring disorders. In addition, the social worker needs to be aware of the need for consulting with a physician (or, preferably, a psychiatrist) when a pharmacological intervention is required.

In considering social work intervention with persons with mental illnesses, three major theoretical frameworks are most frequently used: systems theory, cognitive-behavioral theory, and psychodynamic theory (Walsh, 2006). These frameworks are adapted into treatment modalities that address specific issues and/or populations. A review of the literature will provide the practitioner with information regarding the best practices use of each framework. The use of the framework should be based on a careful assessment of the presenting issue and the functional level of the client.

In working with persons with addictive illnesses, any of the previously mentioned theoretical frameworks might be considered. However, current best practices frequently use motivational interviewing (Miller & Rollnick, 2002), systems theory, or cognitive-behavioral therapy. The selection of the theoretical framework should be dictated by a careful assessment of the client's substance use. Often a self-help program such as one of the 12-step programs or SMART Recovery is used as an adjunct. Twelve-step programs (e.g., Alcoholics Anonymous, Narcotics Anonymous, Al-Anon, and Nar-Anon) use a mutual-help model based in spiritual fellowship. The SMART Recovery model, which is also a mutual-help model, uses a cognitive-behavioral framework. All of these programs are available to persons in community, hospital, and correctional settings. Twelve-step programs are available throughout the world.

Persons dealing with co-occurring disorders (mental illness and addictive illness) require careful assessment to determine the most appropriate level of intervention, which includes the selection of the theoretical framework to be used. All of the frameworks mentioned earlier for use with mental illness and addictive illness are likely to be considered. Persons within this population usually require consultation with a physician for a pharmacological evaluation (Peterson, Nisenholz, & Robinson, 2003).

Common Issues

Social workers working in the field of mental health and/or addiction recovery services often encounter similar issues and problem areas. In the area of service delivery, problems encountered include waiting lists for treatment, the ability to obtain required medications, and, with managed care companies, level-of-care authorizations. In the area of clinical issues, nonadherence to treatment plans and subsequent relapses are common, so too are acceptance of illness, medication compliance, attendance at 12-step meetings, and denial of a problem.

Common Practice Settings

Mental health and addiction issues arise in a variety of settings. Social workers practicing in medical settings, courts or correctional facilities, or schools are likely to encounter persons with mental and/or addictive illnesses.

Mental health and addictions services have similar settings from least restrictive to most restrictive but may call them different names depending on what area of the country you are practicing in. These settings, from least restrictive to most restrictive, are self-help groups (only), outpatient care, intensive outpatient care, inpatient care, extended care (e.g., state hospitals, minimum 1-year residential care drug rehabilitation), prison inpatient programs, and aftercare (halfway house, group home, intensive case management). Most practitioners in the fields of mental health, addictions and MICA (mentally ill, chemically abusing) clients recommend self-help groups for the individuals as well as their family and friends. The level of care is based on the severity of the illness.

Social workers who choose to work in mental health or addictions could find themselves with many tasks to complete on behalf of the agency, client, or client's family. These activities include, but are not limited to, advocacy, prevention, assessment, intervention, education, treatment, and/or case management. Regardless of the setting, the social worker must pay attention to the human rights of the clients as well as to provide the best care possible. Social workers will often function as part of interdisciplinary teams providing services to persons with mental and/or addictive illnesses. Depending on the setting, these teams may be made up of medical doctors, nurses, addiction counselors, psychologists, corrections officers, or school personnel (e.g., guidance counselors or child study team personnel). As a member of such teams, social workers may function in various capacities and perform a variety of functions. Social workers may be responsible for assessment, intervention, education, prevention, case management, and/or advocacy services.

Interagency work frequently occurs on behalf of clients. Such work might include contact on behalf of clients with probation or parole officers if your client is involved in the legal system. Educational personnel may also request information. All contacts with outside agencies require consent.

Legal and Ethical Issues

Providing services to persons with mental and/or addictive illnesses requires the social worker to be aware of legal and ethical guidelines that govern practice with these populations. Specifically, providers need to be aware of confidentiality regulations and ethical considerations, informed-consent guidelines, duty-to-care/warn considerations, and licensure/credentialing regulations.

Confidentiality

Persons seeking services for mental and/or addictive illness are often deterred from pursuing treatment because of concerns regarding confidentiality. Practitioners using a social work model are aware of the ethical and legal importance of maintaining confidentiality. Confidentiality is mandated by the NASW *Code of Ethics* (1996), in state laws regarding privileged communication, and in federal HIPAA regulations (see below).

Practitioners in mental health/addictions need to be aware of the impact of age and cognitive functioning when advising clients regarding how confidentiality matters will be handled. The client's right to confidentiality means a practitioner will not divulge any information that the client shares *unless* one of the following exceptions occurs: harm themselves, harm someone else, or when child abuse is involved. The "unless" is known as the *duty to warn*, which will be discussed after we explain confidentiality more fully. The confidentiality extends to the treatment team, therefore sharing information with a member of the team is acceptable, but the client should know the bounds of the confidentiality.

Substance-abusing/dependent clients have historically been difficult to treat for many reasons. One of the impediments to treatment was fear of sharing past history with a practitioner because of possible legal ramifications. In addition, if there was a fear that the social worker could breach confidentiality, the individual with a substance-abuse problem would not seek assistance even when ready to halt substance use. However, social workers providing services to persons with addictive illness are required to follow stricter, federally mandated guidelines regarding disclosure of information. The Drug Abuse Prevention, Treatment and Rehabilitation Act (21 U.S.C. 1175) contains provisions regarding confidentiality for persons seeking rehabilitation services for addictive illness (U.S. Department of Health & Human Services [HHS], 1987). The specific requirements of the Act are provided in section 42 of the Code of Federal Regulations, Part 2 (CFR). These regulations are commonly referred to by addictions counselors as the "federal confidentiality regs" or as "42 CFR-2." These provisions apply to direct-service practitioners and program administrators. These provisions direct how information may be released, to whom it may be released, and when it may be released. It also recommends that clients be informed in writing about limitations to confidentiality.

Social workers working in employee assistance program (EAP) settings with clients seeking addiction recovery services should also be aware of provisions of the Americans with Disabilities Act (ADA) (Public Law 101-336 [42 U.S.C. Sec. 12101]). Provisions within ADA may pertain to clients with addictive illness who are referred for services through EAPs.

Duty to Warn

At times, mental health and addictions professionals are exposed to clients who may be dangerous to other people. Not until the court case of *Tarasoff v. Board of Regents* (1976) did any legislation exist that defined the obligation to report such danger. In *Tarasoff*, a University of California student told his psychologist that he was going to kill his ex-girlfriend. The psychologist alerted the campus police who talked to the student. He denied his intention. The girl, Tatiana Tarasoff, was murdered. The Tarasoff family filed a lawsuit claiming that their daughter should have been notified of the threat. The family won the case. As a result, mental health workers are now obligated to report a client's intent to harm to the potential victim. This "duty to warn" provides an exception to the oath of confidentiality and is applicable to all counseling profession-als in 48 states (the exceptions are Maryland and Pennsylvania) (Lowenberg, Dolgoff, & Harrington, 2000). In making a decision whether to use the duty to warn, the social worker must identify a threat of violence against a specific identified victim.

Voluntary and Involuntary Commitment

The *Tarasoff* decision also raises issues for social workers as to when commitment may be necessary. Commitment in most states may be voluntary or involuntary. "Voluntary" means that the client may sign himself or herself into a psychiatric facility.

Occasionally a client will present a threat to him/herself or others but is not willing to accept the treatment being offered (usually an inpatient psychiatric unit). In this case to keep the client and others safe, an involuntary commitment is necessary. Every state has different procedures for how an involuntary commitment is performed. This process always involves at least a psychiatrist and another doctor. An involuntary commitment has a time limit. The client must go before a judge, who then determines if commitment is still warranted and should be extended or if the client may released. For example, in the state of New Jersey, an involuntary commitment requires three doctors, one of whom must be a psychiatrist, and the hearing must be held in front of a judge within 72 hours.

Informed Consent

Most states mandate that health professionals obtain informed consent for treatment. The concept of informed consent is consistent with social work values and ethics because it underscores the client's right to self-determination (Reamer, 2006).

Social workers, whether working in mental health or addictions, need to be aware of the elements that must be covered when creating an informed-consent document (Levin, Furlong, & O'Neil, 2003; Munson, 2002). Areas to be considered are:

- risks/benefits/discomforts;
- alternative approaches, including medications;
- a statement regarding limitations of confidentiality and maintenance of records;
- emergency contact information;
- voluntary participation (unless mandated);
- fees and accepted methods of payment;
- issues regarding early withdrawal from treatment;
- theoretical framework, treatment philosophy, and methods.

Practitioners who work with persons with mental and/or addictive illnesses must consider the functional level of the client when obtaining informed consent. Issues such as impaired cognitive capacity resulting from trauma, chronic substance use, or dementia may interfere with obtaining consent. Additional factors to consider in this area are the age of the client and cultural issues.

Duty to Care

It is imperative in the mental health/addictions field that social workers conduct a thorough, careful assessment on persons seeking services. Such an assessment is necessary to determine the appropriate level of care for the client. It is the social worker's duty to determine what type and what level of service a client requires.

In the field of addiction treatment, social workers often determine level of care based on the American Society of Addiction Medicine Patient Placement Criteria, commonly referred to as the ASAM Criteria (http://www.asam.org/Frames.htm). These are national guidelines that address placement, length of stay, and discharge criteria for persons with addictive illness.

HIPAA

The Health Insurance Portability and Accountability Act of 1996 (HIPAA) has created many privacy agreements that extend to mental health and addictions professionals (HHS, 1996). The purpose of this Act is to further protect a client's privacy in the age of technology while improving reimbursement for providers. Most agencies will include this information in new-employee orientations and explain their privacy policy and the forms associated with the HIPAA policy.

Assessment and Intervention

An important skill for social workers working with mental health and substance-abuse clients is to accurately and quickly assess the client to determine the diagnosis and how to best intervene. In the process of conducting an assessment the social worker must be able to determine the severity and duration of symptoms. This may lead to a specific diagnosis or addictions screening. It is essential when completing an assessment to screen for indications of suicidality, particularly in correctional facilities where the primary focus is not on mental health. Suicide screening instruments are usually integrated into depression screening instruments.

When conducting an assessment for mental or addictive illness, the social worker needs to assess for appropriate developmental milestones to ensure the client is functioning age appropriately. Cultural factors should also be considered. No one social worker can be an expert in every culture, therefore it must be recognized that the client is the expert regarding his or her specific culture. However, the social worker must be culturally sensitive at all times and elicit from the client how culture informs the presenting problem.

Care needs to be taken in writing any assessment report as it is used to determine what happens next in the client's life. Assessment reports are taken seriously by other professionals.

There are a variety of assessment scales and forms available.

Additional Web sites with screening and assessment tools (all sites retrieved August 21, 2008):

- Massachusetts General Hospital School of Psychiatry
  http://www.massgeneral.org/schoolpsychiatry/screeningtools_table.asp
- Cincinnati Children's Hospital Medical Center: list of free tools for children
  http://www.cincinnatichildrens.org/svc/alpha/c/special-needs/resources/mental-health.htm
- Abuse Screening Instruments
  Adolescent Substance: http://slp3d2.com/rwj_1027/webcast/docs/screentest.html
- National Clearinghouse on Families and Youth
  http://www.ncfy.com/publications/satools/index.htm
- Assessment scales for Juvenile Justice System
  http://www.ncjrs.gov/pdffiles1/ojjdp/204956.pdf
- Minnesota Multiphase Personality Inventory
  http://www.pearsonassessments.com/clinical/adult.htm
- National Institute of Mental Health: http://www.nimh.org
- National Institute on Alcohol Abuse & Alcoholism
  http://pubs.niaaa.nih.gov/publications/arh28-2/78-79.htm
- National Clearinghouse for Alcohol & Drug Information
  http://ncadi.samhsa.gov/
- Substance Abuse & Mental Health Service Administration
  http://coce.samhsa.gov/cod_resources/PDF/ScreeningAssessment(OP2).pdf
- Federal Confidentiality and Substance Abuse law
  http://www.access.gpo.gov/nara/cfr/waisidx_02/42cfr2_02.html

Licensure/Credentialing Requirements

Provision of clinical social work services is governed by licensure in all 50 states. The level and type of care that may be provided is stipulated in the licensure regulations. Social workers should consult their specific licensing board to determine the levels of practice within their states.

States have also begun to license and/or credential counselors providing services to persons with addictions issues. Practitioners should consult with their rerspective state's regulatory boards for information specific to their region.

Practitioner Skill Set

Social workers working in the areas of mental health or addiction recovery need excellent verbal and written language skills. Much of the work required in both of these practice areas involves keeping clear, concise treatment notes and generating written summaries of client's progress.

When working in these areas, social workers need to be aware of the professional jargon used within each area. Although not all social workers may agree with the use of the medical model in treating clients with mental illness, the universal language of the mental health industry in the United States is the *Diagnostic and Statistical Manual of Mental Disorders* (DSM-IV-TR; American Psychiatric Association, 2000). Familiarity and ease of use of this classification system is necessary when working in any mental health setting. If working in addiction settings, use of the *DSM-IV-TR* and knowledge of the ASAM criteria are an asset.

Unless working solo as a private practitioner, most social workers providing services in mental health and/or addiction recovery will be working on interdisciplinary teams. The ability to collaborate, negotiate, and advocate for your discipline's approach are important interpersonal skills. As was stated previously, sound assessment skills are essential when working in these practice areas. An integral part of assessment skills is cultural competence. Most, if not all, social work programs in the United States address this area. Misdiagnosis in mental health and addiction cases can easily occur if the social worker is not aware of the role of cultural nuances in a client's presenting behavior.

Social workers practicing in these areas may be called on to present expert testimony in either civil or criminal proceedings on behalf of a client who is being treated. Report writing for this purpose should be concise, focused on the issue before the court, and use current diagnostic language. Consulting a supervisor and/or an attorney may be helpful. It is important to be aware of the type of written consent required by the client to release such information. Records can be subpoenaed by court. Always check with an attorney knowledgeable about the release of confidential records before responding to the subpoena (see chapter 4 for more information).

VOICES FROM THE FIELD

Lisa Taylor-Austin, NCN, LPC, LMHC, Certified Forensic Mental Health Evaluator Psychotherapist, Forensic Expert Witness, Forensic Mental Health Evaluator

Agency Setting

I currently own a private practice and business located in Connecticut.

Practice Responsibilities

As a psychotherapist I provide counseling to children, adolescents, and adults dealing with issues of loss, depression, anxiety, identity, relationships, and decision making. When working with patients, making a diagnosis, writing treatment plans, obtaining insurance authorization, and keeping a detailed medical record are also required.

As a forensic mental health evaluator I am available to perform comprehensive mental health evaluations on individuals involved in the criminal justice system and on private citizens who are not court involved. Interviewing clients, performing the MMPI-2 and other assessments, report writing, and collaboration with attorneys is required.

As a forensic expert witness I testify in criminal cases across the United States involving death penalty, murder, RICO, gang enhancements, and so on. This work involves reading discovery, interviewing the defendant, conferring with counsel, reviewing case notes, written reports, and providing testimony on the stand.

Written reports are required when completing mental health evaluations and when working on legal cases. Often these reports become court documents that are part of discovery and the legal record.

Expertise Required

A minimum of a master's degree in social work or counseling is required. Licensure and certification are also required. In addition, experience in the legal arena is necessary. When working as an expert witness one must possess an unusually high level of skill, knowledge, and experience in a specific area.

Practice Challenges

Challenges include being self-employed and not having a regularly scheduled paycheck/income.

Common Legal and/or Ethical Issues

It is mandatory to have a neutral approach in this work. All facets require professional observation and assessment, as well as an unbiased view of the client/patient.

Brief Description of Collaborative Activities
With Professionals and/or Other Stakeholders

I work with attorneys (defense and prosecution), psychiatrists, medical personnel, and criminal justice professionals on a regular basis.

Additional Information

My advice for those seeking this work is to complete a minimum of a master's degree, obtain hands-on experience in the legal arena, take courses in criminal street gangs, and have first-hand experience working with gang members. For more information, my Web site is www.gangcolors.com.

Jackie

The case study that follows exemplifies both mental health and addictions issues. The case demonstrates the intersections of multiple systems and levels of assessment and treatment necessary to serve the client best.

Jackie, a 42-year-old, White, single, lesbian female presented for outpatient treatment because friends reported concern regarding her drinking. Jackie reported that she drank at least two six-packs of beer nightly. This level of consumption had occurred for the last 3 years according to her self-report. Friends were concerned that Jackie was often so intoxicated at night that she was unable to speak coherently on the phone.

Jackie reported that she began drinking at around age 11 or 12 by sneaking drinks of various types of wine from her parents' liquor cabinet. Also at around this period, Jackie reports that she became very defiant with her parents and ran away from home on numerous occasions. Subsequently, between the ages of 14 and 18, Jackie was hospitalized for psychiatric treatment and treated with antipsychotic medications.

At the time of intake, client had not been involved in any type of psychiatric care and had not been on medication for at least 8 years. Client was employed full time and had a social support network of friends. She was estranged from her family. She attributed the estrangement from her family as a result of their inability to accept her sexual orientation as a lesbian.

Initial sobriety was obtained in 6 months of individual, outpatient treatment and participation in the fellowship of Alcoholics Anonymous. Jackie was unable to sustain sobriety. It became apparent by Jackie's inability to maintain sobriety that a psychiatric disorder might be present. Closer investigation of the reason for drinking at night revealed that client suffered from "nightmares" that would awaken her and then she would be unable to return to sleep. The nightmares were so disturbing in content that client often awoke sweating and screaming.

Over time in working with the client it was revealed that she had been sexually abused by a family friend, a priest, at age 11. The drinking and running away from home were coping mechanisms as her parents refused to believe Jackie when she told her story of the abuse. Jackie was emotionally and physically abused by her father in response to her accusations of sexual abuse. Jackie did not seek mental health or addictions treatment until she was in her 30s. She did not admit to the sexual abuse until her early 40s and it was not in her best interest (based on her current health status) to pursue legal action against the priest when she was an adult. Diagnosis was revised to include posttraumatic stress disorder (PTSD), dissociative amnesia, and alcohol dependence.

A psychiatric consult was obtained for medication evaluation. As treatment progressed with a PTSD specialist, psychiatric hospitalization became necessary because of suicidal ideation with an executable plan. On discharge from inpatient treatment, supportive services were provided through integrated case management services (ICMS).

Sustained sobriety was achieved through outpatient PTSD treatment, outpatient alcoholism counseling, psychiatric consultation for medication, and participation in the fellowship of Alcoholics Anonymous.

Jack

Jack is 32-year-old, single, White, male employed full time as a salesman for a snack distributor. Jack presents to intensive outpatient treatment (IOP) secondary to a conviction for driving while intoxicated.

Jack reports the use of substances since age 14, when he began drinking. During high school, he reports that he also used marijuana. Jack entered the Navy upon graduation from high school. While in the Navy, he reports the use of alcohol only. Jack went to college after discharge from the Navy. While in college, Jack reports that in addition to using alcohol and marijuana, he experimented with cocaine. He reports that he never smoked "regular" cigarettes. At the time of entering IOP, Jack reports that he is only using alcohol.

Jack is resentful of his conviction for driving while intoxicated. He reports that he was stopped at a roadblock, not for any irregularities in his pattern of driving on the highway. He feels he was able to safely operate his vehicle in spite of registering a .25 on the breathalyzer test (.08 is the legal limit in most states).

Jack reports that this is not his first drunk-driving incident. When he was in the Navy, he was involved in a "minor fender bender" that involved rear-ending another vehicle at a traffic light. That incident was "fixed' by the Navy and did not result in a court hearing. As a result of that incident, which occurred at age 20, Jack reports that he now knows his limit when he drives.

In group sessions, Jack is sarcastic and defensive. He makes it clear that he feels that he does not belong in this program. He reports that he is attending on the recommendation of the counselor at the intoxicated driver resource center (IDRC), to which he was court ordered.

In individual sessions, Jack is witty and evasive. He tries to distract conversation from focusing on his use. Knowledgeable about current affairs and history, he exerts great effort in trying to change the topic to world affairs.

In obtaining a detailed history, it is noted that Jack's drinking significantly increased while in the Navy. Jack served aboard a nuclear submarine while in the Navy. Reluctantly he shared some of the incidents aboard the submarine involving mechanical malfunctions and deaths of shipmates. He reports that he still experiences nightmares from those years. While in the Navy, Jack's drinking went from partying on the weekends to drinking to intoxication whenever possible.

Currently, Jack reports himself as "a controlled, daily drinker." He states that he never drinks before or during work. He reports that he never misses work because of his drinking. Jack describes himself as finishing work, stopping at his favorite bar after work, having a few beers (his drink of choice) with friends, and going home with a six-pack, which he finishes each night.

Jack reports that this has been his pattern of drinking for the last 5 to 7 years. He reports that the number of drinks at the bar depends on the time he gets off work and how many friends are at the bar.

Jack reports that he has not experienced any legal or work-related problems from his drinking. He reports that he does have some financial problems with credit-card debt. He denies any gambling problems.

Jack reports no social or leisure activities. He is distant from his family of origin and has no significant dating relationship with anyone.

Jack was able to attain sustained early recovery from alcohol during his 6 weeks in IOP. He reluctantly participated in AA, feeling that he couldn't get anything from listening to other people's problems. He remained isolated from his family and developed no new friendships through AA. Continued individual therapy was recommended at the time of discharge from IOP. Prognosis is guarded for continued abstinence from alcohol.

Summary and Conclusions

This chapter provided a brief overview of two complicated and demanding areas of practice. It covered a theoretical overview of fields of practice, relevant theoretical frameworks, common issues and practice settings, specific legal and ethical issues, assessment, screening, licensure and credentialing requirements, and necessary skill sets. The intention of this chapter was to assist the reader in developing a deeper awareness of the knowledge, skills, and responsibilities of forensic social workers providing services to persons diagnosed with mental health and/or addictions issues.

Resources

Association of Social Worker Boards—http://www.aswb.org

National Association of Social Workers—http://www.socialworkers.org

National Clearinghouse for Alcohol & Drug Information—http://ncadi.samhsa.gov/

National Council of Alcohol & Drug Dependence—http://www.ncadd.org

National Institute on Alcohol Abuse & Alcoholism—http://pubs.niaaa.nih.gov

National Institute of Mental Health—http://www.nimh.nih.gov

Substance Abuse & Mental Health Service Administration—http://samhsa.gov

References

American Psychiatric Association. (2000). *Diagnostic and statistical manual of mental disorders* (4th ed., text rev.). Washington, DC: American Psychiatric Press.

Americans with Disabilities Act. (1992). Pub. L. No. 101-336 42 U.S.C. Sec. 12101 et seq.

Frances, R. J., Miller, S. I., & Mack, A. H. (Eds.). (2005). *Clinical textbook of addictive disorders* (3rd ed.). New York: Guilford Press.

Levin, C., Furlong, A., & O'Neill, M. K. (Eds.). (2002). *Confidentiality.* Hillsdale, NJ: Analytic Press.

Lowenberg, F., Dolgoff, R., & Harrington, D. (2000). *Ethical decisions for social work practice* (6th ed.). Itasca, IL: F. E. Peacock.

Miller, W. R., & Rollnick, S. (2002). *Motivational interviewing* (2nd ed.). New York: Guilford Press.

Munson, C. (2002). *Handbook of clinical social work supervision* (3rd ed.). Binghamton, NY: Haworth Press.

National Association of Social Workers (NASW). (1996). *Code of ethics*. Washington, DC: NASW Press.

National Institute for Mental Health (NIMH). (2008). *National Institute for Mental Health*. Retrieved August 31, 2008, from http://www.nimh.nih.gov/health/publications/the-numbers-count-mental-disorders-in-america.shtml

Peterson, J. V., Nisenholz, B., & Robinson, G. (2003). *A nation under the influence*. Boston: Allyn & Bacon.

Reamer, F. G. (2006). *Social work values and ethics*. New York: Columbia University Press.

Richmond, M. (1917). *Social diagnosis*. New York: Russell Sage Foundation.

Substance Abuse & Mental Health Services Administration. (2006). *National survey of drug use and health*. Retrieved May 1, from http://www.oas.samhsa.gov/nhsda.htm

Tarasoff v. Regents of the University of California, 131 Cal. Rptr. 14, 551 p.2d 334 (1976).

U.S. Department of Health & Human Services. (1987). Confidentiality of alcohol and drug abuse patient records. *Federal Register*, 42 CFR Part 2, 21796–21813. Washington, DC: U.S. Government Printing Office.

U.S. Department of Health & Human Services. (1996). *Standards for privacy of individually identifiable health information*. Final Rule: 45 CFR Parts 160 & 164. Washington, DC: U.S. Government Printing Office.

Walsh, J. (2006). *Theories for direct social work practice*. Belmont, CA: Thompson Learning.

"Order in the Drug Court": Understanding the Intersection of Substance Abuse and Law

15

Keith Morgen
Lauren Gunneson
Lisa Maietta

As of April 2007 there were 1,699 operational drug courts in the United States with 349 additional drug-court programs in the planning stages (Bureau of Justice Assistance, 2007). However, drug courts vary by jurisdiction and state so a comprehensive and detailed review of all drug-court procedures and policies is outside the scope of this chapter. Here we provide an elementary review of the important issues relevant to a social worker operating within the drug-court system. We will present the basics of drug-court organization and process but encourage the reader to consult her or his county and state judicial systems for the procedures relevant to that jurisdiction (e.g., whether a social worker is permitted to make a diagnosis and work within a drug court; policies on the expungement of the record for a successful drug-court client). In addition, a detailed review of the abundant drug court effectiveness research (including cost-benefit analyses) is beyond this chapter's scope. Because of page limitations, we highlight some of the more recent literature that reviews studies of drug-court effectiveness. Again, we encourage the reader to consult his or her state and county justice systems for drug court effectiveness data relevant to the jurisdiction.

Substance Abuse and Crime

Drug offenders represent the fastest-growing prison population as a result of increases in drug-related arrests and convictions (Auerhahn, 2002, 2004). The most recent Bureau of Justice Statistics data (Mumola & Karberg, 2007) underscore the intersection between substance abuse and crime: 17% of state prisoners and 18% of federal prisoners cited obtaining money for drugs as the motivation for committing their current offense. State prisoners with property and drug offenses were more likely to commit crimes to obtain drug money than state prisoners sentenced for violent and public-order offenses. Federal prisoners sentenced for property offenses were less than half as likely as drug offenders to report a need for drug money as the primary motivating factor for committing their offenses.

Large numbers of state (53%) and federal inmates (45%) reported substance abuse or dependence in the year prior to prison admission. Just under half (47%) of all state prisoners with violent offenses met the criteria for drug abuse or dependence with a little over one quarter of these violent offenders (24%) reporting the commitment of their crime while under the influence of drugs. In addition, one third (32%) of all state offenders committed their current offense while under the influence of drugs.

Consequently, criminal offenders are entering the United States justice system (at the federal and state levels) with serious drug-addiction problems that influence their criminal behaviors. Drug courts serve as a key intervention point where drug-addicted offenders can receive treatment services that will (one hopes) move the offender toward a state of recovery while eradicating the need/desire for criminal behavior.

General Description of the Drug-Court Process

Most drug courts follow the diversion model whereby all charges are dropped if all program requirements are met (Belenko, 2001). Although every drug court may vary (because of differences in personnel, state laws, treatment services available, etc.) all drug courts follow the 10 key operational components described by the National Association of Drug Court Professionals (1997) (see Table 15.1).

Cooper (2003) provides a generic overview of the drug-court process from start to finish. A summary of that process is provided here.

The defendant is arrested for a drug charge. Once arrested, the offender's case is presented to the prosecutor's office for review of drug-court eligibility. This review includes the current charge as well as the offender's past criminal history (e.g., the offender's violence history or risk to the community). This rapid case review is already a vast improvement over how a traditional case is handled as the offender's case would likely not have been reviewed until several months post-arrest.

Once eligible, the defendant is provided the opportunity to enter the drug-court program. The public defender reviews the charges, explains the drug-court system, and provides the merits of drug courts versus the traditional adjudication processes. Once the defendant chooses to enter the drug court s/he is seen at the next available drug-court hearing (typically the following day). The judge will explain the drug-court system and the defendant signs an agreement to participate if s/he is found to have a *Diagnostic and Statistical Manual of Mental Disorders (DSM-IV)*-classified substance-use disorder (American Psychiatric Association, 2000) via the drug court's screening-and-assessment process. It is important to note that criteria for enrollment

15.1 Drug Court Key Components

The following 10 key components come directly from *Defining Drug Courts: The Key Components* published by the National Association of Drug Court Professionals (1997)

Key Component #1: Drug courts integrate alcohol and other drug treatment services with justice system case processing

Key Component #2: Using a non-adversarial approach, prosecution and defense counsel promote public safety while protecting participants' due process rights

Key Component #3: Eligible participants are identified early and promptly placed in the drug court program

Key Component #4: Drug courts provide access to a continuum of alcohol, drug, and other related treatment and rehabilitation services

Key Component #5: Abstinence is monitored by frequent alcohol and other drug testing

Key Component #6: A coordinated strategy governs drug-court responses to participants' compliance

Key Component #7: Ongoing judicial interaction with each drug-court participant is essential

Key Component #8: Monitoring and evaluation measure the achievement of program goals and gauge effectiveness

Key Component #9: Continuing interdisciplinary education promotes effective drug-court planning, implementation, and operations

Key Component #10: Forging partnerships among drug courts, public agencies, and community-based organizations generates local support and enhances drug-court effectiveness

Note: From NADCP (1997).

in a drug court varies by jurisdiction: some mandate that the defendant be diagnosed with a substance-use disorder, whereas other jurisdictions allow for offenders charged with possession of drugs to enter a drug-court recovery program (thus the need to be well acquainted with the rules of the drug court in your jurisdiction). Any defendant not meeting the drug court enrollment criteria is transferred back to the traditional adjudication system. Once enrolled in the drug-court system the defendant will start intensive outpatient substance-abuse treatment (4 to 5 days per week), typically within a few days of his or her arrest.

Court appearances typically begin at the rate of one per week. During these meetings the judge will review the participant's progress, drug-test results, and overall compliance with the drug-court requirements. As the participant establishes a history of compliance with the procedures, the rate of scheduled court appearances may relax.

There are two general types of drug courts: preplea and postplea. In the preplea drug-court process prosecution is deferred and offenders can have all charges dropped on successful program completion. Furthermore, many jurisdictions will also expunge the current arrest record if the offender remains arrest-free for an additional span of time. Postplea drug courts may assist the offender in avoiding incarceration, allow the offender to plead guilty to a misdemeanor rather than a felony crime, or receive a sentence of time-served in the program. Cissner and Rempel (2005) highlight the

15.2   Potential Roles for Social Workers in the Drug-Court System

Conduct preliminary assessment for drug-court placement
Liaison among prosecution, defense, judge, and treatment facility
Develop treatment plan in conjunction with defendant and treatment facility
Maintain records for monitoring and evaluating progress

mixed research findings on pre/postplea drug courts. Though some data indicate the legal coercive leverage indicative in a postplea model may lead to a more effective outcome, other data found preplea offenders have better outcomes, whereas other research theorizes that the coercive element of all drug courts (pre- or postplea) may be an effective facilitator of change in drug use and criminal behavior. Thus, more research is needed to clarify the strengths and limitations of preplea and postplea drug courts.

Role of the Social Worker in the Drug Court

In states and/or jurisdictions in which social workers are permitted to provide diagnoses and work within the drug-court system, the social worker can play a major role operating as a case manager. Social work and case management share a long history (Roberts, 1987) and recent research highlights the important role case management plays in the substance abuse treatment process (Barnett, Masson, Sorensen, Wong, & Hall, 2006; Morgenstern et al., 2006). The social worker (trained in both mental health treatment and advocacy) is well suited to bridging the multiple offices within the drug-court system (prosecution, defense, judge) to provide the most seamless continuity of services and support for the drug-court client (see Table 15.2). Specifically, the social worker operating in the drug-court system (likely as a case manager) must address two key areas that will be described in the following sections: assessment/evaluation and confidentiality pertinent to substance abuse.

Assessment and Evaluation

The social worker/case manager provides a critical service in the opening stages of the application to the drug-court system. Although specific criteria vary per jurisdiction, many drug-court programs typically mandate that all participants meet the *DSM-IV-TR* (American Psychiatric Association, 2000) criteria for substance abuse or dependence. Consequently, the social worker who performs the initial assessment and evaluation serves as the gateway into the drug-court system. The findings of the evaluation are reported to the prosecution, defense, and drug-court judge and are instrumental data in the decision to accept or reject a drug court application. Furthermore, if the applicant is accepted into the drug court, the social worker's assessment and evaluation guide the court's decision process on assigning a type of substance-abuse treatment (e.g., inpatient or outpatient).

The preliminary assessment/evaluation typically starts with a strong and thorough clinical interview lasting at least 45 minutes. The social worker must inquire about specific drugs used and not simply ask, "Do you use drugs and/or alcohol?" All classes of drugs should be addressed (e.g., alcohol, nicotine, depressants, stimulants, cannabis, opioids, other drugs) in a detailed interview. Other important questions address heaviest lifetime use of each drug, evidence of tolerance and dependence, family history, criminal/legal history, prior substance abuse treatment episodes, and psychiatric history. The social worker must always remember that these data will be used to determine eligibility for the drug court and must be comprehensive.

In addition to an interview, many clinicians also use assessment instruments to complement and/or supplement the interview data. The social worker should be cautious in selecting an instrument because many of them (such as the Michigan Alcoholism Screening Test) only target one substance, thus producing incomplete assessment data. However, myriad drug courts (as well as treatment facilities) use the Addiction Severity Index (ASI; McLellan et al., 1992), which is a structured interview assessing past and current (prior 30 days) problems in seven domains: medical, employment, alcohol use, drug use, legal, psychiatric, and family/social problems related to substance use. The ASI has been shown to be both a valid and reliable measure (Kosten, Rounsaville, & Kleber, 1983; Makela, 2004; McLellan, Luborsky, Cacciola, & Griffith, 1985).

The social worker, following the interview, will diagnose the drug-court applicant as meeting the *DSM-IV* criteria for abuse or dependence (see Table 15.3). At this point the social worker/case manager will communicate the results of the assessment/evaluation with the prosecution, defense, and drug-court judge. If the defendant is accepted into the drug-court program the social worker/case manager will typically attend a case conference during which the defendant's data are again presented and a drug-court session is scheduled.

Confidentiality

Throughout the drug-court process the social worker (especially if operating as a case manager) must keep detailed records of each drug-court defendant. Thus, the social worker operating in the drug court (or any substance abuse services organization) must be aware of the specific issues of confidentiality relevant to substance abuse. In brief, federal confidentiality laws and regulations (42 U.S. C.SS 290dd-3 and ee-3 and 42 CFR Part 2; U.S. Department of Health and Human Services, 1987) protect any and all information about an individual if that individual applied for or received drug/alcohol-related services from a program covered under the law. Services covered can include assessment/evaluation, individual/group counseling, or referrals for treatment. From the time the individual enters the system there are restrictions on any data that may identify the individual as substance-abusing or dependent. These data are only permissible after the individual (e.g., defendant in a drug-court case) signs a consent form. Regulations allow for disclosure without consent in medical emergencies, communications between program staff (e.g., between treatment facility and the drug court), or when allowed via court order. In addition, federal laws and regulations do not protect information related to child abuse or neglect, a crime committed at the treatment facility or against any staff of the facility or about a threat to commit such a crime. As one of the handlers of confidential drug/alcohol-related

15.3   DSM-IV* (2000) Diagnostic Criteria for Substance Abuse or Dependence

Abuse One or More of the Following Over a 12-Month Period	Dependence Three or More of the Following
Recurrent substance use resulting in a failure to fulfill work, school, home obligations	Tolerance
Recurrent use in hazardous situations	Withdrawal
Recurrent substance-related legal problems	Taking substance in larger amounts than intended
Continued use despite recurrent interpersonal problems caused or exacerbated by the substance	Unsuccessful effort or persistent desire to control substance use
Never met the criteria for dependence	Great amount of time spent obtaining substance or recovering from effects
	Social, occupational activities given up or reduced because of substance use
	Continued use despite physical or psychological problems caused or exacerbated by the substance

*(American Psychiatric Association, 2000).

information, the social worker is obligated to understand these laws and regulations and obtain the proper consent throughout the drug-court processes. The social worker should consult the National Institute of Justice and her or his state government for all laws and regulations relevant to the state of practice to be certain all confidentiality laws are followed.

Drug-Court Research Review

Program Outcomes

Drug courts are consistently criticized in the areas of research, documentation, and evaluation (Heck, 2006). For instance, the Government Accountability Office (GAO) was recently provided the task of evaluating drug-court programs. Despite a nationwide review the GAO (2005) found only 27 of 117 drug court program evaluations methodologically sound for analysis. A basic summary of this research review indicates that when contrasted with comparison group data fewer drug-court participants were rearrested or reconvicted and had lower rates of recidivism (across various offenses). The National Drug Court Institute (2005) reported on recent field studies of drug courts and found similar positive criminal justice results. Offenders who successfully completed a drug-court program were less likely to be rearrested in the year following drug-court completion and demonstrated a significant reduction in days incarcerated 2 years after drug court program completion.

Despite these strong findings indicating drug court effectiveness at reducing criminal justice recidivism, recent data present mixed results for drug-abuse outcomes (GAO, 2005). For instance, self-report data on drug use showed no significant reduction in drug use for drug-court participants. Drug court completion rates were varied (27% to 66%) and, outside of compliance with drug-court procedures, no other variables effectively predicted drug court program completion.

Research Design Criticisms

In addition to the limitations of only having a small pool of methodologically sound studies to evaluate, numerous methodological flaws limit the generalizability and accuracy of the research findings. As a result it is still difficult to determine the effectiveness of drug-court programs because so many evaluations were built from methodologically unsound research designs and procedures. The primary problem in evaluating drug courts is the lack of a true experimental design. True program evaluation mandates an experimental design that uses a control group with random- ized assignment (Shadish, Cook, & Campbell, 2002). Heck (2006) reports that since randomization is not possible within the drug-court arena, evaluations rely on compar- ison groups (i.e., matched groups) comprised of individuals mirroring the drug- court participants across numerous key variables. Comparison groups never eliminate confounds within nonexperimental design (e.g., systematic bias) but can reduce the possibility and/or impact of bias by using numerous variables for comparison. Thus, when a social worker is evaluating drug-court literature s/he should look for studies using comparison groups matched on a number of key comparison variables.

In addition, Heck (2006) offers suggestions for creating uniform drug court pro- gram evaluation research by listing key variables in need of analysis. For example, process-related questions should address program goals, program compliance, drug court team colleagueship, and the outcomes of incentives and sanctions. Performance indicators should tackle program retention rate, span of time drug-free after drug court, and the postdrug court recidivism rate.

Cost Analyses of Drug Courts

The majority of substance abuse treatment interventions produce an economic benefit to society and drug courts are no exception. For example, Belenko, Patapis, and French (2005) use the benefit–cost ratio (BCR) to evaluate the strength of a drug court's economic benefit. Belenko et al. (2005) defines the BCR as the total benefits of the program divided by the total costs of the program, with a positive BCR greater than one indicative of an economically beneficial program. Although Belenko and colleagues caution that study design, population, time period, and other factors influ- ence the calculation of the BCR, and that more research is needed on treatment effects and follow-up studies, drug court BCR values for three programs ranged between 1.74 and 2.80; consequently, the drug courts evaluated did provide a strong net economic benefit. Additional recent data out of Ohio also underscore the cost-effective- ness of drug courts. Shaffer, Bechtel, and Latessa (2005) noted the small costs associated with drug courts ($5,777) and the larger costs associated with a single new crime

($27,371). Dividing the new-crime costs by the smaller drug-court costs produces a statistic that indicates a net savings of $4.73 for every dollar invested in drug courts.

VOICES FROM THE FIELD

Malinda Lamb, PhD, LISW, CCJP
Clinical Services Manager, 6th Judicial District Department of Correctional Services, Iowa

Agency Setting

From 2000–2004, I worked at Fulton State Hospital, a state psychiatric hospital that maintains the maximum and intermediate forensic units for the state of Missouri. The clientele within the forensic units are primarily individuals being evaluated following the alleged commission of a criminal offense, those receiving services revolving around competency to stand trial, or those who have been found to be not guilty by reason of mental disease or defect. Additionally, these units also provide a variety of treatment programs to meet the needs of the clients it serves.

From 2005 to 2007, I was the Jail Alternatives and Mobile Crisis Coordinator for Johnson County Mental Health and Developmental Disabilities, an agency that provides funding and coordination of services for individuals who have mental health disorders and development disabilities. This agency is responsible for the oversight of the financial aspects and treatment coordination of mental health services for clients within the county. However, through the years it had become apparent that many individuals with mental health disorders were entering the criminal justice system. Therefore, the county approved the hiring of a coordinator to develop and implement a program to address the needs of these individuals within the jail and throughout the criminal justice system.

Currently, I am Clinical Services Manager of the Sixth Judicial District Department of Correctional Services, a community-based corrections agency. The Sixth District is comprised of six counties in the eastern region of Iowa, with two larger communities—a Native American settlement as well as several rural communities. The major function of the agency is to provide supervision of individuals who have been placed on probation or parole.

Practice Responsibilities

Although all of the agencies mentioned are unique and ultimately have different agency roles, the clientele whom I worked with throughout these various agencies are very similar. With the evident and growing number of individuals with mental health disorders within the criminal justice system, agencies are developing and implementing unique programs and interventions for this population. Through all of these professional opportunities, I developed strong collaborations across many fields of practice, which has enabled me to develop and implement new and innovative programming.

While at Fulton State Hospital, I gained a wealth of knowledge through direct service work with clients and research opportunities, I was exposed to a variety of treatment programs and interventions that were available to individuals who found themselves in the state forensic psychiatric hospital setting. Through conducting assessments, evaluations, and treatment interventions, I gained the experience I needed to move forward in my career.

On relocation to Iowa, I was hired by Johnson County to develop and implement a program that would address the needs of individuals with mental health disorders who had become involved in the criminal justice system. This was a new approach for the county, therefore collaboration across the fields of mental health, substance abuse, and criminal justice was essential. I worked to develop regular and ongoing meetings to discuss and address issues that arose as new programs were developed and implemented.

In my current position with the Sixth Judicial District Department of Correctional Services, I have worked with a team to develop a drug-treatment court in two of the counties in the Sixth judicial district. I am also working to develop a unique facility within the district for clients diagnosed with mental health disorders. Construction is currently underway on this new correctional residential mental health facility. This facility is extremely unique, and will be a community-based facility featuring collaboration with various community treatment providers to address both the treatment and the security needs of our clients. Other responsibilities I maintain are making presentations to treatment providers, consumers, advocates, and correctional professionals regarding mental health and the programming that the district is developing and implementing. Although these are only a few of the examples of my responsibilities and the programs that exist within the Sixth district, this district is very innovative and actively works to provide creative and needed interventions to clients.

Expertise

A master's degree in social work or related field allowing for licensure as a clinician is needed to work independently in the positions described. These positions require both experience and knowledge gained through academic preparations and hands-on work. These positions require the ability to work independently across professions and to be seen as an expert within the field of mental health.

Practice Challenges

Many challenges are inherent when working with a variety of agencies and organizations, all of which have unique roles and regulations guiding their practice. Whether it is working directly with clients, or in an administrative capacity, the bureaucratic issues that arise can make it difficult for the clients to get the resources that they need. It can also be difficult to balance the needs of the individual client while ensuring the safety and security of the community.

Common Legal and/or Ethical Issues

When practicing in the field of forensic mental health and/or criminal justice, legal and ethical issues are always present. One must always remember the community and the victims that have been affected by the actions of the clients that we, or our agencies, serve. It is a balancing act to provide for the needs of the client, maintain a safe and secure community, while also adhering to the rights of victims.

Brief Description of Collaborative Activities With Professionals and/or Other Stakeholders

Collaboration has been and continues to be an essential part of the work that I do. Since relocating to Iowa, my career choices have made collaboration a vital part of my work. Although some interactions were going on, I worked to develop a more formalized method of meeting with key stakeholders. Regular meetings were initiated to get mental health providers, substance-abuse providers, and criminal justice professionals together to discuss the issues that affect our clients and to establish a method to work collaboratively to benefit all of our agencies.

Additional Information

I feel that social workers can fill a vital role within the field of forensic mental health and/ or criminal justice. More and more individuals with mental health and/or substance-use disorders are entering the criminal justice system. Through appropriate academic preparation and field experience, social workers approach this population with methods and techniques that are evidence based, while interacting with the individual as more than just an issue or problem. Social workers will be and should be key players in developing and implementing necessary interventions to assist in reducing recidivism and improving the quality of life for our clients.

Summary and Conclusions

The past 10 to 15 years have seen tremendous growth in the implementation of American drug courts. For instance, problem-focused courts have expanded beyond drug treatment to include adult or juvenile drug courts, DUI (driving under the influence) courts, family-based courts, and mental health courts (Huddleston, Freeman-Wilson, & Boone, 2004). Consequently, the field of social work as well as the other associated professions (psychology, counseling) seem destined to practice in the courts more often than ever before. As the substance abuse treatment field moves farther into the 21st century, the reach of treatment, advocacy, and support seems to be stretching deeper into the community. However, as mentioned earlier in the chapter, social workers must consult their county and state justice systems for the specific components of drug courts in their area, which can include the type of court (preplea or postplea), prosecutor reactions to drug courts (some feel they are "soft" on crime), and whether a social worker is even permitted to participate in the drug-court process. Once well versed in the drug-court procedures relevant to her or his jurisdiction, the social worker can play a pivotal role as an advocate for positive change for substance-abusing/dependent criminal offenders.

References

American Psychiatric Association. (2000). *Diagnostic and statistical manual of mental disorders* (4th ed., text rev.). Washington, DC: American Psychiatric Press.

Auerhahn, K. (2002). Selective incapacitation, three strikes, and the problem of aging prison popula-tions: Using simulation modeling to see the future. *Criminology and Public Policy, 1*, 353–388.

Auerhahn, K. (2004). California's incarcerated drug offender population, yesterday, today, and tomor-row: Evaluating the war on drugs and Proposition 36. *Journal of Drug Issues, 38*, 95–120.

Barnett, P. G., Masson, C. L., Sorensen, J. L., Wong, W., & Hall, S. (2006). Linking opioid-dependent hospital patients to drug treatment: Health care use and costs 6 months after randomization. *Addiction, 101*, 1797–1804.

Belenko, S. (2001). *Research on drug courts: A critical review 2001 update.* New York: National Center on Addiction and Substance Abuse at Columbia University.

Belenko, S., Patapis, N., & French, M. T. (2005). *Economic benefits of drug treatment: A critical review of the evidence for policy makers.* Philadelphia: Treatment Research Institute, University of Pennsylvania.

Bureau of Justice Assistance Drug Court Clearinghouse Project. (2007). *Summary of drug court activity by state and county.* Washington, DC: American University.

Cissner, A. B., & Rempel, M. (2005). *The state of drug court research: Moving beyond 'do they work'?* Washington, DC: U.S. Department of Justice.

Cooper, C. S. (2003). Drug courts: Current issues and future perspectives. *Substance Use & Misuse, 38(11-13)*, 1671–1711.

Government Accountability Office. (2005). *Adult drug courts: Evidence indicates recidivism reductions and mixed results for other outcomes.* Washington, DC: Author.

Heck, C. (2006). *Local drug court research: Navigating performance measures and process evaluations. Mono-graph no. 6.* Alexandria, VA: National Drug Court Institute.

Huddleston, C. W., Freeman-Wilson, K., & Boone, D. (2004). *Painting the current picture: A national report card on drug courts and other problem solving court programs in the United States.* Alexandria, VA: National Drug Court Institute.

Kosten, T. R., Rounsaville, B. J., & Kleber, H. D. (1983). Concurrent validity of the Addiction Severity Index. *Journal of Nervous and Mental Disorders, 171*, 606–610.

Mäkelä, K. (2004). Studies of the reliability and validity of the Addiction Severity Index. *Addiction, 99*, 398–410.

McLellan, T. A., Kushner, H., Metzger, D., Peters, R., Smith, I., Grissom, G., et al. (1992). The 5th edition of the Addiction Severity Index. *Journal of Substance Abuse Treatment, 9*, 199–213.

McLellan, T. A., Luborsky, L., Cacciola, J. S., & Griffith, J. E. (1985). New data from the Addiction Severity Index: Reliability and validity in three centers. *Journal of Nervous and Mental Disease, 163*, 412–423.

Morgenstern, J., Blanchard, K., McCrady, B., McVeigh, K., Morgan, T., & Pandina, R. (2006). Effectiveness of intensive case management for substance-dependent women receiving temporary assistance for needy families. *American Journal of Public Health, 96*, 2016–2023.

Mumola, C. J., & Karberg, J. C. (2007). *Drug use and dependence, state and federal prisoners, 2004: Bureau of Justice Statistics Special Report.* Washington, DC: U.S. Department of Justice.

National Association of Drug Court Professionals. (1997). *Defining drug courts: The key components.* Washington, DC: U.S. Department of Justice.

National Drug Court Institute. (2005). *Drug court review, Vol. V, 1.* Alexandria, VA: Author.

Roberts, M. D. (1987). Developing case management as a practice model. *Social Casework, 68*, 466–470.

Shadish, W. R., Cook, T. D., & Campbell, D. T. (2002). *Experimental and quasi-experimental designs for generalized causal inference.* New York: Houghton Mifflin.

Shaffer, D. K., Bechtel, K., & Latessa, E. J. (2005). *Evaluation of Ohio's drug courts: A cost benefit analysis.* Cincinnati, OH: Center for Criminal Justice Research, Division of Criminal Justice, University of Cincinnati.

U. S. Department of Health and Human Services. (1987, June 19). Confidentiality of alcohol and drug abuse patient records. *Federal Register, 42*, U.S. C.SS 290dd-3 and ee-3 and 42 CFR Part 2.

Women at Risk: Legal Involvement Among Mothers in Addiction Treatment

16

Nancy M. Violette
Thomas J. Morgan
Audrey Redding-Raines

This chapter describes a research study that examined women's risk for involvement in the legal system both before and after focused addiction treatment. The program was developed specifically for mothers at risk for involvement in New Jersey's child protection system and was provided in several different treatment agencies throughout the state. Data were collected between the years 2005–2007.

Familiarity with women at risk for involvement in the legal system is of importance to social workers in a variety of settings. Social workers in child protection, social services, addiction treatment, as well as hospital and mental health programs may come into contact with women who have engaged in illegal activities, are on probation, awaiting sentencing, or were recently released from jail or prison. The increased use of drug courts and alternative-sentencing routes makes recommendations for addiction treatment rather than jail time more commonplace. As a result, barriers that formerly had existed between legally involved populations and social workers have been eliminated. As the number of women in the jail and prison system increases, so, too will referrals of women, in particular, to programs where social workers deliver direct services. The research participants described in the study that follows fit the profile of a growing segment of the client population within many addiction programs throughout the country.

The women described in this project received specialized programming designed to address their unique needs as women and mothers. These services, delivered at multiple sites, included clinical services provided primarily by female counselors in counseling groups for women only. Groups focused on topics such as self-esteem, parenting, domestic violence, and sexual abuse. Services important to women including the provision of, or linkage with child-care services, and assistance with transportation were also provided in these programs. A brief discussion of background issues pertinent to women and their risk for legal involvement is explored in the following section.

Background

Prevalence

Evidence suggests that there is a robust relationship between substance abuse and risk for involvement in the legal system, for both men and women. An estimated 80% of offenders in state and federal prison had one of the following characteristics: they were engaged in a drug-related offense, they were under the influence of drugs or alcohol at the time of the offense, they were trying to obtain money to manage a drug habit, or they had a history of substance abuse. A similar profile is identified for 67% of people on probation, and 80% of people on parole (Belenko, DeMatteo, & Patapis, 2007). Given the strong relationship between addiction and subsequent or concurrent legal problems, exploration of factors associated with both is an important area of inquiry (Alleyne, 2006). Further, it is reported that female prisoners were more likely than their male counterparts to have used drugs in the month prior to incarceration (Morash, Bynum, & Koons, 1998).

Women comprise a smaller proportion of the criminal justice population, accounting for 23.2% of all arrestees and 16% of correctional inmates (Greenfield & Snell, 2000). Women also have a different profile than men in terms of the offenses they commit that result in legal supervision. Women are more likely than men to be current drug users and to be incarcerated as a result of actions associated with their drug use, rather than because of their involvement with violent crimes or property offenses (Conly, 1998). Women inmates are more likely to have used crack cocaine in the month prior to their offense, and also at the time of their offense. Similarly, women are more likely than men to have committed a crime to obtain money for drugs (Conly).

Although women are less likely than men to be involved in the criminal justice system, women's incarceration and legal supervision is increasing at a disproportionately faster rate than it is for men (Henderson, 1998). It has been noted that the quadrupling of women's incarceration rate within the past 2 decades may be caused by changes in sentencing policies including the Federal Sentencing Reform Act of 1984 (P.L. 98), as well as an overall increase in arrests of women for petty, or lifestyle crimes, such as prostitution and vagrancy (Alleyne, 2006). Women who have been arrested for drug distribution at the lowest level are subject to stiff minimum sentences without the opportunity for parole. Judges who formerly may have been able to take into account a defendant's home responsibilities are no longer able to do so (Brownell, Miller, & Raimon, 2007).

Psychosocial History

It appears that women of color, socioeconomically disadvantaged women, and, by extension, their children, are especially affected by this phenomenon (Morash et al., 1998). Black and Hispanic women are disproportionately more likely than White women to be incarcerated in both local and state jails and the federal prison system (Greenfield & Snell, 2000).

Most important, as an increasing number of women face incarceration and supervision under the criminal justice system more children are vulnerable to the risks associated with a sudden and prolonged separation from their mothers. The changes faced by these children are severe and life-altering. They include the potential for displacement from their homes and schools; change in caregivers; loss of contact with other siblings whose foster care or family placements may be different from their own; loss of mother's wages; stigma; greater likelihood of involvement with the juvenile justice system; and an unknown range of psychological repercussions depending on the child's age, temperament, resiliency, and social support (Alleyne, 2006; Conly, 1998; Greenfield & Snell, 2000; Morash et al., 1998). The ripple effects on these children's extended families, especially grandparents, already burdened by social conditions associated with socioeconomic vulnerability, are further affected by caring for additional children.

Health Concerns

Women offenders are more vulnerable than men to a wide range of psychological and health risk factors. These problems precede women's incarceration and are exacerbated by their imprisonment. Women offenders are more likely to have a lifetime history of drug and alcohol addiction, especially to more addictive drugs, such as heroin and crack (Conly, 1998). Women have more serious mental health profiles, including a greater likelihood of major depression and dysthymia, for example. In their study of comorbidity among female arrestees, Abram, Teplin, and McClelland (2003) found that compared to men, women had greater psychiatric severity, and higher rates of comorbidity of drug use disorders and mental health problems. They reported that 72% of the women with a severe psychiatric disorder, such as schizophrenia or major depression, also had a current substance-dependence problem. Women in prison have HIV/AIDS at twice the rate of male prisoners (Henderson, 1998). Pregnant women entering jail, or those with gynecological problems such as sexually transmitted diseases, or cancer, may not have the medical care and follow-up necessary for amelioration of their condition, although for some women, a prison or jail medical exam may be the first time they receive a diagnostic test, such as for HIV (Henderson).

It is believed that women under legal supervision are more likely than their male counterparts and women in the general population to have been physically or sexually abused prior to adulthood (Conly, 1998). Not surprisingly, it is estimated that up to 30% of women inmates may suffer from posttraumatic stress disorder (Henderson, 1998). Of concern is the risk of rape or sexual coercion that these women face under imprisonment; certain to add salt to the wounds they already have. Women with a history of trauma may likely face increased mental health risks as a result of a host of stressors associated with incarceration. These considerations, plus the range of health, mental health, substance abuse, and socioeconomic factors associated with women's incarceration illustrate the imperative for social workers to advocate on behalf of women to prevent their incarceration and limit the time spent as an inmate. This issue takes on additional urgency when imagining the affect on their children.

Impact on Children

Nearly three quarters of women under correctional supervision have minor children, with an average of 2.1 children each. These approximately 1.3 million children under the age of 18 are affected directly, and seriously, by the legal involvement of their collective 615,500 mothers (Greenfield & Snell, 2000). Approximately two thirds of women serving time in state prison, and 84% of those in federal prison leave behind children with whom they were living prior to incarceration (Brownell et al., 2007). Furthermore, it is estimated that up to 25% of women "entering prison are either pregnant or delivered a child within the year of their incarceration" (Brownell et al., p. 355). The following section describes a program-evaluation study conducted with mothers who had risk factors for legal involvement, including poverty, substance abuse, and mental health problems similar to the ones that have been described.

The Current Study

Methods

The goal of this research study was to investigate factors associated with legal involvement among a sample of mothers in addiction treatment. Data are derived from a larger project of 250 women who were recruited for a statewide evaluation study of mothers in specialized residential, drug-free intensive outpatient, and methadone-maintained intensive outpatient programs. The intended length of stay for women in the residential treatment was 6 months, and for the intensive outpatient programs, 4 months.

Twenty-six treatment sites participated in the treatment study. These sites were assigned by the state's addiction authority to pilot the specialized women's treatment. The entire universe of programs offering this treatment at the commencement of the evaluation study were selected to participate. The women were either self-referred, or recommended to the specialized women's treatment by their substance abuse counselors or the child protection system as a result of their having an "open case" or risk factors associated with involvement with the child protection system. All women newly admitted into the specialized women's programs were offered the opportunity to be screened for engagement into the research study. The evaluation researchers did not oversee the agency's intake procedures, so it is possible that sampling bias may have occurred. However, the university evaluation team, in working with agency personnel emphasized, throughout the study, the importance of following project referral procedures and the counselor's role in those processes.

University research staff met the women at their treatment programs where they were provided information about the study. At the initial interview with research volunteers, informed consent and locator information were obtained, and a battery of questionnaires was administered. Store vouchers were given to the participants to compensate them for their involvement in the study (first and second interviews,

$20.00 each; final interview, $50.00). Three research interviews were conducted: one at baseline (at the start of treatment), at "end of treatment" (4 to 6 months post baseline), and a final 10–12-month (post baseline) follow-up. This chapter uses data from baseline and "end of treatment" interviews. Additional demographic, substance use, admission, and discharge information on the women was obtained from a state-wide administrative database, the New Jersey Substance Abuse Monitoring System (NJ-SAMS).

We used the Addiction Severity Index, fifth edition, to test the associations of interest and women's legal involvement, the outcome measure (McLellan et al., 1992). The ASI is a semi-structured interview that assesses the occurrence of problems in several discrete problem areas of functioning within the past 30 days, including alcohol and drug use, legal involvement, employment, and family/social functioning. The reliability and validity of this instrument has been established (Alterman, Brown, Zaballero, & McKay, 1994; McLellan et al., 1992).

Findings

Our total sample included 236 women. Their average age was 32.4 (SD = 8.5) years old. They had, on average, 2.4 minor children. More than half of the women (66%) had at least one of their children in an out-of-home placement because of intervention by state child protection authorities. Most participants were not married, were unemployed, and had an average annual income of less than $7,000.00. Forty-eight percent of the women were African American, 38% were Caucasian, and 14% were Hispanic. Fifty-seven percent of the women reported a history of physical abuse, and 44% of the women reported having been sexually abused in their lifetime.

Prior to treatment, women reported that they used drugs on an average of 9 days in the past 30 days, an average use of heroin, 4 days; cocaine/crack, 3 days; marijuana, 2 days; and alcohol, 2 days.

We wanted to examine the risk and protective factors for women who had legal involvement at the beginning and end of treatment. Tests of normalcy were conducted prior to the use of significance tests using t-tests, analyses of variance, and chi squares.

Factors Associated With Legal Involvement Before Treatment

Risk factors for women's legal involvement immediately prior to treatment included the presence of serious psychiatric symptoms ($p < 0.01$, $n =$ 213). Women who spent more money on drugs had more arrests in the month prior to treatment ($p < 0.001$, $n =$ 203), as did those who had a greater number of drug treatments in their lifetime ($p < 0.01$, $n =$ 203). Women with greater likelihood of legal involvement at baseline ultimately attended more days of the targeted addiction treatment ($p < 0.05$, $n =$ 198), a potential prospective protective factor.

Factors Associated With Legal Involvement After Treatment

Women were more likely to be involved legally at the end of treatment if they had more days of alcohol use ($p < 0.001$, $n =$ 208), more days of alcohol use to intoxication ($p < 0.01$, $n =$ 208), more days of heroin use ($p < 0.01$, $n =$ 208), and more days of cocaine/crack use ($p < 0.01$, $n =$ 208). Women who had spent more money on drugs were also at greater risk for legal involvement ($p < 0.001$, $n = 208$) as were those reporting serious psychiatric symptoms ($p < 0.01$, $n = 208$). Women with greater legal risk also attended treatment on fewer days ($p < 0.05$, $n = 193$).

Implications and Recommendations

Women with more severe psychiatric and substance-abuse profiles at both the beginning and end of the study were more at risk for legal involvement at those two time points. Of particular interest was the role of treatment. Women with more legal involvement at the beginning of the study attended treatment on more days. However, by the end of the study period, fewer days of treatment attendance was associated with legal involvement. This is not surprising given the following considerations.

Women in the general population appear to have lower rates of substance abuse than men. However, women with substance-abuse problems are less likely than their male counterparts to use substance abuse treatment services. Women involved with the legal system are more likely than men to have more recent and more severe drug involvement (Henderson, 1998). Given this information, it is not surprising that substance-use severity placed the women in this study at particular risk. However, why would women with more severe legal problems at the end of treatment have attended treatment on fewer days? These findings may reflect difficulty in treatment retention for at-risk women beyond what is identifiable on intake. This suggests that programming designed thoughtfully for women must occur at all levels of intervention to protect women from the possibility of imprisonment.

Program Recommendations

Treatment agencies have an imperative to develop treatment programs that retain women until recovery goals are met. Effective treatment assumes that gender is a key factor in women's lives (Covington & Bloom, 2004) and recovery. Specialized treatment for women that provides basic necessities such as child care (including child treatment services for those who need it) and transportation enable women to attend their treatment programs regularly, without undue absences caused by nagging logistical concerns. By being present in treatment, women can focus on getting well. Programs must include outreach efforts for women who have missed appointments. Intensive case-management approaches also ensure that clients' multiple needs can be addressed in a coordinated fashion.

Programs need to address women's socioeconomic needs, including offering educational and training opportunities to maximize women's ability to care for their children independently, regardless of partner status. By focusing on economic stability, concurrent with addiction and mental health recovery, engagement in criminal acts may be minimized. Legal counsel in the form of inexpensive or free legal clinics must be made available. Social workers can accompany women to court dates to provide advocacy and guidance. For agencies unable to provide these in-depth services, linking women to other community-based providers is an essential role for social work practitioners. Treatment agencies can also develop outreach programs to women already within the jail and prison system, as a way to engage women prior to release.

At the clinical-engagement level, women at risk need to be counseled by social workers who can promote the client's dignity and respect by focusing on a strengths-based perspective. This needs to occur in the context of helping women reinforce the healthy relationships in their lives, including those with family, community, and children (Covington & Bloom, 2004). By reinforcing these connections, women will have access to the resources and social support necessary to weaken the likelihood of at-risk behaviors.

Case Study

A case example illustrates these recommendations. Susan is a 30-year-old mother of two young children. She came to the intensive outpatient program at the strong recommendation of her probation officer. She is not a mandated client, per se, but she has been told by probation that any future drug-related arrests could result in a lengthy sentence, given her prior arrests and conviction record for drug possession and loitering. Her children live with her, but she is under supervision of child protection services.

Susan is scheduled to meet with a social worker this afternoon to develop a treatment plan, assuming she shows up for the appointment, and assuming she agrees to commit to treatment. The social worker, Joanne, conducts a lengthy and thorough assessment with Susan, allocating 2 full hours to meet with her. Joanne understands that treatment retention begins with a multitiered assessment and early attempts at engagement. Her program is designed to permit for lengthy initial sessions. She allows, even invites Susan to take a few "stretch breaks" (really cigarette breaks for Susan) so that she can stay focused and involved during the assessment process. Joanne had learned from the initial telephone screening that Susan has a history of legal involvement; knowing this, she is on the lookout for a likely secondary mental health diagnosis. Joanne is already aware (based on information she has already gotten from the agency's telephone screening form) that Susan's cocaine use has been a persistent problem for the past 7 years.

At the initial session, which includes extensive history-taking on drug, alcohol, and tobacco use; mental health; family background; and physical or sexual abuse, Joanne also administers a few easy-to-fill-out questionnaires designed to measure Susan's treatment readiness and level of motivation. Luckily for Joanne, her agency has provided extensive training on empirically supported treatment approaches that help with engagement and retention. The program, sensitive to the unique needs of the female addicted client, has emphasized that clinicians use collaborative rather than confrontational approaches with even the most challenging clients.

During this initial session, Joanne makes sure to do an extensive assessment of Susan's social network to understand the role that current intimate, family, friendship, and social networks play in her life. Joanne has learned that Susan's drug use developed following the client's introduction to cocaine by her boyfriend, who is currently incarcerated. Susan admits that her legal problems started when she became involved in a high-risk lifestyle introduced to her by this boyfriend.

Susan states that she wants to be a better mother and hopes to learn more about parenting in her new program. Joanne, in understanding the need for intensive case management, contracts with Susan at this first meeting to share the names and phone numbers of her probation officer, child protection case worker, and her mother and sister. Susan signs releases, allowing Joanne to set up phone meetings with probation and child protection, as well as family meetings with her mother and sister.

This case depiction, which only describes the initial session and approach of the social worker, illustrates the ways in which using a context-driven perspective, with a case-management methodology, frees the social worker to augment the usual boundaries of more passive or reactive approaches seen in many treatment settings serving high-risk populations.

Policy Recommendations

At the policy level, social workers need to challenge minimum-sentencing laws. Women's important roles as caregivers need to be taken into account when sentencing women for minor crimes. Social workers can also be active in helping women with addictive or psychiatric histories find an alternative placement to the justice system. The increasing use of drug courts and alternative sentencing programs are also a good start in this direction. Programs and treatments for women need to be developed, piloted, and evaluated to ensure that progress continues in this arena (Morash et al., 1998). These interventions should address mental health/addictions and trauma histories.

Summary and Conclusions

Women with addiction and mental health problems require a range of well-planned, gender-specific interventions to reduce their risk for legal involvement. By ensuring that women remain outside of the legal system, their children are more likely to have access to their mothers. Prevention of legal involvement in the next generation may well start with helping their mothers. Social workers can play a major role in helping to improve conditions for this population.

Acknowledgment

This study was made possible by New Jersey Department of Human Services, Division of Addiction Services.

References

Abram, K. M., Teplin, L. A., & McClelland, G. M. (2003). Comorbidity of severe psychiatric disorders and substance use disorders among women in jail. *American Journal of Psychiatry, 160*, 1007–1010.

Alleyne, V. (2006). Locked up means locked out: Women, addiction and incarceration. *Women & Therapy, 29*(3/4), 181–194.

Alterman, A., Brown, L., Zaballero, A., & McKay, J. (1994). Interviewer severity ratings and the composite scores of the ASI: A further look. *Drug and Alcohol Dependence, 34*, 201–209.

Belenko, S., DeMatteo, D., & Patapis, N. (2007). Drug courts. In D. W. Springer & A. R. Roberts (Eds.), *Handbook of forensic mental health with victims and offenders* (pp. 385–423). New York: Springer Publishing Company.

Brownell, P., Miller, K. M., & Raimon, M. L. (2007). Female offenders and the criminal justice system. In A. R. Roberts & D. W. Springer (Eds.), *Social work in juvenile and criminal justice settings* (pp. 75–86). Springfield, IL: Thomas Books.

Conly, C. (1998). *The Women's Prison Association: Supporting women offenders and their families.* Retrieved September 10, 2007, from http://www.ojp.usdoj.gov/nij

Covington, S., & Bloom, B. (2004, November). *Creating gender-responsive services in correctional settings: Context and considerations.* Paper presented at the meeting of the American Society of Criminology Conference, Nashville, TN.

Federal Sentencing Reform Act of 1984. Pub. L. No. 98-473, 98 Stat. (1987).

Greenfield, L. A., & Snell, T. L. (2000). *Women offenders.* Retrieved August 6, 2007, from http://www.ojp.usdoj.gov/bjs

Henderson, D. J. (1998). Drug abuse and incarcerated women: A research review. *Journal of Substance Abuse Treatment, 15,* 579–587.

McLellan, A. T., Cacciola, J., Kushner, H., Peters, F., Smith, I., & Pettinati, H. (1992). The fifth edition of the Addiction Severity Index: Cautions, additions, and normative data. *Journal of Substance Abuse Treatment, 9,* 199–213.

Morash, M., Bynum, T. S., & Koons, B. A. (1998). *Women offenders: Programming needs and promising approaches.* Retrieved September 10, 2007, from http://www.ojp.usdoj.gov/nij

Suicide-Prevention Programming in the Jail Setting

17

Schnavia Smith Hatcher

In *Elliot v. Cheshire County, N.H.* (1991), a young man with a history of mental health problems, most recently schizophrenia, assaulted his mother. A state trooper responded to the parents' call for help. The trooper was informed that the son had mental health problems and was schizophrenic; however, he was not told of the son's two prior threats to commit suicide. In turn, the trooper did not inform the intake officer of what he did know of the arrestee's mental health and the intake officer did not inquire. A few days later, after some very strange and suicide-suggestive behavior, that is, head banging and statements of wanting to take his life, the man committed suicide while in custody.

The reviewing court found that the trooper did not know of the decedent's prior suicide threats and that the man's demeanor did not suggest suicide. The court did not address the fact that the trooper was provided the man's mental health information and knew of the diagnosis of schizophrenia (*Elliot v. Cheshire County, N.H.*, 1991).

The number of persons incarcerated in jails in the United States has risen dramatically during the past several decades, with a significant increase in inmates with mental health issues. The Bazelon Center for Mental Health Law (2000) revealed that there are between 600,000 and 1 million individuals with mental illness booked into jails each year, representing more than 16% of inmates in detention. Corresponding with the increase of mental health demands within jails nationally, suicide has become one of the leading causes of death in local jails as well. There were 314 reported casualties in 2002 alone, representing the second most common cause of death in detention centers after natural causes, 32% and 52%, respectively (Mumola, 2005).

There have been a number of cases under judicial review which allege that certain jails and detention centers are at fault for custodial suicides, indicating they were preventable fatalities that could have been addressed if the facilities were prepared. Jails are similar to prisons, however, they are different in that they house individuals accused of committing crimes prior to their convictions, and, at times, inmates who are remanded or have short-term sentences. State prisons mostly house long-term-sentenced inmates, those with more than 1 year to serve. Though concepts of correctional justice have evolved throughout the centuries, the primary goal of correctional reform is still to enforce justice—within both jails and prisons. However, *Bell v. Wolfish* (1979) directed that the state must distinguish between pretrial detainees and convicted felons in one fundamental way, the state cannot punish a pretrial detainee. Officials involved in corrections must remain cognizant of this difference and be prepared to respond appropriately to mental health treatment needs and service issues.

This chapter helps to prepare social workers for forensic practice in local detention centers by providing an overview of factors related to suicide in jail settings and the assessment and screening process of inmates. Examples of cases with the rationales for judicial decisions involving custodial suicides and the recommendations of suicide-prevention policies from organizations and professions affiliated with the corrections system will also be discussed. The analyses are then followed by implications for social workers to adopt a sociological approach that augments existing practices through training and policy changes that support enhanced systems of care.

Classification of Suicidal Types

A number of characteristics have been identified that are strongly related to suicide in jail settings, such as intoxication, emotional state, psychiatric history, family history of suicide, lack of a social support system, limited prior incarceration, and various other confinement stressors. Three major classifications of suicidal persons in jails include: (a) inmate facing a crisis, (b) inmate experiencing a major depression, and (c) manipulative and impulsive inmates.

Inmate Facing a Crisis

An inmate facing a crisis is reacting to a real, immediate problem. As in most crisis situations, there is a failure of the person's usual coping methods and some people may function at a lower level than before the event. Table 17.1 provides examples of circumstances that inmates in this classification may face.

Inmate Experiencing a Major Depression

It is normal to react to some problems in life by being sad or despondent temporarily. However, a person defined by a mental health professional as being in a major

17.1 Examples of Personal Crises That Inmates May Experience

Jail officials should closely monitor inmates when the following occurs:

- News occurring outside of the jail

  - Family and friends not supportive
  - Unable to see children
  - Legal decisions within the jail
  - Trial rescheduled
  - Being found guilty
  - New charges added
  - Receiving a long sentence

Feelings of shame, frustration, and hopelessness displayed or stated by inmate

- Inmate-related conflicts
- First offenders
- Persons who have committed a crime of passion
- Professionals and high-profile persons who believe they will lose everything as a result of arrest
- Inmates coming down from drugs and alcohol

depression is experiencing more than a case of the blues. Table 17.2 provides examples of warning signs forensic social workers should notice.

Manipulative and Impulsive Inmates

Many young inmates are immature and impulsive. They act without thinking about the consequences of their actions, with the primary goal being getting some attention from the people in charge. It is frustrating for a correctional officer to try and maintain professionalism and concern regarding suicide prevention when it is suspected that the inmate is threatening suicide as a means of manipulating the corrections officer. However, many inmates have died because their attention-seeking attempt went further than they anticipated. Social workers working in corrections need to remind officers that anyone who would threaten to slash his or her wrists is emotionally unstable and needs professional help.

Suicide Intake Screening and Assessment

Intake screening and ongoing assessment of all inmates are critical to the prevention of suicide attempts within the jail. Screening may be included within the medical screening form or as a separate process performed by jail staff. Some content areas have been previously mentioned as red flags, for example, history of suicidal behavior (ideation and attempts), family history of suicide, or psychiatric history. The inmate's potential risk of suicide can be determined by asking preliminary questions such as: (a) Are you currently thinking of committing suicide? (b) Do you have a plan to

17.2 Examples of Warning Signs for Inmates Experiencing a Major Depression

Physical:

■ Sleeping difficulties: insomnia, irregular hours, early-morning awakening
■ Weight loss or loss of appetite
■ General loss of energy
■ Depressed physical appearance
■ Slumps when walking or sitting

Behavioral:

■ Talks of suicide
■ Cries frequently and/or for no apparent reason
■ Talks of getting out of jail unrealistically
■ Withdrawal, little communication with inmates or officers
■ Expresses feelings of helplessness and hopelessness
■ Gives away personal possessions and exhibits sudden change in behavior, such as making an unprovoked attack on an officer or another inmate.

commit suicide? And if so, (c) What is your plan to commit suicide? Additional intake-assessment priorities include noting current medications for depression/severe mental illness and recent alcohol and/or drug use.

In addition to the basic jail-intake screening process, there are a variety of standardized suicide assessment tools that can determine the threat, plan, or intent of the inmate. One of the most often used standardized suicide-assessment measures is the Scale for Suicide Ideation (SSI). The SSI (Beck, Kovacs, & Weissman, 1979), a 21-item interviewer-administered rating scale, measures the intensity of inmates' attitudes, behaviors, and plans to commit suicide. Items assess suicidal risk factors such as the duration and frequency of ideation, sense of control over making an attempt, number of deterrents, amount of actual preparation for a contemplated attempt, and the incidence and frequency of previous suicide attempts. Each rated item presents three options graded as 0 (low suicidal intensity) to 2 (high suicidal intensity), yielding a total score ranging from 0 to 38. The SSI has been used in a wide variety of settings, with both inpatients and outpatients with mental illness, and has established validity and reliability (Beck, Brown, & Steer, 1997; Beck et al., 1979).

It is recommended that any positive response to a suicidal inquiry (on the SSI or any other assessment), regardless of the total score, be followed up immediately with a clinical interview by a trained mental health professional. Also, along with the use of assessment measures, social workers should note any visual observations made by the correctional staff. These observations will help track behavior during periods when social workers on the mental health staff are not available to monitor the actions and responses of the inmate. As follow-up, mental health staff should also implement regular scheduled appraisals of those who are considered at risk.

Factors Related to Suicide in Jails

Suicide may be linked to many various factors: the offender's health status, feelings of shame and disappointment associated with breaking the law, as well as to any features of the institution itself. The annual national rate of suicide in jails is reported to be approximately 100 to 200 per 100,000 inmates, nine times greater than the rate for the general population (Bonner, 2000). Moreover, in 2002, the suicide rate in local jails was over three times the rate in state prisons (Mumola, 2005). Many jails are ill equipped, underfunded, and unprepared to respond appropriately to detainees' multiple mental health needs.

An abridged profile of suicide victims includes categories of age, sex, and race. In the past, the general rule was: the older the person, the more likely that he would be successful with the suicide attempt. However, there has been an increase in suicide in younger adults. It is also documented that women attempt suicide more frequently than men, but men have a higher rate of completing suicide attempts. Of the number reported during the time frame of Mumola's (2005) study, males were 56% more likely to commit suicide than female inmates and the suicide rate of White jail inmates was more than triple that of Hispanic inmates and was six times the rate for African Americans.

Along with considering personal characteristics, the time served after admission into the facility and housing placement were also intervening variables. According to Mumola (2005), approximately 48% of all jail suicides took place during the inmate's first week of being processed into the jail. These facts do not indicate that administrators should not continue to monitor detainees after this time period, however, almost a quarter of all jail suicides took place either the day of admission to the facility or the following day (Bonner, 2000; Mumola, 2005). Other environmental factors, for example, isolation in cells, held in temporary holding areas, were also shown to be prevalent in the suicidal deaths in local jails and detention centers (Mumola, 2005).

Myths of Suicide Prevention

The following list offers some common misconceptions regarding suicide:

- If you ask them about it, it will make them want to do it more.
- People who threaten suicide do not commit suicide.
- Suicide happens suddenly and impulsively, without premeditation.
- Once a person attempts suicide and fails, the inmate does not try again.
- If someone says he or she wants to kill him or herself, there is usually no way to prevent it.
- If the immediate crisis passes for the inmate, then the risk is over.

All of these misconceptions about suicide attempts can occur in jails. Belief in these and other misleading notions by correctional officers can be detrimental to a crisis situation. Forensic social workers need to emphasize that an inmate exhibiting a positive change in behavior during a suicidal watch should still be monitored and still considered to be in a critical period. Correctional staff attitudes reflected in statements such as "if they want to kill themselves, we can't stop them" and "we can't watch these suicidal people all the time" can be potentially harmful and suggest a lack of training in recognizing symptoms and the treatment of mental illness and suicidal behavior in the inmates whom they observe daily (Hatcher, in press). Social workers can make correctional staff, particularly officers, aware that factors that make jails a particularly high-risk environment include: the large proportion of inmates who have mental illness, their co-occurring disorders of alcohol and drug abuse, and the traumatic effect that criminal incarceration can have on an inmate's personal life (Goss, Peterson, Smith, Kalb, & Brodey, 2002).

Standards for Jail-Suicide Prevention

Acknowledging the need to address suicide occurrences, the American Correctional Association (ACA) (1981) and the National Commission on Correctional Health Care (NCCHC) (1987, 2003) contributed recommendations for jail-suicide-prevention programs. The guidelines are standards that can help forensic social workers develop prevention programs that improve the health of inmates, increase the efficiency of their health services delivery, and strengthen the organizational effectiveness of the jail. Twelve essential components that can establish and facilitate maintenance of acceptable health services systems are:

1. identification
2. communication
3. training
4. intervention
5. assessment
6. notification
7. monitoring
8. reporting
9. housing
10. review
11. referral
12. critical-incident debriefing (NCCHC, 2003).

Details are provided that outline the prevention process, including housing recommendations—an accessible cell free of all obvious protrusions and break-away objects; levels of observation—close (intervals of 15 minutes or less) and constant (uninterrupted); and intervention strategies—initiate and continue life-saving measures until relieved by appropriate medical personnel. The components also address necessary communication from mental health staff to correctional staff and provide critical information on high-risk periods when inmates may become suicidal.

Guidelines and standards have also been offered by individuals who work integrally with the criminal justice system. Hayes (2005) provided approaches—eight components derived from national correctional standards—to facilitate the care and optimal treatment of the inmate: staff training, intake screening and assessment, communication, housing, levels of observation, intervention, reporting, follow-up, and mortality review. For a more detailed discussion of the eight recommendations, the reader is directed to the review by Hayes (2005).

Referencing all of the recommendations, including those of the ACA and NCCHC, provides a preliminary safe space for the inmate with suicidal tendencies. Nonetheless, jail administration should be cautioned to remember that the assessment of suicide risk is an ongoing process.

Custodial Suicides and Legal Interpretation

In a recent case, *Perez v. Oakland County* (2005), 18-year-old Ariel Perez, Jr. hanged himself from a bed sheet tied to a vent in his single cell in the Oakland County Jail in Pontiac, Michigan, resulting in his death 3 days later. Perez had been on a suicide watch during previous stays, and had told jail staff of suicide attempts and about hearing voices telling him to hurt himself. He tried to commit suicide approximately half an hour after he was admitted by tying his pants around his neck and to the bars of his cell. He was taken off suicide watch by a case worker and returned to the general population after he said his attempt was a means to obtain medication. Jail officials later canceled his medication request after learning he wasn't taking the medication and did not feel he needed it.

Perez's father brought action in the district court against Oakland County, Michigan, the caseworker/counselor at the jail, the Oakland County Sheriff, several of his deputies, and the jail psychiatrist. He stated that Perez was diagnosed with attention-deficit/ hyperactivity disorder (ADHD) at age 6 and with schizophrenia shortly before his death. The plaintiff argued that the defendants violated Perez's right to be free from cruel and unusual punishment by failing to provide appropriate mental health treatment and suicide monitoring. The U.S. District Judge dismissed the lawsuit, saying the jail caseworker may or may not have acted with deliberate indifference, but the official and the county were entitled to a form of government immunity (*Perez v. Oakland County*). The summary judgment indicated that although the decisions in the case were questionable, they were not in violation of existing law.

Deliberate indifference exists when the plaintiff can show an unusual risk of harm; defendants' actual knowledge of, or willful blindness to that risk; and defendants' failure to take obvious steps to address the risk (*Bowen v. City of Manchester*, 1992; *Estelle v. Gamble*, 1976). Based on these criteria, the case facts presented previously and in *Elliot v Cheshire County, N.H.* (1991) seem to indicate proof of deliberate indifference, however, the reviewing court determined otherwise.

There are other examples of how standards of deliberate indifference have been interpreted and provided the defacto rationale for the courts' decisions, for example, *Dobson v. Magnusson* (1991), *Kocienski v. City of Bayonne* (1991). The decisions underscore that the Constitution outlaws cruel and unusual "punishments," not "conditions," and the failure to alleviate a significant risk that a correctional staff should have perceived, but did not, cannot be condemned as the infliction of punishment.

A Place for Social Work

Because suicides usually are attempted in inmate housing units often during late evening and on weekends, very few suicides are actually impeded by social work, mental health, medical, or other professional staff. Although qualified mental health professionals, such as a licensed clinical social worker, should receive the referral requests for full clinical assessments from intake staff to determine the inmate's risk of suicide and treatment needs, once housed in the facility, it is usually the primary duty of the correctional staff to conduct the follow-ups. Social workers can be a vital presence within the jail during these times by becoming intrinsically involved in training the correctional officers—the front line of defense—in preventing the attempts. Basic elements needed for initial and refresher training include identifying: (a) individual risk factors, for example, warnings, signs, and characteristics of inmates; (b) institutional risk factors, for example, staff attitude about suicide, facility configuration; (c) the benefits and barriers to a good suicide-prevention program; (d) the steps in critical-incident debriefing; (e) liability issues and other legal redress; and (f) challenges with the facility's current suicide-prevention plan.

Social workers should also be responsible for supporting the development and implementation of all relevant health policies with the detention center. While first understanding and appreciating the criminal justice system, social workers should advocate for changes in policy and legislation that improve social conditions and promote social justice for their clients in detention centers. Once positioned with the right tools, the profession can take an active leadership role in formulating and providing for the delivery of adequate mental health services to the incarcerated population.

Although this chapter primarily focuses on management and prevention efforts of providers and administrators within the correctional facilities, social workers must also prepare to take a lead in the treatment provisions for inmates with mental health issues. Promising clinical treatment with inmates who are depressed and/or self-injurious include dialectical behavior therapy (DBT) (Ivanoff & Hayes, 2001; McCann, Ivanoff, Schmidt, & Beach, 2007) and motivational interviewing (Britton, Williams, & Conner, 2008). Scholars are continuing to identify the most effective interventions in mental health corrections that will facilitate health promotion within the facility.

Finally, establishing a system within the jail that focuses on continuity of care is essential in increasing the chances of improved health and decreasing the possibility of recidivism for the offender with mental illness (OMI). Transitional planning, one of the most vital aspects of successful reentry, is still not being provided even in some of the largest jails in the nation (Osher, Steadman, & Barr, 2002; Steadman & Veysey, 1997). Hatcher (2007) suggests that just referring standard, which most times are limited, mental health resources from jail for OMI is not enough for them to survive in the community. Aims need to transcend basic institutional (correctional) objectives and promote the client to achieve a healthier well-being. A collaboration of efforts bringing together correctional systems and community-based organizations is crucial to achieving optimal living for these clients.

Summary and Conclusions

Suicide, on its own, does not warrant liability. On the contrary, it is when suicide is somehow foreseeable that officials become responsible. The failure to develop and implement a suicide-prevention policy, deliberate indifference to a suicidal risk, and improper correctional and mental health staffing currently stand as exemplar dynamics in liability cases. Given that the current practice provides margin for substandard conditions, interpretation, and an infringement on an inmate's civil rights, it appears that the requirements for jail-suicide prevention should be more prescribed by recommended standards and, quite possibly, move toward mandated benchmarks. Social workers can work with correctional administration and staff to address these needs by facilitating the development and implementation of thorough prevention guidelines, maintaining the training and continuing education of the prevention standards and techniques, and becoming a vanguard for the provision of quality care and thorough assessment of inmates within the facility.

Online Resources

American Association of Suicidology: http://www.suicidology.org

American Foundation for Suicide Prevention: http://www.afsp.org

National Center on Institutions and Alternatives: http://www.ncianet.org

National Commission on Correctional Health Care: http://www.ncchc.org

References

American Correctional Association. (1981). *Standards for adult local detention facilities* (2nd ed.). College Park, MD: Author.

Bazelon Center for Mental Health Law. (2000). *1999 annual report*. Washington, DC: Author.

Beck, A., Brown, G., & Steer, R. (1997). Psychometric characteristics of the Scale for Suicide Ideation with psychiatric outpatients. *Behavior Research and Therapy, 11*, 1039–1046.

Beck, A., Kovacs, M., & Weissman, A. (1979). Assessment of suicidal intention: The Scale for Suicide Ideation. *Journal of Consulting and Clinical Psychology, 47*, 343–352.

Bell v. Wolfish, 441 U.S. 520 (1979).

Bonner, R. (2000). Correctional suicide prevention in the year 2000 and beyond. *Jail Suicide/Mental Health Update, 9*(3), 1–4.

Bowen v. City of Manchester, 966 F.2d 13 (1st Cir. 1992).

Britton, P., Williams, G., & Conner, K. (2008). Self-determination theory, motivational interviewing, and the treatment of clients with acute suicidal ideation. *Journal of Clinical Psychology, 64*(1), 52–66.

Dobson v. Magnusson, 923 F.2d 229 (1st Cir.1991).

Elliot v. Cheshire County, N.H., 940 F2d. 7 (1st Cir. 1991).

Estelle v. Gamble, 429 U.S. 97 (1976).

Goss, J., Peterson, K., Smith, L., Kalb, K., & Brodey, B. (2002). Characteristics of suicide attempts in a large urban jail system with an established suicide prevention program. *Psychiatric Services, 53*, 574–579.

Hatcher, S. (2007). Transitional care for African American offenders with mental illness in jail: Mapping indicators of successful community reentry. *Best Practices in Mental Health: An International Journal, 3*(2), 38–51.

Hatcher, S. (in press). Deliberate indifference in jail suicide litigation: A fatal judicial loophole. *Social Work in Public Health, 24*(5).

Hayes, L. (2005). Suicide prevention in correctional facilities. In C. Scott & J. Gerbasi (Eds.), *Handbook of correctional mental health* (pp. 69–88). Washington, DC: American Psychiatric Press.

Ivonoff, A., & Hayes, L. (2001). Preventing, managing, and treating suicidal actions in high-risk offenders. In J. Ashford, B. Sales, & W. Reid (Eds.), *Treating adult and juvenile offenders with special needs* (pp. 313–331). Washington, DC: American Psychological Association.

Kocienski v. City of Bayonne, 757 F.Supp. 457 (D.N.J. 1991).

McCann, R., Ivanoff, A., Schmidt, H., & Beach, B. (2007). Implementing dialectical behavior therapy in residential forensic settings with adults and juveniles. In L. Dimeff & K. Koerner (Eds.), *Dialectical behavior therapy in clinical practice: Applications across disorders and settings* (pp. 112–144). New York: Guilford Press.

Mumola, C. (2005). *Suicide and homicide in state prisons and local jails.* Washington, DC: U.S. Department of Justice, Office of Justice Programs, Bureau of Justice Statistics.

National Commission on Correctional Health Care. (1987). *Standards for health services in jails.* Chicago, IL: Author.

National Commission on Correctional Health Care. (2003). *Standards for health services in jails* (7th ed.). Chicago, IL: Author.

Osher, F., Steadman, H., & Barr, H. (2002). *A best practice approach to community re-entry from jails for inmates with co-occurring disorders: The APIC model.* Delmar, NY: National GAINS Center.

Perez v. Oakland County, 380 F. Supp. 2d 830 (E.D. MI. 2005).

Steadman, H., & Veysey, B. (1997). *Providing services for jail inmates with mental disorders.* Washington, DC: U.S. Department of Justice, National Institute of Justice.

Part VI

Forensic Practice in Juvenile and Criminal Justice

Juvenile Justice and Social Work

18

Tina Maschi
Nancy M. Violette
Nancy Scotto Rosato
Jennifer Ristow

Social workers who deal with at-risk youth, families, and communities often have varying levels of involvement with the juvenile justice system. Their work generally falls within a continuum of care that involves prevention or intervention efforts geared toward decreasing adverse health, mental health, and/or behavioral outcomes among youth, especially juvenile delinquency. For example, at one end of the continuum are social workers engaged in prevention activities, such as skills training, aimed at children or their parents in a community agency setting. At the other end of the continuum are clinical social workers and administrators engaged in correctional rehabilitation efforts, such as providing treatment services for incarcerated youth with mental and behavioral problems in a maximum security facility. Despite their differing levels of involvement with the juvenile justice system, both types of practice demand that social workers be knowledgeable of the social and legal factors affecting these populations. Understanding the impact of sociolegal factors can assist social workers in developing or improving prevention and intervention strategies at any point on the continuum of care.

This chapter is designed to assist social workers in maximizing their practice effectiveness with youth by providing knowledge and skills for practice that intersects with the juvenile justice system. We begin with an overview of the structure and processes of the juvenile justice system. Next, we provide an outline of juvenile delinquency, including the common characteristics of the juvenile justice population that affect assessment and intervention strategies. This is followed by a review of risk and resilience perspectives as well as the common social work practice settings, assessment, prevention, and intervention strategies and skills necessary for effective practice. The chapter concludes with excerpts from a qualitative case study of an incarcerated youth that illustrates common issues that may arise in social work practice with youth involved in the juvenile justice system.

The Juvenile Justice System: An Overview

The term "juvenile justice system" refers to the structure and process of juvenile justice, which the *Social Work Dictionary* defines as: "That part of the criminal justice system that is oriented toward the control and prevention of illegal behavior by young people (those younger than age 22 in some jurisdictions and younger than age 16 or 18 in others) and toward the treatment of a minor engaged in such behavior" (Barker, 2003, p. 235).

The juvenile justice system is not a concrete entity but rather a loose-knit group of service organizations and institutions that are involved in some aspect of the decision-making process with youth (Rosenheim, 2002). What distinguishes the juvenile justice system from the criminal justice system is its authority over youth, generally under the age of 18, compared to the criminal justice system, which presides over adults aged 18 and older. The organizations involved in the juvenile justice system include law enforcement, juvenile courts, juvenile detention centers, and social welfare agencies (e.g., child welfare, foster care in patient mental health, or substance-abuse services) (Drowns & Hess, 2003). Compared to other child-focused institutions (e.g., schools), the juvenile justice system has secondary status and receives less public support and fewer resources. Therefore, social workers whose practice intersects with the juvenile justice system should be aware that the nature of political and public support rests on the shifting political climate, public opinion, and mass media coverage (Rosenheim, 2002).

The Law Enforcement, Courts, and Corrections Continuum

To best serve juvenile-justice–involved populations, social workers should understand the continuum of legal interventions that make up the juvenile justice system. Like the criminal justice system, the juvenile justice system has three basic legal components: the police, the courts, and corrections (Agnew, 2001). The process for youth involved with the juvenile justice system usually begins with an initial contact with the police, followed by the courts, and then corrections. At any juncture in a youth's legal procession through the system, he or she may be diverted out of the system (Bartollas & Miller, 2005). For example, a police officer may use his or her discretionary power to provide a verbal warning and release the juvenile or file a petition for delinquency charges to the court. Pending the outcome of the judge's decision, a juvenile may be recommended for the least restrictive placements (e.g., a community-based diversion program) to the most restrictive placement (e.g., out-of-home placement in a secure-care correctional facility).

History

As illustrated in chapter 2, social work's history is closely interwoven with the history of juvenile justice. The origins of the juvenile justice system can be traced back to the child-saving movement of the late 1800s (Platt, 1969). The child-savers, particularly the "feminist" reformers, such as Jane Addams, were viewed as making an "enlight-ened effort to alleviate the miseries of urban life and juvenile delinquency caused by an unregulated capitalist society" (Platt, 1977, p. xiv). Successful lobbying efforts for a rehabilitative approach made by Jane Addams and fellow reformers resulted in the creation of the Cook County (Illinois) Juvenile Court on July 3, 1899.

The establishment of the Illinois juvenile court system created a justice system for children with the underlying premise of the protection and rehabilitation of youth. This premise was different from the punishment approach taken by the criminal justice system. The juvenile court was also designed to see to the needs of abused and neglected children and delinquent children. By 1925, the juvenile court system model had been adopted across the United States and Canada, as well as by countries in Europe and South America (Justice Policy Institute, 2000), which underscores how the collaborative efforts of social workers and other advocates led to wide-scale legal reform.

The contemporary mission of the juvenile justice system has been described as having three parts: (a) to protect public safety, (b) to hold juvenile offenders accountable for their behavior, and (c) to provide treatment and rehabilitation services for juveniles and their families (Bartollas & Miller, 2005). However, more recent trends for addressing juvenile crime combine rehabilitative and punitive approaches. For exam-ple, rehabilitative approaches include alternatives to detention or community pro-grams that attempt to keep youth in the community and divert them from the formal juvenile justice system (Bruns et al., 2004; Burns & Hoagwood, 2002; Cocozza & Skowyra, 2000; National Mental Health Association [NMHA], 2004). For example, since the 1960s teen courts have been steadily growing as an alternative to juvenile courts, especially for youth aged 10–15 who have been charged with minor offenses (Butts & Buck, 2000). What is unique about teen courts is that sentencing is done by other teens, rather than an "official" judge (Herman, 2002). In contrast, recent punitive approaches feature tougher policies and laws, such as the juvenile waiver to adult court and the death penalty for juveniles (Justice Policy Institute, 2000). Social workers working within this system should be aware of the tension between the rehabilitative approach (which is more consistent with the philosophy of social work) and the opposing punitive approach and how this tension might influence their ability to achieve practice objectives that are consistent with social work's mission to enhance social functioning and increase social justice outcomes.

Scope of the Problem

Social workers may be involved with youth who have received an official court disposition for juvenile delinquency. Therefore, it is essential to understand how the legal system defines juvenile delinquency and classifies juvenile crime.

Juvenile delinquency is defined as "illegal acts committed by persons under the age of 18, including some acts called status offenses which, if committed by someone 18 or older, would not be illegal" (Snyder, 2000, p. 1). The official definition of delinquency places delinquent acts into three categories (or indexes), based on the severity of the offense (Snyder & Sickmund, 2006). The most serious of the three categories are violent crime indexes, for example, forcible rape, robbery, aggravated assault, murder, and negligent manslaughter. Property crime indexes, the second level of offenses, includes burglary, larceny (i.e., theft), motor vehicle theft, and arson. Nonindex offenses, which are generally considered minor acts of delinquency, include stolen property (e.g., buying, receiving, possessing), drug-abuse violations, and status offenses (e.g., liquor law violations, truancy, running away, violating curfew) (Snyder, 2000). Thus, social workers in a variety of settings (e.g., community agencies, schools, and legal settings) face a high likelihood of being involved with youth who have committed minor to severe delinquent offenses or are at-risk of doing so.

Juvenile-Arrest Trends

Juvenile-arrest trends across time are not static but dynamic. In 2004, approximately one out of five arrests in the United States were of juveniles. In other words, juveniles represented 2.2 million (16%) of the 14 million arrests made. As high as these rates may appear, they actually represent a declining trend: the rate in 2004 was 2% less than in 2002 and 22% less than in 1995 (Snyder & Sickmund, 2006). This decrease of delinquency in youth has been attributed to the influence of environmental factors, such as an increase in economic prosperity and the active development of community-prevention and intervention efforts (Butts, 2000). This suggests that systemic interventions, such as better economic conditions and community-based strategies, have tremendous potential for increasing positive outcomes for youth, their families, and their communities.

Common Issues Across the System

The juvenile justice population can be classified as a multineed population because these youth are often affected by a broad range of psychosocial issues. Over two decades of research have documented the psychosocial stressors among juvenile justice populations: histories of trauma or other stressful life events, including being a victim and/or witness to family and/or community violence, school problems, and living in poverty (e.g., Abram et al., 2004; Grisso, 1999; Martin, Sigda, & Kupersmidt, 1998; Maschi, 2006; Potter & Jenson, 2003). Studies also have shown that juvenile justice involves youth who often exhibit a complex array of psychological, cognitive, emotional, and behavioral issues that may include serious mental illness, low cognitive functioning, learning disabilities, substance abuse, self-injurious behavior, suicidal risk behavior, delinquent peer and/or gang involvement, and aggressive behavior (e.g., Government Accounting Office, 2003; Lyons, Baerger, Quigley, Erlich, & Griffin, 2001; Teplin et al., 2005; Vermeiron, 2003). Another major concern is the disproportionate involvement of minority youth, especially among African Americans, in the juvenile justice system (National Council on Crime & Delinquency [NCCD], 2007; Williams, Hovmand, & Bright, 2007). Minority youth are more likely to be subject to police arrest, court referral, and more severe court dispositions, such as placement in secure care rather than community-based settings. In addition, evidence suggests that youth with mental health problems are at risk for more severe juvenile justice sanctions compared to youth without mental health problems (Hirschfield, Maschi, White, Goldman-Traub, & Loeber, 2006; Maschi, Hatcher, Schwalbe, & Scotto Rosato, 2008; Wasserman, Ko, Larkin, & McReynolds, 2004). In addition, although there are a large number of males in the juvenile justice system, trends suggest female juveniles' involvement in the juvenile justice system is increasing at a much greater rate than males (Chesney-Lind & Sheldon, 2004; MacDonald & Chesney-Lind, 2001; Snyder, 2006, Youth Law Center, 2000).

A review of the prevalent psychosocial issues suggests that social workers who serve juvenile justice populations should be prepared to assess and treat youth affected by a wide array of personal, family, and community factors. Adopting a two-pronged approach (using micro- and/or macro-level intervention strategies) that incorporate evidence-based practices can help address the issues facing youth, their families, and their communities. These strategies include the need for social workers to be proficient in providing or designing and implementing trauma-based intervention services (Baer & Maschi, 2003).

Relevant Theoretical Frameworks

The criminological literature has a number of theories that attempt to explain illegal behavior among juveniles and adults. Some theories attempt to explain criminality as a learned behavior (e.g., social learning theory) that can be influenced by interpersonal or situational stressors (e.g., anomie or general strain theory), or societal level controls (e.g., deterrence theory, rational choice theory, and social control theory) and attitudes (e.g., labeling theory), or adverse environmental or neighborhood factors (e.g., social disorganization theory) (Akers & Sellers, 2004; Shoemaker, 2004).

Social workers working with youth and families in the juvenile justice system would benefit from the knowledge of risk and resilience and community-development perspectives. These perspectives are consistent with social work's mission of assisting disenfranchised populations in maximizing their potential.

Risk and Resilience Perspective

Derived from the fields of psychology and education, the *risk and resilience perspective* can be useful in informing assessment and intervention strategies with youth involved in—or at-risk of—juvenile justice involvement. Consistent with social work's biopsychosocial framework, the risk and resilience perspective examines the influence of individual, family, and community risk and protective factors on individual youth-development outcomes (Fraser, 1997; Rutter, 1985, 1987). A critical aspect of this perspective is the focus on protective factors that foster positive youth development (Garmezy & Masten, 1994; Garmezy & Rutter, 1983).

Resiliency is central to this perspective. *Resilience* refers to the "presence of risk factors in combination with positive forces that contribute to adaptive outcomes" and has been defined as "successful adaptation despite adversity" (Kirby & Fraser, 1997, p. 14). Risk factors are vulnerabilities in the individual (e.g., impulsive behavior), family (e.g., family violence), or environment (e.g., living in poverty) that increase the odds of a negative outcome for youth. Risk factors may include impulsive or aggressive behavior; living in poverty; and exposure to family, school, and/or community violence. In contrast, protective factors are internal and external resources that increase the odds of positive outcomes for youth. These protective factors may include personal resources (e.g., high self-esteem, internal locus of control), social resources (e.g., family cohesion, family emotional support), and community resources (e.g., positive reinforcement at school, church, and in the community) (Walsh, 2006).

Community Youth Development Perspective

The *community youth development perspective* evolved from the risk and resilience and ecological perspective literature and integrates youth development with community-development perspectives (Garbarino, 2001). Perkins, Borden, Keith, Hoppe-Rooney, and Villarruel (2003) defined the community youth development perspective as:

> *Purposely creating environments that provide constructive, affirmative, and encouraging relationships that are sustained over time with adults and peers, while concurrently providing an array of opportunities that enable youth to build their competencies and become engaged as partners in their own development of their communities. (p. 6)*

The community youth development model focuses on the interaction between youth and their environment. Positive or negative development occurs as youth interact with their surroundings, including social interaction with others. Intervention strategies should be used to develop or reinforce the connections to individual youths, adults, and the larger community. Intervention strategies that foster community youth development involve providing positive support, competency-building opportunities, and partnerships with youth and stakeholders across the multiple domains (Lerner, 2002; Perkins et al., 2003). What is useful about these combined perspectives for social work practice is that they provide leverage for practitioners working with youth (i.e., micro level) and/or communities (i.e., macro level) across the common practice settings that intersect with the juvenile justice system. A review of these practice settings follows.

Common Practice Settings

Social workers often work in community practice settings as well as in the juvenile justice system. These settings fall within a continuum of care from the least restricted community environment to the most restrictive secure-care environment. Because social workers are present to emphasize the social welfare aspect of juvenile justice, the settings in which social workers are present are often geared toward prevention and/or rehabilitation efforts for youth and their families, including probation, secure-care placement, and after-care services (Drowns & Hess, 2003). For example, social workers who work with juvenile-justice–involved youth may practice in school- or community-prevention programs, school-based counseling services, community-based diversion programs, social welfare agencies, intensive case management programs, outpatient or inpatient treatment centers, residential programs, law enforcement settings, the courts, or secure-care correctional settings (e.g., detention, training schools), and after-care/community reentry programs (Ellis & Sowers, 2001).

These practice settings also may differ from the central mission of the "host" setting, whether it is a medical, mental health, social welfare, or juvenile justice program or institution. To work effectively within these varied settings, social workers should be cognizant of their position in the system as well as how their assessment and intervention decisions may affect the placement of youth in community, residential, or correctional settings. Understanding their position in the system will assist practitioners in delineating effective strategies that can best be used to facilitate change efforts.

Common Practice Activities

Regardless of their job title, social workers involved with any area of the juvenile justice system may engage in a number of "direct" and "indirect" activities, including clinical social work, case management, administration, research and evaluation, advocacy, networking, mediation, advising, education, and policymaking and policy advocacy. The following section describes the individuals (i.e., professionals and nonprofessionals) with whom social workers may interact in the course of collaborative forensic social work activities (Madden & Wayne, 2003; Roberts & Springer, 2007).

Common Practice Skills

Social work activities within the juvenile justice system incorporate generalist and specialized practice skills that span individual, group work, and community practice, such as problem-solving skills; written and oral communication skills (including computer skills); case management skills that involve organizational, coordination, and networking; crisis management skills; trauma, substance abuse, and mental health assessment and intervention; and research and evaluation skills (Baer & Maschi, 2003; Cournoyer, 2005).

This next section highlights four areas that can greatly assist in practicing collaborative forensic social work practice within the juvenile justice system:

- learning the language of the juvenile justice system,
- confidentiality in ethical and legal decision making,
- the use of empathic neutrality, and
- culturally competent/ethnically sensitive practice.

Learning the Language

Because the juvenile justice system focuses on rehabilitation rather than punishment, practitioners should be familiar with the special language used to describe juvenile contact with the legal system. Compared to the criminal justice system and adult offenders, juvenile justice language tends to "humanize" rather than "criminalize" the nature of the legal encounter. For example, juveniles are not "arrested"; they are "taken into custody." Juveniles have "adjudicatory hearings" rather than "trials." Juveniles also are "detained" rather than "jailed." Juveniles are placed in "reform schools" and "youth service centers," not "prisons." When placed in secure-care settings, juveniles are commonly referred to as "residents" rather than "prisoners." When they are released, juveniles are placed in "after-care" rather than on "parole." A debate exists in the profession as to whether the use of these types of euphemisms helps to reduce stigma or whether it is deceptive language that minimizes or rationalizes illegal activities (Barker, 2003).

Confidentiality: An Ethical and Legal Dilemma

It is common for social workers to be responsible for clients in crisis in the juvenile justice system. For example, new intakes into a secure-care setting are often at high risk for suicidal behavior or have engaged in illegal activities that have not come to the attention of authorities. Therefore, practitioners in the juvenile justice system should be aware of the limits of confidentiality. It is also important for practitioners to understand that confidentiality is both an ethical and legal issue (Madden, 2003).

Social workers in direct contact with juvenile justice youths are responsible to review the parameters of confidentiality with their clients—including its exceptions, because of the high-risk nature of this population. Social workers should discuss with their clients that communications between the social worker and client are confidential except when:

- clients pose a danger to themselves or someone else;
- a client under the age of 16 is the victim of incest, physical abuse, or sexual abuse;
- information is subpoenaed in a court case;
- clients request that their records be released to themselves or to a third party (Dickson, 1998).

Social workers may find that ethical dilemmas and legal issues that occur in this work. For example, the tension between punishments versus rehabilitative approaches may cause a value conflict or raise an ethical dilemma for the social worker (Ivanoff, Smyth, & Dulmus, 2007; Needleman, 2007). Although the nature of these dilemmas may vary, social workers can best be prepared by familiarizing themselves with an ethical decision-making model to help navigate practice dilemmas that involve ethical and/or legal issues (see Barker & Branson, 2003; Madden, 2003).

Empathic Neutrality

Empathic neutrality is a useful skill to practice in the juvenile justice system. According to Patton (2002), it is a stance that seeks vicarious understanding (i.e., empathy) without judgment (i.e., neutrality). Empathic neutrality assists with rapport-building and keeping personal biases in check when working with youthful offenders. This empathically neutral stance is achieved by demonstrating openness, sensitivity, respect, awareness, and responsiveness. This technique involves the use of empathy, which is made up of the cognitive and affective components that enable the practitioners to be able to understand the thoughts, feelings, experiences, and worldview of others, whereas neutrality refers to the suspension of judgment (Patton, 2002). This technique enables practitioners to use empathy with a nonjudgmental attitude so as to effectively work with youth, particularly those accused of crimes in which a victim was injured or killed. It is also useful in interactions with interdisciplinary professionals that enable social workers to understand a different perspective using a nonjudgmental stance to facilitate consensus-building.

Cultural Competence

Because the juvenile justice population consists of a diverse group made up of vulnerable populations, cultural competence (i.e., ethnically sensitive social work practice) is a critical element for effective practice with these individuals (Fong & Furoto, 2001). Evidence suggests that a disproportionate number of minority youth (especially Black youth), youth with mental health disorders, and those from impoverished urban neighborhoods become involved in the juvenile justice system (e.g., Cocozza, 1992; Hirschfield et al., 2006; Maschi et al., 2008; National Council on Crime and Delinquency, 2007; Wasserman et al., 2003; Williams et al., 2007; Youth Law Center, 2000). Distinct differences—such as victimization, mental health status, and offending patterns— between male and female youth involved in the juvenile and criminal justice systems also have been found (MacDonald & Chesney-Lind, 2001).

The population characteristics of youth in the juvenile justice system make it critical that practitioners are proficient in the use of evidence-based assessment and intervention strategies that address cultural, mental health, and gender-specific needs (Chesney-Lind & Sheldon, 2004; LeCroy, Stevenson, & MacNeil, 2003; Potter & Jenson, 2007; Wasserman et al., 2003). Practitioners who integrate evidence-based practices with an ethnically sensitive approach will be "knowledgeable, perceptive, empathic, and skillful about the unique as well as common characteristics of clients who possess racial, ethnic, religious, gender, age, sexual orientation, or socioeconomic differences" (Barker, 2003, p. 100).

VOICES FROM THE FIELD

Michael J. Federici, MSW
Juvenile Probation Supervisor

Agency Setting

The Juvenile Probation Department is part of the Court Support Services Division (CSSD); an agency within the State of Connecticut Judicial Branch. There are 13 Juvenile Probation Offices regionally located in Connecticut. Juvenile Probation is responsible for all Delinquent, Family With Service Needs, and Youth in Crisis complaints filed with the courts. I am responsible for the Norwalk Juvenile Probation Department, which oversees the towns of Westport, Wilton, Weston, New Canaan, Darien, and the City of Norwalk.

Practice Responsibilities

As a full-time forensic social worker in the Juvenile Probation Department, I am responsible for assessing all new client intake referrals for judicial or nonjudicial determination. Once the case is assigned to a probation officer, I work collaboratively with the officer to ensure that a complete biopsychosocial history is done. This would include assessing the client's mental health, medical, substance abuse, and educational needs as well as identifying the client's individual strengths and the strengths of that client's entire family / environmental system. The court uses these assessments to determine the most appropriate interventions for the client. At this point the focus shifts from assessment to monitoring and intervention. In this capacity, I work with the probation officers to ensure compliance with court orders, address any violation concerns, implement a strategic plan aimed at assisting the client with change behavior and working collaboratively with families, schools, mental health agencies, and social skills-building programs. Additional responsibilities include monthly supervision with probation officers, case review team presentations, detention triages, and adherence to all CSSD policy and procedures.

Expertise Required

I believe that the forensic social worker involved with Juvenile Probation should have a background in social work, psychology, or a related field. Though the position does not require a master's degree, it is my impression that many of the skills probation officers use during the course of the workday are master's level skills. All probation officers have received extensive training in motivational interviewing, strengths-based probation, crisis intervention, and risk reduction. When hired, each officer is required to complete 80 hours of initial training and an additional 40 hours every year thereafter. Trainings have been clinically focused in the area of suicide prevention, cognitive-behavioral therapy, multisystemic therapy, anger management, child development, as well as officer safety and personal restraint. It is one of the few positions within a criminal justice field that requires a person to obtain a high level of skill competence in both social work and law enforcement principles.

Practice Challenges

Probably the single most difficult challenge that probation officers face is working with families who do not support the client. Because all clients are generally children under the age of 16, families can present quite an obstacle to treatment success. Other challenges include clients who are more than 2 years behind academically within their school settings, significant mental health or substance-abuse issues, and lack of adequate housing or financial stability. In some instances, several or all of these challenges are present, which has resulted in clients being removed from their home environments and placed either in a short-term detention facility or a longer-term residential treatment facility. Despite these challenges, I believe that the training and experience that probation officers have obtained allow for creative thinking in offsetting these deficits and enable them to use whatever strengths the child and/or family presents to assist in maintaining the client in the community.

Common Legal and/or Ethical Issues

One of the most common legal dilemmas facing the courts today is sifting through referrals on clients for noncriminal or status offenses. Clients have routinely been referred to courts for truancy, defiance of school rules, or beyond control behaviors at home, which has created a conundrum of issues for the courts, most notably, how to deal with noncompliance of court orders for a noncriminal offense. I typically divert these types of cases from the courts by establishing and maintaining strong collaborative ties to the faith-based community, mental health providers, and school personnel. Among the many ethical issues that probation officers face, the most complex is trying to separate what is criminal behavior versus what is normal adolescent acting-out behavior. This can be quite daunting especially when you add other issues such as minority overrepresentation within the juvenile justice system, parental substance abuse or incarceration, neglect, and abuse, all of which present with an entire different set of ethical and moral issues.

Brief Description of Collaborative Activities With Professionals and/or Other Stakeholders

I have been a member of the Community Prevention Task force for 13 years, a program designed to address youth violence, substance abuse, and teen-pregnancy prevention. I served as the chairperson for this task force for over 10 years between 1995–2005. I also am a member of the Systems of Care collaborative, which is comprised of mental health, school, Department of Children and Families (DCF), and court agencies. I am also a member of the Urban Youth Initiative, which is a collaboration of police, probation, schools, mental health agencies, and the faith-based community. This initiative addresses issues related to youth violence. As part of my duties as a Probation Supervisor, I head the Case Review Team, which encompasses many of the same principles for case discussion on whether certain clients need to be removed from the community. Additionally, there is a collaborative relationship with DCF, in which detention triages occur, for example, regular meetings with the Family With Service Needs Liaison from DCF and planning meetings with the Area Director are taking place.

Additional Information

I have also been an adjunct trainer for CSSD providing training in Pre-Dispositional Studies, the Juvenile Assessment Generic, and Suicide Intervention. I have also done presentations in the community for various stakeholders concerning the juvenile court process, as well as internal trainings for officers on motivational interviewing. I currently serve as a field liaison for Sacred Heath University, BSW program and have been invited to speak to both the criminal justice program about the juvenile justice process and the social work program about motivational interviewing.

Collaboration in the Juvenile Justice System

Knowledge and skills in interdisciplinary collaboration are essential to serve juvenile-justice-involved clients. As noted previously, collaboration in the juvenile justice system involves different individuals, groups, and organizations across a variety of practice settings. It is useful to conceptualize these individuals (professionals, nonprofessional individuals, or groups) as stakeholders because they all have a vested interest in youth and/or community safety outcomes. The different systems and their stakeholders include:

- the family (e.g., juvenile, parents, legal guardians, siblings, and extended family);
- the community (e.g., neighborhoods and community volunteers);
- the schools (e.g., teachers and other educational staff);
- law enforcement (e.g., police officers, juvenile police officers);
- the juvenile courts (e.g., juvenile court judges, intake officers, probation officers, court-appointed advocates, prosecuting attorney for the state, defense attorney for the youth, and social workers);
- teen courts (e.g., other teens);
- juvenile detention centers (e.g., social workers, mental health and medical professionals, juvenile correctional facilities); and
- social welfare agencies (e.g., social workers), such as inpatient mental health or substance-abuse services (e.g., alcohol and drug counselors), and court-mandated foster care services (e.g., child welfare workers).

The presence of multiple "actors" across juvenile justice systems underscores the need for combining multiple perspectives in assessment and intervention planning that involves youth, their families, and their communities. However, practitioners should be aware that this combination of diverse perspectives may not always result in harmonious interactions. Conflict may occur among interdisciplinary professionals who have been trained with a particular set of personal and professional values and ethics, and professional areas of expertise.

Therapeutic jurisprudence outcomes (e.g., positive outcomes) that address juvenile public policy issues must transcend the expertise of one profession and must include open interactions across the disciplines (Madden & Wayne, 2003). Effective strategies that social workers can use include open communication, cooperation, coordination, and the resolution of disciplinary conflicts through debate (Abramson & Rosenthal, 1995; Garland, Hough, Landsverk, & Brown, 2001; Payne, 2000; Petrucci, 2007). These cooperative efforts, particularly among interdisciplinary professionals, extend to assessment, prevention, and intervention strategies across the juvenile justice system. A review of assessment, prevention, and intervention with the juvenile justice populations follows.

Assessment, Prevention, and Intervention

Assessment, prevention, and intervention efforts occur at each step of the juvenile justice process, from entry in the system (e.g., the courts) to aftercare services (e.g., when a youth is paroled from prison). It is common for assessments of juveniles to be completed by social workers, psychologists, and/or psychiatrists. (Please see a sample psychiatric assessment in Appendix C.) Ellis and Sowers (2001) defined social work assessment as the "examination of the client and his social systems to identify the problems that may contribute to his deviant behavior and the strategies that might be used to curb it" (p. 30).

Biopsychosocial Assessment

Biopsychosocial assessment is a tool that serves the critical function of guiding decision-making processes for youth involved in the juvenile justice system. A biopsychosocial assessment commonly includes information on the presenting problem, the demographic background of the client, and relevant history, including family history, developmental history, educational, vocational training, and employment history, family and peer relations, medical, mental health, substance-abuse history and treatment, and legal history (Vogelsand, 2001).

A social worker conducting a biopsychosocial assessment engages in a broad and comprehensive process that often includes interviews with the youth, collateral contacts, case-record reviews, and a review of the relevant theoretical and empirical literature. An expert consultation is frequently used to help explain information gathered. Obtaining multiple sources of information helps to ensure reliability and validity (Vogelsand, 2001).

The biopsychosocial assessment can have different functions in different settings. For instance, in private agency settings, the information can be used to inform treatment or intervention planning, or to develop community resources. In public settings, such as the court, the assessment may be used to provide information that would assist the judge or jury in decision making related to the juvenile defendant (Ellis & Sowers, 2001).

For social workers, particularly clinical social workers, a biopsychosocial assessment plays an important role in expert testimony. Vogelsand (2001) had several recommendations on how social workers can best prepare for court testimony, including knowing how to define psychosocial assessment and being able to explain one's area of expertise and training in conducting biopsychosocial assessments. A sample psychosocial assessment for use by a social worker with juvenile justice and criminal justice populations can be found in the Appendix A.

Specialized Assessment

In additional to general assessments, there are also specialized risk assessments at every stage of the judicial decision-making process for youth (Roberts, 2004). These assessments provide recommendations that may serve to influence placement decisions and the type of treatment received. Some of the more specialized assessments include an assessment for danger to self (i.e., suicidal assessment) or others (e.g., violence and sexual offending behavior), mental health issues (e.g., competency and need for treatment), and substance abuse (Borum & Verhaagen, 2006; Hoge & Andrews, 1996; Perry & Orchard, 1992).

Suicide Risk Assessment

Suicide risk assessment often occurs in the juvenile justice system. Youth, especially those detained for the first 72 hours, may be at an elevated risk for suicidal behavior. A suicidal risk assessment attempts to determine the level at which a youth is a danger to him or herself. This assessment includes determining the presence of recent stressors, the degree of suicidal ideations, suicidal intent, suicidal plans, and past suicidal history. Risk assessment for an offender's potential for being a danger to others (e.g., violence) attempts to determine the propensity of risk for repeat offending (Borum & Verhagaagen, 2006; Perry & Orchard, 1992). Often conducted by a psychologist or psychiatrist, recommendations from these reports may significantly influence the placement of youth.

Substance-Abuse and Mental Health Assessments

Substance-abuse and mental assessments may also be conducted with youth involved in the juvenile justice system (Roberts, 2004). Substance-abuse evaluations attempt to determine the level to which a youth has a substance-abuse problem. This type of assessment may include the degree to which juveniles use alcohol or drugs and whether this constitutes dependence or abuse and/or the need for treatment (American Psychiatric Association [APA], 2000).

Mental health evaluations are designed to determine a youth's level of mental health competence or his or her need for treatment. Youth may be assessed for competency at various points in the juvenile justice process. For example, before making an arrest, police may need to assess a youth's ability to comprehend his or her Miranda rights. Court officials may need to determine a youth's ability to stand trial or whether a waiver to criminal court is warranted (Grisso, 1998; Hoge & Andrews, 1996). Examples of mental health screening instruments used in the juvenile justice system are the *Massachusetts Youth Screening Instrument* (*MAYSI-2*; Grisso & Barnum, 2006) and the *Brief Symptom Inventory* (*BSI*; Derogatis, 1993).

Massachusetts Youth Screening Instrument

The *MAYSI-2* is one of the most widely used mental health screening tools; it may be used at entry or transitional points during the juvenile justice process (e.g., intake, probation, or pretrial) (Grisso & Barnum, 2006). Designed for youth aged 12 to 17, the *MAYSI-2* takes approximately 15 minutes to administer and identifies youth with special needs (e.g., alcohol/drug use, suicidal ideation, anger and irritability, depression, and trauma histories).

Brief Symptom Inventory

The *BSI* is the short version of Symptom Checklist-90-Revised (SCL-R-90; Derogatis, 1993). It is a 53-item instrument self-report instrument and takes 8 to 12 minutes to administer. It identifies psychological symptoms in adolescents and adults using a 5-point Likert scale (0 = not at all to 4 = extremely) to measure one's level of distress (e.g., somatic complaints, anxiety, depression, hostility, paranoia, and psychoses) over the course of 7 days (Derogatis, 1993).

Primary, Secondary, and Tertiary Prevention Strategies

In addition to assessment, there are prevention and intervention strategies social workers use to address youth concerns.

Primary Prevention

Prevention and intervention strategies geared toward enhancing youths' positive developmental assets may occur at the primary, secondary, and/or tertiary levels (Rapp-Paglicci, Dulmus, & Wodarski, 2004). The first level, *primary prevention*, involves a universal approach. Primary prevention programs target all youths in community and school settings. An example of a violence-prevention approach for all children is the Second Step: A Violence Prevention Curriculum (D. C. Grossman et al., 1997). It is an emotional literacy program that was developed to increase the social and emotional skills of youth. This program includes modules on empathy, anger management, and emotional learning. Research on the Second Step Program has shown that youth who have participated in this program increased their social and emotional skills and decreased their use of physical and verbal aggression and disruptive behavior (D. C. Grossman et al., 1997; McMahon, Washburn, Felix, Yakin, & Childrey, 2000).

Secondary Prevention

Secondary prevention strategies specifically target at-risk youth populations. The focus of secondary prevention activities is on preventing repeated occurrences of problem behavior through targeted interventions (Howell, 2001). For example, a social worker can provide a student who has more than one disciplinary referral for fighting in a given month special instruction in conflict resolution or social skills. Another example of a secondary prevention strategy is establishing mentoring programs in neighborhoods with high levels of youth gang affiliation. These programs provide at-risk youths the opportunity to bond with prosocial adults or peers. Mentoring programs, such as the Juvenile Mentoring Program (JUMP) and Big Brothers/Big Sisters (BB/SS), are examples of evidence-based mentoring programs that can improve prevention or treatment outcomes for at-risk youth (J. B. Grossman & Garry, 1997; Keating, Tomishima, Foster, & Alessandri, 2002). Evidence suggests that at-risk youth who participate in mentoring programs are less likely to engage in antisocial activities, such as substance use and violence, than youth who do not; mentoring programs also improve the participants' academic performance (Blechman, 1992; Office of Juvenile Justice and Delinquency Prevention, 1998).

Tertiary Prevention

The most intensive level of support is *tertiary prevention*. Tertiary prevention strategies specifically target delinquent youth, especially serious and chronic offenders. Interventions are geared toward reducing the impact of a condition or problem on the individual's ability to function in the least restrictive setting (Catalano, Arthur, Hawkins, Berglund, & Olson, 1998; Howell, 2001). Wraparound services and multisystemic therapy (MST) are examples of tertiary-level interventions.

Wraparound Services

Wraparound services are designed to enable children with severe, multiple needs and risks (including delinquency) to remain at home rather than be placed in institutionalized care. They generally refer to a set of individualized services for youth and their families being helped by multiple agencies. These services may include treatment as well as personal support services. These services emphasize a partnership among the families, educators, and service providers responsible for the child (Burns & Hoagwood, 2002). The National Mental Health Association (NMHA) and Substance Abuse and Mental Health Services Administration's (SAMHSA) Center for Mental Health Services (CMHS) have endorsed this approach and since the 1990s have promoted it as part of its systems of care initiatives (NMHA, 2004). Wraparound services generally include a collaborative, community-based interagency team, a formal interagency agreement, care coordinators, child and family teams, a unified plan of care, and systematic, outcome-based services. Social workers may work in wraparound services as a program administrator or as a practitioner providing services.

Multisystemic Therapy

Multisystemic therapy (MST) is an intervention strategy designed to help identified youth reduce antisocial behavior (e.g., disobedience, running away, drug use, arson, vandalism, theft, and violence against persons). MST provides multilevel intervention strategies in individual, family, and community domains (Henggeler et al., 1991; Swenson, Henggler, Taylor, & Addison, 2005). There is a debate over the effectiveness of MST (Henggeler, Schoenwald, Borduin, & Swenson, 2006; Littell, 2006). Proponents of MST cite methodologically sound outcome studies for treating violent and chronic juvenile offenders and their families from diverse backgrounds, including offending behavior and substance-use problems (Brown, Borduin, & Henggeler, 2001; Henggeler et al., 1991; Swenson et al., 2005). MST also has been shown to provide cost savings, especially among substance-abusing juvenile offenders (Schoenwald, Ward, Henggeler, Pickrel, & Patel, 1996). In contrast, Littell and colleagues' systematic review of published and unpublished studies on MST (conducted for the Campbell and Cochrane Collaborations) found that MST is not as effective as previously thought (Littell, 2005; Littell, Popa, & Forsythe, 2005).

Case Study

Not all social workers are involved in the juvenile justice system as practitioners or administrators. Some social workers in the juvenile justice system are researchers. Social work researchers may use both qualitative and quantitative methods to study why youth engage in delinquency or how effective certain interventions (e.g., MST) are at preventing and treating juvenile offenders. The following case study of a young man named Lee illustrates the contribution of qualitative methods to gain a better understanding of the problems, strengths, and needs of juvenile-justice–involved youth.

At intake, a licensed psychologist completed a comprehensive intake assessment by reviewing Lee's case records and conducting an in-person interview with Lee. Based on this assessment, the psychologist recommended psychiatric treatment, mental health counseling, and sex-offender and anger-management counseling. Based on these recommendations, the intake social work staff referred Lee for services with the mental health department, which was made up of three licensed clinical social workers (LCSWs), one licensed psychologist, and one psychiatrist. On completion of his 3-year sentence, a multidisciplinary team of prison administrators, psychologists, psychiatrists, and social workers deemed Lee "unsafe" to return to society. He was involuntarily committed to a state hospital for violent offenders with mental health problems where he would be held until the mental health team deemed that his rehabilitative goals had been met.

At the time of the qualitative interview, Lee had been incarcerated for 1 year. He had been attending weekly mental health and anger-management counseling with a social worker in a secure-care setting. Records indicated he was compliant with prescribed psychotropic medication. What follows is a detailed description of significant events in Lee's life and his reactions to them. This case study provides practitioners with a real-life example of a juvenile detainee and uses some of his own words. The case study also highlights similar information that might be shared during an intake interview or counseling session.

War Scars and Symbols: The Story of Lee

Lee is a 17-year-old African American male serving a 3-year sentence in a secure-care facility. Lee's official records indicate a prior-offense history that included property crimes (i.e., theft and burglary), sexual offenses (i.e., harassment, lewdness, and criminal sexual contact), and violence (i.e., simple assault and aggravated assault). Yet, the story behind the case record reveals a resilient youth who, despite many adversities, including parental loss and child sexual abuse, maintained a hopeful and positive attitude about himself and the world. Records indicate a history of mental health issues, multiple suicide attempts, and self-mutilation.

As part of a qualitative interview, Lee shared the story behind his face sheet (i.e., cover sheet for official records). Lee lost both of his parents by the age of 4. Lee revealed, "My dad was an alcoholic, and my mom was...she died of drugs." He described a snapshot-like memory of his parents and a prolonged sadness over their loss: "I remember bein' so little you know, seein' her, I could only see her knees, she was a heavyset lady. I can't see her face. It's blank, yo. My dad's face is blank. Makes me sometimes wanna cry, yo."

After the death of his parents, Lee reported that he was separated from his brother and placed in foster care. His most vivid memory of this experience is of being sexually abused in early adolescence by a foster parent. He recalled his thoughts and feelings about this incident:

> I was sexually abused as a child. I was 9, or 10, or 11. I felt scared, trapped, until we went to a meeting. I told on him. I just got enough strength to tell on him. I said, "I can't go back and do this again, yo. I'm tired of this." I was there for a year straight. A year of my life that really didn't mean nothin,' didn't teach me nothin. Nothin. It was a waste of time. I mean I learned more things in prison!

Presence of Psychological, Emotional, and Behavioral Consequences

Lee reported a history of psychological, emotional, and behavioral issues. He was diagnosed with multiple mental health disorders, including intermittent explosive disorder, conduct disorder, attention-deficit/hyperactivity disorder, impulse control disorder, and substance abuse. He currently is taking Depakote but in the past was prescribed other psychotropic medications, such as Paxil, Risperidol, Haldol, Lithium, and Ritalin.

Lee also reported having engaged in self-destructive behaviors such as self-mutilation and 10 suicide attempts, which involved an attempt by hanging, slitting his wrists, and jumping off of a building. Lee shared how stress, especially being separated from his brother, heightened his feelings of depression and anger, which in turn, fueled his self-destructive behavior.

> *I tried to kill myself over 10 times. Over 10 times. By hangin' myself, uh, bangin' my head against the wall, tryin' to knock myself out, and cuttin' myself, slittin' my wrist, I did that. Some of the scars went away though. I was young. When I moved to Jersey, after I was in a program. So, about 15, 16 years old. I tried ten times in the last 2 or 3 years. It was all the stress in programs. Not seein' my brother. That was the main reason. That's when I started. Not seein' my brother. So uh, well I did it. I did it outa anger too. I was angry at everything, man. Everything. They said you get war scars. A symbol. You understand. There's no way to hide that. I felt depressed and angry at the same time. When you start thinkin'...I always had one problem. And I used to say, "Dag, man...you see, this leads onto this, and that's why this and this is happenin,' " you know what I mean.*

Presence of a Positive Attitude

Despite many prior adverse life events, Lee maintained a positive outlook about himself and the world. Lee admitted responsibility for his past negative behaviors but displayed a positive attitude. He regarded his future as a positive one in which he was granted a second chance at childhood. He said:

> *I'm a good kid. I am, yo! And people don't realize it. I don't like to hurt nobody. I gotta play this game, that's how I figure it. I gotta be rough, like tough, you know what I mean. I can't show my real self like some others. I like, I like, I wanna get back all those childhood things, like I never had a childhood, and I'm gonna make up for all that, yo. I don't wanna treat anybody bad. And if I do, I'll just ask God for forgiveness. Ask God to forgive me for doin' stuff to that person.*

Lee also shared his personal creed of resilience, which reflected his attitude that he could triumph over adversity:

> *Ah, man! I'm most proud of myself for living on experience. Livin' life experience. Sometimes I'm not glad I learned the hard way. I had to bump my head. Knock myself out. I'll still be achieving my goals. You know. And that's my creed.*

Where Does the Social Worker Go From Here?

Two years after completion of this interview, Lee was involuntarily committed to a secure-care facility for serious and violent offenders with mental health problems. In that setting, his treatment team would consist of multidisciplinary professionals, including social workers. At this point, a social worker might work with Lee as he receives mandated inpatient treatment. The social worker might help him process his feelings of betrayal toward prison staff and "the system," to help him adjust to his new environment, to better manage his anger and violent outbursts, to learn to be more accountable for his behavior, and to help reinforce a positive outlook with positive actions. A successful outcome would result in his rehabilitation and release to the community.

Summary and Conclusions

This chapter explored the practice of social work with youth involved in the juvenile justice system and their families and communities. Social work history reveals the importance of social work reformers in the establishment of the juvenile court system. In 1899, the juvenile court system was created and promoted a rehabilitative approach to juveniles who commit delinquent acts. Recent trends have shifted the juvenile court's focus from a purely rehabilitative approach to one that incorporates a punitive approach. Social work might be well served by revisiting the closing commentary from Jane Addams's book, *The Spirit of Youth and the City Streets:*

> *We may smother the divine fire of youth or we may feed it. We may either stand stupidly staring as it sinks into a murky fire of crime and flares into intermittent blaze of folly or we may tend it into a lambent flame with power to make clean and bright our dingy city streets. (Addams, 1972, pp. 161–162)*

Collaborative forensic social work might be the lambent flame that Addams spoke of. To achieve that goal, social work should actively pursue a two-pronged approach to improve social functioning and social justice outcomes for youth, their families, and their communities. Social workers whose practice intersects with the juvenile justice system must engage in a multifaceted approach, which requires them to be knowledgeable and skillful in navigating the different facets of the juvenile justice system, interacting and collaborating with system professionals and family and community members, problem-solving ethical/legal dilemmas, and able to apply multi-level assessment and intervention skills using a multicultural lens. It is these skills and strategies that may kindle the free spirit of youth.

The additional chapters in this section address forensic social work practice in correctional institutions and community reentry, particularly with adults. Special topics, such as the disproportionate waiver of minority youth to the adult system, and restorative justice approaches for social work practice with victims and offenders are also reviewed.

Juvenile-Justice–Related Online Resources

Juvenile Justice System: Structure and Process

OJJDP Case Flow Diagram: http://ojjdp.ncjrs.org/ojstatbb/structure_process/case.html

Prevention, Assessment, Intervention, Diversion, and Reentry Resources

Friends: http://www.friendsnrc.org/outcome/toolkit/
Juvenile Justice Evaluation Center: http://www.jrsainfo.org/jjec/

National Center for Mental Health & Juvenile Justice: http://www.ncmhjj.com/resource_kit/Default.htm

Special Issues

American Bar Association (Gender Issues): http://www.abanet.org/crimjust/juvjus/girls.html
Building Blocks for Youth (Minority Youth): http://www.buildingblocksforyouth.org/justiceforsome/
Center for the Promotion of Mental Health in Juvenile Justice: http://www.promotementalhealth.org/
National Center for Mental Health & Juvenile Justice: http://www.ncmhjj.com/

General Resources

American Bar Association: http://www.abanet.org/dch/committee.cfm?com=CR200000 Bureau of Justice Statistics: http://www.ojp.usdoj.gov/bjs/
Child Advocate: http://www.childadvocate.net/
Children's Defense Fund: http://www.childrensdefense.org/site/PageServer
Children's Law and Policy Center: http://www.cclp.org/
Juvenile Law Center: http://www.jlc.org/
National Center for Criminal Justice Reference Service: http://www.ncjrs.gov/index.html
National Center for State Courts: http://www.ncsconline.org/
National Council on Crime and Delinquency: http://www.nccd-crc.org/
Office of Juvenile Justice and Delinquency Prevention: http://ojjdp.ncjrs.org/
Youth Law Center: http://www.ylc.org/

Measurement Tools on the Web: Children and Adolescents

Buros Institute of Mental Measurements: http://www.unl.edu/buros/
Child and Family Review Instruments: http://www.acf.hhs.gov/programs/cb/cwrp/tools/
Multicultural Measurement Tools: http://www.multiculturalcenter.org/test/

References

Abram, K. M., Teplin, L. A., Charles, D. R., Longworth, S. L., McClelland, G.M., & Dulcan, M. K. (2004). Post traumatic stress disorder and trauma in youth in juvenile detention. *Archives of General Psychiatry, 61*, 403–410.

Abramson, J. S., & Rosenthal, B. S. (1995). Interdisciplinary and interorganizational collaboration. In R. L. Edwards (Ed.), *Encyclopedia of social work* (19th ed., pp. 1479–1489). Washington, DC: NASW Press.

Addams, J. (1972). *The spirit of youth and the city streets.* Urbana IL: University of Illinois Press.

Agnew, R. (2001). *Juvenile delinquency: Causes and controls.* Los Angeles: Roxbury.

Akers, R. L., & Sellers, C. S. (2004). *Criminological theories: Introduction, evaluation, and application* (4th ed.). Los Angeles: Roxbury.

American Psychiatric Association. (2000). *The diagnostic and statistical manual of mental disorders* (4th ed., text rev.). Washington, DC: American Psychiatric Press.

Baer, J., & Maschi, T. (2003). Random acts of delinquency: Trauma and self-destructiveness in juvenile offenders. *Child & Adolescent Social Work Journal, 20*(2), 85–99.

Barker, R. L. (2003). *The social work dictionary* (2nd ed.). Washington, DC: NASW Press.

Barker, R. L., & Branson, D. M. (2003). *Forensic social work: Legal aspects of professional practice* (2nd ed.). Binghamton, NY: Haworth Press.

Bartollas, C., & Miller, S. J. (2005). *Juvenile justice in America* (4th ed.). Upper Saddle River, NJ: Pearson Prentice Hall.

Blechman, E. A. (1992). Mentors for high-risk minority youth: From effective communication to bicultural competence. *Journal of Clinical Child Psychology, 21*, 160–169.

Borum, R., & Verhaagen, D. (2006). *Assessing and managing violence risk in juveniles*. New York: Guilford Press.

Brown, T. L., Borduin, C. M., & Henggeler, S. W. (2001). Treating juvenile offenders with mental health disorders in community settings. In J. B. Ashford, B. D. Sales, & W. H. Reid (Eds.), *Treating adult and juvenile offenders with special needs* (pp. 445–464). Washington, DC: American Psychological Association.

Bruns, E. J., Walker, J. S., Adams, J., Miles, P., Osher, T., Rash, J., et al. (2004). *Ten principles of the wraparound process*. Portland, OR: National Wraparound Initiative, Research & Training Center on Family Support & Children's Mental Health, Portland State University.

Burns, B. B., & Hoagwood, K. (2002). *Community treatment for youth: Evidence-based interventions for severe emotional and behavioral disorders*. New York: Oxford University Press.

Butts, J. A. (2000). *Youth crime drop*. Washington, DC: Urban Institute.

Butts, J. A., & Buck, J. (2000). *Teen courts: A focus on research*. Washington, DC: Office of Juvenile Justice Delinquency Prevention.

Catalano, R. F., Arthur, M. W., Hawkins, J. D., Berglund, L., & Olson, J. J. (1998). Comprehensive community and school based interventions to prevent antisocial behavior. In R. Loeber & D. P. Farrington (Eds.), *Serious and violent juvenile offenders: Risk factors and successful interventions* (pp. 248–283). Thousand Oaks, CA: Sage.

Chesney-Lind, M., & Sheldon, R. G. (2004). *Girls, delinquency and juvenile justice* (3rd ed.). Belmont, CA: Wadsworth.

Cocozza, J. J. (1992). *Responding to the mental health needs of youth in the juvenile justice system*. Seattle, WA: National Coalition for the Mentally Ill in the Criminal Justice System.

Cocozza, J. J., & Skowyra, K. (2000). Youth with mental health disorders: Issues and emerging responses. *Juvenile Justice, 7*(1), 3–11.

Cournoyer, B.R. (2005). *The social work skills workbook* (4th ed.). Belmont, CA: Brooks/Cole.

Derogatis, L. R. (1993). *BSI Brief Symptom Inventory. Administration, scoring, and procedures manual* (4th ed.). Minneapolis, MN: National Computer Systems.

Dickson, D. T. (1998). *Confidentiality and privacy in social work: A guide to the law for practitioners and students*. New York: Free Press.

Drowns, R. W., & Hess, K. M. (2003). *Juvenile justice* (4th ed.). Belmont, CA: Wadsworth.

Ellis, R. A., & Sowers, K. M. (2001). *Juvenile justice practice: A cross-disciplinary approach to treatment*. Belmont, CA: Wadsworth.

Fong, R., & Furuto, S. (2001). *Culturally competent practice: Skills, interventions, and evaluations*. Boston: Allyn & Bacon.

Fraser, M. W. (1997). *Risk and resilience in childhood: An ecological perspective*. Washington, DC: NASW Press.

Garbarino, J. (2001). An ecological perspective on the effects of violence on children. *Journal of Community Psychology, 29*, 361–378.

Garland, A. F., Hough, R. L., Landsverk, J. A., & Brown, S. A. (2001). Multi-sector complexity of systems of care for youth with mental health needs. *Children's Services: Social Policy, Research, & Practice, 4*(3), 123–140.

Garmezy, N., & Masten, A. S. (1994). Chronic adversities. In M. Rutter, E. Taylor, & L. Herson (Eds.), *Child and adolescent psychiatry* (pp. 32–47). Boston: Blackwell Scientific.

Garmezy, N., & Rutter, M. (Eds.). (1983). *Stress, coping, and development in children*. New York: McGraw-Hill.

Government Accounting Office. (2003, April). *Child welfare and juvenile justice: Federal agencies could play a stronger role in helping states reduce the number of children placed solely to obtain mental health services* (GAO-03-397). Washington, DC: United States House of Representatives Committee on Government Reform-Minority Staff.

Grisso, T. (1998). *Forensic evaluation of juveniles*. Sarasota, FL: Professional Resource Press.

Grisso, T. (1999). Juvenile offenders and mental illness. *Psychiatry Psychology & Law, 6*, 143–151.

Grisso, T., & Barnum, R. (2006). *Massachusetts Youth Screening Instrument, Version 2: User's manual and technical report*. Sarasota, FL: Professional Resource Press.

Grossman, D. C., Neckerman, H. J., Koepsell, T. D., Liu, P. Y., Asher, K. N., Beland, K., et al. (1997). The effectiveness of a violence prevention curriculum among children in elementary school. *Journal of the American Medical Association, 277*, 1605–1611.

Grossman, J. B., & Garry, E. M. (1997, April). Mentoring—A proven delinquency prevention strategy. *Juvenile Justice Bulletin*. Washington, DC: Office of Juvenile Justice and Delinquency Prevention.

Henggeler, S. W., Borduin, C. M., Melton, G. B., Mann, B. J., Smith, L., Hall, J. A., et al. (1991). Effects of multisystemic therapy on drug use and abuse in serious juvenile offenders: A progress report from two outcome studies. *Family Dynamics of Addiction Quarterly, 1*(3), 40–51.

Henggeler, S. W., Schoenwald, S. K., Borduin, C. M., & Swenson, C. C. (2006). Methodological critique and meta-analysis as Trojan horse. *Children & Youth Services Review, 28*, 447–457.

Herman, M. M. (2002). *Teen courts: A juvenile justice diversion program. Report on trends in the state courts*. Williamsburg, VA: National Center for State Courts.

Hirschfield, P., Maschi, T., White, H. R., Goldman-Traub, L., & Loeber, R. (2006). The effect of mental disorders on juvenile justice involvement. *Criminology, 44*(3), 1–31.

Hoge, R. D., & Andrews, D. A. (1996). *Assessing the youthful offender: Issues and techniques*. New York: Plenum Press.

Howell, J. C. (2001). Juvenile justice programs and strategies. In R. Loeber & D. P. Farrington (Eds.), *Child delinquents: Development, intervention, and service needs* (pp. 305–322). Thousand Oaks, CA: Sage.

Ivanoff, A., Smyth N. J., & Dulmus, C. N (2007). Preparing social workers for practice in correctional institutions. In A. R. Roberts & D. W. Springer (Eds.), *Social work in juvenile and criminal justice settings* (3rd ed., pp. 341–350). Springfield, IL: Charles C Thomas.

Justice Policy Institute. (2000). *Second chances: 100 years of the Children's Court: Giving kids a chance to make a better choice*. Washington, DC: Author.

Keating, L. M., Tomishima, M. A., Foster, S., & Alessandri, M. (2002). The effects of a mentoring program on at-risk youth. *Adolescence, 37*, 717–734.

Kirby, L. D., & Fraser, M. W. (1997). Risk and resilience in childhood. In M. W. Fraser (Ed.), *Risk and resilience in childhood: An ecological perspective*. Washington, DC: NASW Press.

LeCroy, C. W., Stevenson, P., & MacNeil, G. (2003). System considerations in treating juvenile offenders with mental disorders. In J. B. Ashford, B. D. Sales, & W. H. Reid (Eds.). *Treating adult and juvenile offenders with special needs*. Washington, DC: American Psychological Association.

Lerner, R. M. (2002). *Adolescence: Development, diversity, context, and application*. Upper Saddle River, NJ: Prentice Hall.

Littell, J. H. (2005). Lessons from a systematic review of effects of multisystemic therapy. *Children & Youth Services Review, 27*, 445–463.

Littell, J. H. (2006). The case for multisystemic therapy: Evidence or orthodoxy? *Children & Youth Services Review, 28*, 458–472.

Littell, J. H., Popa, M., & Forsythe, B. (2005). Multisystemic therapy for social, emotional, and behavioral problems in youth aged 10–17. *Cochrane Database of Systematic Reviews, 3* (Art. No.: CD004797. DOI: 10.1002/14651858.CD004797.pub4). Retrieved January 1, 2006, from http://www.cochrane.org/reviews

Lyons, J., Baerger, D., Quigley, P., Erlich, J., & Griffin, E. (2001). Mental health service needs of juvenile offenders: A comparison of detention, incarceration, and treatment settings. *Children's Services: Social Policy, Research, & Practice, 4*, 69–85.

MacDonald, J. M., & Chesney-Lind, M. (2001). Gender bias and juvenile justice revisited: A multiyear analysis. *Crime & Delinquency, 47*, 173–195.

Madden, R., & Wayne, R. H. (2003). Social work and the law: A therapeutic jurisprudence perspective. *Social Work, 48*, 338–347.

Madden, R. G. (2003). *Essential law for social workers*. New York: Columbia University Press.

Martin, S. L., Sigda, K. B., & Kupersmidt, J. B. (1998). Family and neighborhood violence: Predictors of depressive symptomatology among incarcerated youth. *Prison Journal, 7*, 423–438.

Maschi, T. (2006). Exploring the link between trauma and delinquency: The cumulative versus differential risk perspectives. *Social Work, 1*, 59–70.

Maschi, T., Hatcher, S., Schwalbe, C., & Scotto Rosato, N. (2008). Mapping the social service pathways of youth to and through the juvenile justice system: A comprehensive review. *Children and Youth Services Review*, doi:10.1016/j.childyouth.2008.04.006.

McMahon, S. D., Washburn, J., Felix, E. D., Yakin, J., & Childrey, G. (2000). Violence prevention: Program effects on urban preschool and kindergarten children. *Applied & Preventive Psychology, 9*, 271–281.

National Council on Crime & Delinquency. (2007). *And justice for some: Differential treatment of youth of color in the justice system*. Retrieved September 12, 2008, from http://www.nccd-crc.org/nccd/pubs/2007jan_justice_for_some.pdf

National Mental Health Association. (2004). *Mental health treatment for youth in the juvenile justice system: A compendium of promising practices*. Alexandria, VA: Author.

Needleman, C. (2007). Conflicting philosophies of juvenile justice. In A. R. Roberts & D. W. Springer (Eds.), *Social work in juvenile and criminal justice settings* (3rd ed., pp. 186–190). Springfield, IL: Charles C Thomas.

Office of Juvenile Justice and Delinquency Prevention (OJJDP). (1998, December). *1998 report to Congress: Juvenile mentoring program (JUMP)*. Washington, DC: U.S. Department of Justice, Office of Juvenile Justice and Delinquency Prevention.

Patton, M. Q. (2002). *Qualitative evaluation and research methods* (4th ed.). Thousand Oaks, CA: Sage.

Payne, M. (2000). *Teamwork in multiprofessional care*. Chicago: Lyceum Books.

Perkins, D., Borden, L., Keith, J. G., Hoppe-Rooney, T., & Villarruel, F. (2003). Community youth development: Partnership creating a positive world. In F. Villaruel, D. Perkins, L. Borden, & J. Keith (Eds.), *Community youth developmemt: Programs, policies, amd practices* (pp. 1–24). Thousand Oaks, CA: Sage.

Perry, G. P., & Orchard, J. (1992). *Assessment and treatment of adolescent sex offenders*. Sarasota, FL: Professional Resource Press.

Petrucci, C. (2007). Therapeutic jurisprudence in social work and criminal justice. In A. R. Roberts & D. W. Springer (Eds.), *Social work in juvenile and criminal justice settings* (3rd ed., pp. 287–299). Springfield, IL: Charles C Thomas.

Platt, A. M. (1969). The rise of the child-saving movement: A study in social policy and correctional reform. *Annals of the American Academy of Political & Social Science, 381*, 21–38.

Platt, A. M. (1977). *The child savers: The invention of delinquency* (2nd ed.). Chicago: University of Chicago Press.

Potter, C. C., & Jenson, J. M. (2003). Cluster profiles of multiple problem youth: Mental health problem symptoms, substance use, and delinquent conduct. *Criminal Justice & Behavior, 30*, 230–250.

Potter, C. C., & Jenson, J. M. (2007). Assessment of mental health and substance abuse treatment needs in juvenile justice. In A. R. Roberts & D.W. Springer (Eds.), *Social work in juvenile and criminal justice settings* (3rd ed., pp. 133–150). Springfield, IL: Charles C Thomas.

Rapp-Paglicci, L. A., Dulmus, C. N., & Wodarski, J. S. (2004). *Handbook of preventive interventions for children and adolescents*. Hoboken, NJ: Wiley.

Roberts, A. R. (Ed.). (2004). *Juvenile justice sourcebook: Past, present, and future*. New York: Oxford University Press.

Roberts, A. R., & Springer, D. W. (2008). *Social work in juvenile justice and criminal justice settings* (3rd ed.). Springfield, IL: Charles C Thomas.

Rosenheim, M. K. (2002). The modern American juvenile court. In M. K. Rosenheim, F. E. Zimring, D. S. Tanenhaus, & B. Dohrn (Eds.), *A century of juvenile justice* (pp. 341–359). Chicago: University of Chicago Press.

Rutter, M. (1985). Resilience in the face of adversity: Protective factors and resistance to psychiatric disorders. *British Journal of Psychiatry, 147*, 323–356.

Rutter, M. (1987). Psychosocial resilience and protective mechanisms. *American Journal of Orthopsychiatry, 57*, 316–331.

Schoenwald, S. K., Ward, D. M., Henggeler, S. W., Pickrel, S. G., & Patel, H. (1996) Multisystemic therapy treatment of substance abusing or dependent adolescent offenders: Costs of reducing incarceration, inpatient, and residential placement. *Journal of Child & Family Studies, 5*, 431–444.

Shoemaker, D. J. (2004). *Theories of delinquency: An examination of explanations of delinquent behavior* (4th ed.). New York: Oxford University Press.

Snyder, H. N. (2000). *Juvenile arrests 1999*. Washington, DC: U.S. Department of Justice, Office of Justice Programs, Office of Juvenile Justice & Delinquency Prevention.

Snyder, H. N. (2006). *Juvenile arrests, 2004*. Washington, DC: U.S. Department of Justice, Office of Justice Programs, Office of Juvenile Justice & Delinquency Prevention.

Snyder, H. N., & Sickmund, M. (2006). *Juvenile offender and victims: 2006 national report.* Washington, DC: U.S. Department of Justice, Office of Justice Programs, Office of Juvenile Justice & Delinquency Prevention.

Swenson, C., Henggler, S., Taylor, S., & Addison, W. (2005). *Multisystemic therapy and neighborhood partnerships: Reducing violence and substance abuse.* New York: Guilford Press.

Teplin, L. A., Elkington, K. S., McClelland, G. A., Abram, K. M., Mericle, A. A., & Washburn, J. J. (2005). Major mental disorders, substance use disorders, comorbidity, and HIV-AIDS risk behaviors in juvenile detainees. *Psychiatric Services, 56,* 823–828.

Vermeiron, R. (2003). Psychopathology and delinquency in adolescents: A descriptive and developmental perspective. *Clinical Psychology Review, 23,* 277–331.

Wasserman, G., Ko, S. J., Larkin S., & McReynolds, M. (2004). *Assessing the mental health status of youth in juvenile justice settings.* Washington DC: Office of Juvenile Justice and Delinquency Prevention.

Vogelsand, J. (2001). *The witness stand: A guide for clinical social workers in the courtroom.* Binghamton, NY: Haworth Press.

Walsh, J. (2006). *Theories for direct social work practice.* Belmont, CA: Thompson Learning.

Williams, H. B., Hovmand, P. S., & Bright, C. L. (2007). Overrepresentation of African Americans incarcerated for delinquency offences in juvenile institutions. In D. W. Springer & A. R. Roberts (Eds.), *Handbook of forensic mental health with victims and offenders: Assessment, treatment, and research* (pp. 213–225). New York: Springer Publishing Company.

Youth Law Center. (2000). *Building blocks for youth: And justice for some.* Retrieved September 1, 2001, from http://www.buildingblocksforyouth.org

Prisons as a Practice Setting

19

Rebecca Sanford
Johanna Foster

Like child welfare, health care, and educational systems, the criminal justice system is a major social institution shaped by the intersection of race, class, and gender inequality, and one that sits at the center of U.S. social relations. Within the larger criminal justice system, the enormous expansion of the U.S. prison system, in particular, has deeply affected the social landscape of the United States. Although it may be safe to say that in the past, a relatively small proportion of the U.S. population had been directly affected by incarceration, the criminal justice system today organizes everyday social interactions so pervasively that a startling number of people in our nation are now living a significant portion of their lives in prison, or are under some other kind of criminal justice system surveillance. As a result, contemporary scholars have begun to argue that the rise of mass incarceration has become one of the most pressing social problems of our time (Mauer & Chesney-Lind, 2002). In this context, an understanding of the prison system as an extremely powerful and far-reaching practice setting, and one fundamentally connected to all of the other fields addressed in this text, is essential for any effective social worker in the 21st century.

Overview of Practice Setting

As the social institution responsible for enforcing the laws of our society and meting out the penalties for those who break these laws, it is more accurate to frame the criminal justice system as a set of interrelated, though often disconnected, social institutions—including prison systems—that sometimes coordinate functions, but often do not. As Sheldon and Brown (2003) argued, the U.S. criminal justice system consists of over 50,000 separate public and private agencies and organizations, including city, state, and federal law enforcement agencies; municipal, state, and federal court systems; probation agencies; parole agencies; juvenile justice systems; jail systems; military facilities; territorial prisons; Bureau of Immigration/Customs Enforcement (ICE) facilities; and the state, federal, and privately operated prison systems. Within the operations of the prisons alone, which are meant to confine people serving sentences longer than 1 year, there were 1,668 state and federal prisons in 2000, which is 204 more correctional facilities in operation than just five years before (Stephan & Karberg, 2003). There were 264 privately operated (i.e., for-profit) prisons under contract with state or federal authorities in 2000 as well (Stephan & Karberg, 2003). Although the total annual cost of the criminal justice system was estimated at $193 billion in 2004 (Bureau of Justice Statistics [BJS], 2007), U.S. taxpayers spent $38 billion in 2001 to maintain the state prison systems alone (Stephan, 2004).

Moving from the level of the system to the level of the individual, approximately 2.3 million people are in prison in the United States (Harrison & Beck, 2006), with two thirds confined to state or federal prisons, and the remaining third in local jails (BJS, 2005). Another 5 million people are awaiting sentence, on probation, or on parole (Mauer, 2004). Although individuals convicted of violent crimes constitute a significant proportion of the prison population, individuals are more commonly convicted of offenses that are increasingly nonviolent, overwhelmingly drug related, and disproportionately endured by economically and socially marginalized people and their families (Boyd, 2004). Perhaps not surprising, then, these patterns of confinement, which ensnare 7 million people each year, make the United States the country that imprisons more individuals, both per capita and in absolute numbers, than any other country in the world (Sifakis, 2003).

To be the world's largest jailor has also required the U.S. criminal justice system to expand its employment ranks in recent decades, making corrections the " 'fastest growing function' of all government functions," employing more people than any Fortune 500 company with the exception of General Motors (Sheldon & Brown, 2003, p. 5). Today, the U.S. Department of Justice reports that nearly three quarters of a million people are employed in corrections (BJS, 2004), with an estimated two thirds of state and federal prison employees working as correctional officers (Stephan & Karberg, 2003). These figures do not include those who work in related state agencies connected to the criminal justice system, or those who work in the nonprofit sector in an effort to ameliorate the impact of both crime and the effects of the punishment system on individuals, families, and communities. This map of the structural arrangements within the criminal justice system suggests the troubling emergence of what Sheldon and Brown (2003) call the "crime control industry" in the United States, or a set of social institutions that not only includes the criminal justice system itself, but also corporate, nonprofit, academic, and other public agencies that enable individuals to "profit either directly or indirectly from the existence of crime[,] from attempts to control crime," and from collective attempts to manage and solve the individual and social problems caused by our modern prison system (p. 5).

Historical Background

Although the penitentiary has long had its place in U.S. society, its seeming ubiquity, and its capacity to reproduce a range of social harms on such a wide scale, is unique to this historical period. In fact, the earliest penitentiaries in the United States were designed in the late 18th century and hailed by religious reformers as humane alternatives to the then common method of official punishment, which was corporal punishment or death by torture (A. Y. Davis, 2003). Inspired by Enlightenment ideals of reason and the importance of individual rights, as well as religious notions of the redemptive power of acts of solitary penitence, early prison reformers advocated for the construction of a seemingly progressive social institution: prisons that were not merely temporary holding cells for those condemned to die (as had been the customary purpose of such confinement), but structures intended to isolate deviants by themselves in long-term and silent confinement to provide the conditions that would bring about repentance for their crimes through a soul-searching process of personal deprivation (A. Y. Davis, 2003). Although early prisons would come to vary somewhat in their practices, they would put in motion a set of confinement practices that would become notorious features of the U.S. criminal justice system in the century to come.

Indeed, despite reformers' claims that the penitentiary was a more principled and effective response to social deviance, the early prison system, like the current system, reflected and maintained class, gendered, and racialized notions of the time. In its capacity as a political tool of the elite to regulate so-called "unruly" populations, the prison has, from its inception, functioned as an institution of economic, gendered, and racial social control.

A shift in the highly racialized dimensions of the penal system occurred, ironically, during what criminologists call "the Reformatory Period" (Sheldon & Brown, 2003), or the era between 1870 and 1900 when the penitentiary system came under fire for its own built-in brutality. As the name suggests, reformers ushered in the concept of "the reformatory," that is, a system in which deviants would be "rehabilitated" through, among other elements, the use of indeterminate sentencing, vocational, and educational training, and a reinvigorated emphasis on the values of Christianity, democracy, and obedience to authority. The reformatory period aimed to reproduce law-abiding members of the poor and working classes through the infusion of military-style discipline into the penal system, the reframing of deviance as a medical problem to be cured, and the management of prisoners through the use of early-release incentives, such as "good time" and parole, to promote compliance with newly articulated "treatment plans."

By the late 19th century, women prison reformers had successfully campaigned for separate women's reformatories built "cottage-style" in bucolic settings, home-like structures where female matrons would instill in women offenders the "proper" gendered values of chastity and domesticity. As was true for men, the system for women was highly racialized: Women of color were more likely than White women to be labeled as "incorrigible" and sent to custodial prisons, whereas White women were more likely to be sent to reformatories where there was at least some hope of a "program of rehabilitation" (Rafter, 1985).

In 1900, the Reformatory Period gave way to the growth of the industrial prison, which could house thousands of prisoners in enormous structures, closely resembling a mega-factory in form and function. This "Big House" model of prisons lacked the rehabilitative promise of the early reformatory era, and remained central to the penal landscape until the post-World War II era's "new penology" brought in "correction-alists," who restored the focus on criminality as an individual problem that can be cured through treatment. For the first time, functions of this "rehabilitation" system would be performed by workers who were required to be professionally trained, often through a college education, to manage "inmates" (no longer "convicts"), whether as "correctional officers" (no longer called "guards"), correctional administrators (no longer "wardens"), correctional educators, psychologists, or social workers, armed with, among other tools, new classification instruments and specialized treatment plans designed by teams of experts (Sheldon & Brown, 2003). Indeed, the "prison" itself "disappeared" and was replaced by "the correctional facility."

Despite the professionalization of state punishment in the mid-20th century, schol-ars agree that the prison system has never been truly organized around the goal of rehabilitation (Sheldon & Brown, 2003), and by the beginning of the 1970s, prisoner unrest and discontent was palpable, culminating in the deadly Attica riot of 1971 where prisoners demanded a range of human rights protections for incarcerated people—such as the right to decent food, health care, basic educational services, and religious freedom. Although the immediate impact of the Attica action was a pendulum swing in popular opinion toward prison reform in the early 1970s, the growth of a prisoners' rights movement coincided with the passage of the notorious Rockefeller Drug Laws, which required mandatory minimum sentences for the possession or intent to sell even small amounts of controlled substances, and the ramping up of the newly declared "War on Drugs" that would soon explode the prison population in the decades to come. Repressive drug laws would be just the first of a set of strict sentencing guidelines (e.g., the No Early Release Act [NERA]) that would proliferate into the 1980s and 1990s. These policies would significantly increase both the number of people in prison and the amount of time they would serve, and would open the door to the current period in penology widely recognized as the era of the "prison-industrial complex" (e.g., M. Davis, 1995).

The era of the prison-industrial complex has brought with it one of the most consequential social changes of the last century as the rate of imprisonment began to increase steadily and phenomenally each year beginning in the early 1970s (Travis, Sinead, & Cadora, 2003). By 2005, the rate of imprisonment in the United States was 491 per 100,000, or one out of every 136 U.S. residents (Harrison & Beck, 2006). Other scholars put the current rate of incarceration at closer to 700 per 100,000 people (Mauer, 2004), remarking that the pervasiveness of incarceration today has created a "new American apartheid" that rivals the patterns and importance of residential racial and class segregation (Sheldon & Brown, 2003).

Recent Demographics

Of the over two million people who are currently imprisoned in the United States, many are serving lengthy sentences for relatively minor offenses; most people in the United States today are arrested for driving under the influence, drug use, assault, and larceny. Since the emergence of strict drug laws in the early 1970s, drug convictions, in particular, now represent one of the largest categories of convictions in both state and federal prison, as well as in U.S. Bureau of Immigration and Customs Enforcement (ICE)-operated facilities. Indeed, more than one out of three arrests in the United States in 2000 were directly related to drug and alcohol use alone, a figure that does not include arrests related to drug sales or *indirectly* related to drug and alcohol use or sales (Sheldon & Brown, 2003).

More specifically, according to the U.S. Department of Justice, close to half of those now incarcerated in the United States have been convicted of nonviolent offenses, charges that—in other parts of the world—would only bring on a fine or community service (Silverstein, 2003). In 2003, 19% of people confined in state prison were serving time for drug offenses, whereas another 21% were incarcerated for property offenses (Harrison & Beck, 2006). In federal prisons, about 54% of those incarcerated in 2003 were convicted of drug offenses, making it the most common category of crimes in the federal system, followed only by immigration-related offenses, which constituted 10% of the total federal convictions in the same year (Harrison & Beck, 2006). Also in 2005, there were 19,562 detainees in ICE-operated facilities in the United States being held on immigration charges, double the number of detainees held in 1995 (Harrison & Beck, 2006). Across all categories of convictions, the national average length of sentence in state prison in 2002 was 53 months (Durose & Langan, 2005).

Offenders by Gender

Even though women account for only 7% of state and federal prisoners, they are the fastest growing group of incarcerated people. Black and White women constituted approximately equal shares of the total female population in 2002 and in the past 20 years alone, the rate of incarceration for Black women increased by 571%, compared to 131% for Latinas, and 75% for White women (Young & Adams-Fuller, 2006). Although the "War on Drugs" has had dire consequences for men and women alike, and although data are clear that men use and sell drugs more frequently than women (Boyd, 2004), women of all races and ethnicities are significantly more likely than men to be imprisoned on drug charges. Although 30–34% of imprisoned women in 2003, compared to only 19% of men, were serving time for drug offenses (Harrison & Beck, 2006).

Social Class

Those with class privilege in the United States are also significantly less likely to be incarcerated than those who are economically marginalized. Recent data show that only 60% of men and only 40% of women report being employed full time prior to their incarceration (Bloom, Owen, & Covington, 2003), and that approximately one third of all prisoners in the U.S. had prearrest annual incomes of less than $5,000 (Fortunato, 2006).

Given the intersection of race, gender, and class inequalities, it is not surprising that rates of chronic illness, mental illness, drug addiction, HIV/AIDS-related illness, and previous victimization among incarcerated people are each at crisis levels. A 2004 survey by the U.S. Department of Justice found that 73% of women and 55% of men in state prisons, and 61% of women and 63% of men in federal prisons, suffered from a mental health problem, the most common illnesses being mania, depression, and psychotic disorders (BJS, 2006). Of those in state prisons who had reported mental health problems, 13% said they were homeless prior to arrest (BJSa, 2006). And only one in three state prisoners and only one in four federal prisoners had received any treatment since commitment; of those who had reported treatment, the most common type was prescription medication (BJS, 2006).

Health and Behavioral Health Characteristics of Prisoners

The U.S. Department of Justice also reports that an overwhelming majority of people living in prison today were alcohol and/or drug dependent prior to incarceration. In 2004, 74% of state prisoners said they were addicted to drugs or alcohol in the year before arrest, and 34% were using drugs or alcohol at the time of the offense (BJS, 2006). In addition, a significant number of prisoners live with serious health conditions at higher rates than those in the general population, most notably HIV/AIDS and Hepatitis C. Between 2003 and 2004, there were over 23,000 HIV-positive people incarcerated in state and federal prison systems, and the rate of confirmed AIDS cases in 2004 (6,027) was more than three times higher than in the total U.S. population (BJS, 2006). In 2000, HIV/AIDS accounted for more than 6% of all deaths in state and federal prisons (Walton, 2007).

These patterns form a demographic picture that suggests that those who are currently at the greatest risk for incarceration are also those who, given their disadvantaged social locations, are also most likely to be victimized themselves. Finally, given the current structure of the criminal justice system and the lack of reentry services available postrelease (see chapter 20), the chances that one will return to prison within 3 years are extraordinarily high: The national rate of recidivism is now nearly 70%. Some scholars have argued that given the complicated patterns of social, economic, and political marginalization, recidivism is better understood as a process of "revictimization."

VOICES FROM THE FIELD

Katie Heffernan, LCSW
Office of the Public Defender, New Haven, Connecticut

Practice Responsibilities

I assist public defenders in pretrial, trial and sentencing of cases. I conduct psychosocial evaluations and mental status examinations of indigent defendants. I obtain past medical, psychiatric, substance-abuse and education records for background and mitigation purposes. I assess and determine the need for competence to stand trial, criminal responsibility, psychiatric, psychological, or medical assessment and evaluation by experts. I assist public defenders by presenting written and verbal reports to the judge and prosecutor in pretrial discussions and through testimony. I coordinate the referral, admission, and monitoring of psychiatric, substance-abuse, and medical treatment of the defendants for pretrial and sentencing purposes. I am liaison for community treatment and probation providers. I have served as an expert witness and consult in the voir dire process. I supervise graduate social work students in field placements.

I regularly make presentations and conduct training on sex offender probation, psychiatric disabilities, cognitive disabilities, and competence to stand trial. I and other Public Defender Office staff frequently speak in the school system to educate students on issues such as sexual assault, drug and gun laws. I am one of the founding members of the Criminal Justice Collaborative and co-facilitate the Collaborative's training for police officers on how to assess and communicate with individuals who have cognitive disabilities.

I have also worked with the Connecticut Innocence Project: I counsel inmates who have been sentenced for at least 10 years for a conviction that they claim to be innocent of as evidence from the original crime is being DNA tested. I prepare them for possible new trial and reintegration to the community. I worked on the case of James Tillman—the first man in Connecticut to be exonerated.

Expertise Required

I believe a master's degree in social work is necessary as well as experience in a variety of clinical settings as my job requires a vast knowledge of community resources, as well as psychiatric and cognitive disabilities. Knowledge of the criminal justice field is equally important. The position requires strong and broad expertise, including the ability to review medical records, interview and assess defendants and family members, liaison with other clinical experts, community providers, jail/probation/parole personnel, and to advocate for appropriate clinical services for the defendants. An important role for the forensic social worker is convincing judges to order treatment as an alternative to incarceration or as part of the overall sentence.

Practice Challenges

The primary practice challenges faced can be traced to the realities of the population served and resource issues. Because I work with defendants who are accused of the most serious crimes (i.e. murder, arson, sexual assault, robbery, etc.), I sometimes have the difficult task of developing sentencing plans that are both supportive of the defendant and responsive to the concerns of the state's attorney and the judge regarding recidivism and protection of the community. To minimize potential accusations of bias because I am a member of the defense team, it is not unusual for me to face the additional task of identifying and hiring "independent and neutral" experts to perform evaluations and provide recommendations that support my plan. Each case is unique. There are a variety of psychological, psychiatric, cognitive, substance-abuse, and environmental issues that lead our clients to being accused of or committing crimes. It is important to have good assessment and evaluation skills to determine the underlying cause of their criminal behavior. Then it is important to have knowledge of the community and state treatment systems to develop and implement a realistic clinically appropriate alternative to an incarceration plan. It is also important to have the knowledge and skills to hire the most appropriate expert (psychiatrist, psychologist, social worker, etc.) to assist in the defense as needed.

Common Legal and/or Ethical Issues

The biggest issue for a social worker on the defense team is following the "attorney–client privilege" when in other settings, the social worker would be a mandated reporter. The other difficulty is when you are working with defendants who have caused harm to others—especially children—and you have to assess the underlying cause of the offense. The clients that I work with have all been accused of felonies (murder, arson, sex assault, robbery, etc.)—it's hard at times to focus on the issues of the defendant rather than the crime for which he/she is accused. Community agencies feel that the court should either incarcerate the defendants for life or should come up with their own treatment facilities instead of referring the defendants back into the community systems from whence they came.

Brief Description of Collaborative Activities
With Professionals and/or Other Stakeholders

As mentioned previously, I must collaborate with expert witnesses and community providers when working with a defendant. Connecticut's resources have lessened over the years and community providers have been feeling the strain of long waitlists. Some community providers have the notion that the court has its own programs to service clients and will, at times, have clients arrested from their group homes, hospitals, etc. to send a message that the client is held accountable for assaults, vandalism, etc. even when in a decompensated state. The community providers also sometimes feel that it's okay to send the clients to the criminal justice field under these circumstances because they will be afforded the treatment that they need. Unfortunately, the courts do not have treatment programs and probation officers are not adequately trained to supervise clients with psychiatric and/or cognitive difficulties. Once a client is arrested, he/she is often incarcerated because community providers fill their beds—once they think the client will be treated elsewhere—and the defendants are placed on long waitlists. Our offices take as many opportunities that we can to educate community providers to treat—not arrest so that they are aware that there are no treatment programs through the courts.

Additional Information

Don't be afraid to call people who are already in the field. Don't just look at books; talk to people who are doing it, find out how it works and what's the best way to be prepared. That was the most helpful thing to me, and I find it's the most rewarding thing to me now when people call me and say, 'Can you tell me about your job?' I don't think there'd be one professional who'd say 'I can't help you' if approached by somebody who really wants to pursue a career in this area."

Current Trends

Contemporary scholars of the current prison system argue that the most important trends in corrections today include the boom in prison construction, the emergence and centrality of the for-profit prison and other efforts to privatize correctional functions, the increased prevalence of the supermax facility, and the rapid increased in the rate of women's imprisonment. Although each of these developments deserves its own treatment, we will focus here on the growing number of women in prison, as this trend may be one that most directly impacts the routine practice of social work for many practitioners. Although still a relatively small proportion of the total prison population, women now constitute the fastest growing demographic of prisoners in our nation (Templeton, 2004). Since 1980 alone, the rate of imprisonment for women has increased 654% (Boudin & Smith, 2003). As is the case for men, the majority of women newly committed to state prison have been convicted of nonviolent offenses. Despite the similarities to men's patterns of incarceration, the persistence of the unequal gendered relations in education, employment, and the family, among other gendered institutions, creates a set of structural arrangements for women that promotes both victimization and criminality simultaneously (e.g., Boyd, 2004; Renzetti, Goldstein, & Miller, 2006). More specifically, over 70% of women incarcerated in state prison were convicted of nonviolent crimes, largely property and nonviolent drug offenses (Greenfeld & Snell, 1999), with Mauer, Potler, and Wolf (1999) reporting an 888% increase in drug-related convictions for women between 1986 and 1996.

Scope of the Problem

In the context of the material we have reviewed above, we argue that the scope of the problem of incarceration cannot be overstated. At the level of the social system, the public expenditure of billions of dollars each year for a correctional system that, by all accounts, is failing to reduce crime is raising serious political questions in a nation where funds for public education, housing, and health care are nonetheless being appropriated to build new prisons. As large numbers of poor people and people of color are increasingly warehoused in prisons, they lose access to education and employment skills, severely limiting their human capital and the ability to contribute to the vitality of families, communities, and to the larger society. As we will discuss in the text that follows, the experience of incarceration is deeply traumatizing, a horrific experience that goes largely untreated for millions of people, and with consequences that go well beyond just the individual person recovering from prison.

Relevant Theoretical Frameworks

Volumes of social science research have been dedicated to theorizing crime and deviance and the institutional mechanisms employed to regulate crime and deviance in societies. Because a review of this research is beyond the scope of this chapter, we aim instead to briefly address those theoretical frameworks that we assert have the most currency today in understanding the growth of the prison system in the United States. Perhaps an obvious explanation for the rise of mass incarceration is that there has been an increase in the number of actual crimes committed during this same period, particularly violent crimes. However, many scholars agree that there is little support for the idea that prisons have grown to accommodate an increasingly violent society, citing a lack of positive correlation between an increase in violent crime and an increase in rates of incarceration (e.g., Silverstein, 2003). In fact, in some recent periods when the rate of incarceration has increased, we have actually witnessed a decrease, or leveling off, of violent crime (Sheldon & Brown, 2003). So, why, then, are prisons so prevalent in America today?

Critical/Marxist Theories

Some of the most important theoretical analyses of the rise of the prison-industrial complex in the United States emerge from critical criminologists who examine the criminal justice system using a Marxist lens. From a critical/Marxist perspective, the criminal justice system primarily serves the needs of the capitalist or ruling class by protecting the exploitative and plundering practices of wealthy individuals and corporations while at the same time punishing threats to private property interests from the working classes primarily through the incarceration of surplus laborers, the use of prison labor as cheap labor, the privatization of prisons as for-profit industries, and the criminalization of poverty itself.

Critical Race Theory

Despite the theoretical power of critical/Marxist analyses, such perspectives have historically been taken to task by other contemporary progressive theorists for the singular, or at least primary, focus on political economy, and for lacking a more nuanced analysis of the intersection of class and race. Critical race theorists approach the expanding criminal justice system, in its disproportionate ensnarement of native-born people of color and non-White immigrants, as one that has emerged in the postindustrial context to do much of the work that slavery and racial segregation did in the past, and in doing so, contributes to the escalation of the United States as the new postcolonial empire increasingly capable of imposing its own criminal-processing practices throughout the world in highly racialized ways.

Intersectionality Theory

Although critical race theorists have added a multidimensional analysis of the prison-industrial complex other than traditional Marxist scholarship, we argue that the most useful analyses of the crisis of mass incarceration today take an intersectional approach, or one that understands class, race, and nation, but also gender and sexuality, as central and interlocking systems of structural inequality. In this paradigm, which accepts much of the theoretical foundations of both a critical/Marxist perspective and critical race theory, these intersecting systems of inequality form what Patricia Hill Collins (1991) has called a "matrix of domination" that creates greater risks of incarceration for some groups than others, but also shapes the very institutional arrangements in which prisons have expanded. Informed most directly by multiracial feminism, an intersectionality perspective on the criminal processing system takes the analytical starting point that prisons as they exist today serve to maintain not only class and racial hierarchies but what bell hooks would call a system of "white supremacist capitalist patriarchy" (2000, p. 159).

Common Issues

Prison Culture

Social workers in the prison setting are dealing with complex and nuanced client issues. Many prisons across the country, and most women's prisons, are located in more rural areas and away from major population centers. This poses issues for inmates maintaining family and social support network relationships, as visiting without access to public transportation or across large distances may prove impossible for an economically disadvantaged family. However, it also creates difficulty for administration at the facilities to be able to hire appropriately trained and credentialed professionals, because of the facilities' locations. In addition, health care access problems and separation from existing social support systems are two common issues in the prison setting.

One readily observable dynamic of relationship acknowledgment was the familial title bestowed on a friend. Many women, in describing their closest friendships, both within the prison as well as outside the prison context, would explain how "she's like a sister," to indicate the depth and significance of that relationship. Rubin (1986), who studied friendship formation, discussed her participants' conceptualization in terms of the idealized family, or the kinds of ties we would most want in our familial relationships, because realistically, her participants reflected that they often did not have the depth and disclosure in their family relationships that were consistent with indicating a friend was "like family" and meaning it in a complimentary manner.

However, within the prison setting, the comparison is frequently dropped and people become "sisters" and "cousins," even "mothers" and "daughters." In addition, romantically linked partners will also consider and reference their romantic partners as their "wives." These familial titles are often confusing for the staff, who are not sure and often have no way to confirm legal or blood extended-family relationships.

Instead, the recreation of familiar relationships and the bestowing of familial titles, thus creating fictive kinship networks, serves several purposes for an incarcerated person. First, the title itself legitimates and reinforces the depth of relationship in a way that calling someone a friend cannot. Essentially, these titles give a layer of meaning that includes inherent assumptions about the significance and expectations of the relationship. In the same way, for example, that in a hospital setting, kin are permitted to visit a person in intensive care whereas friends may not be able to do so, labeling someone as a family member automatically brings access and respect.

In addition, familial titles, when employed across a large group of people, serve as a source of solidarity and support. If a woman becomes close to an in-prison "mother," who also has several other in-prison "daughters" (and occasionally, "sons," who are also women) and "sisters," this woman gains a family support structure. She has people who operate within many of the same parameters of support and obligation typically associated with a blood or legal family network, including the sharing of food and supplies, support for difficult times (most notably health problems and child custody issues), and visiting or gift-giving behaviors.

Prison Gangs

Interestingly, prison gangs serve many of these same family support functions within correctional facilities; according to Inside Prison, an independent research organization for criminal justice issues, the term "prison gang" is used for convenience. Many groups officially called "gangs" actually identify as families, nations, and/or organizations. The scope of the gang literature reaches beyond this chapter, but it should be noted that prison gangs and street gangs may be different from one another, both in terms of ideology and in terms of operations (Knox, 2005).

Knox (2005) argues that prison gangs represent not only a security threat to the institution(s) in which they operate, but also that they may be exploiting religious freedoms within the facility, and even using religious freedom to distribute hate messages. Knox further clarifies:

> *A prison gang, correctly defined, is any gang (where a gang is a group of three or more persons who recurrently commit crime, and where the crime is openly known to the group) that operates in prison. However, a tradition has developed "in practice" within the context of applied ideas about prison gangs, where the correctional practitioner defines a prison gang exclusively as "a gang that originated in the prison." (Knox, 2005, p. 25)*

Thus, gangs like the Aryan Brotherhood and the Black Guerilla Family and the Melanics would be "pure prison gangs" in this respect, because these were not street gangs imported into the prison system, these are gangs that originated within the prison system itself. The Lyman (1989) definition of prison gang is centered on the "commission of crime, without the crime a prison group could violate rules and regulations and still be a security threat group" (pp. 3–4).

According to Gaes and associates (Gaes, Wallace, Gilman, Klein-Saffran, & Suppa, 2001), gang affiliation by an inmate is associated with an increase in misconduct offenses, violence, and serious violence for most gangs; the most frequent areas of violence and misconduct involve drugs and property (p. 16). Having no gang affiliation is associated with an inmate's lower likelihood of violent behavior while incarcerated (p. 16). Thus, an awareness of gang behavior and a client's gang affiliation, or lack thereof, may prove useful for the social worker in terms of determining treatment options and probability of success for the inmate.

Whether or not affiliated with a gang, when a new inmate enters a correctional facility and adjusts to the confinement, she faces high levels of stress (Pollock, 2002). Not the least of her worries is her children, Belknap (2001) notes that

> *Incarcerated women are far more likely than incarcerated men to be the emotional and financial providers for children. Although four out of five women and three out of five men entering prison are parents, research indicates that almost all incarcerated women have custody of their children prior to the imprisonment while fewer than half of the men do....Thus, one of the greatest differences in stresses for women and men serving time is that the separation from children is generally a much greater hardship for women than for men. (p. 176)*

Prison Stress

In addition to economic hardship, separation from loved ones, crowded living conditions, bad food, and poor medical care, another cause of stress faced by women inmates is the potential for sexual abuse. Despite fears and worries, the new inmate must figure out how to spend the next few months or years at this new home, deciding how involved to become in the prison's programming and what sorts of offerings are of interest and available. These practical considerations must be contemplated against the backdrop of "counts" and searches, mandatory and oppressive institutional control, limited visitation with children, and unlimited time to reflect and remember. It is at this juncture of classification, restriction, and opportunity that the inmate and the social worker may first encounter one another.

Domain-Specific Legal and Ethical Issues

The practice of incarceration is made possible by a system of laws that produce the conditions of confinement, including drug laws and three-strikes laws, but this same legal system, as well as a system of ethical responsibilities in the field, also defines the rules for how people can be treated once they are imprisoned. Although it is commonly understood that imprisonment, by definition, means the removal of fundamental civil liberties guaranteed to those who are free, prisoners nonetheless retain some fundamental rights in theory, if not in practice.

Relevant Policies, Laws, and Legal Precedents

The American Civil Liberties Union (ACLU) reports that there are at least three major categories of prisoners' rights that all incarcerated people, their families, and those who work with prisoners should know, namely, rights involving disciplinary sanctions, protection from assault and the unnecessary use of force, and access to medical care (ACLU, 1999). Incarcerated people are protected from cruel and unusual punishment under the 8th Amendment to the U.S. Constitution, and are in part, afforded due process rights articulated by the 14th Amendment. For instance, prisoners are entitled to challenge disciplinary sanctions that are brought against them during the course of their incarceration, although the 1995 *Sandin v. Conner* Supreme Court ruling requires prisoners to demonstrate that the disciplinary sanction created an "atypical and significant hardship," and that "a state regulation or statue grants prisoners a protected liberty interest in remaining free from that confinement or restraint" (ACLU, 1999, p. 1).

Likewise, prisoners are legally protected from assault, including rape and sexual assault, from both correctional staff and other inmates. However, prisoners are not protected from inmate assault if they cannot prove that staff, in their duty to protect prisoners from such abuse, acted with "deliberate indifference" or "reckless disregard" for the safety of an inmate. Moreover, prisoners are not protected from assault by prison staff if they cannot prove that staff used "force maliciously and sadistically for the very purpose of causing harm" (ACLU, 1999, p. 3). In the case of sexual assault, federal statutory provisions expressly prohibit sexual contact between prisoners and corrections staff, defining such contact as—in essence—sexual misconduct (Human Rights Watch, 1996).

Yet, these laws only apply to federal prisons, and only 27 states and the District of Columbia criminalized sexual contact between corrections staff and prisoners as of 1996, and with a range of varying definitions of what constitutes criminal custodial sexual assault (Human Rights Watch, 1996). In addition, despite the promise of the 2003 Prison Rape Elimination Act (PREA), legislation that emerged in large part as a much-needed response to the crisis of sexual terrorism and prisoner rape that continues to organize men's prisons, data suggest that little effort has been made in practice to protect women prisoners from the same kind of gender violence, particularly as it is perpetuated by correctional staff who are still disproportionately men (Human Rights Watch, 1996).

The 8th Amendment also obligates all prison officials, whether publicly or privately employed, to provide incarcerated people with adequate medical care, including mental health care. Incarcerated people have the constitutional right to claims of inadequate medical treatment, but to do so must show that prison officials acted with "deliberate indifference" to their medical needs.

Fourth Amendment rights to privacy and rights to be free of unreasonable search and seizure, as well as First Amendment rights to freedom of expression, are also limited for prisoners, although not entirely removed.

There are other important legal precedents with which social workers must become familiar. Discrimination based on racial segregation is prohibited in prison unless it is deemed necessary for the security of the facility. Under the Americans with Disabilities Act of 1990 discrimination against prisoners with disabilities is also prohibited, and government is required to provide auxiliary aids and services such that a disabled prisoner has equal access to prison routines and programs (Schneider & Sales, 2004). An additional matter of reproductive freedom not directly related to medical care but also central to social work practice are the laws that permit parents to have regular visits with their children. Nonetheless, a devastating law for families with incarcerated adults has been the passage of the Adoption and Safe Families Act of 1997 (ASFA), which mandates termination of parental rights of children who have been in foster care 15 of the last 22 months, regardless of whether the parent is incarcerated or not (Halperin & Harris, 2004). Not only is family stability comprised for prisoners as a result of legal barriers, but access to education is as well: Most states do not guarantee access to educational services in prison unless an incarcerated person tests below a high school level, and although some access to higher education in prison was once possible in the second half of the 20th century, the Violent Crime Control and Law Enforcement Act of 1994 banned the use of Pell Grant funding for postsecondary correctional education and effectively eliminated most higher education programs in prison.

Yet, despite the fact that prisoners may have more access to constitutional rights than we might have originally imagined, the ability for prisoners to ensure that these rights are enforced was severely limited in 1996 when Congress passed the Prison Litigation Reform Act (PLRA). In brief, the PLRA stipulates that prisoners may not file suit in federal court until they have thoroughly exhausted the prison grievance process, that prisoners must pay their own court fees, that the courts have the right to dismiss any lawsuit brought forth by a prisoner and penalize prisoners who incur three case dismissals, that prisoners cannot sue for mental or emotional injury unless they can show physical injury as well, and finally that federal prisoners risk losing merit time if the suit is deemed an attempt to harass those named in the case, or if the prisoner is found to have lied or misrepresented information (ACLU, 1999, p. 2).

Finally, aside from these matters of law, each prison system functions using a set of standard operating procedures, including a strict code of conduct, that prison staff as well as prison volunteers must abide by when working in prisons, policies that also include restrictions on developing personal relationships—whether sexual or platonic—with prisoners. Along with an understanding of each system's administrative policies, the set of standard ethical principles in the field of social work must also be applied with an understanding of the unique constraints of the prison. As the prison is a total institution (Goffman, 1961), and one in which prisoners have no practical ability to fully give or refuse consent to any institutional mandate, including what to wear or eat, when to wake up or move from one location to another, or what rehabilitation program to pursue, providing services to clients in ways that do not violate important principles of ethical behavior, and basic human decency, is a regular and daunting task.

Assessment, Prevention, and Intervention

Screening, assessment, and intervention in the prison setting will occur in a variety of ways for the social worker. Because many female inmates are mothers and care-providers of their children upon sentencing, family-based intervention and assessment may be necessary. In addition, if women enter the criminal processing system while they are pregnant, assessment and planning for their pregnancies, postdelivery child placement, and parental rights may be necessary. It is not uncommon for inmates to enter the system with existing mental illness, nor is it uncommon for inmates to feel suicidal, and both conditions would require appropriate assessment and, if necessary, intervention. Maintenance of family relationships is perilous while incarcerated, and the social worker may be able to assist in this regard with assessment of the family arrangements and access to family-maintenance programs available in the state where the prison is located. Health care assessment would not be conducted by the social worker herself, but assessment of medical adherence in chronic conditions may be part of a screening completed by the social worker. In addition, the social worker is able to advocate on behalf of an incarcerated person; may work to improve policies that are ineffective or unhelpful; and even create programming options where a need exists, but is not being met at the facility or for a specific population within a correctional setting.

Because much of the incarcerated population is serving time for drug-related offenses, the need for addiction-treatment programming is widely recognized in correctional settings. For example, drug-abuse education is offered at every institution operated by the federal Bureau of Prisons in both nonresidential and residential treatment formats (BJS, 2007). Although debate continues as to what "works," especially at the large-scale policy level, and in light of the dually punitive and rehabilitative roles correctional facilities may serve in society (see, e.g., Gendreau, 1996; Martinson, 1974), recidivism remains at issue for all levels of criminal processing system workers. Arguments that some types of treatment are effective at reducing criminal behavior, or addiction-related behavior, are interesting and helpful (see, e.g., Gendreau, 1996). However, increasingly, the ability to tap into long-range programming and treatment options, instead of small-scale, limited interventions, may be the most promising avenue for incarcerated people to limit the probability of returning to prison. Thus, the social worker who is able to access information and resources that extend beyond the correctional facility and into the community, may be more effective in assisting clients in remaining out of prison for longer periods of time. (See chapter 20 on prison reentry.)

Practitioner Skills

Inmate health care issues are an area that can really only be addressed in a helpful way by other in-prison people, be they the formal employees of the department of corrections or, frequently, the social network of inmate friends and fictive kinship. When an inmate is sick, access to high-quality health care is nearly impossible and access to any intervention is often fraught with problems. To lower costs, many states have begun to outsource their medical care to for-profit corporations. On-site medical care is often not available all the time, and even if it is available, it means having someone assess whether you are really sick enough to seek help. To be fair, abuses of the system by chronic complainers or inmates looking for a way out of a work detail must be part of the history of health care limitations, but the results are often problematic. As a social worker, you will undoubtedly come into intervention-based contact with inmates in need of health care for chronic issues (diabetes, in particular, but also Hepatitis C and HIV are common among inmate populations) as well as for limited-term health conditions, such as pregnancy.

Health care problems abound in prison facilities; we can speak to this phenomenon from first-hand awareness of health care misadventures. Most U.S. prisons have underfunded, ill-equipped, and understaffed health care departments that cannot keep up with the needs of their population. Most diagnostic tests require trips to a hospital about 70 miles away from one of the facilities in which we work; few procedures are performed at the facility. In the time that the authors have been working with the women in this facility, about 10 years, there have been numerous deaths, many seemingly senseless.

The waiting time to be seen by a medical care professional is often lengthy, even for inmates with chronic or life-threatening illnesses. When seen, the inmate risks not being taken seriously, especially if her complaint includes pain or if she has a past addiction. Add to the list of health care dilemmas the fact that inmate health care co-payments for a medical visit are $5.00 for each visit. This often means a woman will put off seeking treatment until she can better afford to pay for it. As a result, supportive functions served by friends in prison include both assistance in managing the system as well as care-taking behaviors to help with symptoms or conditions not adequately controlled. For example, when a woman has a friend who is sick, she may offer to share her snacks or stamps so the sick friend is able to pay for the medical visit (inmates cannot transfer money from one commissary account to another, nor do they have a way to pay for each other's health care service fees).

As a social worker in the prison setting, you will likely have limited, if any, ability to provide medical services, or even influence an inmate's access to receiving medical attention. That does not mean that you will not hear about a variety of illnesses or be able to counsel patient-inmates through illness and treatment. One of the common health conditions for female inmates, with a generally more positive outcome, is pregnancy. Although pregnancy and birth-preparation counseling may be available, one of our current colleagues, who gave birth in prison, reports that postpregnancy counseling is vital. Whether or not this is her first pregnancy, giving birth while being an inmate has its own special circumstances and women should be prepared for the experience in advance. A social worker may be able to bridge the gaps between the mother, the custodial staff, and the medical care providers.

VOICES FROM THE FIELD

Kimberly D. Leitch
NYS Licensed Clinical Social Worker
Director of Social Work

Agency Setting

I work for a maximum-security hospital where we provide secure treatment and evaluation for the forensic patients and courts of New York City and Long Island. Most patients are received through the courts under Criminal Procedure Law (CPL) or through state psychiatric hospitals. Treatment is provided in accordance with the current standards of professional care outlined by the Joint Commission of Accreditation of Health Organizations (JCAHO).

Practice Responsibilities

I am responsible for supervising the social work department, which includes seven social workers and two social work interns. They each work on one of seven wards within the hospital and are included in the ward's interdisciplinary Team. Clinically I have been assigned to wards, more specifically the high-acuity ward, which houses the more symptomatic and aggressive patients in the state.

Expertise Required

The expertise required for my position is administrative experience. I am a social worker who concentrated in law while at graduate school in Fordham, which assisted me in acquiring this position. I started as a ward social worker with the high-acuity patients and then took an administrative position as a Team Leader, which is the head of the ward. Subsequently, I was offered the position of Director of Social Work, which I have had for the past 2 years.

Practice Challenges

Some of the challenges that I have had to deal with involve the population that I work with. They are severely mentally ill and I describe it as mental illness in its rawest form. Aside from this would be working with a patient who is dangerous and significantly violent. If those issues have resolved, then I would say that there are cognitive issues and/or psychotic issues that impede progress.

Common Legal and/or Ethical Issues

Because we are a forensic facility there are always legal issues meaning that we get our patients from the legal system. Specific issues we have had to deal with are the fitness cases. We oftentimes get patients who are malingerers and take advantage of the system. On the other hand we can also restore a patient to fitness, discharge them to the Department of Corrections to have them decompensate, and then be readmitted.

Additional Information

Part of my job requirement is that I sit on a Hospital Forensic Committee (HFC). For lack of a better term it is somewhat of a "parole board" for our CPL 330.20 patients who have been found Not Guilty by Reason of Insanity of a crime. For the patient to be transferred to a civil facility s/he needs to pass all phases, the last being an HFC. It is probably the most interesting part of my position. It is an interdisciplinary committee comprised of a board-certified psychiatrist, licensed psychologist, and a licensed social worker. The social worker on the committee holds the responsibility for writing the HFC report that is submitted to the courts.

Summary and Conclusions

This chapter has presented the context of prison as one in which the social worker may have many potential roles. An understanding of the prison system as an extremely powerful and far-reaching practice setting, and one fundamentally connected to all of the other fields addressed in this text, is essential for any effective social worker because she will be working in concert with a variety of other human services and administrative services providers in this position. We have briefly reviewed the history of women's incarceration and highlighted special issues surrounding women's incarceration needs, including the ways in which the social worker may be called in to assist with these needs.

References

American Civil Liberties Union [ACLU]. (1999). *ACLU position paper: Prisoners' rights*. Retrieved June 13, 2007, from http://www.aclu.org/FilesPDFs/prisonerrights.pdf

Belknap, J. (2001). *The invisible woman: Gender, crime, and justice* (2nd ed.). Belmont, CA: Wadsworth.

Bloom, B., Owen, B., & Covington, S. (2003). *Gender-responsive strategies: Research, practice, and guiding principles for women offenders* (NIC Accession No. 018017). U.S. Department of Justice, National Institute of Corrections. Washington, DC: U.S. Government Printing Office.

Boudin, K., & Smith, R. (2003). Alive behind the labels: Women in prison. In R. Morgan (Ed.), *Sisterhood is forever: The women's anthology for the new millennium* (pp. 244–266). New York: Washington Square Press.

Boyd, S. C. (2004). *From witches to crack moms: Women, drug law, and policy*. Durham, NC: Carolina Academic Press.

Bureau of Justice Statistics (BJS). (2004). *Nation spends $167 billion on criminal and civil justice services: Since 1982, justice expenditures average 8% growth annually* [Press Release]. Washington, DC: U.S. Department of Justice, Office of Justice Programs. Retrieved June 20, 2007, from http://www.ojp.usdoj.gov/bjs/pub/press/jeeus01pr.htm

Bureau of Justice Statistics (BJS). (2005). *Nation's prison and jail population grew by 932 inmates per week: Number of female inmates reached more than 100,000* [Press Release]. Washington, DC: U.S. Department of Justice, Office of Justice Programs. Retrieved June 20, 2007, from http://www.ojp.usdoj.gov/bjs/pub/press/pjim04pr.htm

Bureau of Justice Statistics (BJS). (2006). *Study finds more than half of all prison and jail inmates have mental health problems* [Press Release]. Washington, DC: U.S. Department of Justice, Office of Justice Programs. Retrieved June 20, 2007, from http://www.ojp.usdoj.gov/newsroom/2006/BJS06064.htm

Bureau of Justice Statistics (BJS). (2007). *Expenditure and employment statistics*. Washington, DC: U.S. Department of Justice, Office of Justice Programs. Retrieved June 20, 2007, from http://www.ojp.usdoj.gov/bjs/eande.htm

Collins, P. H. (1990). *Black feminist thought: Knowledge, consciousness, and the politics of empowerment*. Boston: Unwin Hyman.

Davis, A. Y. (2003). *Are prisons obsolete?* New York: Seven Stories Press.

Davis, M. (1995). Hell factories in the field: A prison-industrial complex. *The Nation, 260*, 229–234.

Durose, M. R., & Langan, P. A. (2005). *State court sentencing of convicted felons, 2002* (BJS Publication No. 05/05 NCJ 208910). Washington, DC: U.S. Department of Justice, Office of Justice Programs, Bureau of Justice Statistics.

Fortunato, M. (2006). *Prison facts*. Retrieved June 20, 2007, from http://www.heartsandminds.org/prisons/facts.htm

Gaes, G. G., Wallace, S., Gilman, E., Klein-Saffran, J., & Suppa, S. (2001). *The influence of prison gang affiliation on violence and other prison misconduct*. Washington, DC: Federal Bureau of Prisons.

Gendreau, P. (1996). Offender rehabilitation: What we know and what needs to be done. *Criminal Justice and Behavior, 23*, 144–161.

Goffman, E. (1961). *Asylums: Essays on the social situation of mental patients and other inmates*. Garden City, NY: Anchor Books.

Greenfeld, L. A., & Snell, T. L. (1999). *Women offenders* (BJS Publication No. 12/99 NCJ 175688) [Electronic Version]. Washington, DC: U.S. Department of Justice, Office of Justice Programs, Bureau of Justice Statistics. Retrieved June 20, 2008, from http://www.ojp.usdoj.gov/bjs/pub/pdf/wo.pdf

Halperin, R., & Harris, J. L. (2004). Parental rights of incarcerated mothers with children in foster care: A policy vacuum. *Feminist Studies: The Prison Issue, 30*, 339–352.

Harrison, P. M., & Beck, A. J. (2006). *Prisoners in 2005* (BJS Publication No. 11/06 NCJ 215092). Washington, DC: U.S. Department of Justice, Office of Justice Programs, Bureau of Justice Statistics.

Hooks, B. (2000). *Where we stand: Class matters.* New York: Routledge.

Human Rights Watch. (1996). *All too familiar: Sexual abuse of women in U.S. state prisons.* New York: Human Rights Watch. Retrieved June 12, 2007, from http://hrw.org/reports/1996/Us1.htm

Knox, G. W. (2005). *The problem of gangs and security threat groups (STG's) in American prisons today: Recent research findings from the 2004 prison gang survey.* Washington, DC: National Gang Crime Research Center.

Lyman, M. D. (1989). *Gangland: Drug trafficking by organized criminals.* Springfield, IL: Charles C Thomas.

Mauer, M. (2004). Thinking about prison and its impact in the twenty-first century. *Ohio State Journal of Criminal Law, 2*, 607.

Mauer, M., & Chesney-Lind, M. (2002). Introduction. In M. Mauer & M. Chesney-Lind (Eds.), *Invisible punishment: The collateral consequences of mass imprisonment* (pp. 1–12). New York: New Press.

Mauer, M., Potler, C., & Wolf, R. (1999). *Gender and justice: Women, drugs, and sentencing policy.* Washington, DC: Sentencing Project.

Martinson, R. (1974). What works? Questions and answers about prison reform. *Public Interest, 35*, 22–54.

Pollock, J. (2002). *Women, prison, and crime.* Belmont, CA: Wadsworth Thomson.

Rafter, N. H. (1985). *Partial justice: Women in state prisons, 1800–1935.* Boston: Northeastern University Press.

Renzetti, C., Goodstein, L., & Miller, S. L. (2006). *Rethinking gender, crime and justice.* Los Angeles: Roxbury.

Rubin, L. B. (1986). *Just friends: The role of friendship in our lives.* New York: Harper Perennial.

Sandin v. Conner, (93-1911), 515 U.S. 472 (1995). Retrieved March 8, 2008, from http://www.law.cornell.edu/supct/html/93-1911.ZS.html

Schneider, N. R., & Sales, B. D. (2004). Deaf or hard of hearing inmates in prison. *Disability & Society, 19*(1), 77–89.

Sheldon, R. G., & Brown, W. B. (2003). *Criminal justice in America: A critical view.* Boston: Allyn & Bacon.

Sifakis, C. (2003). *The encyclopedia of American prisons.* New York: Checkmark Books.

Silverstein, K. (2003). Introduction. In T. Herivel & P. Wright (Eds.), *Prison nation: The warehousing of America's poor* (pp. 1–3). New York: Routledge.

Stephan, J. J. (2004). *State prison expenditures, 2001* (BJS Publication No. 06/04 NCJ 202949). Washington, DC: U.S. Department of Justice, Office of Justice Programs, Bureau of Justice Statistics.

Stephan, J. J., & Karberg, J. C. (2003). *Census of state and federal correctional facilities, 2000* (BJS Publication No. 08/03 NCJ 198272). Washington, DC: U.S. Department of Justice, Office of Justice Programs, Bureau of Justice Statistics.

Templeton, R. (2004). She who believes in freedom: Women who defy the prison industrial complex. In V. Labaton & D. L. Martin (Eds.), *The fire this time: Young activists and the new feminism* (pp. 254–277). New York: Anchor Books.

Travis, J., Sinead, K., & Cadora, E. (2003, November). *A portrait of prisoner reentry in New Jersey.* Washington, DC: Urban Institute.

Walton, R. G. (2007). *Chairman's remarks.* The National Prison Rape Elimination Commission. Retrieved May 15, 2007, from http//www.nprec.us/chairmans_remarks

Young, V. D., & Adams-Fuller, T. A. (2006). Women, race/ethnicity, and criminal justice processing. In C. Renzetti, L. Goodstein, & S. Miller (Eds.), *Rethinking gender, crime, and justice: Feminist readings* (pp. 185–199). Los Angeles: Roxbury.

Reentry in the Twenty-First Century

20

Patricia O'Brien

"Reentry" is the term commonly used to describe the experience of the 600,000 to 700,000 men and women returning to communities every year after they have served terms in state and federal prison facilities all over the United States. Prisoner reentry has begun to receive national attention from policymakers, practitioners, and researchers (Petersilia, 2003; Travis, 2005). Scholars have examined the factors correlated with recidivism (Langan & Levin, 2002); the causes of desistance from crime (Giordano, Cernkovich, & Rudolphe, 2002; Laub & Sampson, 2003; Maruna, 2001); and what is referred to as the "collateral consequences of imprisonment," including voter disenfranchisement (Mauer & Chesney-Lind, 2002), limited options for employment (Pager, 2003), and impact on family and community (Hairston & Rollin, 2003; Travis, 2005). Attention to prisoner reentry is clearly justified: Except for those inmates who die while they are incarcerated, every person who is sent to prison experiences reentry—the process of leaving prison and returning to society (Travis, 2005).

Sometimes referred to as an "outcome," as in successful readjustment and resumption of citizenship after release or failure when the adult recidivates when rearrested, reconvicted, or reincarcerated, reentry is also a complicated and multilayered process that provides social workers many opportunities for assessment and intervention.

This chapter discusses the conditions and challenges of adults returning to the community after having completed a sentence in jail or prison and then will describe some of what is known about effective psychosocial interventions.

Reentry: The Outcome

According to federal statistics, the U.S. incarcerated population defined as those adults being held in local jails and sentenced to state and federal correctional facilities to serve sentences, has grown from 0.5 million in 1980 to 2.4 million by year-end 2006, more than quadrupling in little more than a quarter century (Sabol, Couture, & Harrison, 2007). The number of offenders either incarcerated or back in the community is projected to increase from roughly 7.1 million to 8.5 million by 2012 (Travis, 2005). As a result, the public sector is now turning to the discussion of who is returning from prison and how best to respond to the estimated thousands each day who come home to communities ill-equipped to address their needs so as to optimize the former inmates' possibilities for success.

One outcome related to reentry that is consistently reported in discussions of the growth of the number of incarcerated adults in this country is their associated failure rate after release. A national follow-up study of released inmates found that within 3 years after their release in 1994, two thirds had recidivated and more than 50% were back in prison, serving time for a new prison sentence or for a technical violation of their release, like failing a drug test, missing an appointment with a parole officer, or being arrested for a new crime (Langan & Levin, 2002).

A report on state sentencing reforms (King, 2007) recognizes the effect of determinate sentencing, which has exerted upward pressure on prison populations in many states, including mandatory sentencing laws for drug-related crimes and other offenses, harsher sentencing provisions, and cutbacks in parole release. At the same time, the report describes reforms driven by a number of factors, including budget crises at the state level, the development and expansion of a range of programs offering alternatives to incarceration, and the falling crime rate. These reforms provide a context for forensic social workers to have more influence in the development and implementation of effective responses to the needs of persons exiting correctional custody.

Characteristics of Released Adults

Prisoner reentry is not just about the greater number of prisoners returning home, although that is certainly what is most apparent to those correctional and other professionals charged with providing ever-increasing services with decreasing state and federal resources. It also involves changes in sentencing guidelines in every state and in the federal system that have contributed to the increasing use of prison, especially for drug charges. This increase has had a noticeable impact on the bulking up of the prison population and on other trends within the correctional system. These include a greater proportion of sentences being served in custody (rather than on parole), increasing disconnection from family and community because of the location of prison facilities and greater restrictions on visitation as prisons operate at capacity and overcapacity, and greater prevalence of untreated alcohol and drug dependency as well as other co-occurring medical conditions and mental health disorders.

Theories of Desistance

Criminologists describe desistance as the life events that lead to a decrease and eventual extinction of criminal behaviors. Sheldon and Eleanor Glueck's early study of juveniles (1940) found that maturation was the key factor in explaining desistance from crime. This was extended later to a theory that indicates that age has a direct effect on criminal behavior, reflecting a spontaneous desistance unrelated to other factors (Renzetti, Curran, & Carr, 2003). Although many scholars maintain that the "aging out" theory is the most influential explanation, others have argued that age alone cannot explain such change. Sampson and Laub (2005) have developed a more sophisticated theory related to social control and conformity that adults may strive for—these include ties to social institutions such as marital attachment and commitment to stable employment that may contribute to the process of reform. Although there is some empirical evidence for the theory from longitudinal studies work that Laub and Sampson (2003) have conducted over multiple cohorts, their research has been criticized as simply reflecting the reality of their White male sample. Within a gender- and racially stratified social system, access to stable jobs, to "good" marriages, and advancement across class levels is unequally distributed.

Laub and Sampson (2003) also integrate elements of the broader life-course perspective (Elder, 1998) to explain childhood antisocial behavior, adolescent delinquency, and criminality in early adulthood. They argue that serious delinquency and adolescent events (such as incarceration) attenuate social and institutional bonds (such as employment) in adulthood that increase the likelihood of continued offending. However, Golder and associates (Golder, Gillmore, Speiker, & Morrison, 2005) found that strong adult social bonds aid in the gradual desistance from problem behaviors (e.g., substance use leading to other criminal behaviors).

Other researchers argue that desistance is not merely a product of external forces of social control, but rather a result of human agency. To better understand the processes that facilitate reform, some theorists have focused on pathways out of criminal behavior as a function of self-identity, choices, actions, and lifestyle. Developing a theory of cognitive transformation, Giordano and colleagues (2002, pp. 1000–1001) describe four stages in the transformation or desistance process: (a) openness to change, (b) exposure to "hooks for change" or turning points, (c) fashioning an "appealing and conventional 'replacement self,' " and (d) a lifestyle transformation in the way the actor views the deviant behavior. Although many of these cognitive shifts may occur together, Giordano et al. (2002) claim that essentially a solid replacement of one's old self may be the central factor in long-term behavioral change.

Several brief case examples demonstrate some of these necessary processes. "Gloria" is almost 60 years old when she exits prison for the last time. She has spent more than half of her adult life in and out of prison facilities in multiple states under multiple identities. She narrates that her crimes have all been thefts to get money for heroin, which she used daily. She also talks about the thirst for excitement that motivated her to take risks and only feel satisfied when she was behaving badly. She talks about her turning point being a realization that she was "tired" of her lifestyle on the streets and at the same time recognized the opportunity to stay at a residential halfway house as offering the possibility of a different life. She now talks proudly about being a "citizen," having an ID card in her real name, and having her own place where she can feel safe and secure about the life she is constructing.

Maruna (2001) claims that for former prisoners to successfully abstain from committing crimes they must make sense of their criminal past and rationalize their decision to desist from crime. He argues that self-narratives present individuals with the opportunity to redefine their checkered pasts in a way that provides meaning in their lives. The way many ex-offenders derive purpose in their lives is by helping other individuals who find themselves in trouble with the law, which includes working as mentors, social workers, counselors, or volunteering and becoming an active participant in the community (Maruna, 2001).

"Joel" is a former drug dealer who is now in a master's program in social work. His days of dealing came to an end when during the course of his incarceration, he recognized that other inmates came to him for assistance in filing papers and taking care of legitimate business. He felt good about being able to help the other guys out. He saw that he had something to contribute to society that was meaningful and that could make a difference in the lives of others.

Many prisoners returning to the community indicate that taking on the role of a responsible, productive citizen is important in reintegrating into their neighborhoods (Maruna, 2001). However, depending on state and federal laws, returning prisoners face numerous barriers, such as the loss of the right to vote, to serve on juries, to hold elective office, as well as limited employment opportunities and more limited housing choices, depending on the type of conviction (Pager, 2003). These barriers, also referred to as "collateral consequences," often hinder and delay successful reintegration (Mauer & Chesney-Lind, 2002).

Thus, although some researchers state that structural transitions (i.e., getting married and finding a job) alone explain reform, others maintain that a personal decision to desist itself produces behavioral change (Gloria being "tired," for example). However, others claim that neither structure nor individual action alone can adequately explain the underlying mechanisms of desistance. Refining their earlier work, and using a life-course perspective, Sampson and Laub (2005) contend that both structural support and human agency are important elements in constructing trajectories over the life course. They conclude that "[c]hoice alone without structures of support, or the offering of support alone absent a decision to desist, however inchoate, seems destined to fail" (Sampson & Laub, 2005, p. 43). In other words, both changes in societal forces and an individual's resolution to change are implicated in the process of reform of criminal behavior.

Despite research findings on the predictive validity of desistance, gender is largely omitted in studies on desistance. Only a handful of studies have examined the lives of women released from prison (Maidment, 2006; O'Brien, 2001). O'Brien (2001) chronicles the lives of formerly incarcerated women who successfully transitioned from prison despite the obstacles in their way. Maidment (2006) examines the postincarceration experiences of Canadian women who took pathways in and out of crime.

Differential Trends:
Race, Gender, and Mental Disorders

Formerly incarcerated adults are still mostly male (93% of all incarcerated adults), disproportionately minority, and unskilled. Within these general categories are some specific trends that both indicate significant changes in the overall population and have implications for social services.

Nearly 4 decades ago, President Richard Nixon launched the war on drugs. In 1969 he declared, "Winning the battle against drug abuse is one of the most important, the most urgent national priorities confronting the United States today." Today, many law enforcement officials and researchers say drugs are now cheaper and more potent, and as easily available as ever, with different trends of use and addiction across the country. What the war did do is help quadruple the nation's prison population, with urban Blacks and Latinos hardest hit—a dramatically disproportionate result of the different networks that developed to distribute drugs (Travis, 2005). According to federal data, Blacks make up just 13% of the nation's illicit drug users, but they are 32% of those arrested for drug violations and 53% of those incarcerated in state prisons for drug crimes (Mauer & Chesney-Lind, 2002).

As the U.S. continues its escalation of increasing incarceration, the number of female inmates has increased to over 112,000 (Sabol et al., 2007). Although the current rate of incarceration for women continues to be much lower than the rate for men (68 per 100,000 women versus 943 per 100,000 men), the growth rate in the number of female inmates has exceeded that of males every year since 1995, making them the fastest growing segment of the prison population (Harrison & Beck, 2006). As is true of Black men overall, Black women are also disproportionately incarcerated as compared to their White and Hispanic counterparts. In 2006, Black women were incarcerated in prison or jail at nearly four times the rate of White women and almost twice the rate of Hispanic women (Sabol et al., 2007).

Persons with mental illness are increasingly criminalized and processed through the corrections system instead of the mental health system. Draine and associates (Draine, Wolff, Jacoby, Hartwell, & Duclos, 2005) discuss this in the context of the restructuring of the mental health system of care away from a hospital-based system to a community-based system of care. Although there may be differences in arguments about how social policy trends have had an impact on the prevalence of mental disorders among the incarcerated population, an estimated 16% of returning citizens have serious mental illness (Ditton, 1999), which must be considered in the trajectory of obtaining success in reentry after release from prison.

Reentry: The Process

Men and women in transition from prison to home face major challenges as they attempt to manage their lives once they are released. Many individuals leaving prison face reintegration obstacles, such as securing employment, finding shelter, reuniting with family and children, and recovering from substance addiction (O'Brien, 2001; Petersilia, 2005; Travis, 2003). Petersilia (2005) suggests that a gradual shift from formal social control to informal social control facilitates formerly incarcerated adults by developing a stake in conformity as they move toward greater investment in participation in citizenship. There are, however, specific components of what constitutes avenues toward full citizenship that may need to be individually recognized and addressed for the returning adult at different points on the way home. Each of the following sections describes a particular system of focus and specific roles for social workers for increasing the odds of successful reentry after an adult has completed his or her sentence of incarceration.

Preparation for Release

According to Petersilia (2003), the average prisoner in the United States spends about a total of 4.4 years under correctional supervision, including jail, prison, and parole. An overarching question is how much of that time is spent in helping detainees, inmates, and parolees to address any of the problems that led them into criminal involvement initially? Today, it is estimated that only about one third of all prisoners released will have received vocational or educational training while in prison, despite their having serious deficiencies in these areas. And despite the fact that three quarters of all inmates have alcohol or drug-abuse problems, just one fourth of all inmates will participate in a substance-abuse program prior to release. As the prison population boomed, money to support rehabilitation programs has lessened. Prison programs of any sort have not kept pace with the demand. Despite the recognition that a higher proportion of individuals entering prison were abusing drugs or may be drug dependent, Petersilia reports from a federal survey that found that 45% of state prisons had no substance-abuse treatment of any kind. Although some state systems are beginning to reconsider their mission of inmate rehabilitation as a result of high recidivism or failure rates, implementation of targeted initiatives for preparation of inmates for reentry has been slow and fragmented.

The role of the social worker at this stage of intervention is focused on assessment and planning for the initial period after release, bridging the worlds of correctional control and the "free world" where the inmate recovers responsibility for decision making and choices. Assessment includes identifying both potential challenges and internal and external resources that can be drawn on to meet the challenges of release.

Parole Supervision

"Parole" refers to the after-release period of time during which the adult remains under the community surveillance of the sentencing jurisdiction for a period of time up to the expiration of the sentence. Parolees are generally released with conditions they must meet, including checking in with the parole officer, participating in one or more treatment programs, not associating with other felons, and not being rearrested. The parole officer has the discretion to determine if the parolee is in violation of any of the mandated conditions and is subject to a revocation of parole status and return to prison. Although in the past this period of supervision has been coupled with the possibility of rehabilitation with the assistance of the parole officer, because of the growing caseloads under supervision, the parole officer in most jurisdictions plays the role of ensuring that public safety goals are addressed by providing the function of surveillance.

With the changes in state and federal sentencing structures to reduce disparities in sentencing, discretionary parole has been eliminated in some states, which means that adults are released to communities after they have completed a certain percentage of their total sentence or have reached sentence expiration without any further supervision or surveillance. In states where there is still a period of mandatory or discretionary parole supervision, and in federal cases where there is always a period of supervision after release from custody, parole can provide the opportunity for a buffer between the prison cell and the streets. Parole officers can, with appropriate training and system support, provide assistance especially related to knowing helpful resources in the location where the individual is released.

The legal status under which an adult reenters the community matters as it can serve to provide an incentive to inmates to earn "good time" that can reduce the period of custody, and provide some possibility for further rehabilitation through the imposition of conditions after release. On the other hand, parole boards have operated with great discretion to make decisions about the readiness of adults to reenter society that often resulted in unwarranted sentencing disparities or racial and gender bias.

Social workers are sometimes employed as parole officers but more often act in a complementary role as case managers or agents of support and referral in assisting parolees to successfully complete parole. Assessment of needs and aspirations as individuals move from the immediate aftermath of release to the more graduated and necessary aspects of maintaining recovery, gaining education and/or employment, and reestablishing positive relationships become the focus for intervention.

Education and Employment Services

Although many incarcerated adults report having little or no prior experience of legal employment and having limited access to vocational and educational programs in prison, they are most often expected to secure a job immediately upon release (Travis, 2003). However, the lack of educational credentials and the stigma of being an ex-convict makes job placement difficult (Pager, 2003). Women's preprison legitimate job experience is less than that of men and women also report more problems such as child care, conflicts with employers and co-workers, and harassment, which influences them both getting and maintaining employment (Maidment, 2006; O'Brien, 2001). For this reason, many women are forced to depend on either their family members—who often have limited resources, or public agencies that have strict eligibility requirements for their services.

Furthermore, former felons are barred from many employment sectors, such as child care, nursing, home health care, education, and security. As ex-felons face blocked opportunities related to finding legitimate employment, the pull toward illegal behaviors to gain income becomes stronger.

Housing

The need for income and educational opportunities is tied to the need to find immediate shelter after release. Finding "home" is the launching pad for all else that can follow in the reentry process. For some men and women, the first address is an emergency, temporary shelter, for others, it is the family member with an available couch who is most willing to take them in. From his survey of former prisoners in multiple states, Travis (2005) reports that the first address for most prisoners is that of a willing family member. Family members may want to help out for a short time but grow impatient when the brother or niece doesn't make progress quickly enough to enable him or her to move on and pay rent independently. Other family members have grown distrustful of the individual's promises to go straight and are not willing to try again. Some families themselves may be embedded in drug and other criminal activities and therefore cannot provide a safe place for former prisoners. Some individuals have spouses waiting for them in the family home with the children, this is more often the case for men than it is for women released from prison.

For some formerly incarcerated adults, living in a residential "halfway house" may be safe and supportive, but others chafe at a whole new set of rules they have to adapt to. Structured residential settings, although serving a relatively small number of former prisoners, have a high rate of success for adults who remain in the setting long enough for the program to take effect.

Specific barriers to securing housing in the private housing market are the overwhelming start-up costs (i.e., security deposits, credit-check fees) that exist for anyone working at minimum wage today. One of the more successful options for men coming out of prison is the single room occupancy (SRO) hotel, where an adult can obtain short-term and more affordable rooms. Additional barriers to affordable housing include the federal prohibition enforced in many states that bars drug felons from accessing public housing. Living with someone in public housing is also a violation of that person's lease and so subjects him or her to possible eviction.

Women report that housing is one of the major challenges for reentry (O'Brien, 2001) related to both finding an affordable option for themselves and for many of them, a place where they can also safely reside with their minor children. "Mandi" (O'Brien, 2001) discussed many of these barriers when she described both the conditions she had to address on parole and the additional conditions she faced in family court to regain legal custody of her children, who had been living with her mother while she was incarcerated. Because she had four children of both sexes, she had to find a place that would meet the criterion for separate bedrooms for the children and a separate bedroom for her, almost an impossibility on the income she earned as an employee at a fast-food restaurant.

Former prisoners who were convicted of a sex offense face a whole slew of community, state, and federal restrictions on where they can reside. Some community-notification registration laws operate as exclusionary practices even to residence in temporary homeless shelters (Travis, 2005).

Reunification With Children

Fathers and mothers who are incarcerated confront a number of obstacles in reestablishing relationships with their children (Mumola, 2000). Major issues include the separation itself, which has a differential effect depending on the relationship of the parent and the children prior to incarceration, the age of the child or children in terms of their developmental stage and capacity for understanding what has happened to the parent, and the abilities of the child or children's caregiver to moderate some of the negative effects of the incarceration. Maintaining contact with the incarcerated parent by letters, phone calls, and especially visits can also maintain the parental bond and relationship with children; this is dependent on where the child is residing and the willingness of the caregiver to transport children for visits.

Gender has an impact on this issue as well because more of the children of incarcerated mothers (than fathers) were living with their mothers before their incarceration, and although the children of incarcerated fathers continue living with their mothers, the children of incarcerated mothers will go into the care of other family members or, if there are no family members available, into temporary state custody, until it is determined that the child or children should be released for adoption (Mumola, 2000).

If the state has custody of children, former inmates must participate in parenting, counseling, and drug-testing programs, as well as have a job and a secure place to live. When a mother attempts to regain custody, her status as an ex-convict can be viewed as an indicator that she is an unfit parent, and this impedes her chances of gaining custody of her children. Multiple reentry barriers already discussed make it difficult for women or men to reestablish themselves as primary caregivers for their children.

Treatment for Substance Abuse

Substance abuse is one of the greatest public health issues associated with the increased number of incarcerated adults, particularly in women, who are arrested often for substance-abuse possession and sales. Given the high portion of the state prison population reporting a history of drug and/or alcohol use as well as using at the time of the event that led to their arrest and incarceration, the need for treatment is evident. According to Travis (2005), the level of treatment for prisoners with drug and alcohol addictions is low and "represents a particularly acute policy failure" (p. 203).

A growing body of research indicates that in-prison drug treatment, when coupled with community aftercare, can reduce the potential for relapse to drug use after release, and thus decrease criminal behaviors and subsequent reincarceration. However, access to drug treatment after release from prison is often fragmented. In her study of opiate-dependent women in one urban community, O'Brien (2006) found that they did not know where the treatment was located or what they had to do to use it, even though they knew they were mandated by parole to get drug treatment. There is often a mismatch between the correctional system mandate and the treatment system availability.

Mental Health Treatment

Given the prevalence of adults with mental illness in prisons, social service professionals must address a myriad of role expectations in working to facilitate reentry with prisoners with mental disorders. These expectations include those related to coordinating multiple systems to ensure compliance with parole conditions as well as linkage of the individual to community mental health services and the social context, which includes housing and productive activities in the community. Draine and associates (2005) describe a conceptual model that they generated from multiple interviews and focus groups with providers, consumers, and criminal justice personnel that enlarges the individual/community dynamic by identifying how community resources can be used to structure and support individual prosocial behaviors after return from prison. They further suggest that "reintegration progresses when the resources and needs of the individual match the resources and needs of the community" (p. 696) leading to inclusion of the individual who is able to reciprocate by contributing to the community.

This model for considering reentry of persons with mental illness could be applicable to reentry in general. It examines not only the service process to determine what it is that adults need, but also the social process that is determined by both relationships on the micro level, and public will on the macro level, to accommodate to the former inmate's needs. Individuals who are identified as having a mental disorder may be further stigmatized on this continuum because of perceptions of dangerousness or risk to public security. An additional complication is the identification of the increased

20.1   Time Frame for Reentry and Social Work Responses

Time Period	Common Issues	Social Work Strategies
Crisis period **(1–6 months out)**	Initial housing Basic needs/clothing Contact with parole officer Initiation of treatment (relapse prevention or aftercare) Health needs Reunification with minor children	Initial assessment of basic needs and immediate concerns Referrals to community agencies Development of plan Assess for mental health issues and required treatment Assess for need for alcohol/drug treatment and/or aftercare
Intermediate **stabilization** **(6–30 months out)**	Employment Housing Relationships	Coach for job placement and training Problem-solve barriers Assess and refer for counseling on relationship issues (with partners/ex-partners, family members, children) Advocacy regarding policy barriers for income, housing, employment
Stability **(30–36 months out)**	Aftercare Completion of parole	Engaged in ongoing recovery mechanisms

proportion of adults diagnosed with co-occurring mental health and substance-abuse disorders (Swartz & Lurigio, 1999). This co-occurrence is often further exacerbated by histories of trauma for women (O'Brien, 2006).

In a social context of potential resistance to providing resources that are needed by returning citizens with mental disorders, correctional staff and social workers serve as collaborators with service providers in the community to facilitate access to effective rehabilitation and community-based interventions, including supportive housing and employment and educational opportunities.

Time Frame of Reentry

In addition to the array of specific issues that adults exiting prison have to address, observers of the reentry process have begun to identify time-specific tasks for reentry (Travis, 2005). Although reentry involves more than formal services, these specified time periods over a trajectory of 3 years out after release bring a focus to different dynamics that change as the reentering adult becomes more securely attached after release from prison. This trajectory of reentry includes the immediate period after reentry that is considered a crisis period, an intermediate stabilization period, and a longer term marker of "making it" forward to full citizenship. Table 20.1 provides a summary of this trajectory by the specific focus of intervention.

The initial crisis period is characterized as months 1 to 6 following release, where securing housing and addressing basic needs are the major foci for intervention or responsiveness to the returning citizen. This period includes the literal "moment of release," which is a moment burdened by both danger and opportunity that is not addressed in prerelease planning. During this period, assessing and planning for reentry considers the specific characteristics of each person's physical and mental status as well as the multiple challenges the released adult must address for making the initial steps toward stability, including identifying the supportive family and social supports that the adult may draw on in times of anxiety. There is a dual emphasis on individual and community characteristics assessing the reciprocal fit of the individual in the community. This period may also include the adult adapting to being outside of a controlled environment and the requirements associated with being on parole. Studies of the time period after release document that this is the period when the former inmate is most vulnerable to rearrest and/or revocation of parole.

The next period that extends to about 2 years out can be considered the intermediate stability period. During this period, the former prisoner has moved from emergency or temporary housing to more permanent housing, has a regular source of legal income, is in drug treatment or counseling if indicated, is complying with all parole requirements, and has begun rebuilding relationships that may have been diminished by the separation during the former prisoner's incarceration. What is most evident during this period is a more graduated engagement with others building on small steps that reinforce the adult's self-efficacy as well as the community efforts to be responsive and restorative.

In the final stage leading to long-term citizenship, beginning 2 1/2 to 3 years out after release, the goals are to achieve permanent housing, find a job that pays a living wage and provides benefits, more reciprocal exchanges with family members, reunification with children, if possible, attention paid to health concerns, earned reduced supervision or early release from supervision on parole, and a reciprocal role within the citizen's community. The challenge for social service and correctional professionals working with formerly incarcerated adults is to integrate expectations effectively that can facilitate assessing individual and community strengths to activate mechanisms to move the adult along the trajectory to reach this final stage of successful reentry.

Summary and Conclusions

The needs of returning prisoners are serious and varied. Those with mental illness are particularly in need of help and in addition, perceived as undesirable by many social service agencies and communities. Likewise, individuals with identified addictions are often considered somewhat intractable in their abilities to stay "clean and sober" after release from enforced abstinence. Individuals who have been convicted on violent offenses or for sex offenses are feared and sometimes hated, regardless of time served to pay for their wrongdoing. The implications for social workers engaged with these more "intractable" groups of people is to first see each person as an individual. Studies of motivational interviewing (Bellack, Bennett, Gearon, Brown, & Yang, 2006) have much to offer social work as a means of working with people to resolve ambivalence about making necessary changes in their lives.

There is little likelihood that reentering adults are able to "make it" without concentrated support from the communities to which they are returning. Although social workers cannot arrange for services that do not exist, they can document the gaps, be proficient in conducting needs assessments, and facilitate program develop-ment that can lead to the creation of new resources and new entry points to community services that offer a broader array of services for prisoners reentering the community. Ultimately, to help meet the needs of the thousands of individuals returning to commu-nities across the nation every day, communities will need to devote substantial, varied, and innovative resources to this purpose and reduce the policy barriers already enacted to deny adults access to those resources.

Social service professionals will have to become ever-more thoughtful about how to assess the match between individuals' diverse and challenging needs and the broader community resources that can be tapped to respond to them. In addition, social workers will need to become more knowledgeable about working across systems to identify common elements of success, regardless of the explicit setting where issues of involvement with the criminal justice system are identified. The National Institute of Corrections initiated a useful process that enabled community stakeholders to understand the dispositional decision points that led to women's increasing incarcera-tion. This process helped people know about different access points to the criminal justice system, where interventions potentially could be made. Churches have also become a likely point for partnership as there has been recent funding for faith-based reentry initiatives.

In conclusion, Travis (2005) suggests five principles for reentry that are parallel to what can be considered effective social work practice. These include: preparation for reentry, building bridges between prisons and communities, seizing the moment of release, strengthening the circles of support, and promoting successful reintegration. These principles require social workers to be proactive in recognizing opportunities for establishing a different context for efforts aimed at improving returning prisoners' prospects for success. In addition to focusing on short-term programs to make individ-ual transitions easier, proponents of successful reentry should also advocate for longer term initiatives that remove some of the unnecessary barriers to adults reclaiming their human dignity and possibilities for moving forward into full citizenship.

References

Bellack, A. S., Bennett, M. E., Gearon, J. S., Brown, C. H., & Yang, T. (2006). A randomized clinical trial of a new behavioral treatment for drug abuse in people with severe and persistent mental illness. *Archives of General Psychiatry, 63,* 426–432.

Ditton, P. M. (1999). *Mental health and treatment of inmates and probationers.* Washington, DC: Bureau of Justice Statistics, NCJ 174463.

Draine, J., Wolff, N., Jacoby, J. E., Hartwell, S., & Duclos, C. (2005). Understanding community re-entry of former prisoners with mental illness: A conceptual model to guide new research. *Behavioral Sciences and the Law, 23,* 689–707.

Elder, G. H. (1998). Life course and development. In R. M. Lerner (Ed.), *Handbook of child psychology Vol. 1: Theoretical models of human development* (5th ed.). New York: Wiley.

Giordano, P. C., Cernkovich, S. A., & Rudolphe, J. L. (2002). Gender, crime, and desistance: Toward a theory of cognitive transformation. *American Journal of Sociology, 107,* 990–1064.

Glueck, S., & Glueck, E. (1940). *Juvenile delinquents grown up.* New York: Commonwealth Fund.

Golder, S., Gillmore, M. R., Spieker, S., & Morrison, D. (2005). Substance use, related problem behaviors and adult attachment in a sample of high risk older adolescent women. *Journal of Child and Family Studies, 14,* 181–193.

Golder, S., Ivanoff, A., Cloud, R. N., Besel, K. L., McKiernan, P., Bratt, E., et al. (2005). Evidence-based practice with adults in jails and prisons: Strategies, practices, and future directions. *Best Practices in Mental Health, 1*(2), 100–132.

Hairston, C. F., & Rollin, J. (2003). Social capital and family connections. *Women, Girls & Criminal Justice, 4*(5), 67–69.

Harrison, P. M., & Beck, A. J. (2006). *Prisoners in 2005.* Washington, DC: Bureau of Justice Statistics, NCJ 215092.

King, R. S. (2007). *Changing direction? State sentencing reforms 2002–2006.* Washington, DC: The Sentencing Project.

Langan, P. A., & Levin, D. J. (2002). *Recidivism of prisoners released in 1994.* Washington, DC: Bureau of Justice Statistics, NCJ 193427.

Laub, J. H., & Sampson, R. J. (2003). *Shared beginnings, divergent lives: Delinquent boys to age 70.* Cambridge: Harvard University Press.

Maidment, M. R. (2006). *Doing time on the outside: Deconstructing the benevolent community.* Toronto: University of Toronto Press.

Maruna, S. (2001). *Making good: How ex-convicts reform and rebuild their lives.* Washington, DC: American Psychological Association.

Mauer, M., & Chesney-Lind, M. (Eds.). (2002). *Invisible punishment: The collateral consequences of mass imprisonment.* New York: New Press.

Mumola, C. (2000). *Incarcerated parents and their children.* Washington, DC: Bureau of Justice Statistics, NCJ 182335.

O'Brien, P. (2001). *Making it in the "free world:" Women in transition from prison.* Albany, NY: State University of New York Press.

O'Brien, P. (2006). Maximizing success for drug-affected women after release from prison: Examining access to and use of social services during reentry. *Women & Criminal Justice, 17*(2/3), 95–113.

Pager, D. (2003). The mark of a criminal record. *American Journal of Sociology, 10*, 937–975.

Petersilia, J. (2003). *When prisoners come home.* New York: Oxford University Press.

Renzetti, C. M., Curran, D. J., & Carr, P. J. (2003). *Theories of crime.* Boston: Allyn & Bacon.

Sabol, W. J., Couture, H., & Harrison, P.M. (2007). *Prisoners in 2006.* Washington, DC: Bureau of Justice Statistics, NCJ 219416.

Sampson, R. J., & Laub, J. H. (2005). A life-course view of the development of crime. *Annals of the American Academy of Political and Social Science, 602*(1), 12–45.

Swartz, J. A., & Lurigio, A. J. (1999). Psychiatric illness and comorbidity among adult male jail detainees in drug treatment. *Psychiatric Services, 50*, 1628–1630.

Travis, J. (2005). *But they all come back: Facing the challenges of prisoner reentry.* Washington, DC: Urban Institute Press.

The Disproportionate Legislative Waiver of Minority Youth Into the Criminal Justice System

21

Leon Banks
Schnavia Smith Hatcher
Edward A. Risler

Under the legal structure commonly referred to as the legislative waiver, youth charged with serious violent crimes such as those involving aggravated assault, robbery, rape and other sexual offenses are subject to the same sentencing guidelines as adult offenders (Risler, Sweatman, & Nackerud, 1998). This chapter discusses three specific issues related to the legislative waiver movement in juvenile justice that impact forensic social work practice with juveniles. A brief history and description of the variations in legislative waivers will be presented, followed by a critical analysis of the legislative waivers and the differential impact on youth tried in adult courts. The chapter will conclude with suggestions and implications for social work practice.

A History of Treating Youth in Court

Remarkably, the court's viewing youths as adults is not a novel notion. In the early 1800s, several prominent individuals from across the country instituted a form of social control in an attempt to respond to the growing numbers of wayward children roaming the streets of large urban cities. They established penitentiaries and work houses to provide youth with what, they believed, were the habits necessary to function as law-abiding citizens in a capitalistic society (Mennel, 1982). Over the next several years the courts began to criminalize behaviors that were associated with what would today be considered as normal youth development, such as not listening to parents.

The wayward-child laws embodied the prevailing assumption of the time that children who engaged in troublesome behavior would inevitably graduate to a life of crime. During this time it was believed that the state had a duty to take in hand young people who exhibited the warning signs of criminality (Garlock, 1979). In principle, the reform schools of the 1800s and early 1900s were designed to socialize deviant youth; in practice, however, they were institutions for the exploitation of child labor (Pisciotta, 1983).

As word of the practices and the many atrocities that often occurred in the work houses spread there was a public outcry for more institutional regulations (Mennel, 1982). During this time, the notion of a separate court especially designed to be in the "best interest of the child" began to take hold. This led to the formation of the first juvenile court in 1899 in Cook County, Illinois. This juvenile court, and those that soon followed throughout the country, were founded on the principle of *parens patriae* meaning that the state had the responsibility to act as the parent (Mennel, 1982). The premise of this doctrine was to provide protection for children whose parents could not provide adequate supervision and that the court's main purpose was to reform children. In theory, these courts were considered civil rather than legal and judges had significant discretion when rendering decisions from the bench.

The Honorable Judge Richard S. Tuthill of Cook County, Illinois (1899), who presided over the first juvenile court, defined the fundamental principal of juvenile court by stating: "That no child under 16 years of age shall be considered or be treated as a criminal; that a child under that age shall not be arrested, indicted, convicted, imprisoned, or punished as a criminal" (Tanenhaus & Drizin, 2003, p. 642). The influence that the early juvenile court had on children grew into a formal, legal institution with wide powers. The juvenile court allowed states to treat juveniles as a separate class of offender and had the power not only to intervene when youth commit criminal acts, but also when they showed signs of a reckless lifestyle (Platt, 1969).

Not surprisingly, the differential treatment of young offenders based on race and class began to emerge during this time (Pisciotta, 1983). For example, Shelden (1976) found that between 1900 and 1917, the majority of poor African American youth who committed criminal acts in Memphis, Tennessee, were tried as adults, whereas their White counterparts appeared in juvenile court. Furthermore, Platt argued that the establishment of the juvenile court was based on class bias because it was directed at rehabilitating poor youth and reaffirming middle-class values. It appeared that the juvenile court movement did not address the structural roots of poverty in America.

In reality, the purpose of the juvenile courts has not always been demonstrated in practice. By the 1920s, the courts began to see the informal transferring of some juvenile offenders to adult criminal court, as a viable prosecutorial option for serious and violent juvenile offenders (Tanenhaus & Drizin, 2003). The juvenile court judges easily rationalized this decision by stating that actively transferring some cases to adult court was a means of protecting younger children already housed in reform schools. Even though there were some critics of the effectiveness of the juvenile court system, no one criticized the court's compassionate intent (Mennel, 1982). Based on the best interest of the child, the juvenile court continued along this path for the next 90 years.

Toward the later part of the 20th century, as a number of youth began committing more serious crimes and treatment approaches were viewed with growing skepticism, policymakers began formally responding to the public's cry to protect society from such youths. Juvenile courts came under pressure to abandon the *parens patriae* doctrine in favor of more punitive methods. The courts believed that providing harsher sentences and limiting treatment options was the answer to juvenile delinquency, which gave way to the formal legislative waiver movement during the 1990s.

Legislative Waivers

Legislative waivers are laws that provide a specific provision for courts to deal with juveniles who commit serious or violent offenses by allowing them to be waived to the jurisdiction of the adult court and tried accordingly. The four main types of legislative waivers currently in use are discretionary, presumption, mandatory, and prosecutorial waiver.

The discretionary waiver allows judges to waive jurisdiction over individual cases involving minors to adult court (Mears, 2003). As the name implies, a judge has discretion in considering factors in a case before making a decision. For example, if a youth commits a violent crime, the judge could review other mitigating factors such as the youth's cognitive functioning or the circumstances surrounding the crime.

The presumption waiver designates a category of circumstances involving juveniles in which transfers to superior court are assumed to be appropriate. For example, if a youth is charged with murder, the presumption is that the case will be waived to adult court (Mears, 2003). However, if representatives for that youth can persuade the court that other mitigating factors (i.e., self-defense or cognitive delays) were contributing factors, then the case could be heard in juvenile court.

The third type of waiver is the mandatory waiver, which allows juvenile courts to waive cases under certain conditions (Klug, 2001). For example, Georgia, Indiana, and South Carolina are mandatory-waiver states in that if a juvenile commits one of a series of identified violent crimes, then the case is automatically waived to superior court (Klug).

The final type of waiver is the prosecutorial waiver. In this instance, the discretion to waive a juvenile to superior court is determined solely by the district attorney (Klug, 2001). Typically, with this type of waiver, the district attorney reviews the case and makes a determination to have the case tried in either juvenile or superior court.

Factors such as the type of offense, the youth's prior record, or age can determine when and how a court may implement each of these waivers (Mears, 2003). Although most states do adhere to one or more of the different waiver options, it is not uncommon for some to implement a combination of transfer provisions when determining which youth will be charged as adults (Klug, 2001). For example, Georgia, a mandatory state, also has provisions for discretionary waivers.

By 1997, 46 states had discretionary judicial waivers, 14 had mandatory judicial waivers, 15 had presumptive judicial waivers, 15 adhered to the prosecution discretion waiver, and 31 states had a once-an-adult–always-an-adult provision-—meaning all subsequent cases will be addressed in criminal court (Mears, 2003). More than 40 states have passed policies for increased prosecution of juveniles in adult court (Finley & Schindler, 1999).

Differential Treatment

Early on, Thornberry (1979) found that, although socioeconomic status had an influence on sentencing, other variables such as previous record, race, and seriousness of crime were not mutually exclusive. Thornberry also found that African American youth who were from poor families received harsher sentences than White youth who had similar backgrounds. Likewise, Wolfgang and Thornberry (1987) found that Whites who were from higher socioeconomic backgrounds were more likely not to re-offend in childhood and adulthood than were non-Whites from lower socioeconomic backgrounds. These researchers provided two explanations for this conclusion. First, Whites from higher socioeconomic backgrounds could have continued to commit crimes or delinquent acts but were not caught for the subsequent acts. Another explanation was that they had more resources available (i.e., better schools, recreational centers, positive peers, and financial support) to prevent them from committing crimes (Wolfgang & Thornberry).

Leiber and Stairs (1999) suggested that race must be considered when discussing differential treatment in sentencing. They observed that in jurisdictions in Iowa, African Americans received jail sentences, whereas Whites charged with the same crimes received treatment options. Joseph (1995) furthered the argument on the relevance of differential treatment by stating that in Florida between 1980 and 1990, the percentage of Black male youths transferred from juvenile court to adult court increased from 47 to 55%. Joseph also stated that in 1989, 86% of youth waived to adult court were Black.

Myers and Reid (1995) suggest that prosecutorial waivers must also be considered when discussing the differential treatment of youth. In the majority of states, the decision to waive juveniles to criminal courts is made by the local district attorney or prosecutor. Joseph (1995) found that in New Jersey, in 1984, 73% of all waivers filed were against minority youth. Joseph also stated that in 1989 Black juveniles in Florida were incarcerated in adult prisons $8\,1/2$ times as often as their White counterparts. Cinatron (2006), in addressing the overrepresentation of Latinos in the juvenile justice system, contends that Latinos receive harsher treatment than White youths when charged with the same crime.

Woodhouse (2002) suggested that the problem in poor families was not a lack of parenting skills, but a lack of economic opportunities that led to parents having to work two to three jobs rather than having time to supervise their children, which then results in youth committing delinquent acts. In some of his earlier studies, Hirschi (1969) suggested that a lack of supervision contributes to delinquent behavior in youth. The literature suggests that the link between youth who come from poor families receiving differential treatment is very strong and policies for youth sentenced as adults are geared toward poor and minority groups.

VOICES FROM THE FIELD

Melissa H. Nolan, MS, LCSW
Social Work Manager, Maryland Office of the Public Defender

Agency Setting

The Maryland Office of the Public Defender (OPD) is a state agency with offices located in 12 districts throughout the state. A district public defender runs each office. His/her staff also consists of a deputy district public defender, assistant public defenders, investigators, and support staff. Ten of the 12 districts also employ social workers in their adult and/or juvenile units. The Office is responsible for providing legal representation to indigent people charged with criminal offenses. In addition to the 12 districts this agency also has a capital defense and two neighborhood defense divisions that employ social workers to work with assistant public defenders to provide mitigation, sentencing recommendations, and reentry services. There are also statewide divisions including Appellate, Innocence Project, Child In Need of Assistance (CINA), Juvenile Protection, and Legislative Affairs.

We recently adopted the team approach in which certain offices' social workers are assigned to teams with a supervising attorney, assistant public defenders, investigators, social workers, and law interns. The teams meet regularly to discuss cases and work together on the best approach for the client's defense. We also expanded social work services by incorporating social workers or social work interns in the following statewide divisions: Child In Need of Assistance (CINA), Juvenile Protection, and Legislative Affairs.

Practice Responsibilities

When I first came to the office in 1992, I was assigned to the Juvenile Court Division in District I (Baltimore City). My primary responsibilities were to conduct psychosocial assessments of juvenile clients. This included working with the client, family, juvenile justice, social services, and local education systems in designing disposition plans. My advocacy skills were used in interagency meetings and court hearings. I prepared psychosocial evaluations that were used in transfer-of-jurisdiction cases in which I also provided expert testimony on these cases. As the division grew, my responsibilities changed to include supervision of staff social workers. In addition, I had an opportunity to develop a social work intern program that included providing field instruction to area undergraduate and graduate social work students.

After a recommendation to the administration to hire social workers to be placed in the local districts, my responsibilities changed once more to my current position. I provide clinical supervision to social workers working on their advanced licenses, consultation to administration, district public defenders, and social workers; I hire and train new social workers; and I coordinate with area colleges and universities to place social work interns in district offices.

To ensure appropriate placements for our clients, I designed a resource book, "Residential Resource Guide for Juveniles: Instate & Out of State." This guide is used both internally by social workers and assistant public defenders, as well as other court personnel throughout the state. It is updated on a regular basis.

Expertise Required

The Social Work Manager of the OPD Forensic Social Work Program is a graduate of an accredited graduate social work program and holds an advanced social work license (i.e., in Maryland: Licensed Certified Social Worker–Clinical [LCSW-C]) to be able to provide clinical supervision to other social workers. A successful manager should have experience working directly with clients represented by the agency and have experience or expertise in the areas of mental health, health, substance abuse, and cognitive impairments. The social work manager needs to have strong advocacy and writing skills, as well as knowledge of local and state resources to better equip him/her to provide competent supervision and mentoring to staff social workers. Because district offices are located in urban, suburban, or rural areas, it is essential that he/she have experience working in different offices to understand local practices, resources, and systems. Knowledge of the trends in forensic social work practice and the needs of individual districts are essential for the social work manager to provide solid recommendations to the administration.

Regarding the expertise required for all staff social workers, they are graduates of an accredited graduate social work program and hold either the Licensed Graduate Social Work (LGSW) license or the LCSW-C license. In addition, all OPD social workers need to have experience or expertise in the areas of mental health, health, substance abuse, and cognitive impairments. OPD social workers need to have strong advocacy and writing skills, as well as knowledge of local and state resources. They work collaboratively with other state, residential, and community-based agencies to advocate for appropriate services for their clients. Assistant public defenders also rely on staff social workers to prepare mitigation and sentencing reports to be able to testify at court hearings. Staff social workers are often asked to conduct preliminary assessments for competency and criminal responsibility. These preliminary assessments provide the assistant public defenders the necessary information to hire outside experts who conduct additional evaluations (i.e., neuropsychological, psychological, psychiatric, and psychosexual evaluations). As the racial and ethnic makeup of our clients change, the need to have bilingual social workers is becoming more necessary.

Our Office is committed to providing comprehensive training on the law, the legal system, and working on an interdisciplinary "defense-based" team. We are also in the process of obtaining the permission to hold continuing-education seminars in-house to assist with maintaining appropriate licensure. These seminars will also assist social workers with staying on the forefront of practice issues as they relate to our clients.

Practice Challenges

My primary challenge is identifying and understanding the unique needs of the individual districts, especially in the area of social work service requests and resources. Most staff social workers have limited experience in forensic social work, so I need to balance training the social workers in "defense-based advocacy" and "neighborhood defense" and training the districts in the wide range of services a social worker can provide to a case.

In my experience, a primary challenge of the staff social workers is to link their clients to appropriate resources. Their clients are charged with a range of serious offenses, from simple assault to first-degree murder, these clients need treatment or rehabilitative services. However, these charges have a stigma attached to them. Balancing the client's needs and protecting the community is a challenge, especially in areas with scarce or inappropriate resources. An example is trying to find substance-abuse treatment for a client with mental health diagnoses and cognitive limitations, who is charged with an aggravated assault.

Common Legal and/or Ethical Issues

A major legal/ethical issue our office has faced is explaining the attorney/client privilege to social workers and the difference between the privilege a client has with his/her attorney and the privilege a client has with a social worker. This required a concerted effort by the training division, general counsel, and administration regarding social workers being covered under the attorney/client privilege while working on the defense team. A policy on privilege was drafted and presented to the State Board of Social Work Examiners. Continual training is done with the district public defenders, assistant public defenders, and social workers on this ethical/legal issue.

A second ethical issue our social workers face is developing appropriate sentencing/disposition plans that balance what is in the "best interest" of a client and what the client wants. Because all the staff social workers have some experience working in the mental health or substance-abuse fields they are skilled in assessing those areas and determining the need for services. However, their clients tend to have limited insight into their problem areas and at times resist necessary treatment and just want "what is needed to do as little time as necessary."

Brief Description of Collaborative Activities With Professionals and/or Other Stakeholders

Collaboration is an essential part of my job. I collaborate with area colleges and universities to provide internship opportunities for social work students. I also collaborate with OPD district offices to help them identify best approaches to working with social workers and how to allocate limited resources.

The collaborative activities that OPD staff social workers engage in depend on the specific districts or divisions they work in. Examples of collaborative activities include: developing education groups for families with incarcerated family members and groups for reentry with the local detention centers, working on palliative care issues with local detention centers, working with court personnel (i.e., judges, assistant states attorneys, Department of Juvenile Justice and Parole and Probation) to advocate on behalf of client who is involved in specialty court (i.e., Drug and Mental Health Courts). Working with other state agencies (i.e., Substance Abuse, Mental Health and Developmental Disabilities) to develop appropriate substance-abuse treatment for mentally ill and cognitively limited clients.

A social work intern was assigned to the Legislative Affairs Division. She works on identifying legislative issues, which she presents to the Division and then presents it to delegates to determine how our office can affect legislation on behalf of our clients.

Additional Information

Developing more forensic social work positions starts with advocating in undergraduate and graduate social work programs to develop more curriculums targeting this practice and then developing more internship opportunities. Starting with the schools will help broaden the students' minds to the importance of advocacy in the criminal justice system both at the micro and macro levels.

Case Study

Brian, a 14-year-old Hispanic American, was charged with first-degree murder. Brian was accused of fatally shooting a 16–year-old after a gang-related argument at the park. There were several shots fired and the individual who was fatally wounded also had a weapon. Brian is the product of a single-parent home and his family's income falls below the poverty line. Because of the family's distressed economic situation, Brian was not able to make bail or afford an attorney. Upon reviewing the facts of the case, the prosecutor argued that this case should be tried in adult court. Brian's attorney argued against the case being waived because of lack of maturity of his client and the possibility of cognitive defects. Because of Brian's court-appointed attorney's lack of resources and insufficient time for Brian, coupled with the city's tough stance on gang-related violence; the judge ordered the case be tried in adult court.

This case is just one example of how a number of juveniles with similar profiles are processed in the waiver system. The issue of differential treatment is not solely contingent on one variable but as cited in the preceding example, the convergence of several variables, such as race and economic status, can result in a juvenile being expedited to adult court.

Policy Practice Implications

Many legislators believe that an effective deterrent to juvenile crime is to provide tougher laws and harsher sentences. Unfortunately, these views are shortsighted because they ignore the larger, more systemic problems of poverty, discrimination, and family instability. It is vital that policymakers reexamine their stance on juvenile crime and begin implementing laws that will address the root causes of juvenile crime instead of creating laws that only address the end results of delinquency.

This chapter should be a reminder to forensic social work practitioners who work with at-risk juveniles to examine every aspect of the child's life before deciding on the appropriate treatment plan. It should also remind the practitioner not to enter into a therapeutic relationship with a youth with an inherent bias about the contributing factors of his or her delinquency. It has been a long-held belief that African American youth from urban neighborhoods have a greater likelihood to commit crimes. However, when these stereotypes are internalized by the social work community without sound empirical evidence, they tend to create an atmosphere of prejudice and unsubstantiated fear for the community in which these youth reside, which negatively impacts service delivery. Other segments of the population (i.e., rural, non-Black youth) also are affected by misinformation, with interventions only modeled for the "at-risk" community.

Risler et al. (1998) concluded that the relationship between poverty and juvenile crime is not mutually exclusive; more research is needed to determine the strength of this relationship to ensure effective treatment and equity in the criminal justice system. Banks (2007) also stated that connection between geographic residence and juvenile crime has to be further explored. It is imperative that social workers become more cognizant of the different personal and environmental factors that contribute to juveniles being charged as adults. The rise in the number of heinous crimes committed by juveniles illustrates the critical need for social workers to provide meaningful research, practice, and advocacy for this population.

References

Banks, L. (2007). *Georgia Senate Bill 440: An examination of determining factors of youth who are waived to superior court and the effectiveness of juvenile waivers as a deterrent to recidivism.* Unpublished doctoral dissertation, University of Georgia, Athens, GA.

Cinatron, M. (2006). Latino delinquency: Defining and counting the problem. In E. V. Penn, H. T. Greene, & S. L. Gabbidon (Eds.), *Race and juvenile justice* (pp. 29–40). Durham, NC: Carolina Academic Press.

Finley, M., & Schindler, M. (1999). Punitive juvenile justice policies and the impact on minority youth. *Probation, 63*(2), 11–16.

Garlock, P. D. (1979). Wayward children and the law, 1820–1900: The genesis of the status offense jurisdiction of the juvenile court. *Georgia Law Review, 2,* 341–447.

Hirschi, T. (1969). *Causes of delinquency.* Berkeley, CA: University of California Press.

Joseph, J. (1995). *Black youth, delinquency, and juvenile, justice.* Westport, MA: Praeger.

Klug, E. A. (2001). Geographical disparities among trying and sentencing juveniles. *Corrections Today, 1,* 100–107.

Leiber, M. J., & Stairs J. M. (1999). Race context and the use of intake diversion. *Journal of Research in Crime & Delinquency, 56*(87), 56–87.

Mears, D. (2003). A critique of waiver research: Critical next step in assessing the impacts of laws for transferring juveniles to the criminal justice system. *Youth Violence and Juvenile Justice, 1,* 156–172.

Mennel, R. M. (1982). Attitudes and policies towards juvenile delinquency in the United States: A historiographical review. In P. M. Sharp & B.W. Hancock (Eds.), *Juvenile delinquency: Historical, theoretical, and societal reactions to youth* (pp. 19–40). Upper Saddle River, NJ: Prentice Hall.

Myers, L. B., & Reid, S. T. (1995). The importance of county context in the measurement of sentence disparity: The search for routinization. *Journal of Criminal Justice, 23,* 223–242.

Piscotta, A. W. (1983). Race, sex and rehabilitation: A study of differential treatment in the juvenile reformatory, 1825-1900. *Crime & Delinquency, 29,* 254–270.

Platt, A. M. (1969). *The child savers: The intervention of delinquency.* Chicago: University of Chicago Press.

Risler, E. A., Sweatman, T., & Nackerud, L. (1998). Evaluating the Georgia legislative waiver's effectiveness in deterring juvenile crime. *Research on Social Work Practice, 8,* 657–667.

Shelden, R. G. (1976). *Rescued from evil: Origins of the juvenile justice system in Memphis, Tennessee, 1900–1917.* Unpublished doctoral dissertation. Southern Illinois University, Carbondale, IL.

Tanenhaus D. S., & Drizin S. A. (2003). "Owing to the extreme youth of the accused": The changing legal response to juvenile homicide. *Journal of Crime, Law and Criminology, 92,* 642–708.

Thornberry, T. P. (1979). Towards an interactional theory of delinquency. In P. Cordella & L. Siegel (Eds.), *Readings in contemporary criminological theory* (pp. 207–222). Boston: Northeastern University Press.

Woodhouse, B. (2002). The end of adolescence: Youthful indiscretions: Culture, class, status, and the passage to adulthood. *DePaul Law Review, 51,* 743–768.

Wolfgang, M. E., & Thornberry, T. (1987). *From boy to man, from delinquency to crime.* Chicago: University of Chicago Press.

Restorative Justice: What Social Workers Need to Know

22

Katherine van Wormer

Forensic social workers, like other social workers, often deal with the stresses and tragedies of life. In the juvenile and criminal justice systems, they may work as correctional officers and correctional counselors in prisons, with juvenile offenders, in programs for sexual offenders, and in victim assistance programs. And as indicated in the other chapters of this volume, forensic social work also relates to legal issues in traditional social work settings, such as child welfare. Although restorative justice is associated in the public mind more with the correctional arena than with child welfare, the principles of this philosophy cut across all areas of social work, wherever there is conflict caused by wrongdoing that needs to be resolved.

Unlike child welfare, the correctional arena has been largely overlooked by the social work profession as a major area of specialization and employment. This abandonment of the field, no doubt, was accelerated by the increasingly punitive nature of corrections (Gumz, 2004). A related factor may be the marginal status that social services hold throughout the criminal justice system (Orzech, 2006).

However, the role of social work within the legal system is changing significantly. Rehabilitation of adult and juvenile offenders has returned as a major focus. Innovative approaches under the rubric of restorative justice are changing the landscape of social work practice, particularly in the criminal justice system.

What Is Restorative Justice?

Let's start with some real-life examples:

- After several meetings with the facilitator-counselor, a woman visits her grandson in prison; the grandson is serving time for the murder of his father (his grandmother's son). As the youth cries at the pain he has caused, grandmother and grandson express their love for each other in a deep embrace.
- A boy who had burglarized a friend's home sat with his family members in a circle that included the victim and the victim's family; after the victim told her story of fear and anguish and the offender apologized, arrangements were made for restitution.
- A big boy, "the school bully" listens to his victims tell of their misery caused by the threats and ridicule they have experienced from this classmate; shaken by what he has heard, the "bully" promises not to continue acting like that and to get help for his problems.
- In a Native American peacekeeping circle, members of the community open the session with a prayer and a reminder that the circle has been convened to discuss the behavior of a young man who assaulted his sister in a drunken rage; an eagle feather is passed around the circle, held by each speaker as he or she expresses feelings about the harmful behavior.

These examples are descriptions of actual cases in which restorative strategies were used to help repair a wrongdoing and bring about peace among parties in a dispute. The first two examples are known to me personally; the latter two are based on those found in the restorative justice literature. So what is restorative justice? As defined by the *Encyclopedia of Social Work* (National Association of Social Workers [NASW]):

> Restorative justice *is an umbrella term for a method of handling disputes with its roots in the rituals of indigenous populations and traditional religious practices. A three-pronged system of justice, restorative justice is a non-adversarial approach usually monitored by a trained professional who seeks to offer justice to the individual victim, the offender, and the community, all of whom have been harmed by a crime or other form of wrongdoing.* (van Wormer, 2008, p. 531)

Operationalizing Restorative Justice

Derived from indigenous and religious forms of justice, restorative justice is a concept that transcends national borders. Today, restorative initiatives are being introduced worldwide in its many varieties as forms of resolving conflict and of meting out justice to victims of wrongdoing. Along with members of the legal profession, child welfare workers, and school authorities, social workers have been actively involved in this movement.

Current trends in dispensing justice fall within three general areas—family group conferencing, victim–offender conferencing, and reparations. These trends in restorative justice are highly relevant to social work values and practice frameworks. At the intersection of policy and practice, restorative initiatives closely parallel the empowerment and strengths-based perspectives of social work.

Restorative justice not only refers to a number of strategies for resolving conflicts peacefully but also to a political campaign of sorts to advocate for the rights of victims and for compassionate treatment of offenders. Rather than emphasizing the rules that have been broken and the punishment that should be imposed, restorative approaches tend to focus primarily on the persons who have been harmed (United Nations, 2006). A restorative justice process does not necessarily rule out all forms of punishment (e.g,. fine, incarceration, and probation), but its focus remains firmly on restorative, forward-looking, and least restrictive alternatives. Instead of incarceration, for example, the option of community service coupled with substance-abuse treatment might be favored. Instead of the death penalty in homicide cases, a long prison term might be seen as more humane and reflective of the values of a just society.

A growing international movement, restorative justice neatly achieves the NASW ethical standard (NASW *Code of Ethics*, 1996, 6.04c) which states that "social workers should promote conditions that encourage respect for cultural and social diversity within the United States and globally." The United Nations, in fact, has taken notice of alternative forms of justice, such as offender/victim mediation and informal means of dealing with certain crimes as a development consistent with human rights initiatives.

Worldwide, restorative justice has come a long way since two probation officers first pushed two tentative offenders toward their victim's homes in 1974 in Ontario (Zehr, 1995). Restorative justice has variously been called "a new model for a new century" (van Wormer, 2001), "a paradigm shift" (Zehr, 1995), and "a revolution" (Barajas, 1995,). This model originated in practice and experimentation; the concepts and the theory came later (Zehr, 2002).

The peacemaking powers of the restorative process are well recognized. Instituting such programs entails a new way of thinking about justice and change of heart as well as a change of mind. The best known restorative justice programs offer victims a carefully facilitated encounter with either their personal offender or offenders of other victims (Zehr, 2001). This vision of justice comes in many forms and shapes, as a visit to www.restorative.org will confirm. Restorative principles are seen in the settlement of school disputes, such as bullying on the playground, as well as in the formalized meeting of a murderer and the victim's family years after the crime for the purpose of enhancing healing. Sometimes forgiveness even occurs, most often not. But research generally shows that the participants report a high level of satisfaction following encounters in which crime victims confront their offenders in victim–offender mediation (Umbreit, 2001).

Review of the Social Work Literature

As of August 16, 2008, *Social Work Abstracts* lists 9 articles and other writings under the heading "restorative justice" from 1998–2008. (In contrast, *Criminal Justice Abstracts* lists 497 during the same time period.)

Turning to relevant sources not listed in *Social Work Abstracts*, restorative justice got its start with the work of Mark Umbreit, the Director of the Center for Restorative Justice and Mediation and Professor of Social Work at the University of Minnesota, who clearly is the most prolific and widely cited of all the writers in this field. Although his books (for example, *The Handbook of Victim Offender Mediation,* 2001) do not take any special note of the social work profession, two of his articles do so. His groundbreaking article on victim–offender mediation details the role played by two co-mediators, both trained social workers, in mediation between an offender and the victims he had burglarized (Umbreit, 1993). In his analysis of data from several Canadian community programs, Umbreit acknowledges the vital role that social workers play in victim–offender mediation as community organizers, program developers, trainers, and mediators.

Barsky (2001), who also has a Canadian perspective, makes a strong case for the social work curriculum to include the theory and principles of family mediation. Skills of group conferencing can be applied to dealing with concerns between the child welfare agency and family in parent–child conflict, for example. In interdisciplinary teams, social workers can advocate for culturally appropriate models and raise awareness of gender-based power imbalances in relationships and of the possibility of wife abuse. Two Canadian social work educators, Burt Galaway and Joe Hudson (2006), have edited the volume, *Restorative Justice: International Perspectives.* This volume is especially useful in providing detailed descriptions of Canadian indigenously based practices, such as circle sentencing. Both social work educators who got their training in Canada, Galaway and Hudson (2006) have also edited the definitive study on family group conferencing. Their text, *Family Group Conferencing: New Directions in Community-Centered Child and Family Practice,* describes one model of which all social workers interested in child welfare innovation and juvenile justice should be aware.

Elsewhere, restorative justice has been presented as an antidote to oppressive judicial practices in *Confronting Oppression, Restoring Justice* (van Wormer, 2004). More recently the extent to which social work's strengths perspective is compatible with the principles of restorative justice has been shown. As a result an integrated model known as the strengths-restorative approach has been constructed (van Wormer, in press). The paradigms of justice as presented in van Wormer's recent text are designed to attend to female victimization issues, including male and female sexual offending within a combined strengths-based and restorative justice context. The paradigm compares the assumptions of the standard retribution model with those of an approach that seeks to restore peace by building on people's strengths. In the paradigm a table is divided into three sections to correspond to each of the three components of restorative justice—victim, offender, and community—that are most strongly affected by crime or some other act that has generated harm. Whereas assumptions of the retribution model focus on wrongdoing as an act against the state, the strengths-based restorative model sees crime as an act against the person and the community as well as the state. The emphasis is on reparation and healing for all parties, rather than on punishment. In contrast to the winner and loser concept of the adversarial system of justice, here dialogue and truth-telling, prevention of further wrongdoing, and empowerment for all parties are stressed.

The field of corrections is one in which treatment professionals such as social workers and correctional counselors have been less prominent since the 1970s, when the focus on punishment and mandatory sentencing replaced the focus on rehabilitation (Gumz, 2004; van Wormer, 2006). A clash between the values of members of the helping professions and correctional administrators in the criminal justice system became apparent. Correctional counselors were socialized into the predominant ideology of the Samenow school of treatment—an approach aimed at the errors in thinking that offenders have "a criminal mind." Although this one-size-fits-all approach continues to be taught to those working with male and female offenders, rehabilitation is making a comeback in hopes of reducing the very high recidivism rates that are associated with the present system (van Wormer, in press). The introduction of restorative strategies, especially within prison walls, is a part of this new emphasis.

Varieties of Restorative Justice

All of the models discussed in this section—victim–offender conferencing, reparative boards, family group conferencing, healing circles—are relevant to forensic social work and collaboration. Victim–offender conferencing is relevant to victim advocacy work; family group conferencing to child welfare work and to work with minority groups within extended family structures; and healing circles to school social work, addictions treatment, and community organization. Policy advocates and lobbyists will want to keep abreast of treatment-evaluation findings so they can conduct cost-effectiveness analyses. (The best U.S. resource for current data on treatment evaluation is found on the Web site of the University of Minnesota's Center for Restorative Justice and Peacemaking at http://ssw.che.umn.edu/rjp.)

At the *micro* level, restorative justice is played out as conferencing between victims and offenders; the rituals take place in family groups and healing circles. At the *macro* or societal level, where the wrongdoing has been on a global scale, restorative justice takes the form of reparations or truth commissions to compensate for the harm that has been done. Common to all these models is restoring justice. The magnitude of the situations ranges from interpersonal violence to school bullying to mass kidnappings to full-scale warfare. Of most relevance to social work practice are the following forms of restorative strategies: victim–offender conferencing, reparations, family conferencing, and healing circles.

Victim–Offender Conferencing

In its most familiar variation, victim–offender conferencing operates through the criminal justice system. In a court-referred process, victims and offenders meet in a circle to communicate their feelings and work out restitution agreements (for a full description, see Bazemore & Umbreit, 2001).

Social work professor Marilyn Armour (2002), Director of the Institute for Restorative Justice and Restorative Dialogue at The University of Texas at Austin, writes enthusiastically of the emerging initiative of victim–offender dialogue in cases of homicide. Because family victims often crave information about the crime that took their loved one, as Armour states, they sometimes request a meeting at the prison with the murderer. Such a process, when well planned and monitored, accords the homicide survivors the recognition they were previously denied by the state's need to bring the murderer to justice. Moreover, such a process is affirming in offering the survivors the opportunity to tell the offender how the crime affected them.

Increasingly common are victim-impact panels in which victims/survivors give a presentation to reveal the impact of a crime on their lives. These panels, typically, are arranged by victim assistance programs, correctional staff, and trained volunteers. Sometimes following extensive preparation, victims/survivors meet with the very offenders who have so altered their lives. Within prison walls, members of victim-impact panels speak to inmates. The purpose of these panels is to enable offenders to empathize with victims or family members for their loss.

Social workers are actively involved in every area of victim–offender conferencing. As noted by Umbreit (2006), mediation, as an expression of restorative justice, is an emerging area of social work practice with youth in the justice system. During the 1990s, as Roberts and Brownell (1999) indicate, steady progress was made toward implementing a community restorative justice model in various parts of the United States. Forensic social workers are leading the way in expanding restorative programs nationwide.

Within the field of corrections, there are few better examples of evidence-based practices than victim–offender mediation, according to Umbreit (interviewed by Fred, 2005). In *Facing Violence*, which focuses on restorative programs in Texas and Ohio that handle cases involving severe violence, Umbreit, Vos, Coates, and Brown (2003) found that 8 out of 10 participants (victims and offenders) in the dialogue sessions reported major life changes occurring as a result of the program.

Reparations

The traditional means of righting wrongs often occurs through a lawsuit followed by the threat of an adversarial trial. As described by Zehr (2001): "The adversarial setting of the court is a hostile environment, an organized battlefield in which the strategies of aggressive argument and psychological attack replace the physical force of the medieval duel" (p. 192).

One side wins and one side loses in such cases. Great legal expenses are involved in cases that make it to court, and sometimes huge winnings to the plaintiff and his/her representing law firm. But lawyers choose their personal injury cases carefully. Most situations do not qualify for economic reasons, mainly because the potential defendants do not have sufficient resources to make a lawsuit worth the effort and expense. The threat of a lawsuit serves some purposes in society in protecting the public from harm, but in most situations is not a practical means of resolving disputes and compensating victims.

Sometimes reparations do not involve money at all as in the Hawaiian ritual of *ho'oponopono*. Social workers in Hawaii have been quietly incorporating this Native Hawaiian culturally based tradition into their human service interventions. Hurdle (2002) chronicles how social workers in collaboration with Hawaiian elders worked to revitalize the use of *ho'oponopono*, an ancient Hawaiian conflict-resolution process. This model is embedded in the traditional Hawaiian value of extended family, respect of elders, need for harmonious relationships, and restoration of good will or *aloha*. The process is ritualistic and follows a definite protocol. With a facilitator in tight control of communication, the opening prayer leads to an open discussion of the problem at hand. The resolution phase begins with a confession of wrongdoing and the seeking of forgiveness. Uniquely, as Hurdle relates, all parties to the conflict ask forgiveness of each other; this equalizes the status of participants. This process effectively promotes spiritual healing and can be used in many contexts. In drawing on guidance of the Kupanas (or wise elders) and a reliance on the family as a natural resource in relieving social problems, social workers are tapping into the community's natural resources, a cardinal principle of the strengths perspective (Heffernan, Johnson, & Vakalahi, 2002).

An example of reparations that involve monetary awards is described in one rare case of resolution following a proven complaint of sexual abuse perpetrated by a priest. This case, described in a newspaper article, involved an especially flagrant example of priest abuse from the diocese of Providence, Rhode Island (Carroll, 2002). This matter involved lawsuits filed by 36 people who were sexually abused. What is remarkable about this resolution is that it was arrived at not through adversarial procedures but through marathon conferencing sessions. Church representatives treated the survivors with empathy. Instead of attacking the victims' stories, church officials showed compassion; sincere apologies were offered. Final settlements varied in amounts proportionate to the severity of the abuse and the extent of pain and suffering. Consistent with the principles of restorative justice, the emphasis was on helping the victims, church, and community heal from the wrongs that had been done.

Restorative initiatives are not limited to work with individuals and families, but also can be successfully applied to the unjust treatment of whole populations. At the macro level, reparation is the form of restorative justice that occurs outside of the criminal justice and child welfare context. In these scenarios the violator is the state: Wartime persecutions, rape of the land, slave labor, and mass murder are forms of crimes against humanity that demand some form of compensation for survivors and their families, even generations later, as long as the wounds are felt. The Truth Commission held in South Africa to address the wounds inflicted by Apartheid is one of the most powerful examples of restoration. Compensation came in the form of public testimony and apology (Green, 1998).

Reparations often involve monetary exchange in addition to public acknowledgment of responsibility for the crimes against humanity. Demands for compensation by African Americans for the cruelty inflicted on their ancestors through the slave trade and subsequent slavery have received much attention in recent years, but the wrongs have not been redressed. Similarly, the Australian government continues to deny reparations to the aboriginal people for their "stolen childhoods," a reference to the earlier policy of removing the children of mixed blood and placing them with White families. Reparations have also been denied to the Korean relatives of innocent civilians slaughtered during the American–Korean war.

Successful examples of reparations are U.S. compensation to families of Japanese-Americans held in concentration camps during World War II, and German compensation to survivors of slave-labor camps. Although social workers have not been involved in any official way in the rewarding of reparations, the values represented in this peacemaking process are highly consistent with social work values, most particularly in regard to social justice, human rights, and empowerment of marginalized populations.

Family Group Conferencing

Developed from the Maori tradition in New Zealand, where it has become a state-sanctioned process, family group conferencing involves the community of people most affected by a situation in need of resolution. Child abuse is a typical example of a problem that can be resolved by a conference of caring and responsible members of the extended family. The similarities between restorative and aboriginal forms of justice coupled with the failure of the existing criminal justice system to deal with the problems of indigenous populations has enhanced its enthusiastic acceptance in New Zealand as in Northwest Canada (Roach, 2000). With the passage of the Sentencing Act of 2002, New Zealand enacted new legislation to make restorative justice processes that had formerly been used with juveniles and families in the child welfare system also available for adult offenders ("New Zealand Expands," 2002).

Actively involved in setting up the conference, social workers then take a back seat to allow the participants to come up with an appropriate sanction or solution. This process is empowering to the community and highly applicable not just for resolution in the criminal justice realm, but also in matters pertaining to child welfare as addressed by the child welfare system (Adams, 2002). Social workers help oversee and monitor the arrangements reached by extended family members as to how the child's safety can be ensured.

Healing Circles

This innovative approach is relevant for work with victims/survivors who need family and or community support following the trauma caused by a crime. The format is ideal for recovering alcoholic/addicts who wish to be reconciled with loved ones. The Toronto District School Board has adopted this approach for situations in which students have victimized others at school ("Healing Circle Shows," 2001). All the people touched by the offense gather together, review the incident or incidents, try to make sense of it, and, they hope, reach a peaceful resolution.

Common to all these examples of restorative strategies are an emphasis on face-to-face communication, truth-telling, personal empowerment, and healing by all parties to the wrongdoing. Relevant to social work innovators, all four of the strategies just outlined can be developed on a collaborative basis, involving, where appropriate, criminal justice agencies, social service agencies, and community associations (United Nations, 2006). In the absence of collaborative arrangements, it is likely that difficulties will be experienced in securing referrals from the courts, the prosecutor's office, victim-assistance organizations, and other required supports.

Relevance to Social Work Values and Education

The mission of social work is rooted in a set of core values. According to the NASW *Code of Ethics* (1996: Preamble), the core values of social work are: service, social justice, dignity and worth of the person, importance of human relationships, integrity, and competence. Restorative justice clearly relates to all these values but most especially to *social justice* or fairness in treatment under the law and to integrity because of its emphasis on truth-telling in these person-centered proceedings (van Wormer, 2004).

The standards for social work education, which went into effect in July 2002, stress the necessity for social work programs to include spiritual development as central to an understanding of human behavior in the social environment (Council on Social Work Education, 2002). This important addition to the *Educational Policy and Accreditation Standards* recognizes the key role that religion and spirituality play in the lives of many of our clients and of the strengths that may accrue through these sources. The rituals pertaining to healing circles often start and end with prayers, depending on the religious preferences of the participants.

Peacemaking circles, as Pranis (2001) indicates, engage the spiritual dimension of human experience in theory and practice. Enhancing empathy for another's pain, as Pranis further suggests, is a powerful for social justice, and defining restorative justice in terms of empathy takes us out of the confines of religion into the realities of community living and decision making. Nevertheless, there is often a religious aspect to restorative practice as well. This aspect arises in much of the victim–offender work, religious devotion on the part of volunteers, religious conversion by the offenders in prison, and the whole forgiveness theme.

The teachings of restorative justice are consistent with those of the world's great religions, with the Jewish concept "tikkun"—to heal, repair, and transform the world and with the Christian notion of forgiveness and belief in the duty to overcome evil with good. From the East, Confucianism supports the theory that human nature is basically good. Confucius taught his disciples the principle of *ren* or truthfulness and kindness. Confucianism, according to Hui and Geng (2001), advocates a restorative approach to matters of crime and justice. It assumes, first and foremost, that the first victim of any criminal offense is the offender.

Research Findings Concerning Intervention Effectiveness

The best evidence for treatment effectiveness, as we know, is found in experiments that compare a group that received an intervention with a control group that did not on certain significant variables that can be measured. Such studies in the field of restorative justice have been rare. Most research in the field uses follow-up investigations of the extent to which participants are satisfied with the process; results have been consistently favorable (Umbreit, 2001). In the interests of obtaining more rigorous research results, Strang (2004) conducted a series of randomized controlled trials in Canberra, Australia, in which juveniles who had committed property or violent crimes were assigned to either restorative conferences or court hearings. The research involved over 5,000 participants and took place over several years. The findings on the whole were positive. Compared to victims who were involved in the conventional courtroom form of justice, participants in restorative justice processes expressed significantly reduced fear that the offender would harm them, far fewer of these victims expressed a wish to harm their offender if they had the chance, and the large majority of victims in the experiment received an apology compared to victims who went to court. Conference participants also experienced significant decreases in anger and increases in sympathy toward their offenders, as well as decreased anxiety. Results with the juvenile offenders, especially among aboriginal youth, were less positive. The fact that police officers head the conferencing is suggested as the reason for the poor outcomes.

The Jerry Lee Center of the University of Pennsylvania presently is replicating the Australian study in Britain. Funded by the British Home Office, this research is focused for the first time on adult offenders with conferences introduced both pre- and postsentencing for offenses including robbery, assault, and burglary (Porter, 2006). Research results will be measured across the participants' lifetimes. Other research in Britain on the restorative processes that are taking place provide very encouraging results. More research is needed, however, on effectiveness of restorative interventions in situations of serious violence and more research in general on the impact of this conferencing on offender attitudes and recidivism rates.

Case Study

Sarah was only 14 years old when her father was killed. As an adult, consumed with anger, Sarah had spoken before a parole board, begging them not to release Jeff, her father's killer. Now, more than 2 decades later, she was plagued with memories and a sense of grief and loss. Her role in the restorative justice process is described in an article in *Social Work Today* by Orzech (2006). To guide the process, Mark Umbreit became Sarah's social worker; he spent 1 year working with Sarah as the family survivor to help prepare her for the journey she would make inside the gates of a maximum-security prison to spend 5 hours with the man who had brutally murdered her father. Umbreit also helped prepare the offender, Jeff, for the conferencing that would later take place. Following the meeting with Jeff, "Sarah spoke of how the encounter had been like going through a fire that burned away her pain and allowed the seeds of healing to take root in her life" (Orzech, p. 34). The meeting had an equally powerful effect on Jeff as well.

Restorative justice processes within the criminal justice system, such as this one involving a case of homicide, inevitably are highly emotional experiences for both parties. This is an area that is ripe for forensic social worker involvement. Such innovations within the prison system are creating new professional roles for social workers, as Orzech suggests. In fact, hundreds of similar meetings between victims and offenders involved in violent crimes have taken place in recent years.

Summary and Conclusions

Restorative justice principles effectively bridge the gap between the formality of conventional criminal justice processes and the social work ethos. In its incorporation of activities related to personal and community empowerment, spirituality, conflict resolution, healing of relationships through dialogue, and learning techniques of decision making inspired by indigenous people's traditions, restorative justice effectively links practice with policy.

Restorative justice programs are proliferating around the world and becoming established in this country through cultural transmission. Social work educators can play a major role through theory development and inspiring students to pursue application of restorative principles to a wide range of practice areas. To date, despite the work of a number of dedicated social work researchers, the social work profession, at least in the United States (though not in New Zealand or Canada), has failed to exert leadership in teaching about, writing about, or setting up restorative justice programs.

The challenge to policy planners is to learn ways of making correctional strategies more consistent with social justice and to participate in the planning, research, policy making, and facilitation aspects of this more humanistic form of justice.

Web Resources on Restorative Justice

Center for Restorative Justice and Peacemaking: http://rjp.umn.edu/
Community Justice Institute: http://www.cji.fau.edu/overview.html
International Institute for Restorative Practices: https://www.iirp.org/index.php
Restorative Justice Online: http://www.restorativejustice.org/
Restorative Justice Consortium: http://www.restorativejustice.org.uk
Restore Justice: http://www.restorejustice.com/
Victim Offender Mediation Society: http://voma.org/index.html

References

Adams, P. (2002, February). *Learning from Indigenous practices: A radical tradition.* Paper presented at the Council on Social Work Education Conference, Nashville, TN.

Armour, M. P. (2002). Journey of family members of homicide victims: A qualitative study of their posthomicide experience. *American Journal of Orthopsychiatry, 72,* 372–382.

Barajas, E. (1995) *Moving toward community justice: Topics in community corrections.* National Institute of Corrections. Retrieved from http:alternet.deschutes.org/juvenile/movingtoward.htm

Barsky, A. (2001). Understanding family from a social work perspective. *Canandian Social Work Review, 18*(1), 25–46.

Bazemore, G., & Umbreit, M. (2001, February). A comparison of four restorative conferencing models. *Juvenile Justice Bulletin.* Washington, DC: U.S. Department of Justice.

Carroll, M. (2002, September). $13.5 million settlement in Rhode Island clergy abuse. *The Boston Globe.* Retrieved September 15, 2007, from www.boston.com/globe/spotlight/abuse

Council on Social Work Education (CSWE). (2002). *Standards on educational policy and accreditation.* Alexandria, VA: Author.

Fred, S. (2005, February). Restorative justice: A model of healing. *NASW News,* p 4.

Galaway, B., & Hudson, J. (Eds.). (2006). *Restorative justice: International perspectives.* Monsey, NY: Criminal Justice Press.

Galaway, B., & Hudson, J. (Eds.). (2006). *Family group conferencing: New directions in community-centered child and family practice.* Edison, NJ: Aldine.

Green, C. (1998, January 11). Without memory there is not healing. *Parade,* pp. 5–7.

Gumz, E. (2004). American social work, corrections and restorative justice: An appraisal. *International Journal of Offender Therapy and Comparative Criminology, 48,* 449–460.

Healing circle shows offenders their human toll. (2001, May 26). *Toronto Star,* p. N01.

Heffernan, K., Johnson, R., & Vakalahi, H. (2002, October). *A Pacific Island approach to aging.* Paper presented at the Baccalaureate Program Directors Conference, Pittsburgh, PA.

Hui, E., & Geng, K. (2001).The spirit and practice of restorative justice in Chinese culture. In M. Hadley (Ed.), *The spiritual roots of restorative justice* (pp. 99–118). Albany, NY: State University of New York Press.

Hurdle, D. (2002). Native Hawaiian traditional healing: Culturally-based interventions for social work practice. *Social Work, 47,* 183–192.

National Association of Social Workers (NASW). (1996). *Code of ethics.* Washington, DC: NASW Press.

New Zealand expands official recognition of restorative justice. (2002, October 2). *Restorative justice online.* Retrieved August 2007, from www.restorativejustice.org/rj3/Feature

Orzech, D. (2006). Criminal justice social work—New models, new opportunities. *Social Work Today, 6*(6), 34–37.

Porter, A. (2006, April 13). *The Jerry Lee program research on restorative justice: Promising results.* Restorative Practices E Forum. International Institute for Restorative Practices. Retrieved August 2008, from www.iirp.org

Pranis, K. (2001). Restorative justice, social justice, and the empowerment of marginalized populations. In G. Bazemore & M. Schiff (Eds.), *Restoring community justice: Repairing harm and transforming communities* (pp. 287–306). Cincinnati, OH: Anderson.

Roach, K. (2000). Changing punishment at the turn of the century: Restorative justice on the rise. *Canadian Journal of Criminology, 42,* 249–282.

Roberts, A., & Brownell, P. (1999). A century of forensic social work: Bridging the past to the present. *Social Work, 44,* 359–369.

Strang, H. (2004). *Repair or revenge: Victims and restorative justice.* New York: Oxford University Press.

Umbreit, M. (1993). Crime victims and offenders in mediation: An emerging area of social work practice. *Social Work 38*(1), 69–73.

Umbreit, M. S. (2001). *The handbook of victim offender mediation: An essential guide to practice and research.* San Francisco: Jossey-Bass.

Umbreit, M. (2006). Restorative justice through mediation: The impact of programs in four Canadian provinces. In B. Galaway & J. Hudson (Eds.), *Restorative justice: International perspectives* (pp. 373–385). Monsey, NY: Criminal Justice Press. (Original work poublished 1996)

Umbreit, M., Vos, B., Coates, R., & Brown, K. (2003). *Facing violence: The path of restorative justice and dialogue.* Monsey, NY: Criminal Justice Press.

United Nations (UN). (2006). *Handbook of restorative justice programmes.* Vienna: UN Office on Drugs and Crime.

van Wormer, K. (2001). *Counseling female offenders and victims: A strengths restorative approach.* New York: Springer Publishing Company.

van Wormer, K. (2004). *Confronting oppression, restoring justice: From policy analysis to social action.* Alexandria, VA: CSWE.

van Wormer, K. (2006). *Introduction to social welfare and social work: The U.S. in global perspective.* Belmont, CA: Wadsworth.

van Wormer, K. (2008). Restorative justice. In *Encyclopedia of social work* (20th ed., pp. 531–532). Washington, DC: NASW Press.

van Wormer, K. (in press). *Counseling female offenders: A gender-sensitive approach.* New York: Lyceum Books.

Zehr, H. (1995). *Changing lenses: A new focus for crime and justice.* Waterloo, ON: Herald Press.

Zehr, H. (2001). *Transcending: Reflections of crime victims.* Intercourse, PA: Good Books.

Zehr, H. (2002). *The little book of restorative justice.* Intercourse, PA: Good Books.

Part VII

Diversity, Human Rights, and Immigration

Human Rights: Some Implications for Social Work

23

Rosemary A. Barbera

Social work's commitment to social justice, human rights, and multiculturalism is well known and well documented (Boyle, Nackerud, & Kilpatrick, 1999; Gil, 1998; Ife, 2001; Mama, 2001). "Social work and human rights have a very close relationship" (Eroles, 1997, p. 56). This relationship calls on social workers to be active in the construction of a new reality so that the human rights of all are respected. Human rights issues permeate all parts of the social realities in which social workers find themselves in the United States, both professionally and personally. Social workers are on the front lines, working with those persons and communities that have been exploited by social conditions that perpetuate massive human rights violations. As a result, social workers should be very familiar with human rights (Sánchez, 1989), integrating human rights into their daily practice. In fact, the International Federation of Social Workers (IFSW) and the International Association of Schools of Social Work (IASSW) consider it imperative that social workers commit themselves fully to the promotion and protection of human rights without reservation (Eroles, 1997). Unfortunately, this is not always the case in the United States, where the population is not educated in the language of human rights.

Social workers also "uphold and defend the dignity of each person's worth" (IFSW, 2004), approaching their work with this dignity in mind. However, often the forces of society and structural inequalities mean that "real human beings suffer (because) human rights are not protected" (DaLaet, 2006, p. 1). This is especially true with regard to the prison system in the United States, where human rights violations run rampant (Golembeski & Fullilove, 2005), as youth are tried as adults and minorities are overrepresented. As a result, the dignity and worth of all humans is severely compromised as there is a clear relationship between human rights and human needs (Wronka, 1995). Wronka stated that the goal of human rights is to fill these human needs: biological (to eat and have shelter), social–psychological (to feel affiliated and loved), productive–creative (to work and create), security (to have privacy and be secure in one's person), and spiritual (to worship and find meaning in one's existence). There are clear implications for social workers who strive to respectfully partner with clients to fulfill the client's needs and gain respect for her or his human rights. In fact, in Latin America, social workers recognized that "with the introduction of human rights into the daily work of social workers, the profession became much more meaningful" (Sánchez, 1989, p. 20) and more effective in creating real change.

This chapter addresses the implication of human rights for social workers. It offers some background on the concept of human rights, with emphasis on the relationship between human rights and social work and human rights and the law. It includes a discussion of the implication of human rights for social work education and social work practice, with a focus on building community. It also discusses obstacles to social work practice from a human-rights perspective, and concludes with a discussion on how social work needs to change to have consistency between discourse and action.

Human Rights

"Today, the language of human rights has become a prominent tool" (DeLaet, 2006, p. xiii) that is used throughout the world governments, nongovernmental organizations (NGOs), and social movements. However, although the discourse on human rights has increased, the application of that discourse seems to be lacking as evidenced by the growth of poverty and exploitation related to the growth of neoliberal globalization. When human rights are not protected; that is, when the discourse remains discourse and is not applied, "real human beings suffer" (DeLaet, 2006, p. 1).

The term "'human rights' refers to a significant number of rights that each human being deserves; it is what many jurists of international humanitarian law refer to as 'basic rights' " (Barbera, 2007, p. 68). These basic rights include the right to housing, health, equitable education, a job at a living wage; in sum, to live a life of dignity and worth. And according to "the keystone instrument of human rights, the Universal Declaration of Human Rights (UDHR), adopted unanimously by the United Nations' General Assembly in 1948" (Bricker-Jenkins, Barbera, & Young, 2008, p. 263), "all are equal before the law and are entitled without any discrimination to equal protection of the law" and all have certain rights in front of the criminal justice system (see Articles 7–13 of the UDHR). Given the disproportionate number of people of minority status inhabiting the jails and prisons in the United States, and the disproportionate number of economically exploited persons in prison or jail, we can see that there is a link between violations of certain human rights as defined by the UDHR and imprisonment in the United States. Therefore, the original violations to the human rights of housing, education, and jobs that pay a living wage are exacerbated by further violations of the right to be equal in front of the law, to no cruel or unusual punishment. In this way, there is a clear role for forensic social workers to advocate with and on behalf of people in prison so that their human rights both within and without the penal system and are respected.

Human Rights and Social Work Practice

The basic human rights just mentioned are central to social work practice. "No society can call itself truly civilized, or truly committed to human rights, until this minimal protection of first generation rights is effectively achieved. A social worker that is committed to a human rights philosophy must also be committed to working towards such a goal" (Ife, 2001, p. 95). To successfully work toward the goal of human rights for all, "social workers need to regard human rights violations or denials as systemic in origin and to address fundamental structural issues through their practice" (Ife, 2001, p. 45). Therefore, it is clear that social workers should no longer spend most of their time asking people to adjust to a dysfunctional society; rather, we are called to intervene in ways that change the exploitative, unjust structures that perpetuate injustice, oppression, and violations of human rights. It is, therefore, the role of social workers to denounce violations of human rights (Sánchez, 1989).

This becomes especially clear when we think about the fact that human "rights are intimately linked to the idea of 'quality of life' " (Cáceres, 2000, p. 19) and many people who end up in prisons and jails in the United States do so because of a poor quality of life (Golembeski & Fullilove, 2005). Social workers spend a good deal of their professional time trying to work with people to improve the living conditions that lead to a negative quality of life for the world's vast majority.

Wainwright (2000 p. 251) noted that "economic and social rights can be protected at a time when poverty and exclusion are recognized as major challenges." The lack of respect for economic, social, and cultural human rights further alienates those members of society who already live on the fringe and are already the most vulnerable. Indeed, it is the role of social workers to work in partnership with the most vulnerable members of society to ensure that such rights are respected and to ensure "continuous improvement in living conditions" (Wainwright, 2000, p. 252) and quality of life.

Social work that grows from a human rights perspective helps us attain the very basis of our professional principles: the preoccupation with serving and being useful to the weakest members of society, by specifically confronting social problems until we are able to assure that the necessary conditions which guarantee that all basic necessities are met (Sánchez, 1989). As a result "social workers have as their task the transformation of societal conditions" (Eroles, 1997, p. 26), which is an ethical–political commitment. Therefore, to be ethical, it is imperative that social work practice is rooted in human rights.

Social work practice from [a human rights] framework requires three elements: a theoretical base that gives us a framework for action; action in both the popular/grassroots and professional arenas; and, an organization ideology with three elements: 1) a commitment to basing our work in the knowledge of the people; 2) an ethical commitment to work in partnership with the most affected to ensure human rights; and, 3) interaction with other social actors towards a practice oriented towards social change. (Eroles, 1997, pp. 28, 29)

This framework calls on social workers not to see people as "clients" or "others." Such a viewpoint makes it easier to objectify people and reduce them to their conditions in life. Rather, social workers are called to form partnerships with the people for whom they are working, recognizing that all human beings are actors and can be agents for change.

However, we must be cautious not to fall into the trap of saying one thing while practicing another. "Human rights seems to be a new fad since people from all walks of life and beliefs are discussing this theme....In this way, however, human rights have been distorted" (Johansson, 1989, p. 33). But for social work and social workers, human rights should be the basis of our action and our work. Human rights are nonnegotiable and we must work to change not only the conditions that lead to the violations of human rights, but also the conditions within our agencies and institutions that do not permit us to practice social work from a human rights framework.

Human Rights and the Law

Human rights law represents a significant paradigm shift as it recognizes that humans are not just subjects, but are also actors (DeLaet, 2006). A major step in this paradigm shift occurred in 1948 when the United Nations' Declaration of Human Rights was signed. "As a resolution passed by the General Assembly, the UDHR is a nonbinding document" (DeLaet, 2006, p. 30). Subsequently, two international conventions were developed to codify the aspirations of the UDHR—the International Covenant on Civil and Political Rights and the International Covenant on Economic, Social, and Cultural Rights. "Both documents were signed in 1966 and entered into force in 1976. As treaties that must be signed and ratified in order to enter into force, both covenants are binding under international law" (DeLaet, 2006, pp. 30–31). Because many international human rights conventions have not been ratified by the United States, their conditions or guidelines are not legal here (Williams, 2001, p. 833). Regarding these two covenants, the United States has only signed and ratified the first covenant and not the second.

This is also true of other international conventions. For example, the United States and Somalia are the only countries that have not ratified the UN Declaration on the Rights of the Child. And, in 1996, the United States was the only country to reject the right of housing at the Habitat Conference, and the right to food at the World Food Summit (Mittal & Rosset, 1999, p. xii): "Melissa Kimble, the head of the United States government delegation to the Food Summit, said that the U.S. could not support language around the right to food in the Summit's Plan of Action because the new welfare reform law would then be in violation of international law." This is a clear recognition by a U.S. government official that social policies in the United Stated do not measure up to international human rights' standards.

In this same vein, it is important to note that the original UDHR includes a call to each signatory country to execute the human rights contained as best they can given the country's economic situation. With this in mind, the United States, as the richest country on the planet, has a particular responsibility to ensure that the basic human rights of its residents are being met. This includes the right to housing, health, education, food, respect regardless of race, and jobs at living wages. These issues have significant implications in legal contexts as many people who find themselves within the criminal justice system come from exploited and oppressed groups in society in which these human rights are not respected. Therefore, we could say that although the United States is not violating the letter of the law, because the UDHR is not a legally binding document but rather an aspiration, it is violating the spirit of the law, and "public authorities must operate within the law" (Williams, 2001, p. 833).

By way of comparison, Williams (2001, p. 836) pointed out that in the United Kingdom "public authorities are under a legal duty not to act in a way that is incompatible with a Convention right" because of the British Human Rights Act of 1998. However, any country that has ratified an international human rights convention is equally responsible to uphold the rights explicated in such document, so by not ratifying a document, the United States leaves itself open to violate human rights.[1] According to Goodwin-Gill (1989), there is a "distinctive concept" of rights against the state, once of moral now legal entitlements, of rights inalienable and inherent in humanity, of the rule of law as essential to the resolution of conflicts between rights, is dominant still in debate about human rights (p. 529).

As social workers using a collaborative forensic practice framework in the United States, it is important for us to keep abreast of international human rights law as a way of improving the living conditions under which so many human beings are forced to live. It is also important to be up-to-date on human rights so that we can work more effectively in partnerships with people in client status to make change happen.

Implications for Social Work

Social work must revise itself according to the present reality (Colectivo, 1989) to bring about the conditions necessary for the respect of human rights. Our ethical obligation goes "beyond simply providing the best service available within the social worker's agency; it also necessitates looking at all the person's human rights and making sure they are realised and protected" (Ife, 2001, p. 113). As a result, we need to reconceptualize how we engage in social work practice.

Social Work Practice

Much social work practice in the United States occurs working one-on-one with an individual or family unit. This legacy of casework from the early Charity Organization Societies directs the focus of social workers on individuals when oftentimes the problems or challenges these people are facing are structural in nature. At the same time, through this individualized focus, people continue to feel isolated and alone, not recognizing that the challenges they are facing are also being faced by many others. Social workers who work in solidarity with the Poor People's Economic Human Rights Campaign, for example, work together with people living in poverty to understand the structural issues that exist. This is as true for social workers focusing on issues of housing, education, and jobs as it is for clinical social workers (Jennifer Jones, personal communication, April 1, 2003). What these social workers do is to reorganize their practice in a collective way, recognizing that the focus of human rights is group oriented, therefore individualistic forms of social work do not make sense.

This calls on social workers to live and work in solidarity with people in client status because "social work values the people as historical subjects" (Eroles, 1997, p. 34) who can be agents for change. For this kind of practice to become more widespread, however, more social workers in agencies and institutions need to demand that their practice be consistent with human rights. It also requires social workers to understand that "as social rights have been chipped away, they have been replaced by 'clientelistic' structures, such as social investment funds created to 'alleviate poverty' with funding from the World Bank and other multilateral sources" (Cáceres, 2000, p. 23). These clientelistic structures function best when there is a power differential between social worker and "client," because they are partially about perpetuating the status quo. Social workers who are committed to recognizing the dignity and worth of each human being need to be given the tools to analyze clientelistic structures so as to change them. Forensic social workers, particularly, need to address issues of structural (i.e., systemic) violence in society and within the penal system that lead to human rights violations in and out of prison.

Social Work Education

Although it is true that social work practice needs to change, it is equally true that social work education needs to change. Steen and Mathiesen (2005) pointed out that despite the obvious connections between social work and human rights, and beside the materials made available through the Centre for Human Rights, social work programs in the United States are behind other professional programs in integrating human rights content in their curricula. This is disappointing since "social workers are called to act to change the social condition, not just study it" (Eroles, 1997, p. 3). Because all social work programs in the United States that are accredited by the Council for Social Work Education (CSWE) must include content about vulnerable populations, students often spend a good deal of time studying poverty and other human rights violations. Often, however, these conditions are not presented as human rights violations. And, more often, students are, at the same time, learning social work practice skills that locate problems at the individual level rather than the structural level. Therefore, there is a disconnection between discourse and practice in this area. Social work education must be based in social action (Sánchez, 1989, p. 27), making use of a pedagogy of human rights in which social work relationships are democratic and based in solidarity; this way social action in social work practice can become more prevalent.

Social work does not have to reinvent the wheel, so to speak. The United Nations' Centre for Human Rights has a document that clearly articulates the fit between social work and human rights. "Human rights are inseparable from social work theory, values and ethics, and practice....Advocacy for such rights must therefore be an integral part of social work" (1994, p. 5). Social work programs can use this document as a guide to help integrate the practice of human rights, and not just its theory and values, into their curricula.

> *It is not enough for social workers to profess a commitment to human rights. We have to know how to integrate human rights into our practice. We have to change our educational models so that they integrate theory and practice in human rights. We must generate a style of work that is participative and active. (Sánchez, 1989, p. 28)*

This calls on social work education to bridge the false divide between so-called micro and macro practice.

The human rights approach to ethical practice suggests that a social worker who insists on maintaining the division between macro and micro practice, and only operates within one of them, is also practising unethically, and the same criticism could be made of university departments which perpetuate the macro/micro divide in their curricula. (Ife, 2001, p. 115)

Building Community

Social work committed to human rights must question the "relationships of power that perpetuate exploitation, alienation, discrimination and social exclusion" and act to change those relationships (Eroles, 1997, p. 53). This calls on social workers to work against the forces of individual consumerism and to work toward building communities of solidarity. This is quite countercultural in a society that worships material goods and the maverick spirit.

"We must criticize the role of 'helper' and clientelism that often characterizes social work; our work should be more about partnerships focused on social change, conscientization, organizing and mass mobilizations" (Sánchez, 1989, p. 25). Clientelism prohibits us from developing the horizontal relation of partnership; as we perpetuate the idea that social workers "help" others, we also perpetuate the idea that there is a vertical relationship of unequal power distribution between social workers and a person in client status. The very fact that the social worker is in a position to "help" denotes that there is a power differential and that the act of helping maintains that differential. Therefore, "the practice of social work needs to be committed to the values that define how we live together: solidarity, justice, and freedom" (Sánchez, 1989, p. 20).

Recognizing the Obstacles

Of course, for social workers to be effective human rights advocates and activists, it is necessary to recognize the obstacles that will slow down our work. Issues of state sovereignty present an obstacle because "the principle of sovereignty discourages the use of force for the purpose of influencing the 'internal affairs' of other states" (DeLaet, 2006, p. 3). DeLaet (2006) later commented that "state sovereignty trumps universal human rights" (p. 3). However, it is important to note that there is a double discourse when discussing state sovereignty. Although each state seems to have the right to enforce international human rights laws and standards as they see fit, at the same time there is universal enforcement of international laws that favor multinational corporations, oftentimes leading to the violation of human rights. Social workers, as advocates, educators, and concerned citizens of the world, can and should be in the forefront of the movement(s) to contest this proliferation of exploitation (Barbera, 2006).

Also relevant is the fact that sovereign states typically are the actors most responsible for perpetuating human rights abuses and are simultaneously the actors responsible for promoting and protecting human rights (DeLaet, 2006, p. 4). And because many social workers exercise their profession in state-financed institutions, this becomes problematic.

Another obstacle that exists for social workers in the United States particularly, is that the majority of the population of the U.S. believes that human rights violations occur in other countries, not their own. This is caused in part by the fact that people most often think of human rights in civil and political terms and do not consider that there are also economic, social, and cultural human rights. In this scenario, social workers need to educate (Freire, 1970) the population regarding the full spectrum of human rights.

One final obstacle to be considered here (although there are others that space limitations do not allow us to explore) is that funding agencies might see human rights as too political and this could jeopardize the budgets of social work agencies. Practicing social work from a human rights framework requires a recognition that the very structure of society is warped and needs to be transformed, not just reformed. For those who have power in society, this proposition is scary. As Freire (1970) found in his work with Brazilian peasants, the powerful in society do not want those on the bottom to understand their rights because the newly informed will then demand that their rights be respected. The same is the case in the United States today.

Summary and Conclusions

"It is not enough for social workers to speak the language of human rights and democracy; before they can even engage in social service work, they have to have in their hearts the conviction that all human beings are worthy" (Eroles, 1997, p. 19). Therefore, we must be willing to question our practice and our locations of practice: Do they perpetuate injustice and oppression? Do they question the status quo or accept it? Are they oppressive? How does our practice acquiesce to dominant thinking? Where does financing come from? How does it limit our work? We must not only know methodologies, but we must look at the context in which we practice (Ife, 2001). That is, we must be willing to interrogate all aspects of our social work practice, including our own location in society and how we might benefit from the structures of society as they presently exist. This, of course, can be a scary proposition, but one that is necessary to contribute to building a society in which the human rights of all are respected.

We must be willing to interrogate how our practice of social work might actually perpetuate problems of human rights abuses and inequalities. As Birkenmaier (2001) suggested: "Individualizing problems in direct clinical practice can also serve to maintain unjust social and institutional forces that directly relate to personal problems" (p. 42). Do we knowingly, and against our will, contribute to oppression through our practices? If so, are we willing to make the significant changes necessary to stop this practice? We must ask ourselves these questions and be willing to face the answers.

Social workers in forensic settings must be able to analyze the structures in society that cause many people to turn to crime. We must also be able to reflect critically on inherent injustices and structural violence that exists and that lead to disproportionate numbers of poor and minority persons inhabiting the prisons and jails in the United States. We must work simultaneously to create conditions in which incarcerated persons can empower themselves; change the conditions that lead to human rights violations within the prison system; and change the conditions in society that further exploit, oppress, and violate human rights.

Finally, we must go beyond the idea of individual human rights and think more communally. Human rights are inherently collective. As a result, the idea of social work practice emanating from a perspective of solidarity is essential. Our social work practice must always take into account the "social" in social work; a practice that focuses only on individuals and individual strategies is the antithesis of what it means to be in solidarity, to be "social" workers, working for the advancement of human rights. The remaining chapters in Part VII address issues of human rights and diversity, particularly related to immigrants and refugees in the United States.

Note

1. However, it must be pointed out that the United States did both sign and ratify the U.N. Convention on Civil and Political Rights. One of the rights explicated in this document is the right to not be tortured. The U.S. has continually violated this right, as well as others.

References

Barbera, R. A. (2006). Understanding globalization through short-term international field experiences. *Journal of Baccalaureate Social Work, 12*(1), 287–302.

Barbera, R. A. (2007). La vivienda es un derecho humano. *Revista de Trabajo Social, Universidad Autónoma Nacional de México, 16,* 68–73.

Birkenmaier, J. (2003). On becoming a social justice practitioner. *Social Thought, 22*(2/3), 41–54.

Boyle, D. P., Nackerud, L., & Kilpatrick, A. (1999). The road less traveled: Cross-cultural, international experiential learning. *International Social Work, 42,* 201–214.

Bricker-Jenkins, M., Barbera, R., & Young, C. (2008). Poverty through the lens of economic human rights. In D. Saleeby (Ed.), *The strengths perspective in social work practice* (5th ed., pp. 321–331). Boston: Pearson Education.

Cáceres, E. (2000). Building a culture of rights. *NACLA Report on the Americas, 34*(1), 19–24.

Centre for Human Rights. (1994). *Human rights and social work: A manual for schools of social work and the social work profession.* New York: United Nations.

Colectivo de Trabajo Social. (1989). *Trabajo social y derechos humanos: Compromiso con la dignidad. La experiencia chilena* [Social work and human rights: A Commitment with dignity. The Chilean experience]. Buenos Aires: Editorial Humanitas.

DeLaet, D. (2006). *The global struggle for human rights: Universal principles in world politics.* Belmont, CA: Thompson/Wadsworth.

Eroles, C. (1997). *Los derechos humanos: Compromiso ético del trabajo social* [Human Rights: An ethical imperative for social work]. Buenos Aires: Espacio Editorial.

Freire, P. (1970). *Pedagogy of the oppressed.* New York: Continuum International.

Gil, D. (1998). *Confronting injustice and oppression: Concepts and strategies for social work.* New York: Columbia University Press.

Golembeski, C., & Fullilove, R. (2005). Criminal (in)justice in the city and its associated health consequences. *American Journal of Public Health, 95,* 1701–1707.

Goodwin-Gill, G. S. (1989). International law and human rights: Trends concerning international migrants and refugees. *International Migration Review, 23*(3), 526–546.

Ife, J. (2001). *Human rights and social work: Towards rights-based practice.* New York: Cambridge University Press.

International Federation of Social Workers. (2004). *Ethics in social work: Statements in principle.* Retrieved February 3, 2008, from http://www.ifsw.org/en/p38000398.html

Johansson, C. (1989). Los derechos humanos no se transan en el Mercado de valores [Human rights cannot be compromised by the market]. In Colectivo de Trabajo Social (Colectivo) *Trabajo social y derechos humanos: Compromiso con la dignidad. La experiencia chilena* [Social work and human rights: A commitment with dignity. The Chilean experience] (pp. 31–36). Buenos Aires: Editorial Humanitas.

Mama, R. S. (2001). Preparing social work students to work in culturally diverse settings. *Social Work Education, 20,* 373–382.

Mittal, A., & Rosset, P. (1999). *America needs human rights.* Oakland, CA: Food First Books.

Sánchez, M. D. (1989). Trabajo social en derechos humanos: Reencuentro con la profesión [Social work in human rights. A reunion with the profession]. In Colectivo de Trabajo Social (Colectivo) *Trabajo social y derechos humanos: Compromiso con la dignidad. La experiencia chilena* [Social work and human rights: A Commitment with dignity. The Chilean experience] (pp. 17–30). Buenos Aires: Editorial Humanitas.

Steen, J. A., & Mathiesen, S. (2005). Human rights education: Is social work behind the curve? *Journal of Teaching in Social Work, 25*(3/4), 143–156.

Wainwright, S. (2000). New rights of responsibilities in anti-poverty work? *British Journal of Social Work, 30,* 249–253.

Williams, J. (2001). 1998 Human Rights Act: Social work's new benchmark. *British Journal of Social Work, 31,* 831–844.

Wronka, J. (1995). Human rights. In *The encyclopedia of social work* (Vol. 7, pp. 1405–1418). Washington, DC: NASW Press.

Calling Some "Illegal": Practice Considerations in Work With Undocumented Immigrants

24

Carol Cleaveland

> Throughout its history, immigration policy in the United States has expressed protectionist, exclusionary, and humanitarian impulses. Policies have been liberalized, only to turn again towards exclusion.
>
> —National Association of Social Workers

Whether processed en masse in 1880 at Ellis Island, doused with kerosene in 1907 as part of a "cleaning process" in El Paso, or fleeing *la migra* in 2007 after crossing a deadly Mexican desert, one thing holds true for all immigrants to the United States — the distinction between being welcomed as permanent or temporary, or not welcome at all is always tenuous and subject to change. Such distinctions shift according to the vicissitudes of economics, perceived national interests, and racial fears. Efforts today to address "the problem of illegal immigration" (Welch, 2003, p. 319), as described in a plethora of recent news coverage and political discourse, are a case in point. American lawmakers and news commentators are increasingly preoccupied with the question of entrance to the United States through unsanctioned means, particularly by Mexicans.

The arrival of undocumented migrants (those who enter the U.S. illegally for a limited period to work) and undocumented immigrants (those who enter illegally with the hope of permanent settlement) has brought a new set of challenges for social work practitioners — particularly in finding the means to provide adequate services for these clients despite legal restrictions. It raises the issue of needed advocacy for this vulnerable population, and the need for practitioners to engage in the political process to ensure that human rights for undocumented persons are protected. Activism and political engagement are mandated by the NASW (1999) *Code of Ethics* to ensure social justice and to protect vulnerable populations. Working toward the enactment of policies that would support, rather than further incriminate this population, would be part of a social justice systems theory approach, as would engagement to assist individual immigrants and families to ensure that they attain health care, housing, employment, and education that are consistent with social justice and with advocacy on behalf of vulnerable and oppressed populations.

The question of how to best serve this population is open given the paucity of social work literature on undocumented immigrants and, as will be detailed later in this chapter, the lack of availability of even basic social services. "Social workers, who function at the edge of social science investigation, policies, politics and practice, often lack information related to what is local about the plight of the migrants they encounter in their communities and what is universal or global about such problems" (Martinez-Brawley & Gualda, 2006, p. 62). Thus, many practitioners may not have adequate means to provide supports for undocumented clients, and may lack sufficient understanding of the social, economic, and political factors that compelled their entrance to the United States without permission.

The terms "illegal immigrant" and "illegal alien" clearly confer criminal status, and without scrutiny, could dissuade social workers from empathy or understanding of the circumstances of those individuals who enter the United States without documentation. This chapter explores the social construction of the concept of illegality — and how this concept has been shaped over more than a century by economics, perceived threats to political stability, and racism. The hope is to support practitioners in understanding immigration laws within the context of American history, and to suggest how new efforts to further criminalize new arrivals might affect social work practice. In collaborative forensic practice, social workers should be aware of the legal and political issues relevant to undocumented immigrants, and be prepared to collaborate with immigration attorneys, tenant's rights organizations, health care professionals, and a variety of activist organizations now working on both national and local levels to advocate for immigrants or for specific ethnic groups. In the following sections, a brief history of immigration laws will be used to illustrate how economic and political considerations shape policy and sort groups into categories of acceptable (legal) immigrants, as compared to those deemed unworthy of entrance to the United States (illegal immigrants).

Exclusion, Economics, and Race

The history of immigration to the United States is one that cannot be viewed without consideration of economics, exclusion, fear, and race. This section presents a brief overview of American efforts to contain immigration, and in particular, to restrict access to residence and work depending on certain social and economic factors. The process of immigration, and the question of whether to accept certain groups into the United States, has never been one that is racially neutral (Gyory, 1998; Johnson, 1998). Instead, at various points in U.S. history, certain non-White groups have been singled out for exclusion from legal entrance.

Late 19th Century: Asian Exclusion

Immigration to the United States in the 19th century has been well chronicled, with historians describing the arrival of millions of Europeans to port cities and the contribution of these immigrants to the nation's developing industrial base. Though Chinese laborers were initially seen as necessary for the construction of railroads in the western United States, an economic depression in the 1870s sparked fears of lost jobs for White Americans, and politicians responded with incendiary speeches labeling Chinese immigrants as vicious, disease-ridden, and in one case, compared communities of new arrivals from China to "kennels of mongrel dogs" (Gyory, 1998, p. 5). Thus, in an effort to halt the flow of immigration from China, the nation adopted the first Chinese exclusion laws beginning in 1882, thus establishing the idea that the act of entering the United States could be defined as illegal (Ryo, 2006).

> *Fears of economic competition from Chinese laborers were amplified by the prevailing notion that the Chinese were racially inferior and inherently ....Chinese immigrants were often depicted as wily and devious creatures, whose growing "monopoly" over certain businesses and willingness to work for low wages put white workers out of their jobs. (Ryo, p. 112)*

20th-Century Immigration Quotas

Though millions of new arrivals continued to be processed through such receiving centers as Ellis Island, with the Chinese exclusion laws the United States had taken its first steps toward limiting immigration— thus creating the concept that immigrants could be labeled as "illegal." Newspaper columnists and politicians regularly engaged in hand-wringing over the "quality" of new arrivals, complaining that the latest waves of immigrants were mentally inferior, politically seditious, prone to criminality, or carriers of infectious disease. And race continued to be an underlying concern in all regulations of immigration. The restrictions against Chinese were expanded to all Asians with new legislation in 1917. This was followed by legislation in 1924 that set strict quotas on immigration which ensured that only 15% of immigrants would be of non-northern–European origin—a policy change that would ensure that admission to the United States would virtually be limited to Whites (Johnson, 1998).

The quota system of 1924 eventually served to limit immigration by Italians, Hungarians, and Greeks, as well as Asians and Mexicans. It was finally repealed with the Immigration Act of 1965 though it can be argued that Whites still continue to be favored under certain policies, including bills passed in the 1990s that eased immigration restrictions for Irish and Poles in particular (Johnson, 1998).

Temporary Workers From Mexico

As noted earlier, decisions about who can enter the United States to work and live —and under what conditions—have varied historically according to social and economic conditions. At certain junctures in history, U.S. policy has loosened restrictions to allow temporary workers to migrate to ease shortages of unskilled labor. In the late 19th century, the southwestern United States relied heavily on Mexicans to provide labor for mining, agriculture, and ranching; Mexico was an easy source of unskilled labor because of its proximity, and thus movement across the border was basically unrestricted (DeGenova, 2004). In El Paso, Texas, Mexicans crossing the bridge to work were first required to endure a "cleaning process" supposedly instituted to prevent disease. Mexicans were doused with a caustic combination of soap and kerosene before being allowed to proceed further into the United States. Though new arrivals at Ellis Island were subject to medical examination, they were not subject to compulsory cleaning with kerosene. Historians have argued that Mexicans were singled out because of racial prejudices associating brown skin with dirt and disease (DeLeon, 1983; Markel & Stern, 1999).

With the Great Depression of the 1930s resulting in severe economic deprivation, U.S. immigration policy shifted again. Mexican labor was not needed, and Mexicans were no longer wanted.

> *The more plainly racist character of Mexican illegalization and deportability became abundantly manifest. Mexican migrants and US-born Mexican citizens alike were systematically excluded from employment.... Notably, Mexicans were expelled with no regard to legal residence or US citizenship or even birth in the US — simply for being "Mexicans."* (DeGenova, p. 164)

In the frenzy to move people of Mexican origin south of the border, authorities often were not careful to delineate citizenship or residency status. Thus, children born in the United States—who were therefore citizens—were deported to Mexico with their parents. Mexicans who had obtained permanent residency and even U.S. citizens of Mexican descent were sent south of the border (DeGenova).

But World War II brought a need for low-cost Mexican labor to the United States to support agricultural production, particularly harvesting crops—jobs that would have been performed by Americans who were instead overseas for the war effort. Thus, 4.5 million Mexicans were recruited as convenient, temporary laborers in the now infamous Bracero program, characterized by exploitation and often brutal working conditions (Mize, 2006). Though an agreement between the governments of Mexico and the United States was supposed to guarantee the minimum agricultural wage paid to Americans, veterans of the Bracero program have described erratic hours of employment, payment according to production (piece work), as well as being denied adequate water and food (Mize). Some had costs for such items as use of blankets at night deducted from their pay. Piece work meant lower pay when crops were damaged by insects or mold (Mize).

Faced with such dire working conditions, some migrants left the Bracero employers and sought better employment in the United States by their own means. As the numbers of unauthorized migrants from Mexico escalated, so did antimigrant sentiment. Newspapers in Texas blamed undocumented Mexicans for crime and for driving down wages for American workers (Handbook of Texas, n.d.). In 1954, the U.S. government launched "Operation Wetback," a mass military seizure of undocumented workers who were deported by train, bus, and ship to various points in Mexico. Though "Operation Wetback" targeted Mexicans and was executed primarily in the southwestern United States, it can also be argued to be another consequence of fears and assumptions about the effects of immigration on the nation's economy, and the quality of life of its citizens.

At least since the 1880s, immigrants have been assumed to take jobs away from and to lower wages of native workers, to add to the poverty population, to compete for education, health and social services. Negative feelings were reinvigorated as successive new waves arrived—first the Irish, then the Italians, then Mexicans. (Epenshade, 1995, p. 201)

Recent political discourse has created an atmosphere of hostility and fear surrounding undocumented immigrants, including those from Mexico. During several segments on his hour-long CNN television show, populist pundit Lou Dobbs asserted that illegal immigrants have been responsible for 7,000 cases of leprosy in the United States over a 3-year period. In fact, The Centers for Disease Control and Prevention (CDC) reports that the number of leprosy cases diagnosed in the United States peaked at 361 in 1985 ("Center Urges CNN," 2007). "People who want to reform immigration by putting America in lockdown have not been shy about using fear and revulsion to get their point across. Illegal immigrants, they say, are invading the country to reconquer it, to erode our Anglo-Saxon culture and to make us all sick" (Downes, 2007, Para 1.).

Economics, Social Policy, and Recent Immigration

As has been noted in discussions of forensic social work, laws and the policies that derive from them should be consonant with the values of social justice that are the foundation of the profession. In this section, trade and economic policies will be outlined briefly so that this key piece of the social justice system can be better understood by social workers attempting to intervene on behalf of undocumented immigrants. Whether trying to link with an immigration attorney to assist him or her in becoming a legal/documented immigrant, or organizing undocumented tenants to protest discriminatory local ordinances, social justice forensic practice should include knowledge of recent policies that have contributed to the widely publicized wave of illegal immigration. That is because, as noted previously, a practitioner must be knowledgeable regarding the laws that shape each client's social justice system.

The policies in question include the North American Free Trade Agreement, the Central American Free Trade Agreement, and the decision of the United States to become part of the World Trade Organization. These treaties and organizations were developed to abet the flow of capital and resources across borders and to enhance the profits of large corporate economic interests (Fernandez-Kelly & Massey, 2007). Social workers also need to be aware that the recent influx of migrants from Mexico and other nations is a direct consequence of economic policies and programs that have been embraced by the United States, particularly the North America Free Trade Agreement (NAFTA), which has led to both the privatization of Mexico's collective farms and the loss of agricultural subsidies, forcing many to seek opportunities north of the border (Fernandez-Kelly & Massey).

Despite the increasing militarization of the border between the United States and Mexico, the flow of people hoping to work here has continued to escalate, with some demographers estimating that close to 5 million Mexicans entered the United States in the 1990s, with about 85% arriving without documentation (Fix & Passel, 2002).

The flow of Mexican migrants, in particular, has been abetted by changes in policy designed to benefit global, transnational countries as part of an economic movement known as neoliberalism in which the role of government is to be lessened, and the social welfare state virtually eradicated in favor of privatization and the deregulation of business interests. Hoping to enhance profits by expansion of markets and lowering production costs (which includes lowering wages), business interests have advocated worldwide for expansion of trade across borders globally, and for the establishment of manufacturing plants in developing nations to ensure a ready supply of low-wage labor.

Neoliberalist economics have led to establishment of such treaties as NAFTA and the Central American Free Trade Agreement. Treaties such NAFTA were designed to reduce or eliminate restrictions on the movement of capital and resources across borders, and have been critical factors in compelling Mexican migration (Aguirre & Reese, 2004). Maquiladoras, or manufacturing plants owned by American interests, were supposed to help build the Mexican economy by increasing employment rates and reducing poverty. Given that American business profits are enhanced when the peso is devalued against the dollar, Mexican workers have been forced to contend with a more depressed economy (Aguirre & Reese).

> The engine driving the global economy is predicated on a system in which profits are tied to low wages and poor working conditions for labor… in which worker rights and working conditions are constrained by the pursuit of profit. (Aguirre & Reese, p. 2)

Neoliberalism has led to the scaling back of the welfare state, particularly in the United States, a trend that has emerged in the service of capital's growing need for low-wage laborers, or even marginalized laborers—those workers who can only secure part-time or day-to-day unskilled jobs (Piven, 2001). As has been argued by Piven (2001), business interests have mobilized to promote self-serving policies, including reductions in the number of workers covered by unemployment insurance benefits, decertification of unions, and increased reliance on contingent workers. Business interests have capitalized on a weakened labor movement, the willingness of political parties to support corporate interests, and an ideological embrace of markets and individualism; thus, Mexican migrants who cross the border to work in the United States can find a niche in the American economy, filling those slots for part-time, unskilled, and temporary labor. Migrant earnings are then spent, in part, in the United States on such costs as transportation, housing, and food, though much of their earnings are sent home as "remittances," or Migradólares (migrant dollars) (Hernandez & Coutin, 2006).

Thus, in the engagement of political awareness and activism that is mandated by the National Association of Social Workers, practitioners should be aware of the economic forces propelling mass migration. Understanding that migration is a response to economic deprivation and the need for a living wage is critical when migrants themselves are being labeled "illegal" and thus are designated by current law as having engaged in a criminal act.

Practice Implications

In their work with immigrants, social workers must be equipped with legal knowledge pertinent to all levels of the social justice system. At the national level, social workers must be prepared to advocate for basic human rights in an era in which some lawmakers are pressing to further criminalize this vulnerable population. In 2005, the U.S. House of Representatives voted in favor of a bill sponsored by James Sensenbrenner (R-FL.) that, had it won approval by the Senate and President, would have delineated entrance to the U.S. without a visa as an "aggravated felony" and mandated imprisonment of undocumented migrants (Jonas, 2006). At the time of this writing, the Senate was weighing a number of immigration bills, including one that could offer pathways for undocumented immigrants to become legal residents, though other less benign proposals could subject undocumented immigrants to criminal penalties for assisting family or friends to immigrate illegally. Thus, social workers engaged in forensic social justice practice would need to be knowledgeable about these developments and be prepared to advocate accordingly.

Congress has also weighed bills to impose criminal penalties on Americans who assist undocumented immigrants, including the 2005 Sensenbrenner Bill, which won approval in the House of Representatives. Should a similar bill one day receive the support of the Senate and President, social workers could be prosecuted for the routine execution of those tasks historically associated with the profession's mission, such as helping vulnerable individuals secure social services, housing, and health care. As mandated by the NASW *Code of Ethics*, social workers must engage in political activism and should maintain awareness of social and political issues as they relate to social justice.

Though this law has not passed at the federal level, social workers practicing in Arizona have been required since 2004 to check the legal status of individuals prior to providing services regarded as public benefits (Furman, Langer, Sanchez & Negi, 2007). Further, social workers, nurses, physicians, and others are also mandated under the law to report any undocumented immigrant to authorities. Failure to comply with the law can result in a fine and/or incarceration. A qualitative study of 51 master's degree social work students and 27 bachelor's degree social work students found that some students were willing to follow the law and report undocumented immigrants to authorities, despite the fact that compliance puts practitioners at squarely at odds with the NASW *Code of Ethics* mandating provision to all vulnerable populations (Furman et al.). Others stated they would be willing to provide services in defiance of the law, whereas some discussed ways in which they might make referrals and circumvent the law. Furman and colleagues (2007) argued that as more laws are passed to criminalize immigrants and the people who assist them, social workers may face lower levels of job satisfaction as they are pressed to devise both legal and illegal strategies to assist this population or to comply with the law and practice unethically.

In 2001, the state of Arizona rescinded the right of undocumented persons to receive dialysis, a life-sustaining procedure, in medical nephrology units. Kay Smith, a social worker, organized other nephrology social workers, Southern Arizona Legal Aid, the Arizona Kidney Foundation, the William Morris Foundation for Human Rights, and Senator John McCain (R-AZ) to fight the policy (NASW, 2003).

At the local level, the vulnerability of undocumented migrants has been exacerbated by antiimmigration sentiments in some communities, including hate crimes such as assaults, shootings, and the firebombing of a Mexican family's home in Farmingville, NY (Leuck, 2003). There are visible antiimmigrant groups such as The Minutemen—whose stated goal is to halt migration at the Mexican border and to intimidate migrants in other areas. Town governments across the country have instituted initiatives to discourage migrant residency by passing laws criminalizing the rental of housing to people who cannot prove legal residency. Some towns, including Hazleton, PA, have adopted new housing codes forbidding rentals to undocumented tenants, a policy designed to force them to leave the area or face homelessness. Other municipalities have adopted ordinances restricting day laborers—many of whom are Mexican or from other Central American countries—from congregating in certain areas. Zealous enforcement of traffic laws is meant to deter contractors from picking up prospective workers (Jonas, 2006).

VOICES FROM THE FIELD

Rebecca Bowman-Rivas, MSW, LCSW-C,

Clinic Counselor & Program Manager, The Law & Social Services Program, University of Maryland Clinical Law Office and Partner/Owner, Bowman-Rivas Consulting, LLC

Agency Setting

University of Maryland–Baltimore (UMB) Clinical Law Office— The Law & Social Services Program

The Law & Social Work Services Program is a part of the University of Maryland School of Law's clinical office. I supervise a group of five to eight graduate social work students who provide a variety of services to clients who are receiving pro-bono assistance from the law students, who are supervised by Law School faculty. The students work together to provide holistic services to our clients. The Clinical Law Office is comprised of smaller "clinics," approximately 20 to 25 choices are available each year. Clinical offerings include an Innocence Project, Immigration Clinic, Prisoner Re-Entry Program, HIV/AIDS & Child Welfare Clinic, Juvenile Advocacy, and many others. Subsequently, the social work students have the opportunity to work with a diverse population in need of a wide variety of services.

Bowman-Rivas Consulting, LLC

This is a private practice owned by me and my husband, who is also a forensic social worker. We provide mitigation, alternative sentencing, release planning, and expert testimony in capital and noncapital cases. We also assist with Dorsey hearings and with discharge planning for NCR clients who are court-released. We contract with state and federal public defenders, courts, private nonprofits, and private attorneys.

Practice Responsibilities

At the Law Clinic I am responsible for supervising social work graduate students who are in field placements, as well as supervising summer assistants. I also provide direct services to some clients, and cover the clinic when students are not available. My students have several interdisciplinary bridge classes with various law clinics, with presentations and discussions relevant to the needs of shared clients. I am occasionally asked by law professors to present various topics to their classes. I also testify in court and at administrative hearings for clients. I maintain statistics and program information, assist with grant writing, and present to current and potential funding organizations.

For the consulting business, I interview clients and collaterals in jails, prisons, homes, and other settings; locate and review records; provide written and oral reports to the attorneys, and/or written and oral testimony in hearings. In some cases I assist with strategy and presentation and the identification of additional expert witnesses. In others, I develop release or community safety plans.

Expertise Required

I believe that a master's in social work and advanced/clinical licensure are the minimal requirements for what I do, in both positions. Experience working with high-risk, potentially violent individuals is essential, as is a good background in psychopathology, experience working with substance-abusing populations, and with survivors of trauma. Knowledge of court procedures, the correctional and mental health systems, and local resources is very helpful.

Practice Challenges

Working with attorneys can be challenging. Although we share some common goals and values, our approaches can be very different, as lawyers are accustomed to an adversarial system, and social workers *generally* tend to seek cooperative and peaceful resolutions.

More and more I'm finding that the resources that people desperately need simply don't exist. Waiting lists are extensive and the services that are actually provided are inadequate.

Common Legal and/or Ethical Issues

As a continuation of the challenges noted previously, the differences between confidentiality and attorney–client privilege are substantial. Conflicts regarding our reporting requirements for child/elder abuse or risk of harm to self or others can become a major issue.

As someone who specializes in defense-based advocacy, I think a great deal about the dual responsibilities—to the client and to public safety. There can be substantial pressure to opine or take action in a way that supports the attorney's formulation of the case, even if it goes against one's clinical judgment.

In work with involuntary clients, power issues become a major concern.

Brief Description of Collaborative Activities With Professionals and/or Other Stakeholders

As described in other sections, I work with attorneys on a daily basis, in a number of different capacities. I have contact with other professionals, including doctors, other health/mental health professionals, and educators. I participate in various special projects with systems including schools, prisons, courts, and community organizations. I participate in fundraising and present to potential and existing funding groups. I do presentations and trainings for various conferences and forums.

Case Study

Dedicated activists and social workers have devised ways to support this population despite legal barriers. The following case example demonstrates how activists in a suburban town assisted undocumented Mexican workers at both the mezzo and micro level. Though the case example focuses on work by activists, the tasks described here could be addressed by social workers and nonprofit organizations.

Juan is a 29-year-old father of two who lived in Chiapas, a poor state at the southern tip of Mexico. His wife is 27. Juan and his wife grow a variety of crops but in recent years there have been no commercial buyers for their products. There is no money for clothing, medical care, agricultural equipment, seed, or home repairs. His children are ages 3 and 5.

Juan had been encouraged to emigrate by his older cousins. Despite the dangers of crossing the border, including the risk of death by hyperthermia or gang violence, Juan borrowed $2,000 from a local man who had connections to an organized crime syndicate in Mexico. The man arranged for Juan's trip across the desert. Juan's family was distraught about his leaving. The family discussed the idea of crossing together but agreed the risks with small children were too great.

Juan arrived in a suburban town in New Jersey 2 weeks after leaving Chiapas. He found a two-bedroom apartment shared by six other undocumented Mexican men. Once as the men watched late-night television, they were disturbed by a knock at the door. Juan stood up and answered as the banging became more insistent. He opened the door to find an armed police officer and a man who, in broken Spanish, introduced himself as a housing inspector. The inspector issued each of the men tickets for $250 for overcrowding. They were told that four men must vacate the premises within a month or face more fines.

Later that month, Juan was hired from a street corner by a man who needed workers to dig ditches, move rocks, and plant trees. Juan worked for 3 days. At the end of the third day, he and two other Spanish-speaking, undocumented workers waited for 3 hours for the contractor to return to pick them up from the worksite. The contractor never arrived, so the men walked 3 miles back to town. They were never paid.

Juan learned from an acquaintance about an activist group in the town that was assisting the burgeoning population of *jornaleros*—day laborers. Some of the activists knew Spanish. Juan met an activist, Mary, a town resident who had attended college in Mexico 30 years before. Mary heard Juan's story about the housing inspection ticket and the contractor who failed to pay him for 3 days work. Juan described the housing inspection as terrifying. He thought the police were there to arrest the men or to detain them for deportation. Having been raised in Mexico, Juan had grown to fear police as corrupt and brutal.

Mary informed Juan of his rights: Though he was undocumented, he had a right to file a complaint for theft of wages through the state Department of Labor. She helped him complete the forms after obtaining Juan's description of the man who hired him and the man's truck. Mary recognized the man as a contractor who had been the subject of prior wage-theft complaints. Using her contacts with sympathetic attorneys, Mary was able to assist Juan in filing suit to recoup wages from the employer.

In addition, Mary referred Juan and other men to a local church soup kitchen that served meals at noon each day. By partnering with another church in the area, Mary organized a successful donation drive for work clothes: Men who had crossed the desert from Mexico typically arrived without work boots, gloves, or thermal undergarments. Sympathetic residents donated hundreds of these items to help the men engage in manual labor.

After learning that hundreds of men had been issued tickets in late-night raids by town police and housing inspectors, Mary and other activists contacted a nationally renowned civil rights law firm, which agreed to assist. Legal assistants interviewed Juan about the night his apartment was raided. The firm filed a class-action suit in federal court and won a restraining order against the town. Recognizing that armed, uniformed officers were being used in a deliberate effort to intimidate Mexican residents, the judge ordered that the town cease sending police to housing inspections. The town was also ordered to stop conducting late-night inspections.

Juan described feeling a sense of relief in knowing that he could recoup wages and hold contractors accountable for pay, even despite his undocumented status. He remained in the suburban town several years, sharing an apartment with other men, and sending money home to Chiapas. He eventually began studying English 2 nights a week at a local church where activists had arranged to offer lessons donated by literacy volunteers.

Practice with undocumented immigrants necessitates an understanding of the legal restrictions and deprivation of fundamental rights to social services that are a fact of life for this vulnerable population. It is their vulnerability as a source of low-paid labor that is a distinguishing feature for this population. This fact should be kept in mind in interventions with undocumented migrants, who are aware of the risks of interactions with authorities. "The legal production of 'illegality' provides an apparatus for sustaining Mexican migrants' vulnerability and tractability—as workers—whose labor-power, inasmuch as it is deportable, becomes an eminently disposable commodity" (DeGonova, 2004, p. 161).

This vulnerability is exacerbated by the lack of rights to social service. When the Personal Responsibility and Work Opportunity Reconciliation Act ("welfare reform") was passed in 1996, it included a provision denying cash Food Stamps and Social Security income to all immigrants, including those who are in the country legally (Fix & Passel, 2002). State governments are permitted to offer legal immigrants cash assistance and Medicaid, but undocumented immigrants are barred from receipt of all social services except those deemed necessary to preserve life and safety (Fix & Passel).

Without adequate resources or means to serve this population, social workers must engage in the profession's historic mandate to advocate for changes in laws and policies that deny social justice. Social workers should also recognize that work with this population necessitates viewing the profession, and its mission, with a broader lens than many roles presently embraced by many in the profession. Though some undocumented immigrants may well need the support/assistance of clinicians, hospital social workers, and the child welfare system, many may be faced with needs such as securing housing, organizing with others to advocate for changes in immigration policy, and/or assistance in filing work-related grievances. In one New Jersey community, activists meet with migrants daily as they wait on street corners hoping to be hired by contractors (Cleaveland & Kelly, 2007). Activists teach English as well as fill out and submit pay-complaint forms to the State of New Jersey Department of Labor. Though undocumented immigrants are not legally entitled to work, they are eligible to pursue pay owed them by unscrupulous contractors—some of whom pick up day laborers on street corners, only to deny them pay at the end of the day. These same activists in New Jersey have worked with coalitions of church leaders to provide immigrants with emergency access to food, shelter, and clothing—needs that can become acute given that they are not entitled to work legally.

The National Association for Social Workers (2006) released a statement in support of upholding certain rights for undocumented immigrants that included a "commitment to basic human rights and civil rights for all immigrants regardless of legal status," elimination of antiimmigrant discrimination and racism in employment practices, humanitarian measures and enforcement to prevent human trafficking, and restoration of a safety net of social and medical service for legal immigrants who meet "reasonable length of residence provisions." Though the final provision calling for "reasonable length of residence" begs definition and clarity, and could conceivably uphold denial of services for some, the spirit of the statement—and its support of the rights of all people to medical and social services—could serve as a starting point of advocacy for the profession.

Summary and Conclusions

Effective practice with undocumented immigrants requires that social workers understand the legal restrictions and deprivation of fundamental rights to social services that are a part of daily life for this vulnerable population. Workers who seek to practice effectively with undocumented immigrants must be willing to view the profession through a broad lens that includes advocacy and activism, particularly to challenge repressive national, state, and local legislation. Besides organizing with activists to advocate for changes in immigration policy to uphold human rights, social workers should be prepared to help provide undocumented immigrants with linkages to supportive attorneys to contest discrimination in housing or the withholding of pay by exploitive employers. Given that many towns, such as Hazleton, PA, are now attempting to force immigrants out by using restrictive ordinances described in the previous section, social workers should be prepared to help undocumented immigrants secure shelter. Again, linkages to organizations or faith groups could be crucial in assisting immigrants to receive emergency access to food, shelter, and clothing.

Unfortunately, as of 2009 many social workers are without adequate means or resources to provide support for undocumented clients, and in the worst cases, may be penalized in their efforts to execute their duties in accordance with the *Code of Ethics*. Further, many practitioners may lack sufficient understanding of the social, economic, and political factors that have compelled so many to enter the United States without legal sanction. With the current debate over immigration producing regulations at the local and state levels that are hostile to both undocumented clients and the practitioners who serve them, many social workers may be uncertain as to how they may be able to support these clients and which resources might be available. Thus, both undocumented individuals and practitioners are working in an atmosphere that is uncertain at best and hostile at worse.

> *The profession of social work should then begin to seriously consider the role of immigration policy and its effect on social service delivery through critical assessment of immigration policy as well as lobbying for or against proposed immigration laws that may negatively affect service delivery to clients. (Furman et al., 2007, p. 143)*

To practice ethically, social work practitioners need to actively engage in advocacy for this vulnerable population to ensure that basic needs for medical and social services can be met. The profession's historic legacy and *Code of Ethics* mandate that social workers actively engage in the political process to ensure that that the human rights of all vulnerable populations are protected, including those who are presently undocumented.

References

Aguirre, A., & Reese, E. (2004). Introduction: The challenges of globalization for workers: Transnational and transborder issues. *Social Justice, 31*(3), 1–20.

Center urges CNN to retract false reporting by Lou Dobbs. (2007, May 9). Southern Poverty Law Center. Retrieved July 1, 2007, from http://www.splcenter.org/news/item.jsp?aid=254

Cleaveland, C., & Kelly, L. (2007, August). *Shared social space and strategies to find work: An exploratory study of Mexican day laborers in Freehold, N.J.* Proceedings of the American Sociological Association Annual Meeting, New York, NY.

DeGenova, N. (2004). The legal production of Mexican/migrant illegality. *Latino Studies, 2*, 160–185.

De Leon, A. (1983). *They called them greasers.* Austin, TX: University of Texas Press.

Downes, L. (2007, June 17). When demagogues play the leprosy card, watch out. *New York Times.* Retrieved June 30, 2007, from http://www.nytimes.com/

Epenshade, T. J. (1995). Unauthorized immigration to the United States. *Annual Review of Sociology, 21*, 195–216.

Fernandez-Kelly, P., & Massey, D. S. (2007). Borders for whom? The role of NAFTA in Mexican-U.S. migration. *The Annals of the American Academy of Political and Social Science, 610*(1), 98–118.

Fix, M., & Passel, J. (2002). The scope and impact of welfare reform's immigrant provisions. In *Assessing the new federalism: An Urban Institute program to assess changing social policies.* Washington, DC: The Urban Institute.

Furman, R., Langer, C. L., Sanchez, T. W., & Negi, N. J. (2007). A qualitative study of immigration policy and practice dilemmas for social work students. *Journal of Social Work Education, 43*(1), 1–12.

Gyory, A. (1998). *Closing the gate: Race, politics and the Chinese Exclusion Act.* Chapel Hill, NC: University of North Carolina Press.

Handbook of Texas online: Operation Wetback. (n.d.) The University of Texas, Texas State Historical Association and General Libraries at UT, Austin. Retrieved July 1, 2007, from www.tsha.utexas.edu/handbook/online/

Hernandez, E., & Coutin, S. B. (2006). Remitting subjects: Migrants, money and states. *Economy and Society, 35*, 185–208.

Hospital social worker, Kay Smith, recognized as the NASW Social Worker of the Year 2003. (2003, July 2). *National Association of Social Workers.* Retrieved July 2, 2007, from http://www.socialworkers.org/pressroom/2003/070103_swoty.asp

Johnson, K. R. (1998). Race, the immigration laws, and domestic race relations: A "magic mirror" into the heart of darkness. *Indiana Law Journal, 73,* 1111–1159.

Jonas, S. (2006). Reflections on the great immigration battle of 2006 and the future of the Americas. *Social Justice, 33*(1), 6–20.

Leuck, T. (2003, July 13). New York: Farmingville: Arrests in firebombing. *New York Times.* Retrieved September 19, 2007, from topics.nytimes.com/top/reference/timestopics/subjects/i/immigration_and_ref

Markel, H., & Stern, A. M. (1999). Which face? Whose nation? Immigration, public health, and the construction of disease at America's ports and borders. *American Behavioral Scientist, 42,* 1314–1331.

Martinez-Brawley, E., & Gualda, E. (2006). US/Spanish comparisons on temporary immigrant workers: Implications for policy development and community practice. *European Journal of Social Work, 9*(1), 59–84.

Mize, R. L. (2006). Mexican contract workers and the U.S. capitalist agricultural labor process: The formative era, 1942–1964. *Rural Sociology, 71*(1), 85–108.

National Association of Social Workers. (1999). *Code of ethics.* Retrieved September 19, 2007, from www.socialworkers.org/pubs/code/code.asp

NASW. (2003). *Hospital social worker, Kay Smith, recognized as the NASW social worker of the year 2003.* Retrieved March 7, 2007, from http://www.socialworkers.org/pressroom/2003/070103_swoty.asp?print=1

National Association of Social Workers. (2006). Immigrants and refugees. In *Social work speaks abstracts.* Retrieved September 19, 2007, from www.socialworkers.org/resources/abstracts/abstracts/immigrants.asp

Piven, F. (2001). Globalization, American politics, and welfare policy. *Annals of the American Academy of Political and Social Science, 577,* 26–37.

Ryo, E. (2006). Through the back door: Applying theories of legal compliance to illegal immigration during the Chinese Exclusion Era. *Law & Social Inquiry, 31*(1), 109–146.

Welch, M. (2003). Ironies of social control and the criminalization of immigrants. *Crime, Law and Social Change, 39,* 319–337.

Collaborative Forensic Social Work With Refugees

25

Mary Kay Jou
Leah K. Lazzaro

This chapter seeks to answer the following questions: Who are the refugees, the asylum seekers, and victims of human trafficking? How do they come to the United States? What are the legal processes they must go through? What do social workers need to know when working with these clients? Why are they being included in a textbook about forensic social work?

As the United States continues its heated political debate regarding the current immigration situation, this chapter focuses on a group of immigrants who are usually neither included nor mentioned in the discussion. Refugees/asylees, asylum seekers, and victims of human trafficking comprise a large portion of the U.S. immigrant population.

This chapter is divided into three different sections. The first section focuses on the specific needs facing refugees and asylum seekers, as well as the immigration detention system and recent immigration policies affecting the asylum process. The similarities and differences found when working with refugees and asylum seekers also are discussed. The next section reviews issues related to victims of human trafficking and the specific policies and practices in place for this vulnerable population. The chapter concludes with practical information for social workers about what to expect when working with refugees, asylum seekers, and victims of human trafficking, underscoring the importance of collaborating with both the legal system and law enforcement in the process.

Refugees and Asylees

Refugees constitute one type of immigrant population that enters the United States. A refugee is defined in the Immigration and Nationality Act (INA) as "an alien outside the United States who is unable or unwilling to return to his or her country of origin because of persecution or a well-founded fear of persecution on account of race, religion, nationality, membership in a particular social group, or political opinion" (Jefferys, 2006, p. 1). Thus, refugees receive their legal status before arriving in the United States. They land at the airport with proper documentation and are already linked with a refugee resettlement agency that is expecting them. The only time a refugee would interact with law enforcement is if they are convicted of a crime while in the United States. In such a case, the refugee goes through the same process as an American citizen and does time in a prison facility. However, for refugees, once their sentence for the crime has been completed, instead of being released, they will be transferred to the United States Immigration and Customs Enforcement (ICE, the former INS), where they could possibly be held in immigration detention indefinitely. This is true for immigrants of any status.

Asylum seekers constitute another special population of U.S. immigrants. Asylum seekers must meet the same criteria as refugees. The legal term for an asylum seeker who has been granted asylum is "asylee." Asylees have the same rights as refugees. The only difference between a refugee and an asylee is the person's geographical location at the time of application. A refugee is located outside of the United States at the time of application and an asylum seeker is located in the United States or at a port of entry (Jefferys, 2006).

An individual from another country seeking asylum in the United States needs to complete an asylum application. There are two forms of asylum applications: affirmative and defensive (Wasem, 2007). The type of application that an asylum seeker will complete depends on whether or not he or she arrived in the United States with proper documents. An affirmative asylum seeker enters with a valid visa. On arrival at a U.S. border this individual immediately interacts with our law enforcement system. At the port of entry, an Immigration and Customs Enforcement officer interviews him or her while verifying his or her documents. Once it is found that the visa is valid, he or she is cleared by the ICE officer and is not detained. He or she then has 1 year from the date of entry to apply for asylum. If the year passes without an application being filed, that asylum seeker is no longer eligible to apply for asylum and is deportable (Wasem, 2007).

In contrast, a defensive asylum seeker is held in one of the immigration detention centers around the country. He or she arrives without proper documentation. The ICE officer then begins what is known as a "credible fear" interview with the asylum seeker to verify whether or not the individual has a valid claim for asylum (Knight, 2001; Wasem, 2007). He or she must prove to the ICE officer that he or she meets the definition of a refugee and is afraid to go back to his or her country for fear of persecution. If the individual passes the credible-fear interview, and the ICE officer deems him or her a valid asylum seeker, the individual is immediately hand-cuffed, shackled, and brought to an immigration detention center where he or she will be held until asylum is granted. If there are no beds available at the detention center, he or she will be held in a local county jail. An application for asylum filed by an immigration detainee is called a defensive asylum application (Wasem, 2007).

For example, a young woman from Somalia arrives in the United States with a valid tourist visa. She has no trouble at the airport and is staying with friends. Her friends link her to a lawyer who can help her apply for asylum. She fled female genital mutilation and a forced marriage. Her application is considered affirmative.

On the other hand, an older man from Tibet arrives in the United States. On arrival at the airport the ICE officer realizes that he does not have proper documentation. In talking with the man the officer concludes that he has been persecuted because of his membership in a specific religious group. The man has also stated that he is afraid to go home. The ICE officer immediately calls security and the man is sent to the nearest immigration detention center. His application process is considered defensive.

Scope of the Problem

For successful collaborative forensic social work practice with refugees, one must understand the social and political forces that drive resettlement admissions. An American political response to refugee crises around the world is relatively new. It dates back to the refugee crisis in Europe following World War II. Since then, the United States has accepted more refugees than any other country. "Between 1946 and 1994 the US allowed almost 3 million refugees and other foreigners seeking protection access to permanent residence" (Gibney, 2004, p. 132). More than two thirds of these refugees were from Communist countries. It is important to remember that refugee work is political and changing political climates affect social work practice. Thus, refugee admissions have declined significantly since 2001. In 2002, fewer than 29,000 refugees were admitted in the United States. This is down significantly from the average refugee admissions of almost 76,000 annually from 1996 to 2001 (Martin, 2005). The next section documents the historical trends of U.S. policies on refugees and asylum seekers in the United States (see Table 25.1).

Brief History of Refugee / Asylum Policy

Displaced Persons Act of 1948

Refugee and asylum policy in the United States began in 1948 with the passing of the Displaced Persons Act (DPA) of 1948. This was a "controversial response to the plight of millions of European refugees who had nowhere to turn after World War II" (Waibsnaider, 2006, p. 395).

Immigration Act of 1965

The next major immigration policy, The Immigration Act of 1965, was passed within a year of the passing of the Civil Rights Act of 1964. It was the first time that U.S. borders were opened to non-European immigrants on a large scale.

25.1   Immigration and Related Policies

Policy	Year	Implication
Alien Registration Act of 1940	1940	Undocumented immigrants could obtain permanent residence by showing that deportation would result in extreme hardship.
Displaced Persons Act of 1948	1948	Allowed European refugees to enter United States.
United Nations Refugee Convention	1951	Provides protection to displaced people who cross country borders and become refugees.
Immigration Act of 1965	1965	First legislation to allow non-European refugees to enter the U.S., which included preference for Middle Eastern and Communist countries.
Refugee Act of 1980	1980	Included the formal definition of "refugee" adopted from the 1951 United Nations. The goal was to neutralize refugee resettlement.
Illegal Immigration Reform and Immigration Responsibility Act of 1996	1996	Introduced indefinite detention and expedited removal.
Trafficking Victims Protection Act	2000	Made human trafficking a crime in the United States and provided funding to prevent trafficking, protect victims, and prosecute traffickers.
Uniting and Strengthening America by Providing Appropriate Tools Required to Intercept and Obstruct Terrorism Act (USA PATRIOT Act)	2001	Intended to increase restrictions on asylum and to further criminalize the asylum seekers.
Homeland Security Act of 2002	2002	Functions of the Immigration and Naturalization Service (INS) were transferred to the U.S. Citizenship and Immigration Services (CIS) and the Bureau of Immigration and Customs Enforcement (ICE) in the DHS.
Real ID Act of 2005	2005	Introduced harsher standards for asylum applications.

Refugee Act of 1980

It was not until 1980 that a "neutral" refugee policy was enacted. The United States had recently pulled out of Vietnam partly because of the strong antiwar sentiment and social action. The country was recovering from the turbulent times of the 1960s and 1970s (McKelvey, 1998). The Refugee Act of 1980 was passed with several new stipulations. In this act, the 1951 United Nations definition of a refugee was adopted as the formal definition for the United States (Barnett, 2002).

Illegal Immigration Reform and Immigration Responsibility Act of 1996

The next wave of sweeping immigration policy changes came in 1996 with the passing of the Illegal Immigration Reform and Immigration Responsibility Act (IIRIRA). The Clinton administration signed into legislation a change in policy indicating that asylum seekers would now be indefinitely detained, and immigration detention began to boom (Welch, 2004). Another initiative was also started through the passing of the IIRIRA entitled "expedited removal." In these cases, asylum seekers are turned away at the airport and never enter the country (Barnett, 2002; Welch, 2004). The credible-fear interview that had previously been conducted by a highly trained asylum officer was now being left up to the untrained customs officers at the airport (Crisp, 1997).

Antiterror Legislation as Immigration Policy

This style of defensive immigration reform continued after the 2001 attacks on the World Trade Center. In fact, between September 2001 and December 2003, over 15,000 asylum seekers had been detained. With the lack of detention space, the U.S. government expanded the use of county jail space as holding places (Welch, 2004).

With the passing of the Uniting and Strengthening America by Providing Appropriate Tools Required to Intercept and Obstruct Terrorism Act (USA PATRIOT Act of 2001) in October 2001, several items included in the Act served to increase restrictions on asylum and to further criminalize the asylum seekers (United Nations High Commissioner for Refugees, 2003).

Prior to 2005, there was an annual ceiling of 1,000 persons who could be granted refugee or asylee status under the Coercive Population Control (CPC) provision. The Real ID Act of 2005 (Jefferys, 2006) continued the trend of increasing criminalization and higher standards for asylum applications. The Real ID Act states that asylum seekers are required "to provide documentary, corroborating evidence for their claims" (Immigration Equality, 2005, p. 5).

Current Immigration and Detention Policies

In terms of forensic social work and law enforcement, it is most likely that asylum seekers will find themselves interacting with the newly formed Department of Homeland Security (DHS). Following the attacks on the World Trade Center on September 11, 2001, several intelligence and enforcement agencies were placed under one umbrella. These agencies include: the Federal Bureau of Investigation, the Central Intelligence Agency, and the Immigration and Naturalization Services.

The Department of Homeland Security was created under the Homeland Security Act on March 1, 2003. The DHS is where refugee-protection decisions are made (Human Rights First, 2004). The mission of the DHS from the Title I of the Homeland Security Act of 2002 is to "prevent terrorist attacks within the United States." This was the first time in our country's history that immigration was considered a national security concern linked to terrorism.

Although immigration detention has been used in the United States for many years, it has traditionally been used strictly as a short-term way to verify that an asylum seeker has a valid claim for asylum (Welch, 2004). The longest an asylum seeker would be detained was 48 hours.

With the passing of the IIRIRA in 1996, it became possible to detain asylum seekers indefinitely. They were to be held, not until an application was approved, but until they completed the entire asylum process (Welch, 2004).

In 2005, 53,813 refugees entered the United States and 25,257 individuals were granted asylum. Through the affirmative asylum process, 13,520 were granted asylum and 11,737 were granted asylum defensively. In 2006, detention bed space increased by 6,300 to fund housing for 27,500 immigration detainees. There are approximately 26,000 immigrant detainees housed in 114 federal immigration detention centers or county jails and state prisons awaiting trials (Jefferys, 2006).

Over time, this has led to a trend not only in the decline of successful asylum claims, but also in the number of people seeking asylum. "The total number of persons granted asylum decreased from 27,169 in 2004 to 25,257 in 2005. The number of persons who became asylees affirmatively through USCIS dropped from 14,207 in 2004 to 13,520 in 2005. Likewise, the number of asylees who were granted asylum defensively through an Immigration court (through the Executive Office of Immigration Review or [EOIR]) declined slightly from 12,962 in 2004 to 11,737 in 2005" (Jefferys, 2006, p. 5).

What to Expect When Working With Refugees and Asylum Seekers

To better serve the client, a social worker needs to be aware of the political-asylum process, the role of law enforcement, and immigration detention centers. This section clarifies what it is like to work within the various systems and offers best practices.

The Political-Asylum Process

Some social workers will work with clients who have come to the United States with the hopes of gaining political asylum. Since 2001, with the large backlog in immigration, the length of time an asylum seeker has to wait has gotten longer. Although some clients can be granted asylum within a few months, others have waited several years (Human Rights First, 2003). Many clients experience an increased level of fear, anxiety, and depression as the court date approaches. Court dates get delayed because of a lack of an interpreter or because other cases took longer than expected. Each time a court date is delayed, the client may become even more nervous.

Immigration Detention

Social workers who find themselves helping clients who are in immigration custody in a federal detention center will have even more complicated issues. One common tactic that the Immigration and Customs Enforcement use is to periodically move detainees from one facility to another. This is usually done without letting the person's lawyer or family members know (Tasoff & Tasoff, 2007). The organization Physicians for Human Rights (1998) recently conducted a research study on the impact of immigration detention on asylum seekers. Their results showed that the experience of detention negatively affects the asylum seekers' mental health. The conditions immigrants experience in the United States often remind the asylum seekers of the persecution they endured in their own countries at the hands of law enforcement, prison guards, and soldiers.

Law Enforcement

Social workers who are working with refugees and asylum seekers often find that these clients have a very distinct and strong fear of people in authority. In many cases, the clients come from countries where law enforcement agencies, such as the police, were involved in the persecution that they encountered, and which led to their flight to the United States (Pistone, 1998). The first author has noted in several cases that because of the trauma of torture and other forms of persecution at the hands of legitimate authority figures, even the sight of police in uniform or carrying a gun, may trigger an emotional response in the client. It is important that the social worker has a clear understanding of trauma and posttraumatic stress. It has also been noted that the attainment of political asylum has a dramatic healing component. The clients have expressed being reborn. Their demeanor changes and their self-confidence increases dramatically.

Victims of Human Trafficking

The American response to the refugee crises is new and the response to victims of human trafficking is even newer. This next section briefly discusses the problem of human trafficking, the identification of victims, and the need for collaborative practice as a best practice in working with this population.

Scope of the Problem

Human trafficking is a national and international problem with wide implications for the practice of collaborative forensic social work. Trafficking in persons is among the world's fastest growing criminal activities. The Office to Combat and Monitor Trafficking in Persons (2007) reports that annually 600,000 to 800,000 people are trafficked across borders worldwide, with some 14,500 to 17,500 brought into the United States. Other estimates range from 4 to 12 million people held in trafficking at any given time. It is estimated that 80% are women and girls. Human-trafficking victims come to the United States often because of promises made by traffickers of jobs or other opportunities (U.S. Department of State, 2007).

Trafficking Victims Protection Act

Human trafficking became a crime in the United States in 2000 with the passage of the federal Trafficking Victims Protection Act (TVPA). The legislation defines a "severe form of trafficking in persons" as:

> (a) Sex trafficking in which commercial sex act is induced by force, fraud, or coercion, or in which the person induced to perform such act has not attained 18 years of age; or (b) the recruitment, harboring, transportation, provision, or obtaining of a person for labor or services, through the use of force, fraud or coercion for the purpose of subjection to involuntary servitude, peonage, debt bondage, or slavery. (2000, p. 8)

Ralph F. Boyd, Jr., former Assistant Attorney General for Civil Rights simply stated, "trafficking is a form of modern-day slavery" (Boyd, 2001, p. 1). Regardless of what definition is used, human trafficking occurs when individuals are forced to work in a job that they are unable to leave (Human Rights Watch, 2002). Trafficking victims who were not born in the United States may not have legal passports or immigration documents. Often their documents may be held by the traffickers as a means of coercion (Office to Monitor and Combat Trafficking in Persons, 2004).

The TVPA was the first federal legislation with provisions to prevent human trafficking, prosecute traffickers, and provide funding for protection and assistance to victims. The protections it offers are an example of therapeutic jurisprudence. Training and capacity-building of federal and local law enforcement, service providers, and legal service providers have been a primary means for identifying and protecting survivors. However, more work needs to continue as "deportation remains the primary mechanism for dealing with...trafficked persons" (Araujo-Forlot, 2002, p. 13).

Identifying and Working With Victims

People are trafficked into many forms of work including: farm work, construction, factory work, commercial sex work, domestic services, restaurant work, begging, and so on. Oftentimes trafficking victims are forced to work in unregulated industries. This can make it difficult to recognize victims, as they often are reluctant to volunteer information about their abusive situations. To better understand whether a client is a victim of human trafficking, social workers can ask screening questions such as the following: Are you able to leave your work site? Do you have a passport or identification card? If not, is your employer holding your identification? What is your rate of pay and the conditions of your employment? Are they what you expected? Do you fear that something bad will happen to you or your family if you leave your job? (Office to Monitor and Combat Trafficking in Persons, 2004).

Once a client is identified as a victim of human trafficking, the social worker must discuss with the client if she/he would like to stay in the United States. Adult clients are required to cooperate with the prosecution of traffickers to qualify for a visa or other services. If the client wishes not to cooperate in the prosecution of the traffickers, she or he will be deported. Because trafficking is a federal crime, the social worker and client work with federal law enforcement and immigration services.

A trafficked person works with an immigration attorney to learn whether he or she is eligible for the temporary nonimmigrant visa, often referred to as a T-visa. This temporary nonimmigrant visa allows victims of trafficking to remain in the United States and after 3 years may be able to become lawful permanent residents. Recipients of the T-visas are eligible for work authorization, which allows them to work legally in the United States. Because of the stringent requirements of the T-Visa, immigration attorneys may also explore other forms of immigration relief (U.S. Department of State, 2007).

Once certified (by the federal government) as a victim of trafficking, the individual is eligible for federally funded services to the same extent of a refugee. These benefits include: assistance with housing, shelter, food, income, employment, English-language training, health care, mental health care, and services for victims of torture (Office to Monitor and Combat Trafficking in Persons, 2007). Hence, it is imperative to work from a social justice systems framework and have collaborative relationships with federal law enforcement and legal experts.

Agency collaboration among federal and local law enforcement, service providers, and attorneys is necessary to identify and provide protection to trafficked persons. Across the country federal funding has been allocated to initiate multidisciplinary teams to work with trafficked persons. For example, in New Jersey, the New Jersey

Anti-Trafficking Initiative was funded through the Office of Refugee Resettlement to initiate such a multidisciplinary coalition to provide education and increase the capacity to serve trafficking survivors throughout the state. The Anti-Trafficking Initiative has become a self-sustaining coalition called the NJ Anti-Trafficking Coalition, which is made up of stakeholders, including law enforcement agents at the local, state, and federal level; legal service providers; social service providers; and medical service providers (see Appendix E).

Common Practice Settings

There are many types of settings within collaborative forensic social work where social workers find themselves working with refugees, asylum seekers, and victims of human trafficking. Some examples include: refugee resettlement agencies, private nonprofit agencies, immigration detention centers, and immigration services. The role of the social worker in each of these agencies will vary. This following section provides an overview of the types of practice settings in which social workers will work with refugees, political asylum seekers, and victims of trafficking.

Refugee Resettlement Agencies and Private Nonprofit Agencies

All around the country there are refugee resettlement agencies whose mission is to provide basic, short-term assistance to newly arrived refugees. Social workers in these agencies play the role of case manager, program director, clinician, and clinical supervisor. In many cases, they also advocate for their clients, as well as provide public education and awareness training. Licensed social workers who are trained in conducting psychological evaluations on survivors of torture, can be called on to provide this service for their clients. In addition, they may be called on to write up an affidavit and provide testimony that will be used in court.

Immigration Detention Centers

It is very rare to find social workers working in immigration detention centers, but it does happen. Sometimes these are United States Public Health Service social workers who are placed within the center. Social workers in these facilities serve as advocates for their clients; in some cases they are the only link between the detention center and asylum services found in the community (United States Public Health Services, 2007).

United States Citizenship and Immigration Services

Social workers who work with refugees and political asylum seekers should be aware of the United States Citizenship and Immigration Services. Within the domain of the new Department of Homeland Security is the former Immigration and Naturalization Services, which has been separated into two different sections. Immigration and Customs Enforcement (ICE) and Citizenship and Immigration Services (CIS). Social workers are found working for USCIS in the capacity of Asylum Officer and the newly created Refugee Corps. This is a professional position in which interviews with refugees and asylum seekers are done to substantiate whether there is a valid claim for refugee status or political asylum. Officers in these positions can work either within U.S. borders, or in refugee camps overseas (Human Rights First, 2004).

Professionals Involved

In all of these settings, social workers find themselves working closely with a multidisciplinary group of professionals and para-professionals. These include lawyers (immigration and pro-bono), certified legal representatives and paralegals, refugee case managers, volunteers, and interpreters (Potocky-Tripodi, 2002).

Lawyers, Certified Representatives, and Paralegals

For social workers who work with asylum seekers or victims of human trafficking, it is very important to collaborate with the legal system. One way to do this is to work closely with trained legal representatives. These include immigration attorneys, certified representatives, and paralegals.

Because the immigration system in the United States is very complicated, and because social workers are not trained as lawyers, it is never our job to provide legal counsel. The best service to offer clients is providing linkages to immigration legal services. A social worker can provide case management, interpretation, supportive counseling, trauma counseling, and linkages with other services, but not legal advice.

It is vital to build close working relationships with lawyers who specialize in asylum and trafficking cases. Therefore, it is imperative to create a network of pro-bono lawyers from which to draw on for the clients. Law schools with human rights clinics where students are learning about asylum law and assisting on cases can be a valuable resource.

Much in the same way that social workers are advocates, so are lawyers. What sets them apart is their specialization and profound knowledge of the legal system. In complicated asylum and trafficking proceedings, a well-trained immigration attorney can be a social worker's strongest ally.

Para-professionals and Volunteers

Because of the lack of adequate funding for refugee programs, many programs rely on both para-professionals and volunteers to keep costs down. In many cases, former clients, who have been through the refugee or asylum experience already, and are adapting well to life in the United States, are hired or volunteer to serve arriving refugees. Some common titles are refugee case manager, culture broker, and community liaison (Potocky-Tripodi, 2002).

Interpreters

Interpreters play a vital role for refugees and asylum seekers. Language is one of the biggest barriers facing this group as they adjust to American life. It is very important to find a way to access certified and trained interpreters who understand the interpreter code of ethics regarding confidentiality, and the proper way to interpret. Most refugee resettlement agencies offer interpretation and translation services as one of their programs. Social workers who need to locate interpreters can contact their local agency to find out if they have interpreters and how to access their services (Potocky-Tripodi, 2002).

Summary and Conclusions

U.S. immigration processes are complex and require social workers to have an understanding of the system to be able to advocate effectively for their clients. A social justice systems approach is necessary for social workers who work with refugees, asylum seekers, and victims of human trafficking. Because immigration policy is constantly changing and directly affects the lives of refugees, asylum seekers, and victims of human trafficking, many agencies and workers must collaborate in their efforts with lawyers, para-professionals, volunteers, and interpreters.

Social workers are key contributors to this successful collaboration. For their clients, they serve as information and referral agents and counselors. They can provide the emotional support that is necessary when dealing with complicated systems such as immigration. They can also serve as advocates for change within the systems.

References

Alien Registration Act of 1940; 670-676, 76th Cong., 3rd Sess. (1940).

Araujo-Forlot, A. (2002). Prevention, protection and assistance schemes to victims of trafficking: Policy and examples of IOM prevention and return & reintegration programmes. *Counter-trafficking Focal Point, 2*, 1–15.

Barnett, D. (2002). U.S. immigration policy: Asylum-seekers and refugees. *Journal of Social Political and Economic Studies, 27*, 151–166.

Boyd, R. F. (2001). *Implementation of the trafficking victims protection act. FDCH congressional testimony, November 29, 2001.* Retrieved April 11, 2003, from http://www.usdoj.gov/crt/speeches/1129testimony.htm

Civil Rights Act of 1964, Pub. L. 88-352, July 2, 1964, 78 Stat. 241. (1964).

Crisp, J. (1997). The asylum dilemma. In J. Crisp, M. Ronday-Cao, & R. Reilly (Eds.), *State of the world's refugees: A humanitarian agenda* (pp. 183–223). New York: Oxford University Press.

Displaced Persons Act of 1948, June 25, 1948, ch. 647, 62 Stat. 1009 (50 U.S.C. App. 1951 et seq.) (1948).

Gibney, M.J. (2004). *The ethics and politics of asylum: Liberal democracy and the response to refugees.* Cambridge, UK: Cambridge University Press.

Homeland Security Act of 2003, Pub. L. 108-7, div. L, Feb. 20, *2003*, 117 Stat. 526. (2003).

Human Rights First. (2003). *Refugees, asylum seekers and the new Department of Homeland Security.* Retrieved August 13, 2007, from http://www.humanrightsfirst.org/refugees/refs_032503.pdf

Human Rights First. (2004). *In liberty's shadow: U.S. detention of asylum seekers in the era of homeland security.* Retrieved March 1, 2007, from http://www.humanrightsfirst.org/asylum/libertys_shadow.pdfhttp:// www.unhcr.org/home/PUBL/3ddce817.pdf

Human Rights Watch. (2002). *U.S. state department trafficking report missing key data, credits uneven efforts.* Retrieved April 1, 2003, from http://hrw.org/press/2002/06/us-report0606.htm

Illegal Immigration Reform and Immigration Responsibility Act of 1996, Pub. L. 104-208, div. C, Sept. 30, 1996, 110 Stat. 3009-546 (1996).

Immigration Act of 1965, 382 U.S. 861, 86 S.Ct. 121, 15 L.Ed.2d 99. (1965).

Immigration Act of 1990, Pub. L. 101-649, Nov. 29, 1990, 104 Stat. 4978. (1990).

Immigration Equality. (2005). *The REAL ID Act threatens sexual minority asylum seekers.* Retrieved February 8, 2007, from http://www.immigrationequality.org/uploadedfiles/Real%20ID%20Act-final.pdf

Jefferys, K. (2006). *Annual flow report U.S. legal permanent residents: 2006.* Washington, DC: Department of Homeland Security, Office of Immigration Statistics.

Knight, S. M. (2001). Defining due process down: Expedited removal in the United States. *Refuge, 19*(4), 41–47.

Martin, D.A. (2005). *The United States refugee admissions program: Reforms for a new era of refugee resettlement.* Washington, DC: Brookings Press.

McKelvey, R. S. (1998). Vietnamese Amerasians: The children we left behind. *Mots Pluriels, 7,* 1–2. Retrieved March 8, 2008, from http://motspluriels.arts.uwa.edu.au/MP798rmk.html

Office to Monitor and Combat Trafficking in Persons. (2004). *How can I recognize trafficking victims?* Retrieved September 10, 2007, from http://www.state.gov/g/tip/rls/fs/34563.htm

Office to Monitor and Combat Trafficking in Persons. (2007). *Overview of U.S. government federal agencies' principal roles to combat trafficking in persons (TIP).* Retrieved June 30, 2007, from http://www.state.gov/g/tip/rls/fs/07/87547.htm

Physicians for Human Rights. (1998). *Current asylum issues.* Retrieved September 11, 2006, from www.prusa.org

Pistone, M. R. (1998). *New asylum laws: Undermining an American ideal.* Washington, DC: CATO Institute.

Potocky-Tripodi, M. (2002). *Best practices for social work with refugees and immigrants.* New York: Columbia University Press.

Refugee Act of 1980, Pub. L. 96-212, Mar. 17, 1980, 94 Stat. 102. (1980).

Tasoff, R., & Tasoff, R. (2007). *Detention asylum seekers.* Retrieved August 13, 2007, from http://www.tasoff.com/Detention_Asylum_Seekers.htm

The Real ID Act of 2005, Pub. L. 109-13, div. B, May 11, 2005, 119 Stat. 302. (2005).

Trafficking Victims Protection Act, Public Law U.S.C. 106-386 (2002).

U.S. Department of State. (2007). *Trafficking in persons report.* Retrieved August 10, 2007, from http://www.state.gov/g/tip

United Nations High Commissioner for Refugees. (2003). *UNHCR global appeal: North America & the Caribbean.* Retrieved February 7, 2007, from http://www.unhcr.org/home/PUBL/3ddccb817.pdf

United States Public Health Service. (2007). *About us: Agencies.* Retrieved August 13, 2007, from http://www.usphs.gov/AboutUs/agencies.aspx#20

Uniting and Strengthening America by Providing Appropriate Tools Required to Intercept and Obstruct Terrorism Act (USA PATRIOT Act) of 2001, Pub. L. 107-56, Oct. 26, 2001, 115 Stat. 272. (2001).

Waibsnaider, M. (2006). How national self-interest and foreign policy continue to influence the US refugee admissions program. *Fordham Law Review, 75*(1), 391.

Wasem, R. E. (2005). *U.S. immigration policy on asylum seekers.* Washington, DC: Congressional Information Service, Library of Congress.

Welch, M. (2004). Quiet constructions in the war on terror: Subjecting asylum seekers to unnecessary detention. *Social Justice: A Journal of Crime, Conflict and World Order, 31*(1-2), 113–129.

Human Rights Issues and Research With Prisoners and Other Vulnerable Populations: Where Does Evidence-Based Practice Go From Here?

26

Sandy Gibson

A substantial challenge facing forensic social workers, especially in correctional settings, is providing effective treatment when security and custodial concerns are emphasized over treatment concerns (Karcher, 2004; Weinberger & Sreenivasan, 1994). However, increased efforts at integrating evidence-based practices in correctional settings has significantly grown over the past 2 decades, with correctional administrations realizing the cost-effectiveness of evidence-based treatment services (Nissen, 2006). Rubin (2008) argued that the evidence-based-practice (EBP) process allows social workers to identify which interventions, programs, policies, and assessment tools are supported by the best evidence; find and critically review research studies in seeking evidence to answer clinical questions; and measure treatment progress and outcomes.

Ethics, Human Rights, and Research and Evaluation

The National Association of Social Workers' *Code of Ethics* (1999, 5.02) purports that social workers should promote and facilitate evaluation and research to contribute to the development of knowledge. This underscores both an ethical and a human rights obligation for the need for more prevention and intervention studies with incarcerated individuals.

There is also a need to research services for individuals with legal problems who are not incarcerated. Existing research identifies that a clear link with aftercare services is vital to ensuring continuity of care after release from jail, and that prerelease planning, referral, and community service engagement ensures the forensic client a connection to treatment and support (Solomon & Draine, 1995). Forensic research focusing on the strengthening of this link could serve to strengthen the services received postrelease, enhance multiservice communication and collaboration, and ultimately serve to reduce recidivism.

The substantially high rate of recidivism for incarcerated individuals with mental health diagnoses (James & Glaze, 2006), coupled with the costs associated with incarceration, also demonstrate the need for treatment research associated with forensic clients to move away from penalty only and move toward a more rehabilitation-oriented incarceration and probation/parole.

History of Human Rights and Ethical Violations in Research With Prisoners

History is fraught with human rights violations in research conducted with prisoners. For centuries, prisoners, a population of disadvantaged and vulnerable persons, have been used as subjects of research. Prisoners were considered expendable research subjects (Arboleda-Florez, 2005). The abuses were such that authors would refer to prisoners as "human guinea pigs" (Adams & Cowan, 1971), who were "cheaper than chimpanzees" (Mitford, 1973).

In the mid-19th and 20th centuries, the dominant ideology was that the common good—either for social benefit or the development of science—justified the performance of experiments in humans without respect for their autonomy (Arboleda-Florez, 2005), as exemplified by the following forensic research studies.

Statesville Penitentiary Malaria Study (1945)

The Statesville Penitentiary Malaria Study was conducted by the University of Chicago and the U.S. Army and State Department. Malaria, an infectious disease, which results in extreme illness and death if left untreated, was hindering the military as they fought battles in the Pacific region. Experimental research was needed to quickly develop drugs to fight malaria, and prisoners were used to test these drugs. During World War II, in Illinois, hundreds of prisoners were inoculated with malaria to research effective methods for disease prevention and intervention (Arboleda-Florez, 2005; Final Report of Advisory Committee, 1995; Paulsen, 1973). An unknown number of inmates became ill or died, and a commutation of sentence or parole was later granted to 317 of the 432 research subjects.

Trends in Phase 1 Research (Until the Mid-1970s)

During the postwar years it was common practice for researchers to employ prisoners as research subjects for studies ranging from identifying the causes of cancer to testing new cosmetics. By the early 1970s, the Food and Drug Administration estimated that more than 90% of phase I research in new drugs was first conducted on prisoners (Adams & Cowan, 1971; Arboleda-Florez, 2005). Over the past 2 decades there has been a substantial reduction in the use of prisoners for research. As a result, phase I projects now use nonincarcerated subjects, although these individuals are typically underprivileged.

University of Washington Radiation Study (1963-1973)

From 1963 to 1973, the University of Washington, Seattle, conducted studies on the effect of radiation on human testicular function using inmates at Washington State prison. The effects of the radiation were unknown, and vasectomies were suggested for the inmates on completion of the study as it was unknown what effect such radiation would have on future offspring. Initially, research subjects were not informed of potential risks associated with participation, although there was a vague reference to the possibility of tumors. In 1976, subjects filed a lawsuit alleging a lack of informed consent. During a deposition, the lead researcher, Dr. Heller, indicated "I didn't want to frighten them so I said 'tumor'... I may have, on occasion, said cancer" (Deposition of Heller, 1976). The suit (*Robert Case vs. State of Oregon*) was settled out of court in 1979 for $2,215 in damages, which was shared by nine individuals. In 1994, President Clinton charged an advisory committee to uncover the history of human radiation experiments. The committee ultimately discovered that over 4,000 federal government-sponsored human radiation experiments were conducted between 1944 and 1974 (Final Report of Advisory Committee, 1995).

Human Rights? Responses to Historic Forensic Research Atrocities

There were many national and international responses to these tragic forensic research studies. These documents including the Nuremberg Code, Declaration of Helsinki, the National Research Act, Title 45 Code of Federal Regulations Part 46, and the Belmont Report (National Institutes of Health [NIH], 1979).

The Nuremberg Code is a set of principles for human experimentation established as a result of the Nuremberg Trials at the end of the Second World War. Specifically, the Code was created in response to the inhumane Nazi human experimentation carried out during the war, such as bone transplantation; sterilization methods; and exposure to extreme cold, high altitudes, and mustard gas (Marrus, 1999). The Code includes principles such as informed consent and the absence of coercion. As horrific as these research efforts were, it is important to acknowledge that during the Nuremberg Medical Trial, defense attorneys argued that there was no difference between research conducted in American prisons and the experiments that took place in the Nazi concentration camps (Arboleda-Florez, 2005).

Another response to these historic forensic research atrocities was the Declaration of Helsinki, developed by the World Medical Association (WMA) in 1964 and currently under review for its fifth revision. It was and is a statement of ethical principles that provides guidance to professionals conducting research involving human subjects (DeRoy, 2004).

On July 12, 1974, the National Research Act (Pub. L. 93-348) was signed into law, thereby creating the National Commission for the Protection of Human Subjects of Biomedical and Behavioral Research. In 1979, the National Commission for the Protection of Human Subjects of Biomedical and Behavioral Research, a subsidiary of the Department of Health, Education and Welfare, published the Belmont Report, a set of ethical principles and guidelines for the protection of human subjects of research. The basic ethical principles of this report are respect for persons, beneficence and justice, and the basic applications are informed consent, assessment of risk and benefits, and the selection of subjects (NIH, 1979).

Furthermore, Title 45 Code of Federal Regulations, Part 46, Protection of Human Subjects, scripted in 1991 and revised in 1995, is a document that embodies the ethical principles of the Belmont Report, providing a framework in which researchers can ensure that serious efforts have been made to protect the rights and welfare of research subjects (USDHHS, 2005).

The vulnerabilities experienced by forensic research subjects are recognized and addressed by the United Nations in principle 22 of the Body of Principles for the Protection of All Persons Under any Form of Detention or Imprisonment (1988), which indicates: "No detained or imprisoned person shall, even with his consent, be subjected to any medical of scientific experimentation, which may be detrimental to his health" (p. 1).

Institutional Review Boards

One protective factor for forensic research subjects is the requirement that researchers obtain Institutional Review Board (IRB) approval of their projects prior to implementation. In 1974, the United States Congress passed the National Research Act of 1974, which defined IRBs, and required them to be used for all research involving human subjects. This was done primarily in response to the many aforementioned research abuses. IRBs are independent committees that approve, monitor, and review research proposals and protocols with the purpose of protecting the rights, safety, and well-being of the research subjects. IRBs are regulated by the Office of Human Research Protections, which is overseen by the Department of Health and Human Services (DHHS).

Information obtained from forensic research may be considered valuable to the criminal justice system administration, as it may do things such as help to identify previously unknown criminal behaviors or may help to identify those who are more or less likely to qualify for parole. If criminal justice's (CJ) administration is associated with the IRB process, it may cause the IRB to weaken the protections afforded to research subjects for the administration to gain the insights it feels would enhance its own system. To provide the protections necessary for ethical forensic research, including the absence or appearance of coercion, the knowledgeable and competent assent or consent of the subject, and the subjects' knowledge that they may quit the study at any time, forensic research IRBs must be free from CJ administration oversight (Hillbrand, 2005).

Many of the documents that arose in response to the forensic research atrocities reference the rights of "prisoners." If this is strictly applied to research studies that are prison-based only, it will not afford the same protections to other research subjects who are involved with the criminal justice system, even though they too experience limited freedoms and liberties and are also subject to the possibility of coercion. In fact, in 2004, of the 7 million individuals involved in the U.S. criminal justice system, only 2.1 million were actually incarcerated, with the reminder being on either probation or parole.

Need for Forensic Research

Out of concern that an IRB may deny a proposal that involves subjects who are involved with the criminal justice system (CJS), many studies exclude such potential subjects in their research design. This not only refers to prison-based research, but also to research studies at community mental health or substance-abuse treatment centers, where individuals on probation or parole are often excluded from samples. Not only does this diminish the value of the research, particularly for understanding outcomes as they relate to forensic clients, but it also excludes forensic clients from enjoying the enhancement of self-esteem that comes from having a share in a project aimed at making a contribution on behalf of society (Young, 2005). Everyone loses in the process. Subjects lose the benefits of innovation and improved services, and forensic social workers lose the improvement of knowledge on how best to serve this population.

"The American Academy of Psychiatry and the Law Committee on Institutional and Correctional Forensic Psychiatry takes the position that forensic mental health research is far too important to be allowed to sink into a sea of oversight requirements" (Young, 2005, p. 368). Arboleda-Florez (2005, p. 515) asked a poignant question: "Can persons stripped of their civil rights and subject to years or decades of confinement be free agents who are capable of exercising freedom of choice?" Thus, there is a great need for forensic research. As forensic subjects are a captive population, they are vulnerable subjects in need of special protective measures. However, excessive protection can bring harm to those who it intended to protect. For example, if researchers avoid conducting forensic research because of the extensive protections required of subjects, then they are doing forensic populations a disservice by not developing knowledge on how to best serve these subjects.

As protections to prisoners emerged in the 1970s, the amount of forensic research decreased immensely. This is mostly a result of the fact that much existing research was of no direct benefit to prisoners, but instead was likely to have been convenience research. Stringent oversight requirements, coupled with a lack of societal interest in investing in services to specifically treat forensic clients, has resulted in a rather limited field of experimental research in forensic settings. However, because of the multiple needs, including high rates of substance abuse and mental health problems among this population, there is a great need for prisoners to receive evidence-based mental health and substance-abuse services (Bureau of Justice Statistics, 2004).

Risks

As, one hopes, the past atrocities of forensic research have ended as a result of new protections of subjects, there is now a more common risk concerning emotional distress as a result of research participation. Social risks of research participation are largely related to confidentiality and the damage to one's reputation that can directly result from participation in the study, even if just as a control member (Cloyes, 2006; Overholser, 1987). For example, in a treatment study for sex offenders, individuals who are known participants, even those nonsex offenders who are in the control group, are likely to be viewed by fellow inmates as sex offenders. In the prison-established hierarchy among inmates, sex offenders exist on one of the lowest levels and are viewed quite negatively; they are often subjected to extensive verbal and physical abuses from other inmates.

In addition, some studies elicit information of a highly personal and sensitive nature, and are often audiotaped (Cloyes, 2006; Overholser, 1987). This can be a cause of great concern for forensic clients as information disclosed to researchers, if discovered by the criminal justice system, could result in convictions for additional crimes committed, a denial of parole, or reincarceration of those on probation or parole. For these reasons, the importance of confidentiality and the trust that forensic clients must have for the forensic researcher are imperative.

A different type of social risk entails the potential for coercion or undue influence often found in forensic settings. As forensic subjects lack the freedom and liberties of nonforensic individuals, it has not been uncommon to use incentives associated with greater freedoms or that someway manipulate their quality of life, such as better prison jobs or extended outdoor time (Cloyes, 2006). When subjects receive benefits such as these, the benefits can serve as coercion to participate in exchange for the desirable enhanced freedom. These types of incentives create resentments among nonparticipants, promoting a negative environment and possibly putting subjects at risk of physical harm. The American Psychological Association recommends that parole boards not take into account research participation when reviewing parole eligibility to avoid the possibility of coercion.

To avoid coercion when conducting forensic research, it is essential that economic benefits are limited because of the impoverished nature of prisons. The Code of Federal Regulations (28 C.F.R., section 512.16) recommends that only concrete reinforcers, such as soft drinks and snacks, be used for reimbursement. If at all possible, external awards as incentives for study participation should be avoided altogether. If subjects are to be paid for their participation, the amount should never be more than their hourly wage they earn, which is typically much less than the federal minimum wage, and participation should be in lieu of work time (Arboleda-Florez, 2005; Wettstein, 2005).

Benefits

There are also benefits to subjects of forensic research, such as the provision of access to treatment not otherwise available, immediate personal health gains, knowledge from classes, an opportunity to engage in altruistic behavior not commonly available in prisons, and an enhanced sense of purpose and usefulness (Arboleda-Florez, 2005; Childress, 2006).

As indicated in the Bureau of Justice Statistics Survey of prison inmates (Harrison & Beck, 2005), one in four inmates with a mental health diagnosis does not receive treatment while incarcerated. This means that services are likely unavailable to them, therefore, any treatment research conducted in prisons may lead to the development of services. Research studies may also include attending classes or receiving medical care that wouldn't otherwise be made available to inmates. Most important, forensic research allows this population to "give back" to both other forensic individuals and society.

Forensic Research Methodologies

The National Commission for the Protection of Human Subjects identifies three categories of research in prison settings: convenience research, prison-oriented research, and treatment-oriented research. In convenience research, the accessibility of a large group is the main, if not sole, reason for using prisons for research. This differs from convenience sampling, which indicates that the researcher has intentions of studying forensic populations and simply took the easiest sampling route of studying this intended population. Convenience research means the forensic population is used solely because the entire population is convenient, but the purpose of the research is not intended to serve primarily (or even at all) this population. Forensic populations are simply a convenient population because of their captivity. This research typically has no direct benefit to the prisoners, and therefore nonincarcerated subjects should be used to reduce the likelihood of coercion or manipulation of the vulnerable incarcerated population (Overholser, 1987). An example of convenience research can be found in the pharmaceutical and cosmetic drug research that once was prevalent in prison populations. Because of the many protections now afforded forensic populations, convenience research is unlikely to be approved by an IRB.

Prison-oriented research typically studies the effects of incarceration on areas such as psychological functioning, predicting adjustment to prison life, or identifying characteristics of participants in a riot. Prison-oriented research can be beneficial to prisoners when it involves direct, practical benefits to the prisoners, such as strategies for strengthening families for children of inmates. When this research serves the interests of prisoners and their families, it has value for both the subjects and the greater society (Overholser, 1987). Studies such as exploring who requests psychological services on admission to prison (Diamond, Magaletta, Harzke, & Baxter, 2008) and a national study of social support, gender, and inmate adjustment to prison life (Jiang & Winfree, 2006) are examples of prison-oriented research.

Treatment-oriented research involves the development and evaluation of treatment programs designed specifically to benefit the subjects (Overholser, 1987). This type of research is the most ethically justifiable of the three as it attempts to improve the welfare of incarcerated subjects. Such research should have direct implications for the later development or refinement of prison services or treatment programs. A study of methadone maintenance for male prisoners (Kinlock, Gordon, Swartz, & O'Grady, 2008) and a multisite evaluation of prison-based therapeutic community drug-treatment program (Welsh, 2007) are examples of treatment-oriented research.

There is a substantial rate of mental health diagnoses in prisons. The consolidation of a large group of individuals meeting diagnostic criteria for a variety of psychological disorders facilitates the recruitment, sampling, and retention process of treatment studies (Metzner & Dvoskin, 2006). However, although it is common to find prison inmates with diagnoses, it is important to separate those disorders potentially capable of affecting or producing the criminal behavior from those that are apparently a consequence of the incarceration (Overholser, 1987). In prison studies, it is extremely difficult, without baseline measures, to control for the effects of incarceration on the outcomes under study, which further supports the need to avoid the use of prisoners as research subjects in studies other than prison/treatment-oriented research.

Whether a research study will directly benefit the prison population is not adequate ethical justification to conduct a study with incarcerated subjects. It is also important to consider the degree of relationship between the subject of research and the offenders' crime. If there is no relationship between the subject and the subject under study, then the use of such a prisoner is again merely convenient and should be avoided.

Qualitative Research Methodologies

Qualitative research methodologies lend themselves well to forensic research, particularly because of the lack of existing research, which creates a need for more exploratory methods. Research subjects themselves can be more involved in the research through techniques such as member checks, follow-up interviews, and coidentification of themes in the data, and other forms of feedback and collaboration (Cloyes, 2006). This can enhance trust between the forensic subjects and the researchers, strengthening the outcomes of the study. Participatory action and feminist and ethnographic approaches have introduced a different set of questions about the ethics of forensic interviewing. These often highlight unequal power relations, the positioning of interview participants, and ways to protect vulnerable and marginalized participants from undue stress or harm caused by insensitive or oppressive research (Cloyes, 2006).

Forensic Research With Juvenile Populations

Inclusion of children in forensic research is important. As social workers, it is essential for us to know the best proven interventions to use with this population. This importance is exemplified by NIH's requirement that all of its funded research include children, unless the investigator can provide a valid reason as to why they should not be included. There are special review requirements for IRBs (Inclusion of Children, 45 CFR 46, Subpart D, Sec. 401-409; USDHHS, 2005) that include various protections for child research, varying by the degree of risk involved in the research. These protections vary from simple parental consent, when the research has no greater than minimal risk, to requiring the permission of both the child and the parents, indicating the likelihood that the research is generalizable and specifically related to the child's disorder. In addition, the risk may only be slightly higher than minimal. Reed (1999) indicates the forensic juveniles who are imprisoned become regulatory orphans for purposes of guiding IRBs in their review process. This means that the IRB shall require appointment of an advocate for each child who is a ward, an advocate who is capable of acting in the best interests of the child for the duration of the child's participation in the research and who is not associated in any way with the research, the investigators, or the guardian organization (Additional Protections for Children, 45 CFR 46.409).

As previously discussed, forensic populations require additional protections when participating in research, but it is still critical that forensic research move forward. For the same reasons that we must remain committed to conducting forensic research, we must also remain committed to including children, who do indeed require additional protections beyond that of adult forensic subjects, in our sample populations when appropriate.

Collaboration in Forensic Research

As research with criminal justice populations, especially prisoners, is conducted by various professions such as psychologists, criminologists, social workers, psychiatrists, and others, as well as within various venues of the legal system, such as prisons, probation and social service departments, and court systems, interdisciplinary collaboration is essential. The skills needed for developing and maintaining effective collaborative relationships that can be applied to successfully completing a research study are described in chapter 3.

Data Collection

Forensic research is likely to require data collection from various sources within the criminal justice system, such as attendance records with probation and parole officers, drug-screen results, school records for youths, and criminal histories (i.e., past offenses) It is very important to include these systems in the development of any research proposal. Simply approaching these organizations with a fully developed proposal and asking for their participation is unlikely to result in a productive or open collaboration. Their inclusion in proposal development will also facilitate the identification of accessible and available data opportunities. In the case of prison collaboration, prison administration will understand the safety concerns involved with an outside researcher gaining access to the inmate population, whether there is space available to meet research needs, and the determination of who will pay for the additional security that will be required (Institute of Medicine, 2006).

VOICES FROM THE FIELD

Dr. Jack S. Monell, ACSW
Criminal Justice Instructor

Agency Setting

Presently, I work for the Central Piedmont Community College in Charlotte, North Carolina. Here I serve as a faculty member in the Public Safety department, where I focus on research and instruction in issues pertaining to juvenile justice and community-based corrections.

Prior to this most recent appointment, I served as a Program Analyst for the Court Services & Supervision Agency for the District of Columbia (CSOSA). There I worked on national and local initiatives pertaining to prisoner reentry, focusing on substance-abuse and mental health treatment, vocational and educational needs, and medical services. CSOSA operates an internationally recognized reentry and sanction center that addresses the various needs of offenders returning to Washington, DC, from incarceration within the U.S. Department of Justice's Bureau of Prisons.

Practice Responsibilities

In my present role as a faculty member, it is my duty to stay abreast of the various literature and trends associated with the field of practice relating to juvenile justice and community-based corrections. Outside of classroom instruction and serving as a faculty coordinator for field placements, we maintain a strong connection with local and federal law enforcement entities for the purposes of collaborating on presentations and continued research.

In my prior role as a program analyst, I served in the capacity of a quality assurance specialist and auditor. In that capacity I monitored federally funded substance abuse and sex-offender treatment programs within the DC metropolitan area. In addition to monitoring, I provided technical assistance to deficient programs and conducted internal surveys to assess unit efficacy within our agency. Within that role I worked collaboratively with various federal law enforcement partners, DC government officials, and community-based stakeholders.

Expertise Required

As do many of my colleagues, I believe that to use the term "social worker," or "forensic social worker," one needs to have at minimum a master's degree in social work from an accredited university. I further believe that specializations in criminal justice and/or forensics would prove to increase the marketability and legitimacy of the field. As a former federal employee, my position required a doctorate in social work. As a faculty member, though preferred, the doctorate is not required and one must have a master's degree to instruct most courses.

Practice Challenges

Working in the field of forensic social work for the past 11 years, I have seen many transitions and paradigm shifts in how systems, agencies, and various governments operate. As a juvenile justice practitioner, it was apparent early in my career that adolescents were not receiving the adequate supports they needed to become productive members of our society. Many of the concerns ranged from mental health and substance-abuse issues, which were quite evident as I transitioned into a career with adult federal offenders. Neglect of this population was difficult for me because it was always a belief of mine that without any legitimate aftercare or treatment options, adolescents would unfortunately recidivate back into the judicial system and become hardened criminals as adults.

Common Legal and/or Ethical Issues

As a faculty member, there are indeed certain legal and ethical requirements that one must adhere to as a college employee. Working for the federal government required a high level of legal and ethical considerations. Quite frankly, as a forensic social worker, one should always operate one's practice not only by agency, educational, or government guidelines but by NASW's *Code of Ethics*, which requires a high level of competence and adherence to rules and regulations.

Additional Information

As a faculty member, I encourage students to the field because I feel that it continues to be a vibrant and ever-evolving necessity in the community. As our importance continues to be recognized and noticed within various fields of practice, the need for competent social workers becomes key to our progression. For students and social workers interested in working in criminal justice settings, the need definitely exists and forensic social workers represent the majority of practitioners providing supervision, treatment, correctional treatment, evaluations, and research regarding trends in the criminal justice process.

Summary and Conclusions

In summary, in response to the human rights violations associated with pre-1970s forensic research, many scientific organizations responded with documents indicating needed protections for forensic research subjects, such as the Nuremberg Code, Declaration of Helsinki, the National Research Act, and the Belmont Report. The much-needed response to such human rights violations has, in some scientists' opinions, resulted in overprotections that lead to an underrepresentation of forensic populations in social and scientific research. This in turn makes the service of this population less knowledge-driven. It is important for forensic social workers to recognize their obligation to adapt evidence-based practices. Forensic social workers must recognize the special vulnerabilities of the prison population, most critically their susceptibility to coercion, when designing and implementing research.

Online Resources

Belmont Report: http://ohsr.od.nih.gov/guidelines/belmont.html
Declaration of Helsinki: http://www.wma.net/e/policy/b3.htm
National Research Act: http://www.kent.edu/rags/Compliance/IRB-National-Research-Act.cfm
Nuremberg Code: http://ohsr.od.nih.gov/guidelines/nuremberg.html
Nuremberg Trials: http://www.law.umkc.edu/faculty/projects/ftrials/nuremberg/Nuremb ergDoctorTrial.html
Statesville Penitentiary Study of Malaria: http://www.gwu.edu/~nsarchiv/radia tion/dir/mstreet/commeet/meet10 /brief10/br10g1.txt
Title 45 Code of Federal Regulations, Part 46: http://www.hhs.gov/ohrp/human subjects/guidance/45cfr46.htm
UN Principle 22: http://www.un.org/documents/ga/res/43/a43r173.htm
Washington State Prison Study: http://www.hss.energy.gov/healthsafety/ohre/roadmap/histories/048 1/footnote.html

References

Adams, A., & Cowan, G. (1971). The human guinea pig: How we test new drugs, *World*, 5, 20.
Advisory Committee on Human Radiation Experiments. (1995). *Final report of the Advisory Committee on Human Radiation Experiments 061-000-00-848-9*. Washington DC: U.S. Government Printing Office.
Arboleda-Florez, J. (2005). The ethics of biomedical research on prisoners. *Forensic Psychiatry, 18*, 514–517.
Body of Principles for the Protection of All Persons Under Any Form of Detention or Imprisonment. (1988). G.A. res. 43/173, annex, 43 U.N. GAOR Supp. (No. 49) at 298, U.N. Doc. A/43/49. Retrieved May 9, 2007, from http://www.un.org/documents/ga/res/43/a43r173.htm
Bureau of Justice Statistics. (2004). *Survey of inmates in state and federal corrections facilities*. Retrieved January 18, 2007, from www.ojp.usdoj.gov/bjs/pub/pdf/quest_archive/siljq02.pdf

Childress, H. (2006). The anthropologist and the crayons: Changing our focus from avoiding harm to doing good. *Journal of Empirical Research on Human Research Ethics, 1*, 79–87.

Cloyes, K. G. (2006). An ethic of analysis: An argument for critical analysis of research interviews as ethical practice. *Advances in Nursing Science, 29*, 84–97.

DeRoy, P. G. (2004). Helsinki and the declaration of Helsinki. *World Medical Journal, 50*, 9–11.

Diamond, P., Magaletta, P., Harzke, A., & Baxter, J. (2008). Who requests psychological services upon admission to prison? *Psychological Services, 5*, 97–107.

Harrison, P., & Beck, A. (2005*). Prisoners in 2004.* Bureau of Justice Statistics, Department of Justice (NCJ 210677). Washington, DC: U.S. Government Printing Office.

Hillbrand, M. (2005). Obstacles to research in forensic psychiatry. *Journal of the American Academy of Psychiatry and the Law, 33*, 295–298.

Institute of Medicine. (2006). *Ethical considerations for research involving prisoners.* Washington, DC: National Academies Press.

James, D., & Glaze, L. (2006). *Mental health problems of prison and jail inmates.* Bureau of Justice Statistics. NCJ 213600 US Dept. of Justice Office of Justice Programs. Washington, DC: U.S. Government Printing Office.

Jiang, S. L., & Winfree, T. (2006). Social support, gender, inmate adjustment to prison life: Insights from a national sample. *Prison Journal, 86*, 32–55.

Karcher, A. E. (2004). How prison mental health providers construct their role and work. *Dissertation Abstracts International, 64*, 9-B.

Kinlock, T., Gordon, M., Swartz, R., & O'Grady, K. E. (2008). A study of methadone maintenance for male prisoners: Three-month post-release outcomes. *Criminal Justice and Behavior, 35*, 34–47.

Marrus, M. (1999). The Nuremberg doctors' trial in historical context. *Bulletin of the History of Medicine, 73*, 106–123.

Metzner, J., & Dvoskin, J. (2006). An overview of correctional psychiatry. *Psychiatric Clinics of North America, 29*, 761–772.

Mitford, J. (1973). *Kind and unusual punishment: The prison business.* New York: Alfred A. Knopf.

National Association of Social Workers. (1999). *Code of ethics.* Washington, DC: NASW Press.

National Institutes of Health (NIH). (1979) *Regulations and ethical guidelines.* Retrieved May 9, 2007, from http://ohsr.od.nih.gov/guidelines/index.html

National Institutes of Health, Office of Human Subjects Research. (1979). *The Belmont Report: Ethical principles and guidelines for the protection of human subjects of research.* Publication No. (OS) 78-0013 and No. (OS) 78-0014. Washington, DC: U.S. Government Printing Office.

National Research Act of 1974. (1974). (Pub. L. No. 93-348), 93rd Cong., 2nd Sess.

Nissen, L. (2006). Effective adolescent substance abuse treatment in juvenile justice settings: Practice and policy recommendations. *Child & Adolescent Social Work Journal, 23*, 298–315.

Office of the United Nations High Commissioner for Human Rights. (1988). *Body of principles for the protection of all persons under any form of detention or imprisonment.* Adopted by General Assembly (Resolution 43/173). New York: Author.

Overholser, J. C. (1987). Ethical issues in prison research: A risk/benefit analysis. *Behavioral Sciences & the Law, 5*, 187–202.

Paulsen, C. A. (1973*). The study of irradiation effects on the human testes: Including histologic, chromosomal and hormonal aspects.* Terminal report, AEC Contract #AT(45B1)B2225. Seattle: University of Washington School of Medicine.

Reed, J. (1999). Regulatory orphans: Juvenile prisoners as transvulnerable research subjects. *IRB: Ethics and Human Research, 21*, 9–14.

Robert Case v. State of Oregon et. al., Civil no. 76-500; Paul Tyrell v. State of Oregon et al., Civil no. 76-499.

Rubin, A. (2008). *Practitioner's guide to using research for evidence-based practice.* Hoboken, NJ: Wiley.

Solomon, P., & Draine, J. (1995). Issues in serving the forensic client. *Social Work, 40*, 25–33.

United States Department of Human Services (USDHHS). (2005). *Code of federal regulations.* Retrieved May 9, 2007, from http://www.hhs.gov/ohrp/humansubjects/guidance/45cfr46.htm

Weinberger, L. E., & Sreenivasan, S. (1994). Ethical and professional conflicts in correctional psychology. *Professional Psychology: Research and Practice, 25*, 161–167.

Wettstein, R. M. (2005). Quality and quality improvement in forensic mental health evaluations. *Journal of the American Academy of Psychiatry and the Law, 33*, 368–370.

Young, J. L. (2005). Commentary: Refusing to give up on forensic research. *Journal of the American Academy of Psychiatry and the Law, 33*, 368–370.

Strengths-Based Psychosocial Assessment (Child Welfare and Community Populations and Settings) Example

A

A Strengths-Based Psychosocial Assessment and Treatment Planning for Children and Families in the Global Environment* (Monmouth University Psychosocial Assessment)

I. Identifying Information
II. Reason for Referral/Presenting Problem
    A. Referral source
    B. Summary of the presenting problem
    C. Impact of the presenting problem
III. Client and Family Description and Functioning
IV. Relevant History
    A. Family of Origin History

---

*From I. Bush & N. Smith, The Monmouth Psychosocial, In K. Ward & R. Sakina-Mama (Eds.), *Breaking Out of the Box* (pp. 77–86), 2005, Chicago: Lyceum Books. Copyright 2005 by Lyceum Books. Reprinted with permission.

    B.   Relevant Developmental History
    C.   Family of Creation History
    D.   Educational and Occupational History
    E.   Religious (Spiritual) Development
    F.   Social Relationships
    G.   Dating/Marital/Sexual Relations
    H.   Medical/Psychological Health
    I.   Legal
    J.   Environmental Conditions
V. Workers Assessment (See Appendix)
VI. Treatment Plan (See Appendix for template)

■ Please see the following Appendix to guide your writing within each area.

Appendix

Identifying Information

This section should include such information as age, sex, race, religion, marital status, occupation, living situation, and so on. Information should be factual, based on information from the client, collateral contacts, and case records.

Reason for Referral/Presenting Problem

This section should identify the referral source and give a summary of the reason for the referral. This should include the client's description of the problem or services needed, including the duration of the problem and its consequences for the client unit. Past intervention efforts by an agency or the individual and/or family related to the presenting problem should also be summarized.

In addition, comment on any of the following areas that have been **affected** by the presenting problem:

■ family situation
■ physical and economic environment
■ educational/occupational issues
■ physical health
■ relevant cultural, racial, religious, sexual orientation and cohort factors
■ current social/sexual/emotional relationships
■ legal issues

Client and Family Description and Functioning

This section should contain data *observed* by the worker. Focusing on the first few interviews, include pertinent objective information about:

■ the client's physical appearance (dress, grooming, striking features)
■ communication styles and abilities or deficits

- thought processes (memory, intelligence, clarity of thought, mental status, etc.)
- expressive overt behaviors (mannerisms, speech patterns, etc.)
- reports from professionals or family (medical, psychological, legal)
- Mental status exam (if appropriate)

Relevant History

This section should discuss past history as it relates to the presenting problem. Although this section should be as factual as possible, it is the place to present how the specifics of the client's culture, race, religion, or sexual orientation, for example, affect resolution of the presenting problem.

Include *applicable* information about each of the following major areas or about related areas relevant to your client. (You are not limited by the outline below.)

Family-of-Origin History

Family composition; birth order, where and with whom reared, relationship with parents or guardian, relationships with siblings, abuse or other trauma, significant family events (births, deaths, divorce, separations, moves, etc.) and their effect on the client(s).

Relevant Developmental History

Birth defects or problems around the birth process, developmental milestones, including mobility (crawling, walking, coordination); speech; toilet training; eating or sleeping problems; developmental delays or gifted areas. This section is especially important for clients who are children. It is critical to identify non-Western expectations and practices for child rearing and development for clients from diverse backgrounds. Nature of stressful experiences client has encountered throughout his/her life in relation to ability to handle them; how he or she has solved the "tasks" of various age levels.

Family-of-Creation Interrelationships

Interacting roles within the family (e.g., who makes the decisions, handles the money, disciplines the children, does the marketing); typical family issues (e.g., disagreements, disappointments).

Educational and Occupational History

Level of education attained; school performance; learning problems, difficulties; areas of achievement; peer relationships. Skills and training; type of employment; employment history; adequacy of wage-earning ability; quality of work performance; relationship with authority figures and coworkers.

Religious (Spiritual) Development

Importance of religion in upbringing, affinity for religious or spiritual thought or activity, involvement in religious activities, positive or negative experiences.

Social Relationships

Size and quality of social network, ability to sustain friendships, pertinent social role losses or gains, social role performance within the client's cultural context. Historical patterns of familial and social relationships.

Dating/Marital/Sexual

Type and quality of relationships, relevant sexual history, ability to sustain intimate (sexual and nonsexual) contact, significant losses, traumas, conflicts in intimate relationships, way of dealing with losses or conflicts. Currently, where do problems exist and where does the client manage successfully?

Medical/Psychological

Health problems, including drug, alcohol, or tobacco use or misuse; medications; accidents; disabilities; emotional difficulties, including mental illness; psychological reports; hospitalizations; impact on functioning; use of previous counseling help.

Legal

Juvenile or adult contact with legal authorities, type of problem(s), jail or prison sentence, effects of rehabilitation.

Environmental Conditions

Urban or rural, indigenous or alien to the neighborhood where he or she lives, economic and class structure of the neighborhood in relation to that of the client, description of the home.

Worker's Assessment

This section should contain the thoughts and opinion of the treating social worker. It is based on initial observations and information-gathering efforts; however, it takes the observations and information to a new level. Here, the worker integrates his or her view with an understanding of the client's problem or situation, its underlying causes and/or contributing factors, and the prognosis for change.

The worker summarizes his or her understanding of the client's presenting situation. To do this, he or she draws on what is known about the current and past situation that has lead to the presenting situation; the social, cultural, familial, psychological, and economic factors that contribute to creating the problem and/or support solutions to the problem. As appropriate, the worker comments on such factors as:

- Social emotional functioning—ability to express feelings, ability to form relationships, predominant mood or emotional pattern (e.g., optimism, pessimism, anxiety, temperament, characteristic traits, overall role performance and social competence, motivation and commitment to treatment)
- Psychological factors—reality testing, impulse control, judgment, insight, memory or recall, coping style and problem-solving ability, characteristic defense

mechanisms, notable problems. If applicable, include a formal diagnosis (e.g., *DSM-IV*, Global Assessment Scale, etc.) (APA, 2000).

■ Environmental issues and constraints or supports from the family, agency, community that affect the situation and its resolution. What does the environment offer for improved functioning (family, friends, church, school, work, clubs, groups, politics, leisure time activities)?

■ Issues related to cultural or other diversity that offer constraints or supports from the family, agency, community that affect the situation and its resolution.

■ Strengths and weaknesses in relation to needs/demands/constraints in which he or she functions (ego functioning):
  ■ Capacities and skills
  ■ Activity patterns
  ■ Ways of communicating
  ■ Perceptions of him/herself and others
  ■ How energy is invested
  ■ What disturbs or satisfies him or her
  ■ Capacity for empathy and affection
  ■ Affects and moods
  ■ Control vs. impulsivity
  ■ Spontaneity vs. inhibition
  ■ Handling of sexuality and aggressiveness; dependency needs, self-esteem, and anxiety
  ■ Attitudes toward authority, peers, and others
  ■ Nature of defenses
  ■ Method and ability to solve problems

Conclude the assessment with a statement about the client's motivation for help, the agency's ability to provide help, and anticipated outcome of services to be provided.

Treatment/Intervention Plan

This section should map out a realistic intervention strategy to address the range of problems and your assessment of the factors that underlie them. Your treatment plan should include: (Below you will find a model to organize this plan).

■ Problem(s) chosen for intervention
■ Goals and objectives
■ How the client, with the worker's help, will achieve these goals
■ The worker's role in the interventions
■ The anticipated time frame (e.g., frequency of meetings, duration of the intervention)
■ Potential factors that may affect goal achievement (including client motivation, client willingness to take responsibility for change, client's personal and cultural resources and/or personal abilities or limitations, agency resources or limitations, community resources or limitations)
■ Method(s) by which goal achievement will be evaluated

You may also wish to state whether further exploration is needed, whether you plan to refer the client to another agency or source of help instead of or in addition to your agency's help.

Reference

American Psychiatric Association. (2000). *Diagnostic and statistical manual of mental disorders* (4th ed., text rev.). Washington, DC: American Psychiatric Press.

Rapid Psychosocial Assessment Checklist

B

Name:		Case Number:	

RAPID PSYCHOSOCIAL ASSESSMENT CHECKLIST: PART I

FOR JUVENILE JUSTICE AND CRIMINAL JUSTICE SETTINGS SYSTEM DISCHARGE PLANNING

Service Date:		Start Time:		Stop Time:	

Assessment Battery: ☐ Clinical Interview   ☐ Record Review   ☐ Other:

Assessment Location:

Referred by:

CASE INFORMATION

CLIENT NAME:		CASE #:

STREET ADDRESS:

CITY:	STATE:	ZIP CODE:
PHONE (h):	PHONE (w):	PHONE (other):
EMAIL:	SS#:	SBI#:
GENDER: ☐ Male ☐ Female	I/M#:	DOB:

RACE/ETHNICITY: ☐ African-Am. ☐ Caucasian ☐ Hispanic ☐ American Indian/Pacific Islander ☐ Other

US CITIZEN: ☐ Yes   ☐ No

> If no, what is the country of origin?
>> If no, does he/she have green card or work visa?   ☐ Yes   ☐ No
> Please explain:

LANGUAGE: Does he/she speak English?   ☐ Yes   ☐ No

> If no, in what language is s/he fluent?
> Does he/she read/write English?   ☐ Yes   ☐ No
> If no, does s/he read/write another language?

CREDENTIALS: Does he/she have a copy of birth certificate?   ☐ Yes   ☐ No

> If no, can he/she get one?

VETERAN: Is he/she a veteran?   ☐ Yes   ☐ No

> If yes, in what branch of service did he/she serve?
> If yes, honorable discharge?   ☐ Yes   ☐ No

> Additional Comments:

INCOME/ FINANCIAL SITUATION

What is his/her income source? ☐ Job ☐ Social Security ☐Pension☐ Municipal Welfare ☐ SSI ☐SSD

☐ Other, please specify:

☐ Additional Sources of Income, please specify:

   Monthly income $

Does he/she have medical insurance? ☐Yes   ☐No

If yes, what type of insurance? ☐ Medicare ☐ Medicaid ☐ HMO (Name of Company):

☐ Charity Care (Name of Hospital):   ☐ Commercial (Name of Company):

☐ Other (Please specify):

Policy #:	Group #:

Does he/she have a prescription plan? ☐Yes   ☐No

If yes, what type of plan? ☐ PAAD ☐ ADDP ☐ City Welfare   ☐ Other:

HOUSING/LIVING ARRANGEMENTS

Is he/she currently homeless? ☐Yes ☐No	If yes, does he/she stay in shelters? ☐Yes ☐No
*FOR INMATES: Is he/she likely to be homeless when released from prison? ☐Yes ☐No ☐N/A	
Has he/she ever been homeless? ☐Yes ☐No	Was he/she homeless when arrested? ☐Yes ☐No
Does he/she need housing now? ☐Yes ☐No	Is housing needed for children also? ☐Yes ☐No
Is housing needed with staff on site: ☐Yes ☐No	Is housing needed that is wheelchair accessible: ☐Yes ☐No
Are there any restrictions that limit his/her ability to obtain housing (e.g., sex offense hx)? ☐Yes ☐No	

Name:	Case Number:

If yes, please explain:	

Please describe any other additional housing concerns:

EMPLOYMENT

Is he/she employed? ☐ Yes   ☐ No

If yes, is he/she employed? ☐ Full time ☐ Part time ☐ Receives unemployment ☐ Other:

If yes, what is his/her occupation?

Where is he/she employed?

If not employed, what is the work history?

If not employed, are there any problems related to obtaining employment? ☐Yes   ☐No

If yes, please specify:

EDUCATIONAL/VOCATIONAL STATUS

Last year of school completed:

Special Education History: ☐ No ☐ Yes, please describe:

☐ Discipline Problems n School: ☐ No ☐ Yes, please describe:

School/s Attended:

Vocational Training (Please list):

Marketable skills (Please list):

Additional comments:

TRANSPORTATION

Is he/she eligible for a driver's license?   ☐Yes   ☐No

Does he/she have a valid driver's license?   ☐Yes   ☐No

Does he/she have transportation available if needed?   ☐Yes   ☐No

Please list any transportation concerns:

FAMILY RELATIONALSHIPS & OTHER SOCIAL SUPPORT

Marital Status: ☐ Single ☐ Married ☐ Significant Other ☐ Divorced ☐ Widowed ☐ Separated

Is he/she emotionally supported by family members? ☐Yes   ☐No

Is he/she financially supported by family members? ☐Yes   ☐No

If applicable, please list family member/s who are aware of he/she's criminal charges:

Does he/she have other social support systems? ☐ Yes   ☐ No

If yes, who are the sources of major support?

Does he/she have a religious affiliation? ☐ Yes   ☐ No

If yes, name of religious affiliation?

If yes, what is his/her level of involvement with religious organization? ☐ High ☐ Medium ☐ Low

Additional Comments:

PSYCHOSOCIAL ASSESSMENT CHECKLIST PART II: CLINICAL INTERVIEW

I. PRESENTING PROBLEM (Reason why individual is seeking services):

PAST MEDICAL HISTORY

Medical Hospitalizations: ☐ No   ☐ Yes (please specify):

Surgeries: ☐ No   ☐ Yes (please specify):

Physical Limitations: ☐ No   ☐ Yes (please specify):

Allergies:

Any additional comments:

MENTAL HEALTH HISTORY

Name:			Case Number:	

PSYCHOTROPIC MEDICATION HISTORY: ☐ No ☐ Yes (please specify):

Current Medications, including psychotropic, over-the-counter, herbal remedies (include all meds taken over past 6 months):

Current Medications	Dosage	Frequency	Prescribed By

Is individual compliant with medications? ☐ Yes ☐ No ☐ Intermittent Compliance

If not, please explain:

Past Suicide Attempts: ☐ No ☐ Yes (If yes, please provide additional details dates, methods used, reasons for attempts):

Past Psychiatric Hospitalizations: ☐ No ☐ Yes (If yes, dates and reasons for hospitalizations):

Physical Abuse History: ☐ No ☐ Yes (Please specify):

Sexual Abuse History: ☐ No ☐ Yes (Please specify):

FAMILY/SOCIAL HISTORY

Family/Social History:

MENTAL STATUS ASSESSMENT *(This Section To Be Filled Out by Certified Mental Health Professional Only)*

Describe any deviation from the norm under each category.

APPEARANCE: ☐ Well Groomed ☐ Disheveled ☐ Bizarre ☐ Other:

ORIENTATION: ☐ Within normal limited (Oriented times 3) ☐ Oriented only to: ☐ Person ☐ Place ☐ Time

MOOD: ☐ Normal ☐ Depressed ☐ Anxious ☐ Euphoric ☐ Irritable ☐ Other:

ATTITUDE: ☐ Cooperative ☐ Uncooperative ☐ Suspicious ☐ Guarded ☐ Belligerent/Hostile ☐ Other:

AFFECT: ☐ Appropriate ☐ Inappropriate ☐ Sad ☐ Flat ☐ Angry ☐ Constricted ☐ Labile ☐ Other:

SPEECH: ☐ Normal ☐ Soft ☐ Loud ☐ Pressured ☐ Incoherent ☐ Slurred ☐ Limited ☐ Other:

MOTOR ACTIVITY: ☐ Calm ☐ Hyperactive ☐ Agitated ☐ Tremor/Tics ☐ Lethargic ☐ Other:

THOUGHT PROCESS: ☐ Intact ☐ Tangential ☐ Circumstantial ☐ Loose Associations ☐ Other:

THOUGHT CONTENT: ☐ Normal ☐ Morbid ☐ Aggressive ☐ Paranoid ☐ Obsessive ☐ Other:

HALLUCINATIONS: ☐ Denies ☐ Auditory ☐ Visual ☐ Other:

COMMAND HALLUCINATIONS: ☐ Denies ☐ Self Harm ☐ Other Harm ☐ Resists Commands ☐ Other:

BIZARRE DELUSIONS: ☐ Denies ☐ Thought Broadcasting ☐ Thought Insertion ☐ Other:

DELUSIONAL BELIEFS: ☐ Denies ☐ Religious ☐ Somatic ☐ Persecutory ☐ Grandiosity ☐ Other:

COGNITIVE FUNCTIONING (Check all that apply): ☐ No Known Disability ☐ Developmental Disability ☐ Personality Diagnosis Diagnosis

DAILY LIVING ACTIVITIES: ☐ Able to function independently ☐ Unable to function independently

SUICIDE RISK: ☐ Denies ☐ Ideation ☐ Chronic ☐ Acute ☐ Recent Suicidal Behavior ☐ Other:

SUICIDE RISK FACTORS: ☐ None ☐ Intent ☐ Plan ☐ Means to Carry Out Plan Other:

DANGER TO OTHERS: ☐ Denies ☐ Has Identified Target ☐ Other:

RECENT STRESSORS/LOSSES: ☐ No ☐ Yes (please specify):

OTHER HIGH-RISK BEHAVIORS: ☐ Denies ☐ Cutting ☐ Head banging ☐ Impulsivity ☐ Anorexia/Bulimia

Additional comments:

DIAGNOSTIC INFORMATION: Code(s) & Label(s)

Source of Information:					Date of Evaluation:

Axis I:	Code				
	Code				
	Code				
Axis II:	Code				
	Code				
Axis III:	Code				
	Code				
	Code				

Axis IV:	Check all that are appropriate and specify the problem:		
☐	Problems with primary support group	Specify:	
☐	Problems related to the social environment	Specify:	
☐	Educational problems	Specify:	
☐	Occupational problems	Specify:	
☐	Housing problems	Specify:	
☐	Economic problems	Specify:	
☐	Problems with access to health care services	Specify:	

Name:		Case Number:	
☐	Mental Health Problems	Specify:	
☐	Problems Related to Sex-Offense Charges	Specify:	
☐	Other problems with legal system/crime	Specify:	
☐	Other psychosocial & environmental problems	Specify:	
☐	None	Specify:	

Axis V:		

DRUG/ALCOHOL ASSESSMENT

SUBSTANCE USE HISTORY (Include experimentation & accidental ingestion; include alcohol, tobacco, and caffeine)

Drug	Method	Age 1st used	Age last used	Onset of heavy use	# days used in last 30	Amt. used in last 48 hrs.	1st as RX?	Last used when?	Amt used daily/weekly?

Additional comments:

Past Inpatient Substance Abuse Treatment: ☐ Yes ☐ No
   If yes, was treatment: ☐ Voluntary ☐ Court Mandated ☐ Participated in both voluntary & court-mandated treatment
   Number of programs participated in: Number of programs successfully completed:
   Additional comments:

Past Outpatient Substance Abuse Treatment: ☐ Yes ☐ No
   If yes, was treatment: ☐ Voluntary ☐ Court Mandated ☐ Participated in both voluntary & court-mandated treatment
   Number of programs participated in: Number of programs successfully completed:
   Additional comments:

Past Other Outpatient Mental Health Treatment: ☐ Yes ☐ No
   If yes, was treatment: ☐ Voluntary ☐ Court Mandated ☐ Participated in both voluntary & court-mandated treatment
   Number of past outpatient programs participated in: Number that were successfully completed:

Past Sex Offender Treatment: ☐ No ☐ Yes (If yes, please provide details):
   If yes, was treatment: ☐ Voluntary ☐ Court Mandated ☐ Participated in both voluntary & court-mandated treatment
   Number of past outpatient programs participated in: Number that were successfully completed:

Additional comments:

LEGAL HISTORY: GENERAL

☐ No Prior Legal Involvement

☐ Violence History	☐ Arson History	☐ Escape History
☐ Parole/Probation Violations	☐ Incarcerated 2 or more times	☐ Currently incarcerated w/ pending release date
☐ Sex Offense History *(If Yes, Fill out Form Below)*	☐ Child Support Fines	☐ Other Outstanding Warrants/Legal Fines

Additional details related to prior legal charges:
Any pending legal charges?   ☐ Yes ☐ No
Current legal status: ☐ Parole ☐ Probation ☐ CSL Supervision ☐ In Prison ☐ Other
   For how long?
Name of Supervising Officer:
Additional Comments Related to Offense History:
If applicable, please list parole release conditions:

FUNCTIONAL SUMMARY & RECOMMENDATIONS:

INCOME/FINANCIAL SITUATION	☐ STRENGTH ☐ CONCERN ☐ N/A
HOUSING/LIVING ARRANGEMENT	☐ STRENGTH ☐ CONCERN ☐ N/A
EMPLOYMENT	☐ STRENGTH ☐ CONCERN ☐ N/A
EDUCATIONAL/VOCATIONAL	☐ STRENGTH ☐ CONCERN ☐ N/A
TRANSPORTATION	☐ STRENGTH ☐ CONCERN ☐ N/A
FAMILY RELATIONSHIPS &/OR SOCIAL SUPPORTS	☐ STRENGTH ☐ CONCERN ☐ N/A
MEDICAL	☐ STRENGTH ☐ CONCERN ☐ N/A
MENTAL HEALTH	☐ STRENGTH ☐ CONCERN ☐ N/A
DRUGS/ALCOHOL	☐ STRENGTH ☐ CONCERN ☐ N/A
DAILY LIVING ACTIVITIES	☐ STRENGTH ☐ CONCERN ☐ N/A
LEGAL: GENERAL	☐ STRENGTH ☐ CONCERN ☐ N/A
LEGAL: SEX-OFFENDER SPECIFIC	☐ STRENGTH ☐ CONCERN ☐ N/A
OTHER:	☐ STRENGTH ☐ CONCERN ☐ N/A
OTHER:	☐ STRENGTH ☐ CONCERN ☐ N/A
OTHER:	☐ STRENGTH ☐ CONCERN ☐ N/A

SERVICE RECOMMENDATIONS FOR INDIVIDUAL/FAMILY:

☐	Financial Assistance	☐	Social Security Administration	☐	Welfare Assistance
☐	Housing Assistance	☐	Group Home/AFC	☐	Room/Board
☐	Employment Assistance	☐	Educational Assistance	☐	Vocational Training
☐	Transportation Assistance	☐	Department of Motor Vehicles	☐	Public Trans. Information
☐	Case Management Services	☐	Psycho-education	☐	Mental Health Assessment
☐	Community Support	☐	Self Help Group	☐	Social Activity/Recreation
☐	Referral to PC Physician	☐	Referral to Health Care	☐	Nursing Support

Name:				Case Number:	
		Specialist			
☐	Physical Health Assessment	☐	Occupational Therapy	☐	Physical Therapy
☐	Psychiatric Consultation	☐	Psychological Evaluation	☐	Medication Assistance
☐	Individual Therapy	☐	Group Therapy	☐	Sex–Offender-Specific Therapy
☐	Anger Management	☐	Social Skills Training	☐	Family Therapy
☐	Dual Diagnosis Group	☐	Family Education	☐	Substance-Abuse Assessment
☐	Services for the Hearing Impaired	☐	Substance Abuse Tx-Inpatient	☐	Substance Abuse Tx-Outpatient
☐	Legal Assistance	☐	Other:		

ADDITIONAL RECOMMENDATIONS:

☐ Family Independence Agency		☐	Community Action
☐ Assistance with Benefits		☐	Money Management
☐ Home Health		☐	Housekeeping
☐ Adult Foster Care		☐	Medication Management Instruction
☐ ADL Instruction		☐	Other:
☐ Other:		☐	Other:

Summary of Strengths, Abilities, Needs, & Preferences:

Possible Obstacles/Barriers to Successful Outcomes:

_____   _____

Signature/Credentials   **Date**

_____

Print Name

Psychiatric Evaluation Example

C

Juvenile and Criminal Justice Settings and Populations*

Doe, John   STATE # 00000   0/0/00

OBJECTIVE: "To discuss medications, I guess."

HISTORY OF PRESENTING PROBLEM: 18-year-old Caucasian male referred due to suicidal gesture, past history of treatment for depression, family history of depression. States he is currently feeling "alright." Sleeping and eating well. Denied suicidal ideation/homicidal ideation/psychosis. States he cut his wrist to "get out of youth house and go to crisis center." Has some impulsive behaviors.

PSYCHIATRIC HISTORY: Has seen psychiatrists and counselors on and off since about 10 years old. Family problems, court mandated, medications. Diagnosis of "depression"—Paxil ("messing with my attitude and mood"), Prozac, Serzone, history of inpatient and outpatient drug treatment.

---

*This example is fictitious and not based on an actual case.

FAMILY PSYCHIATRIC HISTORY: Mother was on Wellbutrin for depression and panic. Sister (18 years old)—depression. Maternal grandmother—depression, ADHD, panic.

SUBSTANCE USE: Started smoking marijuana and drinking alcohol at age 11. States he has tried "most of the drugs out there." Marijuana, alcohol have been drugs of choice. Marijuana use was $1/4$ ounce a day, drank alcohol on weekends—beer, OCC, hard liquor. Has had drug treatment—see above.

MEDICAL: No medical or surgical history. Paxil—?Allergy—disagreed. Seasonal allergies.

LEGAL: Possession VOP. Sentence of 18 months. Original charges: burglaries, theft, criminal mischief, assault (simple), possession, VOP, shoplifting.

SOCIAL/DEVELOPMENTAL: Grew up with mother/father and 18-year-old old sister. "Alright," parents fought a lot when he was younger—physical fighting, breaking things, and throwing things.

SCHOOL: Was in gifted-and-talented enrichment. Thrown out of enrichment in 6th grade for "disrespect." Fighting out of school, finished school with a tutor. Regular junior high school—kicked out for dirty urine. Stopped going to school. Had child study team evaluation in 7th grade. Completed 9th grade and currently in 10th grade. Completed 9th grade, was in alternative for 10th grade—Brookfield Academy.

MENTAL STATUS EVALUATION: 16-year-old Caucasian male, cooperative, motor within normal limits, speech within normal limits, mood "alright, I guess." Affect was constricted, denied thought disorder, denied psychosis. Denied suicidal/homicidal ideation. Insight and judgment—impaired.

DIAGNOSTIC IMPRESSION:

Axis I: Conduct Disorder, History of ADHD, R/O Dysthymia

Axis II: Deferred-Narcissistic Traits

Axis III: Seasonal allergies

Axis IV: Incarceration, Conflicts in Family

Axis V: 65

RECOMMENDATIONS:

1. Inmate does not wish to take medication. Does not have severe psychiatric symptomatology to warrant medications at this time. Will follow mood/behavior.
2. Counseling.

_____

Psychiatrist's Signature

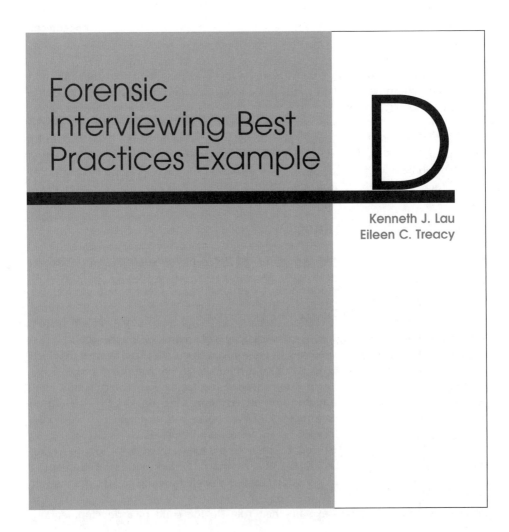

Forensic Interviewing Best Practices Example

D

Kenneth J. Lau
Eileen C. Treacy

New York State Forensic Interviewing Best Practices

This example provides an illustration of guidelines that an interviewer may follow when conducting a forensic assessment, the New York State Office for Children and Families supported the development of guidelines in 2002. These guidelines were designed with the goals of minimizing trauma and gathering accurate information from the child that is free of contamination. There are 12 distinct steps in the guidelines outlined here.

Step One: Preparing for the Interview of Child

The interviewer must consider the logistics of conducting the interview, including who will transport the child to the interview, who needs to be involved in the interview, the physical setting of the interview, and the immediate needs and safety issues of the child and family. Here are some factors that need to be considered prior to the first interview: Before the interview, learn as much as possible about the child and family and determine who will conduct the forensic interview of the child. In doing so, consider the purpose of the interview and the key issues to address. The interviewer should make sure the room is ready and prepared for the child and there should be no interruptions. The cognitive and developmental level of the child should be considered, as well as the tone of the interviewer's voice. The interviewer's greeting should be polite, friendly, and warm. The interviewer should be prepared to explain or expand the questions (New York State Children's Justice Task Force, 2004; Sattler, 1998).

Step Two: First Contact

The purpose of the introduction is to acclimate the child to the interview process; the interviewer uses a relaxed and patient tone that will be carried throughout the session. Sometimes children were not informed or were misinformed by a parent or caretaker about the purpose of the interview. When this happens, children are often confused or worried that they are in trouble. After the child and the interviewer are seated, the forensic interviewer begins by giving a brief explanation of his/her job.

It is recommended that forensic interviewers develop a standard manner in which they introduce themselves to the child and the child to the interview process. For example, "My name is ____, and I am a (social worker, police officer, doctor, etc.). My job is to talk to children about lots of different things" (Sorenson, 1997). Children might be confused about being questioned by a police officer or other professional, so interviewers should feel free to explain more about their job.

When children seem distressed it is appropriate to ask them how they are feeling and to provide reassurance about the interview (e.g., "I talk with a lot of children about things"). The purpose of first contact is to acclimate the child and the interviewer to one another and to set a neutral tone for the interview, as well as to allow the interviewer and recorder to explain their roles to the child in a developmentally appropriate manner.

Step Three: Establishing Rapport

It is clear that rapport building is a simple and effective method of increasing accurate information available to forensic interviewers in their search for the truth about what may have happened to the child (Collins, Lincoln & Frank, 2002). During this section of the forensic interview, the interviewer should begin to assess the developmental skills of the child, such as language, reasoning, and any apparent developmental delays. Interviewers need to be aware that rapport building begins with the initial contact with the child. Never assume that the rapport-building stage is unnecessary with any child.

The purposes of rapport building are to make the child comfortable with the interview setting, to get preliminary information about the child's verbal skills and cognitive maturity, and to convey that the goal of the interview is for the child to provide accurate information. Transcripts of investigative interviews show that many interviewers build rapport by asking questions about the child's teacher, family, and child's likes or dislikes. Another technique is to begin with a few focused questions and then shift the discussion to a recent event the child has experienced (Sternberg et al., 1996). By asking the child to recall a personally experienced event, the interviewer can gather baseline information about the child's verbal skills and promote the child's understanding that he/she will be providing information. The personally significant event could be an injury, doctor visit, vacation, school activity, or family event (e.g., getting a new puppy). The child is asked to describe this event in detail from beginning to end, using open-ended questions.

Young children often have little to say about one-time events and will provide only skeletal details (e.g., I fell down off my bike and hurt my leg). If this is the case, it can be helpful to ask the child to describe a recurring, scripted event. A script is a general description of repeated events in a child's life, such as what the child does to get ready for school each morning, how does the child get to/from school, or what happens when the child gets home from school.

The rapport-building stage is a good opportunity to obtain general information about the child's household and his/her relationship with the different people in the home. If a family member is alleged to have been the perpetrator, it is an opportunity to obtain information about the perpetrator in a less threatening way, for example, asking about activities child may do with the alleged perpetrator.

Step Four: Interview Guidelines

Under some circumstances, the child's understanding of the interview process may be assisted by going over some basic interview guidelines. How the guidelines are presented to the child will depend on the age of the child and the circumstances of the interview. Guidelines help to give the child some idea of what his/her role is in the process. The child should have some level of control in the interview, such as taking a break. These guidelines can be integrated throughout the interview process. Studies have shown that children sometimes try to answer questions even when they have no basis for answering or the questions do not make sense (Waterman, Blades, & Spencer, 2002). During this phase, the forensic interviewer should motivate the child to answer accurately with a series of short, simple instructions. The instructions for young children may sound somewhat different than the instructions for older children. Some of the directives one might ask a younger child include: "I want to understand you, tell me if you think I don't get it; if you don't understand me, tell me; tell me if you feel uncomfortable; I don't know everything." "Try to tell me everything that you remember, tell me what you really remember, don't guess. If you are not sure about something, tell me, I will not get angry or upset with you for anything you say; tell me what really happened. Don't make up any stuff" (New York State Children's Justice Task Force, 2004).

Guidelines for older child may include: "If I misunderstand something you say, please tell me. I want to know. I want to get it right; If you don't understand something I say, please tell me. If you feel uncomfortable at any time, please tell me. Even if you think I already know something, please tell me anyway. If you are not sure about an answer, please do not guess; tell me you are not sure before you say it." Please remember when you are describing something to me that I was not there when it happened. The more you can tell me about what happened, the more I will understand what happened. Please remember that I will not get angry or upset with you. Only talk about things that are true and really happened" (adapted from Yuille, Marxsen, & Ménard, 1995).

Step Five: Developmental Assessment

The developmental assessment actually begins during the process of establishing rapport. The purpose of the developmental assessment is to give the interviewer some baseline information about the child's environment and capabilities (e.g., who lives in the home, who visits the home, what are the child's language skills?). This can be done through a series of open-ended questions. The child can be asked about various favorites (e.g., color, food, television show, or teacher). Whenever possible, the interviewer should attempt to prompt the child for more information. For instance, if the child remarks that her favorite class is art, the interviewer could ask, "What do you like about art class?" This will ease the way for specific questioning that comes later in the interview process.

This is also the time to assess the child's expressive and receptive language skills and affective behavior. Children develop at very different rates. What one child does at the age of 6 years may not be possible for another until the age of 8 years. The interviewer should ask the child to describe in detail a verifiable, personally significant event, which is unrelated to the abuse allegation (e.g., a doctor's visit, holiday celebration, family vacation, last field trip). The child's description of a birthday party or a trip to a museum can give the interviewer a picture of the quality and quantity of detail the child can provide about a memorable event. The interviewer can note the level of complexity in terms of syntax and the level of sophistication in the child's vocabulary. By the time the developmental-assessment phase is finished, the interviewer should have a fair idea of how much detail the child normally gives when talking about nonthreatening events. This can be used to compare the child's memory production when the discussion turns to the allegations of abuse.

During the developmental assessment, it is important for the forensic interviewer to know the child's terminology for body parts. The interviewer needs to gather information about how the child refers to male and female body parts, regardless of the child's age. Sometimes dolls and drawings are helpful in identifying the body parts. The forensic interviewer needs to note the child's demeanor and any changes in child's affect when the child provides the names for more sexual parts of the body. It is recommended that the child be asked to identify body parts from head to toe, rather than emphasize the private parts. Drawings should be neutral and nondetailed (e.g., gingerbread drawings, stick figures, baby dolls, teddy bear). It is recommended that anatomical drawings or dolls not be used during the developmental assessment. If they are used, the forensic interviewer must be specifically trained to use these materials.

Step Six: Establishing the Child's Testimonial Capacity

The goal of the forensic interview is to gather accurate and complete information that is free of contamination. Establishing the child's testimonial competence is an essential element of the forensic interview. It should be noted that different states have different rules related to when a child has the capacity to testify and/or swear under oath. Some children may have the capacity to testify, but not be able to testify under oath, and the unsworn testimony of a child must be corroborated to sustain a conviction in many states. A child may have the capacity to testify in that he or she has demonstrated the ability to accurately recount what happened to him or her, yet not be "swearable" under state law.

As a result, it is important for the forensic interviewer to determine the child's ability to distinguish between a truth and a lie. The forensic interviewer must be able to determine if there is a response set (i.e., always selects the first or last item when posed a dichotomous question). The interviewer must establish whether or not the child has a full appreciation of the necessity of telling the truth and the fact that a witness who testifies in court falsely may be punished.

Forensic interviewers should avoid asking the younger child to define these concepts with questions such as, "What does it mean to tell a lie?" or "Can you tell me what the truth is?" These questions are difficult for young children or children with cognitive delays to answer and often lead to confusion. With younger children or older children with developmental delays, the interviewer may use concrete statements such as, "It is raining in the room. Is that true or not true (a lie)?"

The forensic interviewer should simply ask the older child what telling the truth means, what telling a lie means, and what should happen when a person tells a lie and gets caught. If the child does not seem able to define truth and lies, the interviewer can then give a number of statements that are true and false and ask the child whether each statement is the truth or a lie. If this is too abstract, and the child is not able to respond, the interviewer may attempt rephrasing using the words "right" and "wrong" instead of "truth" and "lie." If a child has demonstrated prior knowledge of colors in prior baseline assessments, then colors may be used. For instance, as an example of a lie, if the child is wearing a blue shirt, ask the child, "If I said your shirt was red, is that the truth or a lie?" The forensic interviewer may ask the child if the people should tell the truth or tell lies. Thereafter, ask the child the reason for his/her answer. The interviewer can then reinforce the importance of truth telling in the interview.

If the child does not demonstrate or have the understanding of the concepts of truth and lies or right versus wrong, the interviewer should continue with the interview, but with caution. It should be noted that just because the child can differentiate truth from lies, it does not necessarily mean that the child is telling the truth. Likewise, the inability to distinguish between truth and a lie does not mean the child is telling a lie. Interviewers should not confuse the ability to differentiate truth from lies with the ability to accurately report information.

Interviewers should observe the child's answers to assess if the child used a "response set." A response set is a relatively fixed or stereotyped way in which an individual tends to respond, such as always guessing, always answering "true," or giving socially desirable answers. Begin with a broad approach if the child consistently selects an answer in a particular order (e.g., first or last answer). If this takes place, switch the order of the possible answers and re-ask the question. Continued use of a response set by the child indicates that the reliability of the answers is suspect. It also means that any questioning technique other than open-ended inquiry should be used with caution.

Step Seven: Introducing the Topic of Concern

Prior to introducing the topic of concern the forensic interviewer should consider the *Sexual Abuse Dynamics* (Sgroi, 1983). It is important to determine if the child made a purposeful disclosure or if it was an accidental disclosure indicating the child may still be in secrecy about the allegation. How the forensic interviewer approaches the topic of concern may be very different depending on whether the child is ready to discuss the allegation. In either case, the forensic interviewer should begin with a broad approach followed by a more specific line of questioning. For example, the interviewer may ask, "Do you know the reason you are here to talk to me today?" The child may disclose at this point. If a child does disclose, the interviewer should move immediately into Step Nine (free narrative).

If there is no disclosure at this point, the forensic interviewer needs to explore whether the child may be recanting the initial disclosure or the initial disclosure was an accidental one. The child may not be feeling safe to share what happened with the interviewer, or the initial report was inaccurate. If the abuse is alleged to have happened at school, for example, the interviewer could say, "Earlier you told me you go to school and you are in the 3rd grade. What do you do before school? What do you do after school?" If the child supplies the names of people, the interviewer could explore their roles in the child's life as well as something the child likes about them and something the child does not like. The forensic interviewer could also ask, "What are some different kinds of touch?" or, "What do you know about touching?" The interviewer can verbalize and/or perform a variety of different touches using a prop (e.g. self, doll) and ask the child to label the touches (e.g., pinch, punch, hug, pat, handshake, kiss). The interviewer should never demonstrate the meaning of sexual terms on the child or on the prop. Information about sexual touching should only be communicated verbally. One of the goals at this time is to gather information about the child's perceptions of various touching behaviors. The child can be asked about any experience about touching (e.g., good, bad, confusing, secret touches). Even very young children are able to label various behaviors as being "good" or "bad" (Wellman & Estes, 1986).

If the child does not make a disclosure during the discussion of the different kinds of touches, the interviewer can do further exploration of this topic by asking questions such as: "Have you ever told anyone about any good/ bad/ secret/ confusing touches?" or "If someone touched you, who would you tell?" When the child made a purposeful disclosure and still does not want to talk to the interviewer about what may have happened, then the interviewer may want to ask the child more directly, "Do you remember talking to __ (the person he/she made the initial disclosure to)? What did you tell___?" If the child continues to be reluctant to disclose any information, the interviewer will need to decide whether to continue to probe, take a break, or try to interview the child another day. If there was clear evidence of sexual abuse (i.e., a witness or medical evidence), and the child might be returning to a potentially risky environment, the interviewer may need to use more direct questioning or refer the child for an extended forensic interview.

Step Eight: Free Narrative

Some children begin to discuss allegations without prompting. In such cases, the interviewer should not interrupt until it is clear that the child has finished telling the forensic investigator as much as he/she can remember about an incident. This is the most important step in the interview. The child must be given every opportunity to provide his/her own version of the events. If the allegation is of a single incident of abuse, the interviewer may say to the child something like this, "Tell me everything you remember about what happened, and start from the beginning." The child should not be interrupted during the free narrative, even if the child starts to describe seemingly irrelevant details or begins to contradict herself/himself. The child should be allowed to go at his/her own pace and the interviewer must be patient when the child pauses.

If, however, it seems that the child is not going to continue the account, the interviewer should attempt to restart the narrative. The best method for this is to simply say, "What happened next?" and/or "You were saying that ___ (restating the last thing the child said). And then what happened?" It is critical to allow children to proceed at their own pace. The interviewer should keep a relaxed, nonjudgmental tone throughout the interview. This is particularly true for younger children, who will often provide only a very limited free narrative and, with this type of child, little information will be obtained without additional open-ended questioning.

It is critical that the forensic interviewer thoroughly explore disclosures of multiple incidents of abuse. If the child discloses multiple incidents, the interviewer may respond in a variety of ways, "Tell me all about the first time this happened." "Tell me everything you remember from beginning to end." "Was there ever a time when it was different?" If the child responds affirmatively, the interviewer may say, "Tell me everything you remember about it."

The interviewer can also ask the child if there are any other incidents that she/he remembers. The child might be asked about the incidents that are most clearly remembered. If there are such incidents, the child's free narrative concerning them should be obtained. If the child becomes upset at any point in the interview, during this or any other step, acknowledge the distress and see if the child wants to pause or talk about something else. Sometimes the child may say he/she doesn't want to talk about this anymore. The interviewer might suggest they could talk about something else and then come back to it. For example, engage the child in nonthreatening activity or conversation that helps the child transition away from the potentially anxiety-provoking material to a more normalized state. When the child has regained his/her composure, the interviewer can resume.

It is critical that the forensic interviewer recognize and deal with the child's anxiety. The interviewer needs to create a relaxed tone in the interview. If noted, the interviewer should acknowledge fear and anxiety and indicate its naturalness. The interviewer should try to save the most stressful questions for later in the interview. For example, it may be easier for the child to talk about the sexual touching than the penetration. If the child is showing excessive levels of anxiety, the interviewer should move away from the topic of concern and return to it later when the child is less anxious.

Step Nine: Open-Ended Questioning

After the child has exhausted the free narrative for one incident, the interviewer can begin to ask open-ended questions. The purpose of this step is to assist the child in providing more details about the incident. If an open-ended question causes a child to disclose a new incident, the interviewer can later "go back" a step and obtain a free narrative about that incident.

Open-ended questions are requests for more details about the event disclosed in the free narrative. Examples include: "What else do you remember about the time it happened in the kitchen?" "Who else was in the kitchen?" "How did you get in the kitchen?" "Where were you in the kitchen?" "Tell me more about it." When asking open-ended questions, it is absolutely imperative that the interviewer let the child know, that, when it is true, "I don't remember" is a perfectly acceptable answer.

Interviewers should always use the most open-ended questions possible during questioning and clarification. A useful memory aid during the open-ended questioning step is the construction of a "W–H chart." Take a piece of paper and write on the top the label for the incident and along the side the prompts WHAT, WHO, WHERE and WHEN. Then the interviewer can say something like this, "Tell me everything you can remember about WHO was there during the party." The interviewer would then repeat this for WHERE the party happened, WHEN it happened, and WHAT happened. The interviewer can nonsuggestively obtain essential details that might be missing from the free narrative. The sequential order of these questions is at the discretion of the interviewer.

Walker (1994) discouraged the use of why questions. This kind of questioning is likely to be perceived as critical or evoke defensive feelings. For instance, "Why did you…" or "Why are you…" may result in feelings that interfere with the child's ability to answer questions or force the child to justify her/his statements. In addition, why questions require a number of advanced cognitive skills, including self-reflection, motivations for actions, and the use of language to describe these processes. Instead, questions should be rephrased, for example, "What scared you?" versus, "Why were you scared?" The interviewer can also reframe why questions as the question,"How come you did not tell anyone till now?"

During the open-ended questioning, there is an opportunity to explore issues related to the sexual-abuse dynamics (i.e., engagement, sexual interaction and progression, secrecy, disclosure, and suppression) by asking some key questions. In terms of engagement: How did you like __ before the touching? What kind of stuff did you do with __ before the touching? Who else was around when __ did these things to you? In terms of sexual interaction and progression: What were the first kinds of touches? What kind of touches did __ do next? What did ___ do with his/her own body? What did ___ do with your body? How did it taste? How did it feel? Question regarding secrecy include: What did ___ want you to say about the touching? What did he/she say about telling? In terms of disclosure: What made you decide to tell _____? Who was the first person you told? What did ___ say when you told? What did ___ do when you told? What happened after you told? How did they treat you after you told? Who else did you tell? Has ___ done this to anyone else? What would you like to happen? Questions related to suppression include: How has your mom, siblings, grandparents (separate each questions), been treating you since you told? How do you feel about telling? If you could do it over, what would you do? What is your wish about all of this?

Step Ten: Alternative Hypothesis/Explanations

During a forensic interview, it is important to test rival explanations for the child's statements. The interviewer might ask: What if someone says, "_____ is trying to make _____ say stories?" What if someone says, "____ is asking ____ to make up lies about ____?" Was ___ trying to put medicine on your private areas? Interviewers should consider whether there is any potential secondary-gain motive for the allegations. In other words, does anyone possibly benefit from the allegations? If so, the interviewer must consider asking questions about that possible secondary-gain motive, for example, the child may want the alleged perpetrator out of the home.

Step Eleven: Clarification Questions

The purpose of this step is to provide an opportunity to clarify and extend previous answers. Clarification of events in the child's statement should be questions addressed toward the end of the interview. Probe issues as gently as possible. For example, "You said he put his finger inside you but you also said you had a snow suit on. Can you tell me how that happened?" or "I'm a bit confused. You said_____ then you said ____."

The forensic interviewer should never include information obtained from another source in a question, as in "I understand from your mother that your Uncle Bob took some pictures of you." Instead say, "What do you remember about pictures?" If the child has displayed language and/or knowledge that seems inappropriate for his/ her age, this would be the time to determine where the child learned that knowledge or those words. This also provides an opportunity to rule out rival explanations. Even when the child is using language that is appropriate, the interviewer needs to ascertain the child's own meaning for her/his words (e.g., the child may use the word "rape" when referring to digital penetration).

The interviewer needs to ascertain whether the child's statements are consistent with known facts already provided during the investigation. The interviewer should not be afraid to ask for more clarification. What did you say about ___? Or ask repetition questions like: "Let me ask that question again." The interviewer should examine whether the child has other abuse experiences. At times, the interviewer may need to challenge the chronology of child's report to clarify inconsistencies in a nonchallenging way. The interviewer may state, "I'm having trouble understanding this." In this component of the interview, other potential abuse experiences (e.g., domestic violence, physical abuse, and substance abuse.) should be explored. If the child has a history of prior abuse, it is important to clarify the child's ability to differentiate between the prior abuse and the current allegations.

Step Twelve: Concluding the Interview

It is important for the forensic interviewer to draw the interview to a close by asking questions like: Do you have any questions for me? Questions that can be answered should be answered. The interviewer should explain to the child what will happen next in the investigation. It is important to refrain from making any promises that cannot be kept. No matter what the outcome of the interview, thank the child for participating and give the child a card with a name and phone number of an appropriate contact person.

In the event of a disclosure, address the potential "fall out" from the disclosure. This may be dealt with by saying, "Some children have an easy time after telling, and some kids have a hard time. Some families are glad that the child talked, and others are not. Some of the kids are happy that they told, and others wish they had not. If you have any mixed-up feelings about telling, it's okay to call. I'll be glad to talk to you." Prior to leaving the interview room, the interviewer could engage in a neutral topic of conversation or activity with the child. The purpose of this transition is to allow the child to leave the interview with as little anxiety as possible.

Extended Forensic Interviews

The scope of forensic interviews can be influenced by a number of factors. These include the specific circumstances being investigated (e.g., the child may need to be referred for a medical examination) and the potential need for other interviewing resources (e.g., sign-language interpreter). More in-depth forensic interviews sometimes occur after the initial stages of an abuse investigation. These interviews are usually conducted by specially trained professionals who have graduate-level education in the areas relevant to this type of interviewing (i.e., psychology, social worker, counselor). Carnes (2000) recommends that interviewers should be graduate-level mental health professionals who have previous experience working with children; training in child sexual abuse and child development; experience conducting forensic interviews; and experience testifying in court.

Children are referred for extended forensic interviews under a number of circumstances, including the child did not disclose abuse to investigators, but exhibited behaviors or there was other evidence strongly suggestive of victimization (e.g., sexually transmitted disease, confession, third-party witness). The purpose of the extended forensic assessment is to determine the likelihood of whether or not the child has been abused; to identify suspected perpetrator(s); to gather forensically sound facts necessary for child protection and law enforcement officials to understand what, if anything, has happened; to allow the child to disclose over time in a nonthreatening environment; and to assess the extent and nature of the alleged abuse (Wilson & Pipe, 1989).

Summary

The forensic interview is a critical component of a child-abuse investigation. Forensic interviewers should have knowledge and training about child development; cultural considerations; the legal requirements of Child Protective Services and law enforcement prosecutions; sexual-abuse dynamics; as well as being able to rule in/out other rival explanations for the child's statements and behaviors, other than abuse. The New York State Forensic Best Practice Guidelines provides a step-by-step methodology to conducting such interviews.

References

Carnes, C. N. (2000). *Forensic evaluation of children when sexual abuse is suspected* (2nd ed.). Huntsville, AL: National Children's Advocacy Center.

Collins, R., Lincoln, R., & Frank, M. (2002). The effect of rapport in forensic interviewing. *Psychiatry, Psychology and the Law, 9*(1), 69–78.

New York State Children's Justice Task Force. (2004). *Forensic interviewing best practices*. Albany, NY: New York State Office for Children and Families.

Sattler, J. M. (1998). *Clinical and forensic interviewing of children and families*. San Diego: Jerome M. Sattler Publishing.

Sgroi, S. (1982). *Handbook of clinical intervention in child sex abuse*. Lexington, MA: Lexington Books/ D.C. Heath.

Sorenson, E., Bottoms, B. L., & Perona, A. (1997). *Intake and forensic interviewing in the children's advocacy center setting: A handbook*. Washington, DC: National Network of Children's Advocacy Centers.

Sternberg, K. J., Lamb, M. E., Hershkowitz, I., Esplin P. W., Redlich, A., & Sunshine, N. I. (1996). The relationship between investigative utterance types and the informativeness of child witnesses. *Journal of Applied Developmental Psychology, 17*, 439–451.

Walker, L. (1994) *Abused women and survivor therapy.* Washington, DC: Psychological Association Press.

Waterman, A. H., Blades, M., & Spencer, C. P. (2002). In H. Westcott, G. Davies, & R. Bull (Eds.), *Children's testimony: Psychological research and forensic practice* (pp. 121–134). New York: John Wiley.

Wellman, H. M., & Estes, D. (1986). Early understanding of mental entities: A reexamination of childhood realism. *Childhood Development, 57,* 910–923.

Wilson, J. C., & Pipe, M E. (1989). The effects of cues on young children's recall of real events. *New Zealand Journal of Psychology, 18,* 65–70.

Yuille, J. C., Marxsen, D., & Ménard, K. (1995). *Report of the Systematic Interviewing Project.* Victoria: Ministry of Social Services.

Multidisciplinary Example: NJ Anti-Trafficking Coalition

E

New Jersey Anti-Trafficking Initiative of the International Institute of New Jersey*

From 2003 to 2006, working with the New Jersey State Attorney General's Office, Monmouth University School of Social Work, Safe Horizon, and with support from Congressman Chris Smith, the International Institute of New Jersey created the New Jersey Anti-Trafficking Initiative. The Initiative brought together key stakeholders from throughout the state to increase cooperation and understanding of the problem of human trafficking in NJ. Additionally, the Initiative worked with stakeholders to develop protocols for serving trafficking victims. The intent of these protocols was to help identify how and where stakeholders may obtain crucial resources and describe a statewide system for coordination and communication.

---

*Adapted from: http://www.iinj.org/programs/sections/anti_trafficking.html

Key achievements of the Initiative:

- ▆ Increased knowledge and understanding of the scope of trafficking in New Jersey, the benefits available to victims, how to identify and respond to the special psychological, social, legal, and medical needs of trafficked persons.
- ▆ Identified gaps in services, promoted communication among key stakeholders, coordinated response and made recommendations for change to promote more effective response to victims' needs.
- ▆ Developed a statewide system for coordination and communication among key partners.
- ▆ Developed a statewide resource list of law enforcement, nongovernmental organizations (NGOs), social service agencies, and organizations able to assist victims.

New Jersey Anti-Trafficking Coalition

Additionally, the Initiative organized the New Jersey Anti-Trafficking Coalition. Because the needs of the state are diverse, the Coalition is divided between the Northern and Southern Coalition. Each group meets every other month and increases cooperation among NGOs, service providers and law Enforcement. Since March 31, 2006, the Anti-Trafficking Initiative at the International Institute of New Jersey has transitioned its leadership role in the Coalition to the NJ Division of Criminal Justice Anti-Trafficking Task Force.

Index